HARDIN COUNTY TENNESSEE RECORDS
1820-1860

Compiled by
Thomas A. Hays

Copyright 1985
By: Southern Historical Press, Inc.

All rights reserved. No part of this publication may be reproduced,
stored in a retrieval system, transmitted in any form,
posted on to the web in any form or by any means
without the prior written permission of the publisher.

Please direct all correspondence and orders to:

www.southernhistoricalpress.com
or
SOUTHERN HISTORICAL PRESS, Inc.
PO BOX 1267
375 West Broad Street
Greenville, SC   29601
southernhistoricalpress@gmail.com

ISBN #0-89308-562-6

Printed in the United States of America

DEDICATION

This Book Is Dedicated To The Following:

My Parents, The late Robert Douglas Hays and Charlyne Welch Hays.

My Wife, Rebecca Hannah Brock Hays.

My In-Laws, Reid Hill Brock, Sr., and Barbara Faye Raper Brock.

PREFACE

Hardin County, Tennessee was formed in 1819 from the western lands ceded to the State of Tennessee by the Indians. Some researchers claim that its western boundary stretched to the banks of the Mississippi River, thereby including present-day Shelby County and Memphis. A survey of the county court minutes indicates that there was a great deal of territory, to the west, attached to the county for governance purposes, but not as permanent part of the county. The westernmost point mentioned in the court minutes is the Big Hatchie River in present-day Hardeman County. Hardin County has existed in its present sized and shape since early on. Apparently, the only serious challenge to its property came from the proposed organization of Taylor County in the 1840's. This proposal was never acted upon.

While the county was settled fairly quickly, its population, after an initial surge, seems to have leveled off and has grown at a slow, but steady, rate. However, a great many people passed through the county on the way west to Arkansas and Texas. Some appear to have stopped, for only a season, in order to raise a crop before continuing their westward trek. The following excerpt, taken from a letter written by William Theophilus Shutt of Hardin County to his brother John Wesley Shutt of North Carolina in 1872, offers a good example of the feelings of that time and the early decades of that century as well.

> "Brother i think you would doo well to come to this cuntry and if this cuntry dont sute you go further west. You can doo better heare on rented land than you can own youre land in N.C. and get all you make and you can doo better futher west than you can heare."

Lying as it did on a direct line east of Memphis, one of the great river ports, Hardin County was a natural stopping point for the westward travelers. Being a river county itself, the county had its share of violence. As attested to in the county court minutes abstracted here, murder and death under peculiar circumstances were no stranger.

The material abstracted here represents the vast majority of the records extant for the period 1820 to 1860. The entries cover the appointment of administrators and guardians; indentures and apprenticeships; reports of inquest juries; releasements, removals, and insolvencies from the tax rolls; wills, inventories, administrator and guardian settlements; the registration of free blacks; land surveys and occupant claims; petitions for widow's dowers; acknowledgement of bills of sale for slaves; certification of deeds of conveyance; and other pertinent records. These records were abstracted from microfilm obtained from the Tennessee State Library and Archives in Nashville, Tennessee.

While every attempt was made to ensure that no errors were made, it is acknowledged that there probably are some errors. Apologies are offered. Much of the writing was faded and this made the abstracting quite difficult in some cases. If there is any question concerning the accuracy of any entry, check either the original records at the Hardin County Courthouse or view the microfilm at the State Archives. Further instructions for the use of each section is included at the beginning of each part.

This compilation has been a year in the making. It is hoped that the information provided will assist the researcher in solving their genealogical puzzles. At the same time, a survey of this book can offer the local historian a glimpse of life in a small, rural area during an exciting and tempestuous period in American history.

                                        Thomas A. Hays
                                        Bristol, Virginia
                                        October 28, 1984

THE COUNTY COURT MINUTES

Not all entries in the county court minutes were abstracted. Only those entries providing information on: appointment of administrators and guardians; indentures and apprenticeships; the registration of free blacks; reports of inquest juries; probate of wills; petitions for widow's dowers; acknowledgment of bills of sale for slaves; certification of deeds of conveyance and gift; and other pertinent information. The county court entries are arranged by date and page number.

The name in capital letters at the beginning of each entry is that of the primary subject of the record. Usually, that person's name is also included in the body of the abstract as follows:

DOE, JOHN - Jane Doe appointed administratrix of the estate of John Doe.

Sometimes, the abstract will simply state:

DOE, JOHN - Produced a land grant for 500 acres issued by the state of Tennessee.

In some instances, the entry, when dealing with a minor and the parents are unknown, will read:

DOE, _____ - James Doe appointed guardian of Elizabeth Doe, minor orphan.

The County Court Minutes for 1826 to 1833 no longer exist. They were destroyed in a fire during the Civil War. When entries were found relating to the settlement of an estate of an individual who died during that period, they were included as well. Normally, entries simply stating that an administrator had produced an inventory or settlement were not included because the appointment of that administrator was included elsewhere in the abstracts. (NOTE: This does not include the Will and Inventory Books which were abstracted in their entirety.)

Book G of the minutes, which extends through 1866, is abstracted only through 1860. There are two reasons for this. First, it is the intention of this book to cover the period from the foundation of the county only to the eve of the Civil War. Secondly, the County Court was forced to suspend its activities through most of the war and the minutes were kept sporadically at best.

A conscientious effort has been made to list married women, mostly minors who required a guardian, within entries under their maiden names as shown in the examples below.

DOE, JOHN - David Jones appointed guardian of his wife, Jane Jones, formerly Jane Doe, a minor heir of John Doe.

OR

DOE, _____ - David Jones appointed guardian of his wife, Jane Jones, formerly Jane Doe, a minor.

HARDIN COUNTY COURT MINUTES

BOOK A: 1820 - 1825

3 April 1820

Pg. 9

BERRY, MICHAEL - Last will and testament of Michael Berry presented and proven by Betsy Berry and Mary Berry, subscribing witnesses.

HARDIN, JOSEPH - A deed of conveyance from Joseph Hardin to William Morrow, certified by the Clerk of Green County, Tennessee, was presented in court.

BLACKWELL, JACOB - Henry Mahan appointed administrator of the estate of Jacob Blackwell.

3 July 1820

Pg. 12

KELSEY, SAMUEL - Robert G. Kelsey appointed administrator of the estate of Samuel Kelsey.

RICHIE, SAMUEL - James Hardin appointed administrator of the estate of Samuel Richie.

1 January 1821

Pg. 22

PETITION - A petition by a group of stockkeepers was brought into court. The document was to notify all persons that the petitioners would not suffer stock other than their own on their premises. Signed by: C.B. Neilson, James Boyd, Jno. Boyd, Joseph S. Ashworth, James Boyd sen., and Jno. Choat.

2 January 1821

Pg. 23

COOKE, ISAAC S.W. Esq. - Certified by the county court to practice law.

COMBS, JAMES W. - Certified by the county court to practice law.

KERR, ANDREW - A land grant, issued in the name of Andrew Kerr, was presented in court and certified.

3 January 1821

Pg. 26

BOYD, JOHN - Jesse Morris confessed, in open court, that he bit off the ear of John Boyd in an affray.

2 April 1821

Pg. 28

GARNER, JOHN - Granted a tavern license.

JONES, JESSE - Produced a grant for 150 acres certified by Davidson County, Tennessee and certified in Hardin County.

COULTON, JAMES - Nancy Coulton appointed guardian for Thomas Coulton, Hartgrove Coulton, Sally Coulton, and Milly Coulton, infant children of James Coulton.

COULTON, JAMES - Ordered that the Hardin County Clerk certify to the Clerk of Humphreys County, Tennessee that Nancy Coulton, administrator of the estate of James Coulton, dec'd., had given bond as the guardian of the infant children, and that the court of Humphreys County could send all papers respecting the estate to this county.

2 July 1821

Pg. 36
McMAHAN, JAMES F. - Granted a tavern license.

STANFIELD, POLLY - Benjamin Huddleston appointed guardian of the daughter of Polly Stanfield, an illegimate child.

Pg. 37
ELDRIDGE, _____ - Gabriel Eads appointed guardian of Elijah Eldridge, an orphan age 10, and is to teach him the blacksmith's trade.

COULTON, JAMES - George W. Coulton presented an inventory of the estate of James Coulton which had been forwarded from Humphreys County, Tennessee.

Pg. 38
BRYANT, AARON - An article of agreement between James Hardin and Aaron Bryant for an occupant claim of 160 acres, assigned to Betsy Bryant, was acknowledged in court.

BRYANT, AARON - A deed of gift from Aaron Bryant to Betsey Bryant for 1 sorrel mare, 4 head of cattle, and 2 beds and furniture was acknowledged in court.

BRYANT, AARON - A deed of gift from Aaron Bryant to Polly Bryant for 1 bay mare, 4 head of cattle, and 2 beds and furniture was acknowledged in court.

4 July 1821

Pg. 40
FARRAR, JEFFERSON - Isham Cherry returned an inventory of the estate of Jefferson Farrar.

MOSS, DAVID - A peace warrant sworn out against Stephen Roach whom David Moss has cause to feel intends bodily harm against him.

1 October 1821

Pg. 45
FULLER, _____ - Samuel Harbour, Esq., appointed guardian of Jefferson Fuller.

Pg. 46
BARNES, JAMES - Presented a land grant for 320 acres and is was certified.

McDANIEL, ALEXANDER AND DAVID D. ROBINSON - Both men entered 100 acres on the tax list.

7 January 1822

Pg. 51
    WILLIAMS, HARDIN - Last will and testament of Hardin Williams presented and proven by Charlotte Williams.

    WILLIAMS, JAMES A. - Sally Williams, widow, appointed guardian for her four children Matilda Williams, Lucinda Eliza Williams, Lora Lucinda Williams, and Sebastine Carole Williams children of James A. Williams.

    WILLIAMS, JAMES A. - Sally Williams, widow, and Henry Heik appointed administrators of the estate of James A. Williams.

    TOMPKINS, HARRISON - A deed of gift from Harrison Tompkins to Lucinda K. Thompson and Mary Ann Tompkins was certified by the court.

    WILLIAMS, JAMES A. - Commissioners appointed to lay off a year's provisions for the widow of James A. Williams.

8 January 1822

Pg. 52
    CAREY, JOEL - Licensed to practice as an attorney.

1 April 1822

Pg. 65
    LACEFIELD, _____ - A deed of gift from William Lacefield to Robert Lacefield was presented and proven by Green Weaver and Isaac Northcutt, subscribing witnesses.

Pg. 66
    BEAR, SAMUEL - A land grant for 160 acres, issued to Samuel Bear, was certified.

    BERRIS, _____ - Andrew Berris appointed as his own guardian.

2 April 1822

Pg. 67
    ALLEN, JAROD S. - Licensed to practice law.

    GRAY, HENRY L. - Licensed to practice law.

Pg. 69
    BARNES, JAMES AND JAMES HUDDLESTON - A deed of conveyance from James Barnes and James Huddleston to William Bradshaw for 160 acres was certified.

1 July 1822

Pg. 74
    CHOAT, _____ - James W. Combs appointed guardian for Eliza W.H. Choat, Jane J.C. Choat, and Charles J. Choat.

Pg. 76
    JUDKINS, JAMES W. - Certified to practice law.

2 July 1822

Pg. 77
JUDKINS, JAMES W. - A deed of conveyance from James W. Judkins to Austin Miller and Archilaws M. Hughes for one lease was acknowledged.

Pg. 79
STUART, WILLIAM - Peace warrant issued against Richard Graham whom William Stuart and his wife, Elizabeth, suspect of intending bodily harm against them.

Pg. 80
GRAHAM, RICHARD - Peace warrant issued against William Stuart whom Richard Graham suspects of intending to do bodily harm to him.

7 October 1822

Pg. 89
EADS, GABRIEL - A bill of sale from Gabriel Eads to David Beckham for one negro girl, Amy, was acknowledged.

BLANTON, ALEXANDER - Jacob Dulaney appointed administrator of the estate of Alexander Blanton.

9 October 1822

Pg. 96
ROBINSON AND KINCANNON - A deed of conveyance from David Robinson and James Kincannon to the commissioners of the town of Hardinsville for 50 acres was acknowledged.

9 January 1823

Pg. 107
ALLISON, WILLIAM - Stock mark registered in the name of William Allison. Smooth cross off of right ear.

CASEY, JOEL - Stock mark registered in the name of Joel Casey. Split in each ear.

Pg. 108
THRASHER, ROBERT - Stock mark registered in the name of Robert Thrasher. Swallow fork in left ear and cross and half cross off right ear.

KERR, ANDREW - Petition by William Allison and his wife Rosanna, James Kerr, Isabella Kerr, Margaret Kerr, Thomas Allison, Lettie Falls, and William Kerr. Petition shows that the petitioners were the heirs of Andrew Kerr, dec'd, and that said Andrew had 5,000 acres granted to him in his lifetime in this county by the State of North Carolina, and that his last will and testament was published and that Andrew Neil and James Kerr were his executors and both are dead. Said executors never distributed said property. The petitioners asked that a commission be appointed to divide and lay off said property.

10 January 1823

Pg. 111
THOMPSON, WILLIAM - John Thompson appointed administrator of the estate of William Thompson.

THOMPSON, WILLIAM - Commissioners appointed to lay off a

year's support for Francis Thompson, widow of William Thompson.

Pg. 113
    SWENEY, A.W. - Stock mark registered in the name of A.W. Sweney. Swallow fork in right ear and smooth cross off the left ear. The entry also shows a brand.

7 April 1823

Pg. 115
    JONES, JESSIE - A grant for 160 acres was produced by Jessie Jones and was certified.

8 April 1823

Pg. 118
    NIELSON, CHARLES B. - A bill of sale from Charles B. Nielson to John Kindel, for a negro woman named Nelly, was acknowledged.

Pg. 120
    WIDEMAN, MARK - Martha Wideman appointed administratrix of the estate of Mark Wideman.

    WIDEMAN, MARK - Commissioners appointed to lay off a year's support for Martha Wideman, widow of Mark Wideman.

9 April 1823

Pg. 123
    MOORE, JESSE G. - A bill of sale from Jesse G. Moore to Isham Cherry for 8 negroes. Slaves named: Solomon and his wife Charlotte, James, Joseph, Winny, Sarah, Polly, and Rodah. The bill was acknowledged.

10 April 1823

Pg. 128
    CHOAT, _____ - Commissioners appointed to inquire into the condition of Mrs. Choat.

    CHOAT, _____ - Christopher Choat allowed $100.00 for the upkeep of Mrs. Choat.

Pg. 129
    EDWARDS, _____ - Gabriel Eads released from his bond for a boy named Elijah Edwards who had been bound to him.

11 April 1823

Pg. 136
    PEARKS, SAMUEL - John Allison appointed administrator of the estate of Samuel Pearks.

    PARKS, SAMUEL - Commissioners appointed to lay off a year's provisions for Sally Parks, widow of Samuel Parks.

7 July 1823

Pg. 137
    WILLIAMS, SAMUEL H. - A deed of conveyance from Samuel H. Williams to Joshua McConnell, for 69 acres, was acknowledged.

    TAYLOR, ISAAC - A deed of conveyance from Isaac Taylor to

Robert Hunter, for 1000 acres, was certified.

Pg. 138
    BLANTON, ALEXANDER - Commissioners appointed to lay off a year's provisions to Lacy Blanton, widow of Alexander Blanton.

    EDWARDS, ____ - Elijah Edwards, an orphan boy, bound to James Boyd until he reaches the age of 21.

Pg. 139
    WILSON, JOHN - Willie B. Wilson appointed guardian of Green Wilson, Madison Wilson, Benjamin Wilson, and Columbia Wilson, infant heirs of John Wilson.

8 July 1823

Pg. 143
    HARDIN, BENJAMIN - Acknowledged breaking the peace by striking John Mc. Ross. Fined $1.00.

    MOSS, DAVID - Peace warrant issued against Stephen Roach whom David Moss suspects of intending bodily harm against him.

9 July 1823

Pg. 144
    PYBURN, WILLIAM - Transfer of a plat and certificate for 23 acres from William Pyburn to Richard Ford.

10 July 1823

Pg. 148
    LOWE, AQUILLA - A court case involving debt brought by John Gallory and Caleb Lowe, executors of Aquilla Lowe, versus Alex. McClintock.

Pg. 149
    JONES, HENRY - Transfer of a plat and certificate, for 160 acres, from Henry Jones to Lewis H. Broyles.

6 October 1823

Pg. 152
    BLANTON, ALEXANDER - Lucy Blanton appointed guardian of Lucinda Blanton and Ruthy H. Blanton, infant heirs of Alexander Blanton.

Pg. 153
    ROBINSON, RICHARD - Christian Robinson appointed administratrix of the estate of Richard Robinson.

    HARDIN, BENJAMIN - A deed of conveyance from Benjamin Hardin to Robert Lacefield, for 160 acres, was acknowledged. Proven by A. McClintock and Austin Miller, subscribing witnesses.

    HARDIN, JAMES - A deed of conveyance from James Hardin to Aaron Briant, for 60 acres, was certified.

    HARDIN, JAMES - A deed of conveyance from James Hardin to Thomas M. Duckworth, for 100 acres, was certified.

    HARDIN, JAMES - A deed of conveyance from James Hardin to

James Emmerson, for 60 acres, was certified.

WILSON, JOHN - Willie B. Wilson, guardian for the minor heirs of John Wilson, certified that he had received $140.00 for the children from James Davis and James Wilson.

Pg. 154
RAWLINGS, JOHN A. - Jane L. Rawlings appointed administratrix of the estate of John A. Rawlings.

CROTTS, _____ - Joseph Crotts, an orphan boy, bound to Isaac Hitchcock until the age of 21.

Pg. 155
CROTTS, _____ - Elizabeth Crotts bound out to Elijah Pauley until age 18.

CROTTS, DAVID - Isham Cherry appointed administrator of the estate of David Crotts.

CROTTS, _____ - Isham Cherry appointed guardian for Eliza Crotts.

Pg. 156
CHERRY, ISHAM - A deed of conveyance from Isham Cherry to A.W. Sweeny, for 160 acres, was certified.

EDWARDS, _____ - James Boyd released from his bond for Elijah Edwards, an orphan boy, who had been bound to him.

Pg. 157
CROTTS, _____ - Lewis Crotts bound to Jonathan R. Pickens until age 21. Pickens to teach him the blacksmith's trade.

DEAN, SHEROD - Delpha Dean appointed guardian of Cornelius Dean, Bedford Dean, and Jeremiah Dean, minor heirs of Sherod Dean.

7 October 1823

Pg. 160
WILLIAMS, SAMUEL H. - A deed of conveyance from Samuel H. Williams to Henry G. Garner, for 25 acres, was certified. Proven by Jonathan Courtney and Charles German, subscribing witnesses.

WILLIAMS, SAMUEL H. - Produced a land grant from the State of Tennessee for 25 acres and it was certified.

McMAHAN, JAMES F. - Produced a land grant from the State of Tennessee for 300 acres and it was certified.

8 October 1823

Pg. 161
WILLIAMS, SAMUEL H. - Produced a land grant from the State of Tennessee for 69 acres and it was certified.

CARROLL, FRANCIS - A document, from Jonathan M. Church to Francis Carroll, was produced in court. The document certifies that the said Carroll, a colored man, is to be freed from Church. Proven by David Kincannon, subscribing witness.

5 January 1824

Pg. 168
   WILSON, JAMES - A deed of conveyance from James Wilson and Jacob Humble to Adam Wilson. Proven by John Reynolds and Joseph Wallace, subscribing witnesses.

   LEWIS, _____ - William Lewis, an orphan boy near 10 years old, bound to Ebenezer Gammill until age 21.

Pg. 169
   CROTTS, _____ - Valentine Crotts, an orphan boy about 16 years old, bound to Isham Cherry until age 21.

7 January 1824

Pg. 178
   CHERRY, ISHAM - A deed of conveyance from Isham Cherry to Francis Kincannon and James Kincannon, for 160 acres, was certified.

   KINCANNON, FRANCIS - A deed of conveyance from Francis Kincannon to David Robinson, for 80 acres, was certified.

   BARNES, JAMES - A deed of conveyance from James Barnes to John L. Barnes, for 50 acres, was certified.

Pg. 181
   THOMPSON, JOHN - A deed of conveyance from John Thompson to John Hogan, for 95 acres, was certified.

9 January 1824

Pg. 188
   CROTTS, POLLY - Isham Cherry returned an inventory of the estate of Polly Crotts.

Pg. 189
   JOHNSON, WILLIE RUFUS - Isham Cherry and Noah Lilly appointed as a commission to enquire into the condition of Willie Rufus Johnson. They found that he ought to come under the poor law. His age was listed as 22.

5 April 1824

Pg. 195
   DICKSON, _____ - Elizabeth Dickson appointed guardian for her infant children Alexander, Nancy, Ann, Sarah, John H., and William N. Dickson.

   PHAROAH, JEFFERSON - Isham Cherry appointed guardian of Samuel, Eliza, Rebecca, John, and Madison Pharoah, infant children of Jefferson Pharoah.

6 April 1824

Pg. 200
   PHAROAH, JEFFERSON - Settlement with executrix and executor returned to the court.

7 April 1824

Pg. 205
WILLIAMS, SAMUEL H. - A deed of conveyance from Samuel H. Williams to Thomas Hogan, for 100 acres, was certified.

Pg. 206
DONOVEN AND MILLER - A deed of conveyance from Andrew Donoven and Austin Miller to Willie J. Duckworth, for 60 acres, was certified.

Pg. 207
HUDDLESTON, JAMES - A deed of conveyance from James Huddleston to James Barnes, for 80 acres, was certified.

BARNES, JAMES - A deed of conveyance from James Barnes to James Huddleston, for 80 acres, was certified.

ENGLISH, JAMES - A deed of conveyance from James English to A.W. Sweeny, for 80 acres, was certified.

8 April 1824

Pg. 207
WILLIAMS, J.A. - Order given for an alias writ for laying off the widow's dower to Sarah Rose, widow of J.A. Williams.

ENGLISH, JAMES - A deed of conveyance from James English to Michael Worley, for 80 acres, was certified.

Pg. 208
COMMISSIONERS OF HARDINSVILLE - A deed of conveyance from A.W. Sweeny, Noah Lilly, Hiram Boon, Daniel Smith, John G. Williams, and James Barnes(Commissioners of Hardinsville) to James Scott for one lot in the town of Hardinsville.

Pg. 209
WORLEY, JOHN - Transfer of a plat and certificate, for 40 acres, from John Worley to Joseph Williams.

WILLIAMS, JOSEPH - Transfer of a plat and certificate, for 25 acres, from Joseph Williams to William White.

9 April 1824

Pg. 210
CHERRY, DANIEL - Transfer of a plat and a certificate, for 90 acres, from Daniel Cherry to Gibson Hardin.

CHERRY, DANIEL - Transfer of a plat and certificate, for 11 acres, from Daniel Cherry, by his agent A.W. Sweeny, to David Robinson.

ROBINSON, DAVID - A deed of conveyance from David Robinson and James Kincannon to the Commissioners of the town of Hardinsville, for 50 acres, was certified.

Pg. 211
GOODIN, JAMES - Produced a land grant from the State of Tennessee for 133½ acres.

Pg. 212
GOODIN, JAMES - A deed of conveyance from James Goodin and James Hardin to William Wells, for 133½ acres, was certified. Proven by Daniel F. Barrey and John S. Broyles, subscribing

witnesses to the deed.

5 July 1824

Pg. 214
EVANS, JOSEPH - Isham Cherry appointed administrator of the estate of Joseph Evans.

Pg. 215
THOMPSON, FRANCIS - A bill of sale, for a negro girl named Hannah, from Francis Thompson to John Thompson was acknowledged.

ROBINSON, DAVID - Transfer of a plat and certificate, for 25 acres, from David Robinson to Alexander Reynolds.

Pg. 218
HARDIN, MARTIN - Last will and testament of Martin Hardin presented for probate. Proven by Russell R. Covey and Thomas Hammonds, subscribing witnesses.

HARDIN, JAMES - A deed of conveyance from James Hardin to John Reynolds, for 163 acres, was certified.

HARDIN, JAMES - A deed of conveyance from James Hardin to Samuel Wells, for 160 acres, was certified.

ROBINSON, DAVID - Transfer of a plat and certificate from David Robinson to Wm. Robinson.

Pg. 219
ROBINSON, DAVID - Transfer of a plat and certificate, for 40 acres, from David Robinson to Frances Kincannon, Sr..

6 July 1824

Pg. 223
LACEFIELD, JESSE - A deed of conveyance from Jesse Lacefield to John Thompson, for 160 acres, was certified.

7 July 1824

Pg. 224
SWEENEY, A.W. - A deed of conveyance from A.W. Sweeney to Joel Casey, for 80 acres, was certified.

8 July 1824

Pg. 231
HARBOR, ELIJAH - A bill of sale, for a negro woman named Agga, from Elijah Harbor to Wilie J. Duckworth was acknowledged. Proven by Thomas M. Duckworth, subscribing witness.

9 July 1824

Pg. 231
CHERRY, ISHAM - A deed of conveyance from Isham Cherry to Lewis N. Falkner, for 160 acres, was certified. Proven by Charles W. Ross and John Mc. Ross, subscribing witnesses.

WILLIAMS, JAMES A. - Guardian bond given by Joseph Williams as the legal guardian of the minor heirs of James A. Williams, deceased.

4 October 1824

Pg. 239
HARDIN, JAMES - A deed of conveyance from James Hardin to James Smith, for 30 acres, was certified.

THOMPSON, JOHN - A deed of conveyance from John Thompson to Joseph Williams, for 65 acres, was certified.

Pg. 240
HARDIN, JAMES - A deed of conveyance from James Hardin to Abraham Wells, for 100 acres, was certified.

5 October 1824

Pg. 242
KILCREASE, DAVIS - Court case by Allen Brount and Mahala Kilcrease, administrators of the estate of Davis Kilcrease, versus James Hardin.

6 October 1824

Pg. 245
COMMISSIONERS OF HARDINSVILLE - A deed of conveyance from the Commissioners of Hardinsville to Joseph Buckingham, for Lott 13 in Hardinsville. Gabriel Eads and Robert Netherry, subscribing witnesses.

20 December 1824

Pg. 259
BOYD, JAMES - Last will and testament of James Boyd presented for probate. Proven by James Graham, subscribing witness.

Pg. 260
CHERRY, ISHAM - A deed of conveyance from Isham Cherry to Walter Wood, for 99 poles of land, was certified.

HARDIN, JAMES - Produced a land grant from the State of Tennessee for 152 acres.

HARDIN, JOSEPH - A deed of conveyance from Joseph Hardin to William Morrow, for 1000 acres, was certified.

Pg. 261
HARDIN, MARTIN - Swan Hardin and Mary Hardin qualified as executor and executrix of the last will and testament of Martin Hardin.

HALE, BENJAMIN - Robert Russell appointed administrator of the estate of Benjamin Hale.

21 December 1824

Pg. 263
BOYD, JAMES - Last will and testament of James Boyd proven by Lewis H. Broyles, one of the subscribing witnesses.

BOYD, JAMES SR. - James Boyd appointed administrator of the estate of James Boyd, Sr.

JONES, JESSE - A deed of conveyance from Jesse Jones to

Wesley Delaney, for 60 acres, was certified.

21 March 1825

Pg. 265
HARDIN, JAMES - A deed of conveyance from James Hardin to Moses Smith, for 40 acres, was certified.

Pg. 266
FALKNER, LEWIS N. - A deed of conveyance from Lewis N. Falkner to James W. Combs, for 160 acres, was certified.

KERR, SAMUEL - A deed of gift from Samuel Kerr to Elizabeth Kerr was certified. Proven by Jesse Jones and Lodowick Jones, subscribing witnesses.

Pg. 267
BOYCE, _____ - John Boyce, an orphin boy age 12, bound to John Pybas until age 21.

KELTON, WILLIAM - Petition by heirs of William Kelton to divide the land belonging to the estate.

Pg. 269
CUNNINGHAM, THOMAS - Stock mark registered in the name of Thomas Cunningham. Smooth off left ear and underbit in right ear.

HOLLAND, ASA - Stock mark registered in the name of Asa Holland. Swallow fork in each ear.

22 March 1825

Pg. 270
HARBOR, ELIJAH - A deed of gift from Elijah Harbor to Elisha Harbor was certified.

Pg. 271
THOMPSON, WILLIAM - Francis Thompson appointed guardian of Mary Thompson, Judah Thompson, Nancy C. Thompson, and Frances Thompson, infant heirs of William Thompson.

EDWARDS, THOMAS F. - Sworn in by the court as a practising attorney.

24 March 1825

Pg. 281
DAVIS, MOURNING - A deed of gift from Mourning Davis to Mazzell Cherry was certified. Proven by Isham Cherry, subscribing witness.

25 March 1825

Pg. 282
COMMISSIONERS OF HARDINSVILLE - A deed of conveyance from the Commissioners of Hardinsville to Gabriel Eads, for Lot No. 8, was certified.

COMMISSIONERS OF HARDINSVILLE - A deed of conveyance from the Commissioners of Hardinsville to William Sloan, for Lot No. 19, was certified.

20 June 1825

Pg. 289
CHERRY, ISHAM - A deed of conveyance from Isham Cherry to Samuel Williams, for 190 acres, was certified.

HARDIN, JAMES - A deed of conveyance from James Hardin to Charles T. Polk, for 200 acres, was certified.

Pg. 290
LINSEY, EZEKIEL - Last will and testament of Ezekiel Linsey presented for probate by Isaac Linsey and Elizabeth Linsey, the executor and executrix. Proven by George W. Guthrie, John Reynolds, and Seth Baker, subscribing witnesses.

BARKS, _____ - Patsey Barks bound out to Kenneth Murkinson until age 18.

CHERRY, _____ - Joseph Cherry, who was 16 years old on 17 December 1824, bound to Walter Wood until age 21.

Pg. 291
CHERRY, _____ - Franklin Cherry, over 10 years old, bound to Coonrod Gibbs until age 21.

Pg. 293
GOODIN, JAMES - A deed of mortgage from James Goodin to Samuel Wells, for 160 acres, was certified. Proven by Henry Nixon, subscribing witness.

21 June 1825

Pg. 294
ROSS, WILLIAM B. - Transfer of a plat and certificate from William B. Ross to Martin Hardin's heirs was certified.

ROSS, WILLIAM B. - Transfer of a plat and certificate from William B. Ross to John Nesbitt, for 50 acres, was certified.

VAUGHN, REUBEN - Transfer of a plat and certificate from Reuben Vaughn to Charles R. Walker, for 100 acres, was certified.

23 June 1825

Pg. 302
COMMISSIONERS OF HARDINSVILLE - A deed of conveyance from the Commissioners of Hardinsville to Amos Hardin, for Lot No. 5, was certified.

19 September 1825

Pg. 306
REYNOLDS, JOHN - Elizabeth Reynolds appointed administratrix of the estate of John Reynolds.

Pg. 307
FRIS(?), HUGH - James Barnett appointed administrator of the estate of Hugh Fris(?).

REYNOLDS, JOHN - Commissioners appointed to lay off a year's provisions for Elizabeth Reynolds, widow of John Reynolds.

SLOAN, ALEXANDER - Ruth Sloan appointed administratrix of the estate of Alexander Sloan.

Pg. 308
BRIANT, AARON - A deed of conveyance from Aaron Briant to Elizabeth Briant was certified.

BLANTON, _____ - Lucy Hix Blanton, guardian of Lucinda and Ruth Blanton, returned an account of their holdings.

Pg. 309
FULLER, _____ - Samuel Harbour released from his bond for Jefferson Fuller.

Pg. 310
KERR, JANE - Stock mark registered in the name of Jane Kerr. Smooth cross off right ear and hole in left ear.

21 September 1825

Pg. 319
KERR, ANDREW - A deed of release from William Alison, Rosanah Alison, Lettis Falls, Isabella Kerr, James G. Willoughby, and Margaret Willoughby to James Kerr for a tract of land whereon Andrew Kerr, dec'd, formerly lived in Iredell County, NC. Rosanah Alison and Margaret Willoughby were examined separately from their husbands and asserted that they executed said deed freely without fear of coercion.

23 September 1825

Pg. 327
CHERRY, DANIEL - A deed of conveyance from Daniel Cherry to Francis Kincannon, for 44 acres, was certified. Proven by A.W. Sweeney and Lewis N. Broyles.

Pg. 329
SLOAN, ALEXANDER - Commissioners appointed to lay off a year's provisions to Ruth Sloan, widow of Alexander Sloan.

19 December 1825

Pg. 330
HACKWORTH, JOHN - David Golleher appointed administrator of the estate of John Hackworth.

Pg. 331
LINDSEY, EZEKIEL - Isaac Lindsey appointed guardian of John W. Lindsey, William T. Lindsey, Elizabeth Lindsey, Polly Lindsey, Phebe Lindsey, Josiah G. Lindsey, and Isaac L. Lindsey, infant heirs of Ezekiel Lindsey.

HACKWORTH, JOHN - Commissioners appointed to lay off a year's provisions for Isabella Hackworth, widow of John Hackworth.

21 December 1825

Pg. 338
CHERRY, ISHAM - A deed of conveyance from Isham Cherry to Hiram Boone, for 228 acres, was certified. Proven by A.W. Sweeney and William Milligan, subscribing witnesses.

Pg. 341

HALBERT, WILLIAM - A deed of conveyance from William Halbert to Samuel Harbour, for 80 acres, was certified.

(Note: The following stock mark registrations were added on to the end of this book and are included here. The pages containing these entries were not numbered.)

YOUNT, LARKIN - Stock mark. Two smooth crosses and an underbit in the left ear. 11 April 1842.

COVEY, WESLEY - Stock mark. Two smooth crosses and two overbits. 11 April 1842.

COVEY, RUSSELL R. - Stock mark. Two smooth crosses and an overbit in left ear. 11 April 1842.

HOLT, TILMAN - Stock mark. Smooth cross off of right ear and hole in the left. 29 April 1842.

HOLT, GILES - Stock mark. Smooth cross off of right ear and hole and underbit in the left. 29 April 1842.

STEPHENS, ELIZABETH - Stock mark. Swallow fork and underbit in each ear. 25 May 1842.

BEASLEY, DANIEL B. - Stock mark. Split in right ear and half cross in the left. 28 January 1843.

DAVEY, JOHN L. - Stock mark. Two under half-crosses. 6 --- 1843.

ROBINSON, D.H. - Stock mark. Split in each ear. 1 September 1849.

DAVY, W.T. - Stock mark. Swallow fork and underbit in the left ear and split in the right. 30 November 1849.

BLAKELY, JOHN C. - Stock mark. Hole in left ear and split in right. 31 January 18--.

THORNTON, JOSIAH - Stock mark. Smooth cross off the left ear and half cross in the right ear. 15 March 1852.

THORNTON, S.R. - Stock mark. Smooth cross off each ear and a split in the right ear. 15 March 1852.

BARNES, JOHN L. - Stock mark. Smooth cross off each ear. 19 March 1852.

BASYE, EDMUND - Stock mark. Two underbits in each ear. 3 May 1852.

HUGGINS, THOS. - Stock mark. Cross and split in the right ear and underbit in left. 18 April 1849.

HAYNES, DARLING - Stock mark. Smooth cross off each ear and underbit in left. 18 April 1849.

RUSSELL, JAMES - Stock mark. Swallow fork and underbit in the right and cross and split in the left. 6 September 1852.

LUTHER, JACOB - Stock mark. Smooth cross and split in the right ear. 2 March 1853.

RINK, H.A. - Stock mark. Smooth cross and split in the right ear and cross and half-cross in the left. 5 March 1853.

GILLIS, DOUGAL - Stock mark. Smooth cross off the right ear and swallow fork in the left ear. 7 March 1853.

COUNTY COURT MINUTES

BOOK C: 1834 - 1843

15 September 1834

Pg. 9
McCHAN, JOSEPH R. - Commissioners appointed to lay off a year's provisions for the widow and heirs of Joseph R. McChan.

CRANESHAH, JACKSON - Robert Steele allowed $25.00 for keeping a pauper, Jackson Craneshah.

Pg. 10
WELLS, JAMES - Samuel Wells appointed administrator of the estate of James Wells.

WINSLOW, JOSEPH - Joseph W. Ellis and Joshua Reaves appointed administrators of the estate of Joseph Winslow.

HAIRE, _____ - Martha Haire, age 11, bound to James McClain. Caion(?) Haire, age 8, bound to John Farrar. William Haire, age 5, bound to James Graham.

REYNOLDS, HENRY - Commissioners appointed to lay off a year's provisions to the widow and heirs of Henry Reynolds.

TISDALE, POLLY - John Hogan allowed $85.00 for keeping a pauper, Polly Tisdale.

Pg. 11
REYNOLDS, HENRY - Matilda Reynolds appointed guardian of Polly Perry Reynolds, Tabitha Jane Reynolds, Henry Vernon Reynolds, Sarah Ann Reynolds, Redden Washington Reynolds, and Rita Caroline Reynolds, minor heirs of Henry Reynolds.

SHELBY, MOSES A. - John Houston appointed administrator of the estate of Moses A. Shelby.

JAMES, THOMAS - John Scott appointed administrator of the estate of Thomas James.

PURVIS, CULLEN - James Barnett appointed administrator of the estate of Cullen Purvis.

EOFF, JOSEPH - David Shull, of Wayne County, and Dicy Eoff, of Hardin County, appointed administrators of the estate of Joseph Eoff.

Pg. 12
SHELBY, MOSES A. - Commissioners appointed to lay off a year's

provisions for the widow and heirs of Moses A. Shelby.

EOFF, JOSEPH - Commissioners appointed to lay off a year's provisions for the widow and heirs of Joseph Eoff.

POLLARD, JAMES - Settlement with Swain Ward, guardian of the heirs of James Pollard.

POLLARD, JAMES - Jesse B. Gantt appointed guardian of the heirs of James Pollard.

Pg. 13
WINSLOW, JOSEPH - Commissioners appointed to divide the estate of Joseph Winslow.

JAMES, ENOCH - Last will and testament of Enoch James proven by Robert Thrasher and Zachariah Smyth, subscribing witnesses.

Pg. 14
CHERRY, ISHAM - Settlement with Eli Cherry, executor of the estate of Isham Cherry.

GOODNER, GODFREY - A deed of conveyance from Godfrey Goodner to L.H. Broyles, for 2 acres, was certified.

Pg. 15
KERR, JANE - Thomas W. Poindexter released as security for Thomas Gray and William Wells, executors or administrators of the estate of Jane Kerr.

SHANNON, THOMAS SR. - Petition by the heirs and guardian of the minor heirs of Thomas Shannon, Sr. to divide the estate.

REYNOLDS, HENRY - Last will and testament and codicil of Henry Reynolds presented for probate by Jesse B. Gantt and Elisha Pack, executors. Proven by Jonathan W. Martin, William Pickins, John C. Reynolds, and Jesse B. Gantt, subscribing witnesses.

WHITE, JOHN - A deed of conveyance from John White to Samuel White, for 70 acres, was certified. Proven by James A. Kindel and George White.

Pg. 16
FALKNER, LEWIS N. - A deed of conveyance from Lewis N. Falkner to Godfrey Goodner and Benjamin Brownerin, for 160 acres, was certified.

CRENSHAW, JACKSON - Joseph W. Ellis appointed guardian for Jackson Crenshaw.

16 September 1834

Pg. 17
CRENSHAW, _____ - Daniel Smith appointed guardian for Elizabeth Crenshaw.

Pg. 18
PICKINS, HEZEKIAH - A deed of conveyance from Hezekiah Pickins to John O. Barnett, for 124 acres, was certified. Proven by Jeremiah Burge and Richard Burge, subscribing witnesses.

17 September 1834

Pg. 21
   JAMES, ENOCH - William R. Janes appointed administrator of the estate of Enoch James.

   SATTERFIELD, JEREMIAH - George Johnson appointed administrator of the estate of Jeremiah Satterfield.

18 September 1834

Pg. 26
   KINDEL, W.C. - A deed of conveyance from W.C. Kindel to Lewis H. Broyles for one town lott. Certified on 22 September 1834.

   BEATY, THOMAS - A deed of conveyance from Thomas Beaty to Jonathan M. Church, for 90 acres, was certified on 29 October 1834.

   WILLBANKS, BENNETT - A deed of trust from Bennett Willbanks to James Warr, for use of Dudley C. Johnson for a waggon and 5 horses and gear. Proven by James Huddleston and Robert Gray, subscribing witnesses. Certified on 31 October 1834.

   BURTWELL, JAMES - A deed of mortgage from James Burtwell to George H. Burtwell, for a clock and sundry other articles of personal property, was certified on 13 November 1834.

15 December 1834

Pg. 28
   LEE, SIMPSON - James Robinson appointed guardian of the minor heirs and children of Simpson Lee. Also, commissioners appointed to lay off a year's provisions for the widow and minor heirs of Simpson Lee.

   HANNAH, JOHN - John Houston and John D. Porterfield appointed administrators of the estate of John Hannah.

   WRIGHT, JAMES - James Wright and William Wright appointed administrators of the estate of James Wright. Commissioners appointed to lay off a year's provisions for the widow and minor heirs of James Wright.

Pg. 29
   McCAN, JOSEPH R. - Commissioners appointed to lay off a year's provisions for the widow of Joseph R. McCan.

Pg. 30
   JAMES, SARAH - A deed of mortgage from Sarah James to Joseph W. Ellis, for 50 acres, was certified.

Pg. 31
   CHERRY, NOEL - Eli Cherry presented an account of Margaret Cherry against the three children of Noel Cherry.

   PICKENS, J.H. _ A deed of conveyance from J.H. Pickens to David Nichols, for 105 acres, was certified.

   PICKENS, JEREMIAH H. - A deed of conveyance from Jeremiah H. Pickens to John Cooper, for 40 acres, was certified.

   PICKENS, JEREMIAH H. - A deed of conveyance from Jeremiah

H. Pickens to John Cooper, for 5 acres, was certified.

Pg. 32
FORBES, COLLIN - A deed of conveyance from Collin Forbes to Rix A. Randolph, for an occupant claim of 200 acres, was certified. Proven by Joseph W. Ellis and John Scott, subscribing witnesses.

NEWELL, HU. F. - A deed of conveyance from Hu. F. Newell to Daniel Smith, for 44 acres, was certified.

NEWELL, HU. F. - A deed of conveyance from Hu. F. Newell to Daniel Smith, for 56 acres, was certified.

Pg. 33
SHANNON, THOMAS - Division of land among the heirs of Thomas Shannon. Heirs mentioned: Thomas T. Shannon, Susan E. Hawkins, Wm. H. Shannon, Sarah A. Shannon, Nathan E. Shannon, George W. Shannon, and Jane L. Rawlings.

16 December 1834

Pg. 35
CHERRY, JESSE - A deed of conveyance from Jesse Cherry to David Cherry, for 15 acres, was certified.

Pg. 36
CHERRY, DAVID - A deed of conveyance from David Cherry to William Stricklin, for 40 acres, was certified.

17 December 1834

Pg. 38
CHERRY, ISHAM - Jesse Cherry qualified as executor of the estate of Isham Cherry.

16 March 1835

Pg. 42
THRASHER, JOSEPH - A deed of conveyance from Joseph Thrasher to Isaac Hitchcock, for 40 acres, was certified. Proven by Andrew Stout and Andrew White, subscribing witnesses.

Pg. 43
TUCKER, THOMAS - A bill of sale, for a negro boy named Harry, from Thomas Tucker to Aaron Cunningham was acknowledged.

RUSSELL, ELIZABETH AND ALBERT - A bill of sale, for a negro boy named Harry, from Elizabeth and Albert Russell to Thomas Tucker was acknowledged.

RUSSELL, JOHN T. AND JAMES - A bill of sale, for a negro boy named Killis and a mill, from John T. and James Russell to Thomas Tucker was acknowledged. Proven by John Wilson, subscribing witness.

RUSSELL, ALBERT - A deed of conveyance from Albert Russell to Thomas Tucker, for a mill and an occupant claim, was certified. Proven by Aaron Cunningham, subscribing witness.

RUSSELL, _____ - A bill of sale, for a negro boy named Harry, from Elizabeth, James, Alexander, and John T. Russell to Albert Russell was acknowledged. Proven by John Wilson, subscribing witness.

HARDIN, _____ - Thomas M. Hardin, a minor, requested that Benjamin Hardin be appointed as his guardian. His request was granted.

Pg. 44
NORVILLE, JAMES - Nathaniel Erwin appointed administrator of the estate of James Norville.

HERROD, JOHN - Commissioners appointed to settle with the administrator of the estate of John Herrod.

ROBBINS, _____ - John Robbins, a minor, bound to Robert Stout until age 21.

NOLEN, JOSEPH - Joseph Nolen, a pauper, allowed $75.00 for his maintenance and upkeep.

Pg. 47
POLLARD, JAMES - Jesse B. Gantt released as guardian of the heirs of James Pollard.

17 March 1835

Pg. 51
BUIE, JOHN SR. - John Buie, Sr. presented his declaration for a pension.

21 March 1835

Pg. 56
KINCANNON, DAVID - A deed of conveyance from David Robinson, surviving administrator of David Kincannon, to Samuel Harbour, for 40 acres, was certified.

Pg. 57
HARGROVE, VALENTINE - A deed of conveyance from Valentine Hargrove to Charles W. Ross, for 25 acres and (next entry) 45 acres, was certified.

MERKINSON, KENNITH - A deed of conveyance from Kennith Merkinson to Hu. McCarn, for 320 acres, was certified. Proven by John Burton and Squire Burton, subscribing witnesses.

HUGHES, A.M. - A deed of mortgage from A.M. Hughes to J.H. Pickens was certified. Dated 20 June 1835.

BURGE, JEREMIAH - A deed of conveyance from Jeremiah Burge to John S. Broyles, for 102 acres, was certified. Dated 21 July 1835.

BURGE, JEREMIAH - A deed of conveyance from Jeremiah Burge to John S. Broyles, for 25 acres, was certified. Dated 21 July 1835.

ROBINSON, JAMES - A deed of conveyance from James Robinson to Lemuel Sutton, for 25 acres, was certified. Proven by Temple C. Johnson and Bowen Davy, subscribing witnesses.

DUFF, ROBERT - A deed of conveyance from Robert Duff to James Duff, for 35 acres, was certified. Dated 14 September 1835.

RHOADS, THOMAS AND WILLIAM H. CARTWRIGHT - A deed of conveyance from Thomas Rhoads and William H. Cartwright to Wm. M. Altem, for 200 acres, was certified.

HOUSTON, JOHN - A deed of conveyance from John Houston to Matthew C. Houston, for four town lots in Savannah, was certified.

15 June 1835

Pg. 58
CHANEY, C.C. - A deed of conveyance from C.C. Chaney to T.W. Poindexter, for Town Lott No. 42 in Savannah, was certified. Proven by Jno. P. Clingman, subscribing witness.

Pg. 59
BURNETT, JOHN O. - Stock mark registered in the name of John O. Burnett. Smooth cross in right ear and swallow fork in left ear.

LEDBETTER, JAMES - James Ledbetter, a pauper, let out to William Wilkins, the lowest bidder.

Pg. 60
KIRBY, WILLIAM - A deed of conveyance from William Kirby to J.C. and C. Johnson, for 100 acres, was certified. Proven by Nimrod Morris, subscribing witness.

Pg. 61
NIELSON, C.B. - Robert Hannah appointed administrator of the estate of C.B. Nielson.

AIKEN, _____ - Rix A. Randolph appointed guardian of William Aiken, Patsy Aiken, and Parthenia Aiken.

16 June 1835

Pg. 66
McCONNELL, JOSHUA - Inventory of estate of Joshua McConnell returned by Polly McConnell, administratrix.

PARRISH, K.V. - Commissioners appointed to settle with L.H. Broyles, administrator of the estate of K.V. Parrish.

STRAUN, WILLIAM - A deed of conveyance from William Straun to Thomas D. Mason, for 500 acres, was certified.

MASON, THOMAS D. - A bill of sale, for 3 negroes named Agnes, Emiline, and Rose, from Thomas D. Mason to William Straun was acknowledged.

Pg. 68
HARDIN, _____ - Mark Hardin requested that his guardian be changed from James Irwin to William K. Hardin. His request was granted.

21 September 1835

Pg. 71
SHUTE, PHILIP - A deed of conveyance from Philip Shute, by his agent Jehu Davy, to Jonathan Windsor, for 240 acres, was certified.

CHERRY, NOEL - Eli Cherry and Margaret Cherry entered into bond as guardians of the minor heirs of Noel Cherry.

ASHWORTH, JOSEPH - Last will and testament of Joseph Ashworth presented for probate by James W. Ashworth, executor.

Pg. 72
BELL, JAMES - A deed of conveyance from James Bell, by his agent David Robinson, to Cordy Parrish, for 150 acres, was ordered to be certified.

KAGLE, GEORGE - A deed of conveyance from George Kagle to Jesse Smith, for 100 acres, was certified.

Pg. 73
SHUTE, THOMAS AND CHARLES GRAHAM - A title bond from Thomas Shute and Charles Graham to William Fisher, for 120 acres, was certified.

Pg. 74
HOLLAND, JNO. - A deed of conveyance from Bannister Holland, administrator of the estate of Jno. Holland, to William Strawn, for 569 acres, was certified. Proven by Richard C. Hale and Joseph N. Baker, subscribing witnesses.

SMITH, DANIEL - A deed of conveyance from Daniel Smith to Jno. C. Johnson and Curtis Johnson, for 100 acres, was certified.

WAGNER, DANIEL - Last will and testament and codicil of Daniel Wagner presented for probate. Proven by Jno. P. Baird, M.L. Woods, and A.H. Baird, subscribing witnesses. Martha Wagner and Jno. J. Williams qualified as executrix and executor.

WRIGHT, _____ - Petition by Euphemia Wright for a dower was granted. Commissioners appointed to lay the dower off.

Pg. 75
REED, OZZI - Commissioners appointed to lay off a year's provisions for the widow of Ozzi Reed.

NEILSON, CHARLES B. - Commissioners appointed to lay off a year's provisions for the widow of Charles B. Neilson.

WETHERLY, JOB - Commissioners appointed to settle with Margaret Wetherly, administratrix of the estate of Job Wetherly.

Pg. 76
HERROD, JNO. - Commissioners appointed to settle with Catherine Herrod, administratrix of the estate of Jno. Herrod.

LEE, SIMPSON - Commissioners appointed to settle with P.B. Hawkins and Jehu Davy, administrators of the estate of Simpson Lee.

Pg. 77
REED, OZZI - Amzi Reed appointed administrator of the estate of Ozzi Reed.

GILLIS, ALX. - Jas. Irwin appointed administrator of the estate of Alx. Gillis.

RUSSELL, DELILAH - Alx. Russell appointed administrator of the estate of Delilah Russell.

Pg. 78
ROSS, GEORGE - A deed of conveyance from George Ross to Elisha Harbour, for 100 acres, was certified. Proven by John Mc. Ross

and Elijah Harbour, subscribing witnesses.

ROSS, JNO. Mc. - A deed of conveyance from Jno. Mc. Ross to Jno. Bundy, for 20 acres, was certified.

22 September 1835

Pg. 83
TARKINTON, ISAAC - A bill of sale, for a negro woman named Cynthia, from Isaac Tarkinton to J.G. Hundly was acknowledged.

BATY, THOMAS - A deed of conveyance from Thomas Baty to Robert M. Coretin, of Alabama, for 160 acres, was certified.

23 September 1835

Pg. 85
SAMUEL, ACHILLES W. - A deed of conveyance from Achilles W. Samuel to Newton E. Akin, for 53 acres, was certified.

PHENIX, HENRY - A deed of conveyance from Henry Phenix of Perry County to Willm. Akin of Perry County, for 100 acres in Hardin County, was certified.

21 December 1835

Pg. 91
STOUT, ROBERT - Andrew Stout and Isaiah Stout appointed administrators of the estate of Robert Stout.

VIARS, REBECCA - John Kirby appointed administrator of the estate of Rebecca Viars.

McBRIDE, _____ - Mary Jane McBride, age about 11, bound to Daniel Baine.

McBRIDE, _____ - Robert McBride, age about 9, bound to George Baine.

STOUT, ROBERT - Commissioners appointed to lay off a year's provisions to the widow of Robert Stout.

Pg. 92
NEWMAN, THOMAS - Samuel Newman and Parry B. Hawkins appointed administrators of the estate of Thomas Newman.

BYRD, WILLIAM - John R. Byrd appointed administrator of the estate of William Byrd.

POLK, _____ - Thomas Blakely appointed guardian of Polly Ann Polk.

Pg. 93
THOMAS, ANDREW - Polly Thomas appointed administratrix of the estate of Andrew Thomas.

GARNER, HENRY - George Johnson and Elizabeth Garner appointed administrators of the estate of Henry Garner.

BYRD, WILLIAM - Commissioners appointed to lay off a year's provisions for the widow and minor heirs of William Byrd.

Pg. 94
HAGGARD, JONATHAN - A deed of conveyance from Jonathan Haggard to David K. Wade, for 80 acres, was certified. Proven by Thomas Blakely and Elizabeth Mosely, subscribing witnesses.

HOLLAND, JESSE - A deed of conveyance from Jesse Holland to Asa Holland, for 25 acres, was certified. Proven by Parry B. Hawkins and William H. Shannon, subscribing witnesses.

WRIGHT, _____ - Isaac Wright, a minor, requested that William Wright be appointed as his guardian. His request was granted.

WRIGHT, _____ - James Wright appointed guardian of Rachel Wright, a minor.

Pg. 95
SHUTE, PHILIP AND JEHU DAVY - A deed of conveyance from Philip Shute, by his agent, and Jehu Davy to Lewis Williams, for 240 acres, was certified.

Pg. 99
MADDOX, JOHN - Last will and testament of John Maddox presented for probate. Proven by Joseph Duncan and William Maddox, the subscribing witnesses. Mary Maddox qualified as executrix.

22 December 1835

Pg. 102
HOUSTON, SAMUEL - Hu. Tarbet appointed administrator of the estate of Samuel Houston.

21 March 1836

Pg. 111
BRATTENBOUCHER, JOHN J. - James Robinson and James Irwin appointed administrators of the estate of John J. Brattenboucher.

2 May 1836

Pg. 116
HAWKINS, JOHN T. - James O. Hawkins appointed administrator of the estate of John T. Hawkins.

Pg. 117
TURNER, WASKING B. - Certified to practice law.

Pg. 119
McCANN, JOSEPH R. - Commissioners appointed to settle with Charles Spencer, administrator of the estate of Joseph R. McCann.

RUSSELL, JOHN T. - Commissioners appointed to lay off a year's provisions for Mrs. Russell, widow of John T. Russell.

Pg. 121
RUSSELL, JOHN T. - James Scott appointed administrator of the estate of John T. Russell. The next-of-kin failed to administer. Scott was the largest creditor of the estate.

6 June 1836

Pg. 123
McBRIDE, SAMUEL - Daniel Bain allowed $25.00 for keeping

Samuel McBride for 5 months and for funeral expenses.

Pg. 124
ROBERTSON, SAMUEL - Samuel Robertson appointed administrator of the estate of Samuel Robertson.

Pg. 125
ASHWORTH, _____ - James W. Ashworth ordered to sell the balance of the property of his father's estate which was left in the hands of the widow.

COX, MERIDETH - William Cox and Joseph W. Cox appointed as administrators of the estate of Merideth Cox.

Pg. 126
GARNER, HENRY - Elizabeth Garner, relict and late wife of Henry Garner, dec'd, petitioned for her dower.

Pg. 127
GARNER, HENRY - Daniel B. Beasley appointed guardian for Joshua Garner and James Garner, minor heirs of Henry Garner.

Pg. 128
BRATTENBOUCHER, JOHN JACOB - Noncupative will of John Jacob Brattenboucher presented for probate. It was contested and sent up to the circuit court.

4 July 1836

Pg. 131
HANNAH, ALEXANDER - John Houston appointed administrator of the estate of Alexander Hannah.

Pg. 132
HAIRE, _____ - Richard Haire, an orphan, bound out to Alexander Nevill.

1 August 1836

Pg. 137
DENNUM, _____ - Wilson Dennum, an orphan minor of 6 years, bound and apprenticed to Thomas A. Kerr until age 21.

5 September 1836

Pg. 139
BOOKOUT, JESSE - Henry Bookout appointed administrator of the estate of Jesse Bookout.

JOHNSON, HUGH - Lucinda Johnson appointed administratrix of the estate of Hugh Johnson.

Pg. 140
COOPER, JONATHAN - James B. Grimes appointed administrator of the estate of Jonathan Cooper.

Pg. 142
BOOKOUT, _____ - Commissioners appointed to lay off a year's provisions for the Widow Bookout and minor heirs.

3 October 1836

Pg. 144
    LEE, _____ - Fanny Lee appointed guardian of Elizabeth Lee, a minor.

Pg. 145
    BUNDAY, JOHN - A deed of conveyance from John Bunday to Eliza Kellogg and Samuel Kelog, for a parcel of land, was certified.

Pg. 146
    COOPER, _____ - Commissioners appointed to lay off a year's provisions for the Widow Cooper.

7 November 1836

Pg. 148
    MORRIS, JOHN SR. - Roda Morris appointed administratrix of the estate of John Morris, Sr.

Pg. 149
    HANNAH, _____ - Commissioners appointed to lay off a year's provisions for the Widow Hannah.

5 December 1836

Pg. 153
    JAMES, THOMAS - John Scott gave bond as guardian of Priscilla James, Elizabeth James, Samuel James, and Delilah James, minor heirs of Thomas James.

    KERR, WILLIAM - Securities for William Kerr, who was guardian of his son at last term of court, were to notify said Kerr that he would be delivered up to the court. Said notice was not given and the security was released from further liability.

    TANKERLEY, _____ - James Tankerley, a minor who was 17 in May of 1837, was bound to Charles Wood until age 21.

6 February 1837

Pg. 157
    MILLIGAN, WILLIAM - George M. Milligan and James S. Milligan appointed administrators of the estate of William Milligan.

Pg. 158
    ORR, JAMES - John White appointed administrator of the estate of James Orr.

    WILLOUGHBY, JAMES G. - Stock mark registered in the name of James G. Willoughby. Cross and half cross off each ear.

Pg. 160
    ORR, JAMES - Commissioners appointed to lay off a year's provisions for the widow and minor heirs of James Orr.

6 March 1837

Pg. 161
    NEILSON(?), WILLIAM - A copy of the last will and testament of William Neilson(?) of Buncombe County, North Carolina, was presented.

1 May 1837

Pg. 172
    LEAKY, _____ - Rachel Leaky, an orphan child 13 years old in October 1837, bound to James Sweeny until age 18.

    LEAKY, _____ - Phebe Leaky, an orphan child age 10, bound to Daniel H. Hunter until age 18.

    LEAKY, _____ - Rhody Leaky, an orphan child 9 years old, bound to Thomas Gray until age 18.

5 June 1837

Pg. 175
    McMAHAN, JAMES F. - Last will and testament of James F. McMahan presented for probate. Proven by Jehu Davy and Solomon Hudiburg, subscribing witnesses. Alexander Russell and Nelly McMahan qualified as executors.

Pg. 177
    LEAKY, MARY - Mary Leaky, a pauper, let out to James Sweeny, the lowest bidder.

3 July 1837

Pg. 181
    PORTER, WILLIAM - Eleanor Porter appointed administrator of the estate of William Porter.

    SMITH, THOMAS - Elizabeth Dickson allowed $15.00 for taking care of Thomas Smith and his mother.

7 August 1837

Pg. 184
    WINDSOR, JONATHAN - Jonathan Wellborn appointed administrator of the estate of Jonathan Windsor.

Pg. 187
    WAGGONER, DANIEL - Alexander Nivill and Elizabeth Nivill petitioned the court to have Martha Waggoner and John J. Williams summoned to court to show why they should not be removed as the executrix and executor of the estate of Daniel Waggoner, and why the probate of the will should not be revoked.

4 September 1837

Pg. 188
    RUSSELL, JAMES - Thomas Tucker appointed administrator of the estate of James Russell.

Pg. 190
    POLK, _____ - Thomas Polk appointed guardian of Elizabeth Jane Polk.

    WAGGONER, DANIEL - Probate of the will of Daniel Waggoner revoked and executors removed. Said decision has been appealed.

5 September 1837

Pg. 191
    WAGGONER, DANIEL - John J. Williams appointed guardian of Sarah Williams, Elizabeth Williams, Daniel Williams, and Julia Williams, heirs of Daniel Waggoner.

WAGGONER, DANIEL - Petition for dower by Martha Waggoner, Wido of Daniel Waggoner.

2 October 1837

Pg. 192
RUSSELL, JAMES - Commissioners appointed to lay off a year's provisions for the widow and minor heirs of James Russell.

WILLIAMS, WILLIAM L. - James Warr appointed administrator of the estate of William L. Williams.

6 November 1837

Pg. 195
MORRIS, ROBERT - Robert Morris, coroner, issued a certificate for holding 3 inquests; one on R.B. Stone, one on Wm.P. Freeman, and one on a dead body found in the river at Burtwell's Warehouse.

RUSSELL, ALBERT - John C. Rea appointed administrator of the estate of Alber Russell.

4 December 1837

Pg. 199
RUSSELL, WILLIAM - Robert R. Russell appointed guardian of Hugh Russell, Alexander Russell, John Russell, James Russell, and Polly Russell, minor heirs of William Russell.

Pg. 200
LOYD, OWEN - Owen Loyd, a Revolutionary soldier, made application for his pension.

1 January 1838

Pg. 202
HANNAH, ALEXANDER - George D. Morrow appointed administrator of the estate of Alexander Hannah.

LAKEY, _____ - William C. Hughes appointed guardian of Rachel Lakey, an orphan.

Pg. 203
McCLAIN, JAMES - John Martin and Emanuel McClain appointed administrators of the estate of James McClain.

1 February 1838

Pg. 204
ROBERTS, MARGARET - Margaret Roberts, a mulatto girl who had been treated badly by Washington Turner, bound out to James Barnes the highest bidder.

Pg. 206
PICKENS, _____ - Jonathan R. Pickens appointed guardian for sufficient reasons of Sion R. Pickens, James G. Pickens, Mary Jane Pickens, Elizabeth B. Pickens, and Archibald G. Pickens, heirs of Jonathan R. Pickens who entered into bond.

Pg. 209
LEE, SIMPSON - Widow Fanny Lee allowed $300.00 for keeping Felix Lee, Emily Lee, and Alfred Lee, the three minor heirs of Simpson Lee.

Pg. 192
RUSSELL, JAMES - Commissioners appointed to lay off a year's provisions for the widow and minor heirs of James Russell.

WILLIAMS, WILLIAM L. - James Warr appointed administrator of the estate of William L. Williams.

6 November 1837

Pg. 195
MORRIS, ROBERT - Robert Morris, coroner, issued a certificate for holding 3 inquests; one on R.B. Stone, one on Wm.P. Freeman, and one on a dead body found in the river at Burtwell's Warehouse.

RUSSELL, ALBERT - John C. Rea appointed administrator of the estate of Albert Russell.

4 December 1837

Pg. 199
RUSSELL, WILLIAM - Robert R. Russell appointed guardian of Hugh Russell, Alexander Russell, John Russell, James Russell, and Polly Russell, minor heirs of William Russell.

Pg. 200
LOYD, OWEN - Owen Loyd, a Revolutionary soldier, made application for his pension.

1 January 1838

Pg. 202
HANNAH, ALEXANDER - George D. Morrow appointed administrator of the estate of Alexander Hannah.

LAKEY, _____ - William C. Hughes appointed guardian of Rachel Lakey, an orphan.

Pg. 203
McCLAIN, JAMES - John Martin and Emanuel McClain appointed administrators of the estate of James McClain.

1 February 1838

Pg. 204
ROBERTS, MARGARET - Margaret Roberts, a mulatto girl who had been treated badly by Washington Turner, bound out to James Barnes the highest bidder.

Pg. 206
PICKENS, _____ - Jonathan R. Pickens appointed guardian for sufficient reasons of Sion R. Pickens, James G. Pickens, Mary Jane Pickens, Elizabeth B. Pickens, and Archibald G. Pickens, heirs of Jonathan R. Pickens who entered into bond.

Pg. 209
LEE, SIMPSON - Widow Fanny Lee allowed $300.00 for keeping Felix Lee, Emily Lee, and Alfred Lee, the three minor heirs of Simpson Lee.

2 April 1838

2 April 1838

Pg. 219
BYRD, JOHN R. - John R. Byrd, acting coroner, allowed $5.00 for holding an inquest over the body of Anderson Tally.

3 April 1838

Pg. 220
PHILLIPS, POLLY - Polly Phillips, a pauper, let out to the lowest bidder, Clark Richards.

7 May 1838

Pg. 221
REYNOLDS, JOHN - Joseph Reynolds appointed guardian for B.F. Reynolds, Mary Reynolds, and Gharky Reynolds minor heirs of John Reynolds.

4 June 1838

Pg. 224
OWEN, THOMAS - David Owen appointed administrator of the estate of Thomas Owen.

2 July 1838

Pg. 226
McDANIEL, JOS. - John McDaniel appointed administrator of the estate of Jos. McDaniel.

Pg. 228
WINDSOR, JONATHAN - James Coulter asked to be released as a security for Jonathan Welborn, administrator for the estate of Jonathan Windsor, because he (Coulter) intends to remove beyond the limits of the state.

3 July 1838

Pg. 229
McDANIEL, LUCY - Power of attorney for Lucy McDaniel granted to John T. Petty.

McDaniel, JOEL - Power of attorney for Joel McDaniel, dec'd, vested in John McDaniel, administrator.

6 August 1838

Pg. 230
WINDSOR, JONATHAN - Martha Windsor, widow, appointed administrator of the estate of Jonathan Windsor.

3 September 1838

Pg. 233
LEAKY, _____ - Phebe Leaky bound out to Willis Brumley until age 18.

Pg. 234
EMMERSON, ELI - John Hawk and Terence Emmerson appointed administrators of the estate of Eli Emmerson.

1 October 1838

Pg. 236
REYNOLDS, JOHN - William Wells discharged as guardian of the minor heirs of John Reynolds. Joseph Reynolds appointed guardian in his place.

FREEMAN, ____ - Benjamin Rush Freeman bound to Isaac Thornton. William Andrew Freeman bound to Thomas Blakly, John Lewis Freeman bound to Dawson H. Robinson. James Jasper Freeman bound to W.G. Campbell.

Pg. 237
FREEMAN, ____ - Adaline Catherine Freeman bound to Willie B. Edwards. Sarah Jane Freeman bound to Willis Lucas.

WELLS, ____ - James Duff appointed guardian of Sarah Jane Wells.

DICKSON, JOHN M. - William Dickson appointed administrator of the estate of John M. Dickson.

BUIE, CORNELIUS - John Buie and Elizabeth Buie appointed administrators of the estate of Cornelius Buie.

Pg. 238
FREEMAN, WILLIAM P. - James Robinson appointed administrator of the estate of William P. Freeman.

BUIE, CORNELIUS - Commissioners appointed to lay off a year's provisions for the widow of Cornelius Buie.

Pg. 239
STEVENS, HENRY - Last will and testament presented for probate. Proven by Willis Lucas, subscribing witness.

STEPHENS, HENRY - Elizabeth Stephens, executrix, asked that Willis Lucas be appointed administrator of the estate of Henry Stephens.

5 November 1838

Pg. 241
STRAUN, MARY - Mary Straun, a pauper, let out to L---- McDaniel.

Pg. 242
COOPER, JONATHAN - James B. Grimes appointed guardian of Elizabeth Cooper, John Cooper, and Vachel Cooper, minor heirs of Jonathan Cooper.

FRILEY, MARTIN - Joseph Duncan, coroner, allowed $5.00 for holding an inquest over the body of Martin Friley.

Pg. 243
FRALEY, MARTIN - Andrew J. and Elizabeth Fraley appointed administrators of the estate of Martin Fraley.

FRLY, ____ - Solomon Frly, age about 10, bound out to Andrew J. Frly.

FRLY, MARTIN - Commissioners appointed to lay off a year's provisions for the widow and minor heirs.

3 December 1838

Pg. 245
    AIKEN, _____ - William Aiken, aged 15, bound to Rix A. Randolph.

    KINCANNON, FRANCIS - Last will and testament presented for probate. Proven by David Garner and Nancy Ashworth, subscribing witnesses. Daniel Smith qualified as executor.

7 January 1839

Pg. 246
    EVANS, EGER - Commissioners appointed to lay off a year's provisions for the widow and a large family of minor heirs.

Pg. 248
    WATERS, _____ - Robert Waters, a minor 11 years old, bound to Daniel Owen until age 21.

Pg. 249
    STRAUN, MARY - Mary Straun and her two small children let out to Charles Riddle, the lowest bidder.

Pg. 250
    LADEN, GEORGE - Last will and testament presented for probate. Proven by Archibald Pool and Henry Garrard, subscribing witnesses. Eady Laden qualified as executrix.

    FRALEY, HENDERSON G. - Last will and testament of Henderson G. Fraley presented for probate. Sarah Fraley qualified as executrix.

    COOPER, JONATHAN - William McFerrin appointed administrator of the estate of Jonathan Cooper.

4 February 1839

Pg. 253
    WELLS, _____ - James Duff, who was appointed guardian of Sarah Jane Wells, has removed to the state of Mississippi and has been appointed guardian of said minor in Pontotoc County, Mississippi.

Pg. 254
    GOLDSMITH, WILLIAM - Charles H. Eads appointed administrator of the estate of William Goldsmith.

6 May 1839

Pg. 260
    POLK, CHARLES T. - Green W. Polk and Christopher H. McGinnis appointed administrators of the estate of Charles T. Polk.

    HAMILTON, JOSEPH - Stephen Hosey appointed administrator of the estate of Joseph Hamilton.

Pg. 262
    HAMILTON, JOSEPH - Commissioners appointed to lay off a year's provisions for the widow and minor heirs of Joseph Hamilton.

Pg 263
    HAIR, _____ - James McClain released from all liability in

the indenture of Martha Hair.

HAIR, _____ - Abel Hair appointed guardian of Martha Hair.

(Pages misnumbered. Page numbers given are those in the books.)

5 August 1839

Pg. 286
MARY ANN - Joseph Duncan, coroner, allowed $5.00 for an inquest held over the body of a negro woman named Mary Ann.

3 September 1839

Pg. 290
SHANNON, _____ - James O. Hawkins, guardian of Sarah A. Shannon, made his report.

7 October 1839

Pg. 291
ROBINSON, ALEXANDER F. - Lawson Robinson appointed administrator of the estate of Alexander F. Robinson.

SHANNON, _____ - Jahu Davy appointed guardian of Sarah A. Shannon in place of James O. Hawkins.

Pg. 292
REYNOLDS, HENRY - Daniel Smith removed as guardian of Tabitha J. Reynolds and Francis Coburn appointed in his place.

POLK, CHARLES T. - Commissioners appointed to lay off a year's provisions for the widow of Charles T. Polk.

GRAY AND WHITE - Milton Gray and Sherod White, paupers, to be let out to the lowest bidder.

Pg. 293
DAVEY, RICHARD - Last will and testament presented for probate. Proven by Samuel Perkins and Thomas Davy, subscribing witnesses. George D. Morrow and John Barham qualified as executors.

4 November 1839

Pg. 295
HATLEY, SHERROD - James S. Hatley appointed administrator of the estate of Sherrod Hatley.

OWEN, DANIEL - Nocupative will presented for probate. Proven by Caroline Battles and Sarah Ann Gray. Mary Owen, decedent's mother, qualified as executrix.

Pg. 297
REYNOLDS, HENRY - Daniel Smith resigned as guardian for Henry and Sarah Reynolds, minors of Henry Reynolds.

Pg. 298
REYNOLDS, HENRY - Francis Coburn appointed guardian for Henry and Sarah Reynolds, minors of Henry Reynolds.

REYNOLDS, HENRY - Daniel Smith appointed guardian for Redding W. Reynolds, minor of Henry Reynolds.

THOMPSON, JACKSON - A free boy of colour, named Jackson Thompson, bound to A.B. Campbell till age 21 to learn the tanner's trade.

2 December 1839

Pg. 301
BLOUNT, REDDEN - Jesse B. Gantt appointed guardian for Susan Ann C. Blount, Henry R. Blount, James E. Blount, Emsley P. Blount, John K. Blount, and Rebecca H. Blount, minors of Redden Blount.

REYNOLDS, HENRY - Samuel Harbour appointed guardian for Sarah Ann Reynolds.

February 1840

Pg. 309
WILLIAMS, SAMUEL - Last will and testament presented for probate. Charles Wood and Lewis Williams qualified as executors.

2 March 1840

Pg. 312
GRISAGE(?), _____ - An orphan boy, named James M. Grisage(?), age 11, bound to William Head until age 21.

NICHOLS, MARY - William Nichols appointed administrator of the estate of Mary Nichols.

Pg. 313
NICHOLS, MARY - William Nichols appointed guardian of James B. Nichols, one of the minor heirs of Mary Nichols.

6 April 1840

Pg. 314
ROBINSON, THOMAS - Elisha Pack appointed administrator of the estate of Thomas Robinson.

Pg. 319
CASEY, RILEY - John Hollandsworth appointed administrator of the estate of Riley Casey.

Pg. 320
UNKNOWN - Joseph Duncan, coroner, allowed $5.00 for holding an inquest over the dead body of a white man found in the Tennessee River.

Pg. 321
REDDING, _____ - A boy, age 9 named James M. Redding, bound out to William Wyatt.

Pg. 326
ROBINSON, THOMAS - Commissioners appointed to lay off a year's provisions for the widow and minor heirs of Thomas Robinson.

4 May 1840

Pg. 328
WHITE, SHERROD - A pauper, named Sherrod White, has been removed from the county.

Pg. 329
   THAXTON, WILLIAM - Last will and testament of William Thaxton presented for probate. Proven by David Robinson and Daniel Owen, subscribing witnesses.

Pg. 330
   STOCKTON, THOMAS - Daniel L. Stockton appointed administrator of the estate of Thomas Stockton.

1 June 1840

Pg. 331
   STOCKTON, THOMAS - Commissioners appointed to lay off a year's provisions for the widow and minor heirs of Thomas Stockton.

Pg. 333
   FREEMAN, ____ - Dorson H. Robinson released from his indenture bond of John L. Freeman. Said Freeman bound to Thompson Hurst to learn the house carpenter's trade.

6 July 1840

Pg. 338
   BASEY, JAMES T. - Samuel Wells and Thomas D. Shelby appointed administrators of the estate of James T. Basey.

Pg. 339
   BASEY, JAMES T. - Commissioners appointed to lay off a year's provisions for the widow and minor heirs of James T. Basey.

3 August 1840

Pg. 342
   HUNDLEY, J.Y. - Charles H. Eads appointed administrator of the estate of J.Y. Hundley.

   McDANIEL, JOHN - Murdock McDaniel appointed administrator of the estate of John McDaniel.

7 September 1840

Pg. 345
   OWEN, MARY - Last will and testament of Mary Owen presented for probate. Proven by Sarah A. Gray and Hezekiah Morton, the subscribing witnesses.

Pg. 346
   HUNLEY, JORDAN Y. - Charles H. Eads, administrator, returned an inventory of the estate of Jordan Y. Hunley.

   MOORE, JOSEPH - James A. Nichols appointed administrator of the estate of Joseph Moore.

Pg. 347
   MOORE, JOSEPH - Commissioners appointed to lay off a year's provisions for the widow and minor heirs of Joseph Moore.

5 October 1840

Pg. 348
   FREEMAN, ____ - John L. Freeman, age 13, and Sarah Freeman, age 11, bound to Paschal Whitlow until age 21.

Pg. 349
POLK, JOHN - Thomas Blakely released as guardian for Eliza J. Polk, one of the minor heirs of John Polk.

Pg. 350
FREEMAN, WILLIAM P. - Isaac Thornton appointed guardian of Benjamin R. Freeman, William A. Freeman, John L. Freeman, James Freeman, Sarah Freeman, Adaline Freeman, and Elizabeth Freeman, the minor heirs of William P. Freeman.

WINDSOR, JONATHAN - William Brim appointed guardian of William B. Windsor, minor heir of Jonathan Windsor.

STEPHENS, HENRY - Willis Lucas released as an executor of the estate of Henry Stephens.

Pg. 351
WARD, SWAIN - James Ward appointed administrator of the estate of Swain Ward.

Pg. 352
CAMPBELL, _____ - William Thomas ordered to keep two paupers, Jacob Campbell and his wife Ruth Campbell, until the January Term of the court.

2 November 1840

Pg. 355
FREEMAN, _____ - Elizabeth Ann Freeman, age 4 or 5, bound to Fielder Woodward to learn the "art and mysteries of a spinster" until age 21.

Pg. 356
DOREN, JAMES G. - Alexander Doren and John M. Andrews appointed administrators of the estate of James G. Doren.

OWEN, DAVID - James B. Grimes appointed administrator of the estate of David Owen.

Pg. 357
OWEN, DAVID - Commissioners appointed to lay off a year's provisions for the widow and minor heirs of David Owen.

OWEN, MARY - Joel C. Hancock qualified as executor of the last will and testament of Mary Owen.

Pg. 358
ROACH, JOHN - Joel C. Hancock appointed administrator of the estate of John Roach.

DOREN, JAMES G. - Commissioners appointed to lay off a year's provisions for the widow and minor heirs of James G. Doren.

Pg. 359
ROACH, JOHN - Commissioners appointed to receive the $150.00 worth of property directed to be given to Virginia Roach for the benefit of her son, Daniel Roach, by the will of Mary Owen. Also commissioners are to lay off a year's provisions for the widow and minor heirs of John Roach.

OWEN, THOMAS - William Owen appointed administrator to settle the unsettled administratorship of David Owen dec'd, former administrator of Thomas Owen.

7 December 1840

Pg. 361
RICE, JOHN A. - Richard Parks appointed administrator of the estate of John A. Rice.

Pg. 362
LAYTON, THOMAS - Last will and testament of Thomas Layton presented and proven for probate. John White qualified as the executor.

Pg. 363
ROACH, JOHN - Daniel Smith appointed guardian of Daniel Roach on of the minor heirs of John Roach.

4 January 1841

Pg. 364
MOORE, JOSEPH - Solomon Hudiburg and Rebecca Moore appointed guardians of Mary J. Moore and Elizabeth C. Moore, minor heirs of Joseph Moore.

Pg. 365
COPELAND, _____ - Solomon Copeland bound to Larkin Yount to learn the blacksmith's trade until age 21.

OWEN, DAVID - Noncupative will presented for probate. Proven by John Scott and James West, subscribing witnesses. Witnesses swore that testator stated that he had made a will, but that he wished his wife, Ann, to have $100.00 more than was given to her in said will. One witness stated that the said Owen told him that he wanted his wife, Ann, to have the $100.00 willed to him by his mother, Mary Owen dec'd.

Pg. 366
McCASTIN, _____ - John Hannah made return to the clerk of the bastardy bond of Elizabeth McCastin of $3.12½.

Pg. 369
WARD, _____ - Commissioners appointed to lay off a dower of land for the Widow Ward.

WATSON, JOHN - Last will and testament of John Watson presented for probate. Proven by R.A. Randolph, subscribing witness. Samuel Watson and James L. Watson qualified as executors.

1 February 1841

Pg. 373
RUSSELL, WYATT - Alexander Russell appointed administrator of the estate of Wyatt Russell.

RUSSELL, WYATTE - Commissioners appointed to lay off a year's provisions for the widow and minor heirs of Wyatte Russell.

Pg. 374
TILBY - A coloured girl, Tilby, to be notified that her term of service to William Russell has expired and that she be liberated, and that said Russell be made to comply with this.

Pg. 375
ASHWORTH, JOHN C. - Solomon Hudeburg, former guardian of Joseph Ashworth, a minor heir of John C. Ashworth dec'd, and

grandson of Joseph Ashworth dec'd, is released. Joel D. Lewis has been appointed guardian of said minor in Jackson County, Alabama.

Pg. 376
ASHWORTH, JOHN C. - Certificate from Madison County, Alabama that Henry Lewis has been appointed guardian of John C. Ashworth, infant son of John C. Ashworth, late of this county.

1 March 1841

Pg. 379
FRALEY, MARTIN - Commissioners appointed to lay off a dower of land for the widow of Martin Fraley.

Pg. 380
HAWKINS, JAMES O. - Last will and testament of James O. Hawkins presented for probate. Proven by William G. Rodes, one of the subscribing witnesses, and Percerville S. Hawkins, executor.

WHITE, JOHN - Samuel White and Levi Shelby appointed as the administrators of the estate of John White.

REYNOLDS, JOSEPH - Nathan E. Shannon appointed administrator of the estate of Joseph Reynolds.

5 April 1841

Pg. 382
MOORE, REBECCA - Solomon Hudiburgh appointed administrator of the estate of Rebecca Moore.

Pg. 384
COPELAND, _____ - Solomon Copeland, an orphan boy about 12 years old, bound to Thomas Polk until age 21.

3 May 1841

Pg. 385
WATSON, JOHN - Last will and testament of John Watson produced in court. Proven by Thomas J. Owen, one of the subscribing witnesses.

Pg. 386
ADAMS, SAMUEL - Rix A. Randolph appointed administrator of the estate of Samuel Adams.

Pg. 387
RIDDLE, NATHANIEL - Evin Beachamp appointed administrator of the estate of Nathaniel Riddle.

Pg. 388
ADAMS, SAMUEL - Commissioners appointed to lay off a year's provisions to the widow and minor orphans of Samuel Adams.

WHITLOW, HENDERSON - Last will and testament of Henderson Whitlow presented for probate. Proven by the subscribing witnesses. Milton Whitlow and Daniel B. Beasley appointed executors.

WHITLOW, HENDERSON - Commissioners appointe to lay off a year's provisions for the widow and minor orphans of Henderson Whitlow.

Pg. 389
BASEY, JAMES T. - Richard Taylor appointed guardian of Edmund Basey, minor orphan of James T. Basey.

BRYANT, ELISHA - Commissioners appointed to set apart to Peggy Bryant, widow of Elisha Bryant, the property to which she was entitled.

McBRIDE, _____ - Robert McBride, an orphan about 15 years old, bound to Andrew Kerr to learn the trade of a farmer until age 21.

Pg. 393
OUTLAW, LEWIS - John Kirby appointed administrator of the estate of Lewis Outlaw.

OUTLAW, LEWIS - Commissioners appointed to lay off a year's provisions for the widow and minor orphans of Lewis Outlaw.

Pg. 394
BASEY, JAMES T. - Alexander Doren appointed guardian for America Basey, James Basey, Caroline M. Basey, Susannah Basey, Joseph T. Basey, Elijah Basey, and David Basey, minor orphans of James T. Basey.

7 June 1841

Pg. 396
FILLOWS, THOMAS J.G. - William Adams appointed administrator of the estate of Thomas J.G. Fillows.

ZACHARIAH, OLIVIA - Olivia Zachariah, a coloured woman, came into court and petitioned for papers of freedom. According to a deposition given by Noah Wade, a citizen of Hardin County, she resided in Carrollville in Wayne County, TN. She was born free and that had never been disputed by the residents of Williamson County, TN where she resided with her mother and the rest of her family. The deposition further states that Noah Wade is upwards of 50 years old, and has known a certain coloured woman now known as Olivia Zachariah, who is about 45 years old, since 1814 and that he knew her in Williamson County, TN where she lived with her mother, Elizabeth Franklin, and the rest of her family, all free people. Certificates of freedom were granted.

Pg. 398
NIX, JOSEPH - Thomas White appointed administrator of the estate of Joseph Nix.

FELLOWS, THOMAS J.G. - Commissioners appointed to lay off a year's provisions for Sarah Fellows, widow of Thomas J.G. Fellows.

Pg. 401
CAGLE, _____ - John S. Cagle, an orphan boy about 14 years old, bound to Edward G. Dinkins to learn the farmer's trade until age 21.

ADAMS, _____ - Leroy Adams, a pauper, let out to Joseph Briant, the lowest bidder.

5 July 1841

Pg. 402
HOLT, JOHN W. - Giles Holt appointed administrator of the estate of John W. Holt.

Pg. 403
CAGLE, _____ - Charles Cagle, an orphan boy, bound out to Thomas Gray until age 21.

Pg. 404
CARROLL, SAMUEL - Isaiah Carroll appointed guardian of John Carroll and Thomas Carroll, minor orphans of Samuel Carroll.

Pg. 405
FREE WHITE MALES - Reuben Day appointed at the January Term to take a list of the free white males in Hardin County over the age of 21 reported that there were 1,349.

Pg. 406
BRYANT, ELISHA - John White appointed administrator of the estate of Elisha Bryant.

FREEMAN, _____ - Thomas Blakely released of liability in his indenture bond to William P. Freeman and said Freeman to go at liberty.

ATER, GEORGE - Commissioners appointed to lay off a year's provisions to the minor orphans and a dower to Sarah Ater, widow of George Ater.

Pg. 407
ATER, GEORGE - Sarah Ater appointed administratrix of the estate of George Ater.

2 August 1841

Pg. 409
HAWKINS, JAMES O. - Perces Hawkins resigned as executor of the estate of James O. Hawkins.

HAWKINS, JAMES O. - Last will and testament of James O. Hawkins again presented and proven by Bowen Davy, subscribing witness. Perry B. Hawkins appointed executor.

Pg. 410
CHERRY, ISHAM - Jesse Cherry appointed guardian for Columbus F. Cherry, Isham S. Cherry, and Margaret E. Cherry, minor heirs of Jesse Cherry and grandchildren of Isham Cherry, dec'd.

HURLEY, THOMAS - Last will and testament of Thomas Hurley presented for probate and proven. Rebecca Hurley, widow, qualified as executrix.

6 September 1841

Pg. 412
RIDDLE, BRITTON - Delila Riddle appointed administratrix of the estate of Britton Riddle.

Pg. 413
BAIN, WILLIAM - George Bain and Daniel Smith appointed administrators of the estate of William Bain.

Pg. 414
BAIN, WILLIAM - Commissioners appointed to lay off to Patsy Bain, widow of William Bain, her dowry and a year's support.

SHELBY, MOSES A. - Thomas D. Shelby appointed guardian of Moses W. Shelby, Sarah Ann Shelby, Mary Amanda Shelby, and Elizabeth J. Shelby, minor orphans of Moses A. Shelby.

4 October 1841

Pg. 416
BARNETT, DELILA - Deposition from Ezekiel Teneson and John Stratten, citizens of Hardin County, stating that "they are acquainted with Delila Barnett, a coloured woman who has been a resident of this county and of the State of Tennessee for a long time, and that they were well acquainted with her mother in the State of Virginia and that she always passed for a free person of colour and the said Delila Barnett was born free and that she now lives in this county on the west side of the Tennessee River." Certificates of freedom were granted.

Pg. 417
TRENTHAM, ZACHARIAH - Allen W. Jones appointed administrator of the estate of Zachariah Trentham.

Pg. 418
TRENTHAM, ZACHARIAH - Commissioners appointed to lay off a year's provisions for Sarah Trentham, widow of Zachariah Trentham.

GAMMILL, ELISHA - James Gammill appointed administrator of the estate of Elisha Gammill.

1 November 1841

Pg. 422
BASEY, JAMES T. - Commissioners appointed to lay off a dower to Lydia Basey, widow of James T. Basey.

6 December 1841

Pg. 424
TOWERY, JOHN - Kiziah Towery appointed administratrix of the estate of John Towery.

Pg. 425
TOWERY, JOHN - Commissioners appointed to lay off a year's support for the widow and minor orphans of John Towery.

Pg. 426
WALLACE, WILLIAM - Commissioners appointed to lay off a year's support for the widow and minor orphans of William Wallace.

SHELLY, WILLIAM - Commissioners appointed to lay off a year's support for the widow and minor orphans of William Shelly.

SHELLY, WILLIAM - Thomas Spencer appointed administrator of the estate of William Shelly.

Pg. 430
EAKS, ZACHARIAH - Commissioners appointed to lay off a year's provisions for the widow and minor orphans of Zachariah Eaks.

BAIN, WILLIAM - Commissioners appointed to lay off the dower for Martha Bain, widow of William Bain.

3 January 1842

Pg. 431
ROBINSON, ABSALOM L. - Last will and testament of Absalom L. Robinson presented for probate. David Robinson qualified as the executor.

Pg. 432
ABLE, JAMES H. - Sarah H. Grogan, formerly Sarah H. Ables, returned an inventory of the estate of James H. Ables as the executrix.

ABLE, JAMES H. - Lewis B. Grogan appointed guardian for Laura A. Able, John W. Able, James L. Able, and Manervy A. Able, minor orphans of James H. Able.

Pg. 435
HOGDEN, MARY - A pauper, Mary Hogden, allowed $25.00 from the County Trustee.

SHELLEY, WILLIAM - Commissioners appointed to lay off a year's provisions for the widow and minor orphans of William Shelley.

Pg. 436
WORLEY, GEORGE - Last will and testament of George Worley presented for probate. Jacob Vanhoose and Abram Worley qualified as executors.

Pg. 437
WALLACE, WILLIAM - Rachel Wallace appointed administratrix of the estate of William Wallace.

Pg. 438
CRISSMAN, _____ - Jane Crissman, an orphan girl about 13 years old, bound to Jefferson C. Brumley until age 18.

7 March 1842

Pg. 443
BURGESS, ELIAS - John Cooper appointed administrator of the estate of Elias Burgess.

Pg. 444
BURGESS, ELIAS - Commissioners appointed to lay off a year's support for the widow of Elias Burgess.

PYBURN, WILLIAM - Daniel G. Wood appointed guardian of Samuel Pyburn and Jane Pyburn, minor heirs of William Pyburn and grandchildren of Samuel Williams, dec'd.

4 April 1842

Pg. 448
ROACH, JOHN - Benjamin Gambill appointed guardian of Mary Roach and Daniel Roach, minor heirs of John Roach, in Greenup County, Kentucky on 1 November 1841.

Pg. 452
PARKS, RICHARD - Last will and testament of Richard Parks presented for probate. John Kirby and Isaac Vawney qualified as executors.

Pg. 458
ATOR, JOHN - John Kirby, coroner, allowed $5.00 for holding an inquest over the body of John Ator.

Pg. 459
TOWRY, JOHN AND AMOS BUSBY - John Mc. Ross allowed $10.00 for holding inquests over the bodies of John Towry and Amos Busby.

2 May 1842

Pg. 461
WHITE, _____ - Commissioners appointed to lay off dowry and a year's support for the Widow White and the minor orphans.

Pg. 462
WHITE, KING - Nowell White appointed administrator of the estate of King White.

6 June 1842

Pg. 470
DICKSON, ELIZABETH - Last will and testament of Elizabeth Dickson presented for probate. John H. Dickson and William N. Dickson qualified as executors.

4 July 1842

Pg. 476
CAGLE, _____ - Edward G. Dinkins released from further liability on his indenture bond for John T. Cagle, an orphan, that was bound to him and has since left him.

1 August 1842

Pg. 480
ROBINS, _____ - Sarah Alexander Robins, about 3 years old, bound to David Robinson until age 21.

Pg. 482
WARREN, LEROY - Thomas W. Poindexter allowed $5.00 for holding an inquest over the body of Leroy Warren.

Pg. 485
COOPER, JOHN - Isaac Thornton appointed guardian of Elizabeth Cooper, John Cooper, and Vachel Cooper, minor heirs of John Cooper.

5 September 1842

Pg. 487
RUSSELL, JAMES - Mary Ann Russell appointed guardian of Martha Ann Russell and Susannah C. Russell, minor orphans of James Russell.

Pg. 489
RICE, JOHN A. - William T. Blanton appointed administrator of the estate of John A. Rice.

Pg. 490
ALISON, ADAM R. - Thomas A. Kerr and William Alison appointed administrators of the estate of Adam R. Alison.

3 October 1842

Pg. 495
   GRIMES, JAMES B. - Last will and testament of James B. Grimes presented for probate. Proven by Fielder Woodward, one of the subscribing witnesses.

Pg. 497
   JONES, JONATHAN - Joseph T. Ables appointed guardian of Margarett Ann Ables, Sarah Ables, Silas Ables, and Charles Ables, minor heirs of Joseph T. Ables and grandchildren of Jonathan Jones, dec'd.

   MARTIN, JANE - John Martin and Robert K. Martin appointed administrators of the estate of Jane Martin.

7 November 1842

Pg. 509
   COVEY, LEVEN L. - Last will and testament of Leven L. Covey presented for probate. Noble W. Covey qualified as executor.

   CLINGAN, _____ - Solomon H. Baker released from further liability on his indenture bond to David Clingan, a boy that was bound to said Baker and refuses to stay with him.

Pg. 511
   GRIMES, JAMES B. - Last will and testament of James B. Grimes proven by Samuel Watson, another subscribing witness.

   OWEN, DAVID - Fielder Woordward appointed administrator of the estate of David Owen. Last will and testament of David Owen presented for probate and proven.

Pg. 515
   WHITE, JOHN - Samuel Watson appointed guardian of Martah G. Watson, John W. Watson, and Matilda R.C. Watson, minor heirs of Samuel Watson and grandchildren of John White, dec'd.

Pg. 516
   SMITH, JOHN - Noncupative will of John Smith presented for probate. Notice issued for the widow of said Smith and his next of kin in the County of Hardin, if they are to be found, to appear at next term and contest the will if they think proper.

5 December 1842

Pg. 518
   SMITH, JOHN - Noncupative will of John Smith proven by Aaron Anderson, James Gammill, and William McClain, subscribing witnesses. Widow and next-of-kin appeared and did not object to the will.

Pg. 519
   JAMES, _____ - Prissilla Layton appointed guardian of Mary A. James.

   MITCHEL, _____ - Arthur B. Campbell released from further liability on his indenture bond for Nancy Mitchel, about 8 years old, and that Nancy be bound to Thomas J. Camp(?) until age 21.

2 January 1843

Pg. 531
WRIGHT, JAMES - Alexander Barham and Isaac Wright appointed administrators of the estate of James Wright.

Pg. 532
WRIGHT, JAMES - Commissioners appointed to lay off a year's support and the dower to the widow and minor orphans of James Wright.

7 February 1843

Pg. 536
SMITH, JOHN - Alexander Doren and Hu. Tarbett appointed administrators of the estate of John Smith.

6 April 1843

Pg. 545
SMITH, _____ - Elizabeth Smith appointed guardian for Jarrard Smith.

OUTLAW, LEWIS - Thomas Combs appointed guardian for Lewis Outlaw, Alexander Outlaw, Francis Outlaw, Emaline Outlaw, and Richard Outlaw, minor orphans of Lewis Outlaw.

Pg. 546
MARTIN, JONATHAN W. - Chisley Garrison appointed administrator of the estate of Jonathan W. Martin.

1 May 1843

Pg. 554
SOWELL, NEWTON - John Sowell appointed administrator of the estate of Newton Sowell.

Pg. 555
REYNOLDS, HENRY - William King appointed guardian of Tabitha J. Reynolds and Sarah Ann Reynolds, minor heirs of Henry Reynolds.

5 June 1843

Pg. 558
MITCHEL, _____ - Col. Arthur B. Campbell released from any further liability on his indenture bond for Jackson Mitchel. John Hannah appointed guardian of the said Mitchel to supervise his heiring and the collection of his wages and to apply the proceeds to defraying the necessary expenses of said Jack and his mother.

McCLAIN, KIZZIAH - Manuel McClain appointed administrator of the estate of Kizziah McClain.

COUNTY COURT MINUTES

BOOK D: 1843 - 1850

3 July 1843

Pg. 3
    LEE, WILLIAM C. - Commissioners appointed to lay off a year's support, and the property to which she is entitled, to Elizabeth Lee, widow, and the minor heirs of William C. Lee.

Pg. 10
    FREEMAN, _____ - Paschal Whitlow released from any further liability on his indenture bond for John Freeman, an orphan boy bound to said Whitlow, who has runaway.

Pg. 11
    LEE, WILLIAM C. - Bowen Davy appointed administrator of the estate of William C. Lee.

7 August 1843

Pg. 14
    PYBURN, WILLIAM - (The following entry pertains to a document recorded on 11 October 1842, and approved the January Term 1843, in Randolph County, Arkansas. The document was then recorded in the Hardin County Court Minutes.) William Black, of Randolph County, Arkansas, appointed guardian of Samuel W. Pyburn, 17 years and 11 months old, and Mary Jane Pyburn, 10 years and 5 months old, minor heirs of William Pyburn.

4 September 1843

Pg. 17
    OUTLAW, LEWIS - Thomas Combs resigned as the guardian of the minor orphans of Lewis Outlaw.

    POLK, WILLIAM - Charles M. Polk and Daniel Smith appointed administrators of the estate of William Polk.

Pg. 18
    HUDSON, JOSEPH G. - Alexander M. Hardin appointed adminisrator of the estate of Joseph G. Hudson.

    JACKSON, _____ - Calvin Jackson, an orphan about 11 years old, bound to William Dowdy until age 21.

    O'NEAL, _____ - Mary O'Neal, an orphan girl who now resides at the house of Richard Orton, ordered to be brought before the court.

Pg. 19
    POLK, WILLIAM - Last will and testament of William Polk presented for probate. Contested by John W. Boals and his wife Cyntha, Benjamin F. Lester and his wife Mary C., Michael L. Polk, and Thomas A. Polk, heirs at law of William Polk.

    OUTLAW, LEWIS - William T. Blanton appointed guardian of the minor heirs of Lewis Outlaw.

2 October 1843

Pg. 21
WINBURN, ELIHU - Catharine Winburn appointed administratrix of the estate of Elihu Winburn.

WINBURN, ELIHU - Commissioners appointed to lay off a dowry to Catharine Winburn, the widow of Elihu Winburn, and also to lay off a year's support for the widow and minor orphans.

JOHNSON, JOHN - Joseph Bivens and James S. Hatley appointed administrators of the estate of John Johnson.

Pg. 23
OUTLAW, LEWIS - William T. Blanton resigned as guardian of the minor heirs of Lewis Outlaw.

Pg. 24
JOHNSON, JOHN - Commissioners appointed to lay off a dowry and a year's support to the widow and minor orphans of John Johnson.

POLK, WILLIAM - Commissioners appointed to lay off a year's support to the widow and minor orphans of William Polk.

6 November 1843

Pg. 28
BRUTON, SAMUEL - Wright Barns appointed guardian of Nancy H. Bruton, minor orphan of Samuel Bruton.

WINBURN, ELIHU - All property taken out of the hands of Catharine Winburn, administratrix of the estate of Elihu Winburn, by an execution of the court. She was released as administratrix.

Pg. 29
THAXTON, MARTHA S. - William C. Kincannon appointed administrator of the estate of Martha S. Thaxton.

4 December 1843

Pg. 34
LOWRY, SAMUEL - Last will and testament of Samuel Lowry presented for probate. Proven by Eli Cherry and Samuel White, the subscribing witnesses. Delila Lowry and Alfred H. Kindel qualified as executrix and executor.

Pg. 35
LOWRY, SAMUEL - Alfred H. Kindel appointed guardian of Lucinda Lowry, minor orphan of Samuel Lowry.

Pg. 38
O'NEAL, _____ - Mary O'Neal, an orphan about 16 years old, bound to Larkin F. Bell until age 18.

1 January 1844

Pg. 40
LOWRY, SAMUEL - Commissioners appointed to lay off a year's support for the widow and minor orphans of Samuel Lowry.

Pg. 42
MOORE, JOSEPH - Solomon S. Hudiburgh resigned as guardian for the minor heirs of Joseph Moore.

MOORE, JOSEPH - George M. Polk appointed guardian for Mary Ann Moore and Elizabeth Moore, minor heirs of Joseph Moore.

POLK, WILLIAM - Charles M. Polk appointed guardian of William H. Polk, minor orphan of William Polk.

5 February 1844

Pg. 44
POLK, WILLIAM - Last will and testament of William Polk probated. Accepted as a true document by the Circuit Court.

Pg. 45
RICE, JOHN A. - William T. Blanton appointed guardian of Olliver Rice, Carroll Rice, and John Rice, minor orphans of John A. Rice.

HAMES, CHARLES - Commissioners appointed to lay off a dowry and a year's support for Dillila Hames, widow of Charles Hames, and the minor heirs.

Pg. 46
HAMES, CHARLES - John T. Hames and James L. Smith appointed administrators of the estate of Charles Hames.

Pg. 47
POLK, WILLIAM - Pheraby Polk, widow of William Polk, dissented from the will as no provisions were made for her.

WHITLOW, HENDERSON - Milton Whitlow appointed guardian for Coleman Whitlow and Eyre Whitlow, minor orphans of Henderson Whitlow.

4 March 1844

Pg. 51
REYNOLDS, BENJAMIN F. - John D. Reynolds appointed administrator of the estate of Benjamin F. Reynolds.

1 April 1844

Pg. 60
HURLEY, THOMAS - John Hagy appointed guardian of John R. Hurley, Elizabeth F. Ledbetter, Asa C. Hurley, James C. Hurley, Henry H. Hurley, Polly Hurley, and Thomas J. Hurley, minor orphans of Thomas Hurley.

Pg. 67
OUTLAW, LEWIS - William Clark appointed guardian for the minor heirs of Lewis Outlaw.

6 May 1844

Pg. 69
HUGHS, ALEXANDER M. - James Hughs appointed administrator of the estate of Alexander M. Hughs.

Pg. 71
WILSON, CORNELIUS - Certificate of freedom issued for one Cornelius Wilson, a free man of colour, who has been a citizen of Hardin County for 18 years. Dated 11 May 1844.

WILSON, UNITY - Deposition by William Wells stating that he had known Unity Robertson, sister of Jack Robinson(sic) for 28 or 30 years, and had known their father and mother who were free people of colour. Unity is now known as Unity Wilson. Certificate of freedom granted. Dated 15 May 1844.

ROBERTSON, JACK - Deposition by William Wells stating that he had known Jack Robinson(sic), a free man of colour, for 28 or 30 years, and knew his mother and father who passed as free people of colour. Further stated that Wells was also acquainted with the said Robinson's present wife before he married her. She went by the name Nancy Franklin and her mother, Betty Franklin, was a free woman of colour for some 30 years. Certificate of freedom granted. Dated 15 May 1844.

3 June 1844

Pg. 73
CHESNEY, THOMAS - Levi Cunningham, Esqr., ordered to secure as much as possible of the claim against the estate of Thomas Chesney, dec'd, upon the appraised value of a mare.

Pg. 74
GANNT, _____ - Jesse B. Gannt appointed guardian of James L. Gannt, Jesse V. Gannt, Andrew J. Gannt, Mary Ann Gannt, Nancy C. Gannt, Elijah N. Gannt, Daniel P. Gannt, Absolom B. Gannt, Lucinda A. Gannt, and Robert W. Gannt, minors.

1 July 1844

Pg. 77
REDDING, SAMUEL - William Jones and Jane Redding appointed administrators of the estate of Samuel Redding.

Pg. 79
GANTT, WILLIAM C. - Jesse B. Gantt appointed administrator of the estate of William C. Gantt.

Pg. 80
BROOKS, WILLIAM - Bennett Brooks appointed administrator of the estate of William Brooks.

GAMMILL, JAMES P. - Margarett Gammill, Moses Gammill, and William S. Gammill appointed administrators of the estate of James P. Gammill.

REDDING, SAMUEL - Commissioners appointed to lay off a year's support and a dower for the widow of Samuel Redding.

GORFUTH(?), _____ - Alfred Gorfuth, age 14, bound out to Michael L. Polk until age 21.

Pg. 81
GAMMILL, JAMES P. - Commissioners appointed to lay off a year's support to the widow and minor orphans of James P. Gammill.

WALLACE, HUGH - Janutt(?) Walluce appointed guardian of Stephen Wallace, minor orphan of Hugh Wallace.

GANNT, WILLIAM C. - Commissioners appointed to lay off a year's support for the widow of William C. Gannt.

5 August 1844

Pg. 82
   BENTLEY, _____ - Robert Bentley, a white boy aged 14 or 15 and living with Lot Akin a free negro, ordered to be brought before the court to be bound out.

Pg. 83
   COOPER, JOHN - Elisha Pack appointed administrator of the estate of John Cooper.

Pg. 84
   COOPER, JOHN - Commissioners appointed to lay off a year's support for the widow and minor orphans of John Cooper.

   MITCHEL, _____ Manuel Mitchel, a mullatto boy aged 4, bound to Henry W. Davis to learn "the arts and mysteries of farming."

2 September 1844

Pg. 86
   BARNHILL, WILLIAM - Commissioners appointed to lay off a year's support for the widow and minor orphans of William Barnhill.

   STRATTON, JOHN R. - Ezekiel Tennison appointed administrator of the estate of John R. Stratton.

   VARNER, ADAM - Henry W. Davis appointed administrator of the estate of Adam Varner.

Pg. 87
   ATOR, SARAH - William Strawn appointed administrator of the estate of Sarah Ator.

   ATOR, ANDERSEN - Matthia D. Ator appointed administrator of the estate of Andersen Ator.

Pg. 88
   VARNER, ADAM - Commissioners appointed to lay off a year's support for the widow and minor orphans of Adam Varner.

7 October 1844

Pg. 93
   LANE, WILLIAM T. - Thompson Hurst appointed administrator of the estate of William T. Lane.

4 November 1844

Pg. 96
   GIBBS, C.C. - Commissioners appointed to lay off a dower to Mrs. Gibbs, the widow of C.C. Gibbs.

   LACY, _____ - Climor Lacy, age 7, and Mary Lacy, age 4, mullatto children bound unto James G. Black until age 21. Rachel Lacy came into court and gave her consent to their being bound out.

2 December 1844

Pg. 98
LONG, DANIEL - Isaac Long and Rebecca Long appointed as the administrators of the estate of Daniel Long.

LONG, DANIEL - Commissioners appointed to lay off a year's support to the widow and minor children of Daniel Long.

Pg. 99
HOLLAND, _____ - Thomas J. Holland, a white boy aged about 16 years, bound to John McCorkle to learn farming until age 21.

HOLLAND, _____ - James M. Holland, a white boy aged about 11 years, bound to William M. Holland to learn farming until age 21.

COVINGTON, _____ - Malinda Covington, an orphan living with Jacob Beame, ordered to be brought before the court and disposed of in her best interests.

6 January 1845

Pg. 104
WILLIAMS, LEWIS - Last will and testament of Lewis Williams presented for probate. Proven by David K. Reed and William B. Byrd, subscribing witnesses. Elisha Pack qualified as executor.

POLK, WILLIAM - Martha Polk, a minor heir of William Polk, requested that Thomas A. Polk be appointed her guardian.

Pg. 105
HOGY, WILLIAM C. - Henry C. Hogy appointed administrator of the estate of William C. Hogy.

WHITE, NANCY - Nowell White appointed administrator of the estate of Nancy White.

Pg. 106
HOGY, WILLIAM C. - Commissioners appointed to lay off a year's support for the widow and minor orphans of William C. Hogy.

3 February 1845

Pg. 108
STOGDEN, AMILINTH - Thomas Seaman appointed administrator of the estate of Amilinth Stogden.

Pg. 109
JOHNSON, _____ - George Johnson appointed guardian of Erasmus Johnson and Mary Johnson.

Pg. 110
COVEY, _____ - William W. Covey appointed guardian of Rebecca E. Covey, Margaret E. Covey, Joshua J. Covey, and Noble W. Covey, minors.

FRALEY, MARTIN - Elbert H. Stephenson appointed guardian of David Fraley, James Fraley, Caleb Fraley, John E. Fraley, Sarah A. Fraley, Elizabeth A. Fraley, and Martin Fraley, minor orphans of Martin Fraley.

3 March 1845

Pg. 112
   GIBBS, JOHN - Commissioners appointed to lay off the dower and one year's support for Delilah Gibbs, the widow of John Gibbs.

Pg. 114
   HAM, JACOB - Joseph Smith appointed guardian of Thomas B. Ham and John P. Ham, minor orphans of Jacob Ham.

   BRADLEY, FRANCIS - Elijah Harbour appointed guardian of Francis Bradley, who was judged non compos mentis.

   SCOTT, JOHN - Jame Warr appointed administrator of the estate of John Scott.

7 April 1845

Pg. 123
   COVEY, WESLEY - Last will and testament of Wesley Covey presented for probate. Proven by George D. Morrow and Lewis H. Broyles, subscribing witnesses. Russell R. Covey qualifed as the executor.

   WHITE, JOHN - George Johnson and Margaret White appointed administrators of the estate of John White.

Pg. 124
   WHITE, JOHN - Commissioners appointed to lay off a year's support for the widow and minor heirs of John White.

   BAIN, WILLIAM - George Bain appointed guardian of Sarah A. Bain and Mary E. Bain, minor orphans of William Bain.

   COVEY, WESLEY - Nancy H. Covey appointed guardian of the son, child, and heir of Wesley Covey and Nancy H. Covey, named John M. Covey, about 2 years old.

5 May 1845

Pg. 129
   COVEY, WESLEY - Commissioners appointed to lay off a year's support to Nancy H. Covey, widow of Wesley Covey, and child.

Pg. 130
   BRYANT, ELISHA - George Johnson appointed administrator of the estate of Elisha Bryant in the place of John White, dec'd.

   BRIM, WILLIAM - John Kirby appointed administrator of the estate of William Brim.

   CARTER, SAMUEL - William Carter appointed administrator of the estate of Samuel Carter.

Pg. 131
   CARTER, _____ - Rachel Carter requested that James M. Carter be appointed her guardian.

2 June 1845

Pg. 135
   DEBERRY, BENJAMIN - Henry D. Deberry appointed administrator

53

of the estate of Benjamin Deberry.

DEBERRY, BENJAMIN - Commissioners appointed to lay off a dower to Disha Deberry, the widow of Benjamin Deberry.

7 July 1845

Pg. 137
REYNOLDS, _____ - Francis Coburn resigned as guardian of Telitha J. Reynolds. Daniel Smith appointed guardian in his place.

Pg. 139
WINDSOR, _____ - Thos. Hail appointed guardian of William D. Windsor, a minor orphan.

COURTNEY, JONATHAN - Commissioners appointed to lay off a dower for Tinsy Courtney, widow of Jonathan Courtney, and family.

FREEMAN, _____ - W.G. Campbell released from liability on an apprentice bond for James J. Freeman.

Pg. 140
SCOTT, _____ - Margaret Scott, age 11, bound to William C. Duncan until age 18.

4 August 1845

Pg. 143
DONOHOO, _____ - Elizabeth Hannah appointed guardian of Elinor and Angelina Donohoo.

KERR, ANDREW - Alfred D. Kerr presented a copy of the last will and testament of Andrew Kerr which was admitted to probate in Iredell County, N.C.

1 September 1845

Pg. 145
ALLISON, _____ - Thomas A. Kerr appointed guardian of Mary Jane Allison, minor orphan.

ALLISON, _____ - William Allison, Jr. appointed guardian of Rosanna and Esther Allison, minor orphans.

6 October 1845

Pg. 148
GARNER, _____ - Joshua Garner, a minor, asked that he be bound to Solomon S. Hudiburgh to learn the trade of blacksmithing until age 21.

MITCHELL, _____ - Abby Mitchell asked that her children, William Henry and Manuel Mitchell, be bound to Alexander S. Hardin. Also asked that an indenture bond for her son Manuel to Henry W. Davis be annulled because she was not present and did not consent. Granted.

MITCHELL, _____ - Abby Mitchell asked that her child, Jim Mitchell, be bound to William K. Hardin. Granted.

SCOTT, G.B. - William O. Duncan released from any further

liability on an apprentice bond for Margaret Scott. Further ordered that G.B. Scott take said child and care for her as the father of said child.

Pg. 150
FRANKS, BAZZELL - John Kirby, coroner, allowed $5.00 for holding an inquest over the body of Bazzell Franks.

3 November 1845

Pg. 152
GARNER, _____ - Solomon S. Hudiburgh released from liability on an apprentice bond for Joshua Garner. Garner has run away.

CUNNINGHAM, ARON - Levi Cunningham appointed administrator of the estate of Aron Cunningham.

HARRIS, RICE AND REBECCA - William Wyatt appointed administrator of the estate of Rice and Rebecca Harris.

NORWOOD, JOHN - Giles McBride appointed administrator of the estate of John Norwood.

BROOKS, BENNETT - James M. Brooks appointed administrator of the estate of Bennett Brooks.

Pg. 154
OUTLAW, LEWIS - William H. Clark allowed $45.00 for boarding the minor heirs of Lewis Outlaw.

Pg. 155
BROOKS, BENNETT - Commissioners appointed to lay off a year's support for Maria Brooks, widow of Bennett Brooks, and family.

Pg. 156
MITCHELL, _____ - Elijah Mitchell, a colored orphan age 17, requested that he be bound to Alexander Russell until age 21.

4 November 1845

Pg. 161
LACY, JACOB - Sheriff ordered to bring Ellen and Mary Lacy, minor children of Jacob Lacy and who were bound to D.J.G. Blake, to court. Blake to be summone to show cause why said children should not be given to their father.

1 December 1845

Pg. 162
BRYANT, JOSIAH H. - Alston Hatley and Mary Bryant appointed administrators of the estate of Josiah H. Bryant.

Pg. 166
BRYANT, JOSIAH H. - Commissioners appointed to lay off a year's support to Mary Bryant, the widow of Josiah H. Bryant.

Pg. 167
WHITE, JOHN - Commissioners appointed to lay off a year's support for Margaret S. White, the widow of John White.

5 January 1846

Pg. 167
LOWRY, SAMUEL - Alfred H. Kindel appointed guardian of Sarah Ann Lowry, minor heir of Samuel Lowry.

LOWRY, _____ - A.B.M. Covey appointed guardian of his wife, Minerva Covey, formerly Minerva Lowry.

Pg. 168
REYNOLDS, _____ - Elijah Harbour appointed guardian of Sarah Reynolds.

Pg. 169
SCOTT, JOHN - Jacob Scirratt appointed guardian for William Scott, minor heir of John Scott.

BROOKS, BROWDER - Daniel G. Wood appointed administrator of the estate of Browder Brooks.

Pg. 173
BROOKS, BROWDER - Commissioners appointed to lay off a year's support to the widow and minor heirs of Browder Brooks.

2 February 1846

Pg. 176
TOWRY, JOHN - Seamoure Long appointed guardian of the minor children of John Towry.

Pg. 177
BROYLES, LEWIS H. JR. - Certified to practice law.

2 March 1846

Pg. 180
MATTHEWS, ALSA - Commissioners appointed to lay off a year's support for Eleanor Matthews, widow of Alsa Matthews, and family.

Pg. 181
DUNCAN, _____ - William C. Duncan appointed guardian of Jesse J. Duncan.

BRIM, RALEIGH - John Shull, administrator, returned an inventory of the estate of Raleigh Brim.

TOWRY, JOHN - The order of the court appointing Seamoure Long guardian of the minor heirs of John Towry annulled. Kiziah T. Rogers, mother of the minor heirs and widow of John Towry, to have possession of the lands and property belonging to said children to support them.

Pg. 182
RUSSELL, JAMES R. - Thomas M. Russell appointed administrator of the estate of James R. Russell.

Pg. 183
BRIM, RALEIGH - John Shull appointed administrator of the estate of Raleigh Brim.

LACY, JACOB AND RACHEL - Thomas Maxwell appointed guardian of Eleanor and Mary Lacy, minor children of Jacob and Rachel Lacy.

6 April 1846

Pg. 186
WILLIS, _____ - Archibald Willis appointed guardian of Joel and Mary Willis, minor orphans.

Pg. 187
HAMILTON, GEORGE M. - Certified to practice law.

MATTHEWS, ALSA - William H. Franks appointed administrator of the estate of Alsa Matthews.

Pg. 188
BRUMLY, _____ - Samuel Perkins allowed $30.00 for maintenance and support of Bashabe Brumly.

4 May 1846

Pg. 198
ABELLS, JOHN L. - Last will and testament of John L. Abells presented for probate. Proven by Thomas W. Poindexter and James Graham, subscribing witnesses. Elizabeth Abells qualified as the executrix.

2 June 1846

Pg. 200
WHITE, REUBEN - Thomas White appointed guardian of Henry White, Nicy White, James White, Pernecy White, and Milly Fanas White, minor orphans of Reuben White.

6 July 1846

Pg. 204
HARBOUR, SAMUEL - Last will and testament of Samuel Harbour presented for probate. Proven by Elisha Harbour, Jesse Powers, Arthur Garrison, and John Allen, subscribing witnesses.

Pg. 206
GANTT, _____ - J.B. Gantt appointed guardian for William and Elizabeth Polk Gantt(?).

7 September 1846

Pg. 209
MITCHELL, _____ - Elijah Mitchell bound to Eldridge Clifton until age 21.

Pg. 210
GARNER, ELIZABETH - John H. McConnell appointed administrator of the estate of Elizabeth Garner.

BLOUNT, _____ - Elijah Harbour appointed guardian of Rebecca Blount and John Blount, minor orphans.

Pg. 211
PIG, PRESTON - Charles M. Ross released as guardian for Jesse H. Pig and Paul M. Pig, minor orphans of Preston Pig.

GANTT, J.B. - Newton Thornton appointed guardian of Mary Ann Thornton, minor orphan of J.B. Gantt.

GANTT, J.B. - James Irwin appointed guardian of the minor

orphans of J.B. Gantt.

Pg. 212
GANTT, JESSE B. - Daniel Smith appointed administrator of the estate of Jesse B. Gantt.

GANTT, WM. C. - Elijah Harbour appointed guardian of Main C. and Elizabeth W. Gantt, minor orphans of Wm. C. Gantt.

Pg. 213
GANTT, JESSE B. - Commissioners appointed to lay off a year's support to the widow of Jesse B. Gantt.

5 October 1846

Pg. 216
ABELL, THORNTON T. - W.G. Campbell appointed administrator of the estate of Thornton T. Abell.

2 November 1846

Pg. 219
COLE, JOHN - Wm. T. Blanton and Elizabeth Cole appointed administrators of the estate of John Cole.

Pg. 221
ROBERTS, _____ - Trustee paid Timothy Hanners $6.00 for keeping a pauper named William C. Roberts until the January Term.

7 December 1846

Pg. 226
WORLEY, JOHN - Jacob Vanhoose and Abraham Worley appointed administrators of the estate of William Jones.

Pg. 227
JONES, WILLIAM - W.S. Campbell appointed administrator of the estate of William Jones.

Pg. 228
COLE, JOHN _ Commissioners appointed to lay off a year's support to Elizabeth Cole, widow of John Cole, and family.

Pg. 229
WHITE, _____ - George Johnson appointed guardian for Marshall White, James D. White, Henry A. White, Isaac N. White, John White, Martha A. White, Emily C. White, Margaret A. White, and George M.D. White.

FREEMAN, _____ - Benjamin A. Freeman appointed guardian for James Freeman, Sarah Jane Freeman, Adaline C. Freeman, and Elizabeth Freeman.

UNKNOWN - Inquest. Found by the jury of inquest that an unknown man drowned in the Tennessee River near Coffee's Landing on or about 20 March 1846.

4 January 1847

Pg. 234
WILLIAMS, _____ - J.J. Williams released as guardian for Susan Williams, now Susan Matley. J.F. Matley appointed guardian.

Pg. 235
   ALLISON, WILLIAM - Last will and testament of William Allison presented for probate. Theophilus Allison and William B. Allison qualified as executors.

1 February 1847

Pg. 240
   McQUEEN, ____ - The Widow McQueen bound out Thomas and John McQueen to Isaiah Carroll.

1 March 1847

Pg. 243
   McWHORTER, GEORGE - Matilda McWhorter appointed administrator of the estate of George McWhorter.

   JONES, JEREMIAH - Last will and testament of Jeremiah Jones presented for probate. Esther Jones qualified as executrix. Proven by John Barham and Alexander Hammill, subscribing witnesses.

Pg. 244
   JONES, JEREMIAH - Esther Jones, executrix of the estate of Jeremiah Jones, asked that W.T. Blanton be appointed administrator. Granted.

   WILLIAMS, WRIGHT - B.D. Butler appointed administrator of the estate of Wright Williams.

Pg. 245
   DUNCAN, ____ - William C. Duncan released of any further liability as guardian of Jesse D. Duncan.

5 April 1847

Pg. 246
   WILLIAMS, ____ - John J. Williams released as guardian of Elizabeth Broyles, formerly Elizabeth Williams. L.H. Broyles appointed guardian in his place.

Pg. 247
   McWHORTER, GEORGE - Commissioners appointed to lay off a year's support to Matilda McWhorter, widow of George McWhorter, and family.

Pg. 250
   ROBERTS, WILLIAM C. - In consequence of a physical deformity and bodily infirmity, William C. Roberts was adjudged unable to procure a livelihood by manual labor. Ordered that John Bivins keep, feed, and clothe said Roberts from 1 January 1847 to 1 January 1848.

Pg. 251
   POLK, WILLIAM - Andrew Clark appointed guardian of Martha Clark, formerly Martha Polk, minor of William Polk.

3 May 1847

Pg. 254
   CLARK, KELSY - Inquest. Found by the jury that Kelsy Clark, on 3 April 1847, was "feloniously, willfully, deliberately, and with malice aforethought" struck with a rifle gun and killed by one Wiley Starling.

BASEY, JAMES T. - Jesse V. Gantt appointed guardian of his wife, Caroline M. Gantt, formerly Caroline M. Basey, a minor of James T. Basey.

Pg. 255
BEARD, JAMES - Last will and testament of James Beard presented for probate. Proven by Samuel Perkins, John J. Williams, and George M. Milligan.

DAVIS, SAMUEL - Commissioners appointed to lay off a year's support for the widow of Samuel Davis.

DAVIS, SAMUEL - Geo. F. Benton and E.H. Shelton appointed administrators of the estate of Samuel Davis.

Pg. 256
CLARK, KELSY - Hiram Clark appointed administrator of the estate of Kelsy Clark.

5 May 1847

Pg. 257
LILLY, NOAH - Noah Lilly, former resident of Hardin County, died in Titus County, Texas. He left a last will and testament but appointed no executors. E.H. Shelton appointed administrator of any property still possessed by Noah Lilly in Hardin County.

7 June 1847

Pg. 257
GANTT, JONATHAN W. - Thos. D. Shelby appointed administrator of the estate of Jonathan W. Gantt.

Pg. 258
GANTT, JONATHAN W. - Commissioners appointed to lay off a year's support to the widow and family of Jonathan W. Gantt.

Pg. 259
HARDIN, GIBSON - Last will and testament of Gibson Hardin presented for probate. David Cook and Benjamin Hardin named as executors. Will was contested by Amos Hardin, Gibson G. Hardin, John Hardin, Woodson Wells and Margaret his wife, Joseph A. Hudiburgh and Jane his wife, James W. Ashworth and Sarah his wife, the heirs at law of Gibson Hardin. Proceedings passed to the circuit court for resolution.

HARDIN, GIBSON - Commissioners appointed to lay off a year's support for the widow of Gibson Hardin.

HARDIN, GIBSON - David Cook and Benjamin appointed as the administrators of the estate of Gibson Hardin.

Pg. 260
MOORE, JOSEPH - George H. Polk released as guardian for Mary Jane Laden, formerly Mary Jane Moore, minor of Joseph Moore. John R. Laden appointed guardian in his place.

HARDIN, GIBSON - John Hardin appointed guardian of Robert Hardin and Mary Ann Hardin, minors of Gibson Hardin.

5 July 1847

Pg. 264
STOCKTON, THOMAS J. - James Irwin appointed administrator of the estate of Thomas J. Stockton.

Pg. 266
HARDIN, GIBSON - John Hardin appointed guardian of Joseph J. Hardin minor heir.

Pg. 267
SELLERS, _____ - Riley Sellers, a free Negro age 5, bound to William Russell to learn the saddler's trade till age 21. His mother appeared and consented.

2 August 1847

Pg. 267
COVEY, WESLEY - Nancy Kelly, formerly Nancy Covey, released as guardian of John Covey, minor. Lawson Kelly appointed guardian.

RUSSELL, _____ - Elinor A. Newman appointed guardian of James W. Russell and Larcent(?) Russell.

6 September 1847

Pg. 271
WINDSOR, _____ - Thomas Hail appointed guardian of W.B. Windsor, minor.

GANTT, JOHN - James L. Smith and Nancy E. Gantt appointed administrators of the estate of John Gantt.

Pg. 272
GANTT, JOHN - Commissioners appointed to lay off a years support to widow and children of John Gantt.

ROBINSON, _____ - W.H. Cherry appointed guardian of David V. Robinson, minor.

BRUMLY, _____ - William A. Brumley bound out to E.M. Porter till age 21.

SEAMON, _____ - Thomas Seaman appointed guardian of William Henry Harrison Seaman.

Pg. 273
ROBINSON, DAVID - A.M. Hardin and E.M. Porter appointed administrators of the estate of David Robinson.

4 October 1847

Pg. 275
JOHNSON, WILLIAM - Isaac Northcutt and Nancy Johnson appointed administrator of the estate of William Johnson.

Pg. 276
JOHNSON, WILLIAM - Commissioners appointed to lay off a years support for the widow and heirs of William Johnson.

Pg. 277
GANTT, JOHN - David Cooke appointed guardian of the minor heirs of John Gantt.

Pg. 278
MITCHELL, _____ - Eldridge Clifton released of his apprentice bond binding Elijah Mitchell, a colored boy, to the said Clifton. Elijah Mitchell was then bound out to Robert P. Bailey.

POLK, _____ - William H. Polk, minor, requested that George H. Polk be appointed his guardian.

Pg. 279
UNKNOWN - Inquest. Found that a young man, about 17 or 18 years old, was found drifting in the Tennessee River. Nothing on his person but an empty packet book and a button or two. The inquest jury buried him about 4 miles north of White's Ferry on the Tennessee River. 23 August1847.

1 November 1847

Pg. 281
COOPER, JOHN - Drussina Cooper appointed guardian of Christopher C. Cooper, John L. Cooper, and Jasper B. Cooper, minor heirs of John Cooper.

Pg. 282
COVEY, HULDAH - E.S. Covey appointed guardian of Jane, May, Minneford, Martha A., Robert, Sophina, and Leon Covey, minor heirs of Huldah Covey.

ALFORD, J.N. - James Couch and W.H. Cherry appointed administrators of the estate of J.N. Alford.

HOLLAND, THOS. - Chisly Holland and S.G. Newton appointed administrators of the estate of Thos. Holland.

Pg. 283
BAIN, WILLIAM - Storling L. Foudles appointed guardian of Sarah A. and Mary E. Bain, minors of William Bain.

Pg. 284
REYNOLDS, HENRY - James Mathis appointed guardian of Sarah A. Reynolds, minor of Henry Reynolds.

ALFORD, J.N. - Commissioners appointed to lay off a year's support for the widow of J.N. Alford.

6 December 1847

Pg. 285
FLATT, WILLIAM - Solomon Flatt appointed administrator of the estate of William Flatt.

Pg. 286
ALEXANDER, SARAH F. - James H. Alexander appointed administrator of the estate of Sarah F. Alexander.

Pg. 288
WILLIS, _____ - Jerman Baker appointed guardian of Martha Baker, formerly Martha Willis.

Pg. 290
GUARDIANS - William Wyatt appointed guardian of William Z., Julianna M., Euphrodinia A., and Marinda Harris. Talbot Willis appointed guardian for David Willis. Naham Cannon appointed guardian of Martha J. and Josephine Harris. James

L. Gantt appointed guardian of Andrew J. Gantt. (All one entry)

3 January 1848

Pg. 293
   COOPER, SMITH D. - Thomas W. Meadow appointed administrator of the estate of Smith D. Cooper.

   COOPER, SMITH D. - Commissioners appointed to lay off a year's support for the widow of Smith D. Cooper.

7 February 1848

Pg. 296
   ROBINSON, ALEXANDER F. - A.B. Campbell appointed guardian for Sarah A. Robinson, minor orphan of Alexander F. Robinson.

Pg. 299
   DAVY, JEHU - Last will and testament presented for probate. Proven by John Barham, Alx. Barham, and Isaiah Jackson, subscribing witnesses. Bowen Davy qualified as executor.

6 March 1848

Pg. 302
   LINDSEY, JOSIAH W. - John W. Lindsey appointed administrator of the estate of Josiah W. Lindsey.

Pg. 303
   ABELL, _____ - L.B. Grogan appointed guardian of the minors; James S. Abell, John W. Abell, and Manerva A. Abell.

3 April 1848

Pg. 310
   LEE, T.H. - J.B. Massey appointed guardian of the minor heirs of T.H. Lee.

1 May 1848

Pg. 313
   MATHIS, ALSA - William Franks appointed guardian of the minor heirs of Alsa Mathis.

5 June 1848

Pg. 317
   REA, JOHN C. - Jincy Rea and Charles W. Morris appointed administrators of the estate of John C. Rea.

   REA, JOHN C. - Commissioners appointed to lay off a year's support for the widow and family of John C. Rea.

   UNKNOWN - Inquest. Found that an unknown man, thought to be a boatsman, drowned. 18 April 1848.

3 July 1848

Pg. 320
   DAVY, JEHU - Thomas Davy sworn in as executor of the estate of Jehu Davy.

Pg. 324
HAWKINS, P.B. - Bowen Davy and Scott Hawkins appointed administrators of the estate of P.B. Hawkins.

7 August 1848

Pg. 328
REA, JOHN C. - J.J. Wolfe appointed guardian of the minor heirs of John C. Rea.

OWEN, THOMAS - Russell R. Covey appointed administrator of the estate of Thomas Owen.

Pg. 329
BRYAN, JOSIAH - Willis H. Bryan appointed guardian of the minor heirs of Josiah Bryan.

4 September 1848

Pg. 331
CROCKET, _____ - W.S. Petty appointed guardian for Mary Louisa Elizabeth Crockett, minor orphan.

Pg. 332
GANTT, JESSE B. - James L. Gantt appointed guardian for A.B. Gantt, minor orphan of Jesse B. Gantt.

WILLIS, _____ - Archibald Willis appointed guardian for Joel Willis and Mary Willis, minor orphans.

McQUEEN, _____ - Hiram McQueen bound to R.J. Wilkerson until age 21.

ROWSEY, _____ - Henry C. Rowsey bound to J.C. Steely until age 21.

Pg. 333
HARRISON, WILLIAM P. - Smith H. Harrison appointed administrator of the estate of William P. Harrison.

WILLS, SAMUEL - John S. Broyles appointed administrator of the estate of Samuel Wills.

Pg. 334
GANTT, JESSE B. - J.W. Daniel appointed guardian of Nancy Daniel, formerly Nancy Gantt, minor of Jesse B. Gantt.

2 October 1848

Pg. 338
GANTT, JESSE B. - Newton M. Thornton appointed guardian for E.N. Gantt and E.P. Gantt, minor heirs of Jesse B. Gantt.

Pg. 339
BAIRD, JAMES - Executor refuses to serve. George S. Ross appointed administrator of the estate of James Baird.

BLAGG, C.D. - W.R. McDougal appointed administrator of the estate of C.D. Blagg.

6 November 1848

Pg. 344
    LAYTON, PRICILLA - Thomas Layton appointed administrator of the estate of Pricilla Layton.

    SELLERS, GINNITTON - John Nisbet appointed administrator of the estate of Ginnitton Sellers.

Pg. 345
    ARENDELL, ERASMUS - William Arendell appointed administrator of the estate of Erasmus Arendell.

Pg. 346
    PARKER, POLLY - Moses P. Couch appointed administrator of the estate of Polly Parker.

    PARKER, _____ - W.H. Francis appointed guardian of O.M. Parker.

Pg. 347
    GARNER, HENRY - Henry C. Garner appointed guardian for Joshua Garner and James Garner, minor heirs of Henry Garner.

    ARENDELL, ERASMUS - Commissioners appointed to lay off a year's support for widow of Erasmus Arendell.

4 December 1848

Pg. 348
    LEE, FANNY - Josiah Dodds appointed administrator of the estate of Fanny Lee.

Pg. 349
    GUARDIANS - W.B. Byrd appointed guardian for Rebecca J. Byrd. W.G. Campbell appointed guardian for Elizabeth Abell, minor orphan of J.S. Abell. Alfred Kenniry appointed guardian for Levina A. Gantt, minor of J.B. Gantt. N.M. Thornton appointed guardian for Robert W. Gantt, minor of J.B. Gantt. (All one entry)

1 January 1849

Pg. 356
    BASEY, J.T. - Joseph T. Basey, minor heir of J.T. Basey, requested that W.H. Duckworth be appointed his guardian. Granted.

    BASEY, J.T. - Alexander Doran resigned as guardian for Joseph T. Basey, minor heir of J.T. Basey.

5 February 1849

Pg. 359
    FRALEY, MARTIN - E.H. Stephenson released as guardian for the minor heirs of Martin Fraley. J.J. Fraley appointed in his place.

Pg. 361
    BEASLEY, DANIEL B. - Last will and testament presented for probate by Thos. A. Polk, one of the executors. Proven by Josiah Alexander and Jesse S. Bugg, subscribing witnesses.

    GANTT, _____ - Elijah Harbour resigned as guardian of W.E.C. Gantt. Jessie Hinkle appointed in his place.

Pg. 363
ROBINSON, ALEXANDER F. - T.A. Jones appointed guardian of Sarah A. Robinson, minor orphan of Alexander F. Robinson.

5 March 1849

Pg. 364
KIRBY, JOHN - Josiah Dodds and Richard P. Kerby appointed administrators of the estate of John Kirby.

Pg. 366
HURLEY, THOMAS - John Hagy released as guardian of the heirs of Thomas Hurley.

HURLY, THOMAS - Allen Temples appointed guardian of the minor heirs of Thomas Hurly.

BERRY, WILEY H. - R.C. Hemphill appointed administrator of the estate of Wiley H. Berry.

Pg. 367
HARRIS, RICE AND REBECCA - Nahum Cannon resigned as guardian of the minor heirs of Rice and Rebecca Harris.

Pg. 368
BEASLEY, DANIEL B. - Stanley M. Hargrove and Thomas A. Polk, executors, renounced their executorship.

BEASLEY, D.B. - G.H. Polk and J.H. McConnell appointed administrators of the estate of D.B. Beasley.

2 April 1849

Pg. 370
SCOTT, JOHN - Jacob Surrat resigned as guardian for William Scott, minor heir of John Scott.

Pg. 371
WILLIAMSON, JOHN W. - Levi Cunningham appointed administrator of the estate of John W. Williamson.

WILLIAMSON, JOHN W. - Commissioners appointed to lay off a year's support for the widow and minor heirs of John W. Williamson.

Pg. 372
HARRIS, RICE AND REBECCA - William Wyatte appointed guardian for Martha Jane Harris and Josephine Harris, minor orphans of Rice and Rebecca Harris.

Pg. 374
BERRY, WILEY - Commissioners appointed to lay off a year's support for the widow and orphans of Wiley Berry.

Pg. 375
EAKES, HARVEY - Green Parish and William Donohau appointed administrators of the estate of Harvey Eakes.

EAKES, HARVY - Commissioners appointed to lay off a year's support to the widow and orphans of Harvy Eakes.

HAMILTON, J.J. - John H. Logan appointed administrator of the estate of J.J. Hamilton.

Pg. 376
POWELL, GEORGE - Last will and testament presented for probate. Proven by R.C. Hemphill and Isaiah Garrison. David Roach appointed administrator of the estate of George Powell.

Pg. 377
LEE, FANNY - Josiah Dodds administrator presented a note dated 26 September 1839 for $200.00 from Harry Hooks in partial payment of his freedom. Note was liquidated and discharged.

7 May 1849

Pg. 380
POINDEXTER, P.P. - Commissioners appointed to lay off a year's support for widow and heirs of P.P. Poindexter.

COPELAND, _____ - Thos. Polk appointed guadian of Solomon Copeland.

Pg. 381
BAKER, WILLIAM - Harrison Christian appointed administrator of the estate of William Baker.

BAKER, WILLIAM - Commissioners appointed to lay off a year's support to widow and heirs of William Baker.

POINDEXTER, P.P. - James B. Erwin appointed administrator of the estate of P.P. Poindexter.

Pg. 382
WOLF, JACOB - J.J. Wolf appointed administrator of the estate of Jacob Wolf.

4 June 1849

Pg. 384
ERWIN, _____ - Joseph Duncan appointed guardian for Rebecca Duncan formerly Rebecca Erwin, wife of said Joseph Duncan.

Pg. 385
LEE, _____ - H.J. Lee appointed guardian of Nathan Lee, Leay A. Lee, Martha Lee, George W. Lee.

GAMMILL, LEWIS - Manuel McLain appointed administrator of the estate of Lewis Gammill.

BLACKARD, NANCY - Fountain Tankersley appointed administrator of the estate of Nancy Blackard.

3 July 1849

Pg. 388
PAYNE, THOS. P. - George D. Morrow appointed administrator of the estate of Thos. P. Payne.

Pg. 389
PAYNE, THOS. P. - Commissioners appointed to lay off a year's support to widow and orphans of Thos. P. Payne.

WOLF, _____ - William Wolf appointed guardian of James A. Wolf.

Pg. 390
POOL, JOHN C. - J.C. Roberts and James Haggard appointed administrators of the estate of John C. Pool.

POOL, JOHN C. - Commissioners appointed to lay off a year's support to widow and orphans of John C. Pool.

6 August 1849

Pg. 394
NIX, _____ - Franklin Nix bound to Reason Keeton until age 21.

3 September 1849

Pg. 396
McCARN, HUGH - Last will and testament presented for probate. Proven by Dougold Gillis and Dougald D. Matthews, subscribing witnesses. Elizabeth McCarn, widow, dissented from said will.

McCARN, HUGH - Commissioners appointed to set apart a year's provision for Elizabeth McCarn, widow and relict, and family of Hugh McCarn.

Pg. 397
McCARN, HUGH - Daniel G. McCarn qualified as executor of the estate of Hugh McCarn.

Pg. 398
ROAN, SOLOMON - John Mc. Ross appointed administrator of the estate of Solomon Roan.

Pg. 399
ROAN, SOLOMON - Commissioners appointed to lay off a year's support for the widow and orphans of Solomon Roan.

HUTTON, CHARLES - Martha Ann Hutton, widow, and John Mc. Ross.

Pg. 400
HUTTON, CHARLES - Commissioners appointed to lay off a year's support to Martha Ann Hutton, widow of Charles Hutton.

Pg. 401
APPRENTICESHIPS - Elizabeth Ray bound to J.J. Davidson. Susan Smith bound to Joseph Shell. Robert Byrd and Emanuel F. Roy bound to H.W. Davis.

IRWIN, _____ - Joseph Duncan appointed administrator of the estate of Rebeca Duncan, formerly Rebecca Irwin.

1 October 1849

Pg. 403
LAVERY, _____ - John Lavery appointed guardian of Eliza Lavery and John D. Lavery, minor heirs.

Pg. 406
MATHIS, ELINOR - Last will and testament presented for probate. Proven by subscribing witnesses. James Mathis qualified as executor for the estate of Elinor Mathis.

Pg. 407
CHERRY, _____ - Eli Cherry released as guardian for Isham B. Cherry.

CHERRY, _____ - Elijah Harbour appointed guardian for Isham B. Cherry.

MORTIN, MARY W. - Michael Worley appointed guardian for Lydia M. Worley, Lucinda M. Worley, Louisa M. Worley, Margaret Ann Worley, Rebecca Casey Worley, Susannah Elizabeth Worley, John V.A. Worley, Joel M.W. Worley, minor heirs of Mary W. Worley, formerly Mary W. Mortin.

Pg. 409
STREET, DAVID A. - A.M. Hardin appointed guardian of D.T. Street, Lucy M. Street, Sarah Street, and Thomas Street, children of David A. Street.

Pg. 410
HAGDON, THOMAS - Larkin Yount appointed administrator of the estate of Thomas Hagdon.

HAGDON, THOMAS - Commissioners appointed to lay off a year's support to the widow and orphans of Thomas Hagdon.

SELLERS, _____ - John Sellers, a coloured boy, bound to John D. Donahoo. Consented to by his mother.

3 December 1849

Pg. 411
MORSE - A negro, Morse, emancipated by the will of R. Davey, dec'd, petitioned to remain in the county. Granted upon his putting up a bond for good conduct.

Pg. 412
ALLISON, _____ - William Allison released as guardian of Esther Allison. Theophilus Allison appointed guardian in his place.

ALLISON, _____ - William Allison gave bond as guardian for Rosanna Allison.

ALLISON, _____ - T.A. Kerr gave bond as guardian for Mary Jane Allison.

7 January 1850

Pg. 416
CARPENTER, _____ - Zenith Carpenter appointed guardian of Ann Elizabeth Carpenter.

Pg. 417
MEEK, WILLIAM - Thomas S. Meek appointed administrator of the estate of William Meek.

MEEK WILLIAM - Commissioners appointed to lay off a year's support for the widow and minor heirs of William Meek.

Pg. 418
MILLAR, L.D. - George Millar appointed administrator of the estate of L.D. Millar

MILLAR, L.D. - Commissioners appointed to lay off a year's support for the widow and minor heirs of L.D. Millar.

8 January 1850

Pg. 420
BAYSE, JAMES M. - Edmund Bayse appointed administrator of the estate of James M. Bayse.

Pg. 421
OUTLAW, _____ - W.A. Clark released as guardian of the Outlaw heirs.

MOORE, _____ - G.H. Polk released as guardian of Elizabeth Moore.

MOORE, _____ - P.A. Kelly appointed guardian for Elizabeth Kelly, formerly Elizabeth Moore.

TARKINTON, ISAAC - J.C. Barnes appointed guardian of the heirs of Isaac Tarkinton.

1 February 1850

Pg. 423
HENRY, JESSE - Inquest. Found by the jury that Jesse Henry came to his death on 15 December 1849 by an ax wagon, loaded with grain(?), running over him.

Pg. 424
CASTLEBERRY, _____ - Giles Holt appointed guardian of Syntha Castleberry and Odom Castleberry, minors.

HUTTON, _____ - Willis Hancock appointed guardian of Pricilla C. Hutton.

Pg. 425
FLEMING, W.D. - Benjamin Hardin appointed guardian of the minor heirs of W.D. Fleming.

FLEMING, W.D. - Commissioners appointed to lay off a year's support for the widow and minor heirs of W.D. Fleming.

FLEMING, W.D. - John Hardin appointed administrator of the estate of W.D. Fleming.

Pg. 426
MEEK, WILLIAM - Commissioners report for a year's support for Mary Meek, widow of William Meek, returned.

4 March 1850

Pg. 429
COPELAND, _____ - Thomas Polk appointed guardian for John W. Copeland, minor.

1 April 1850

Pg. 443
GANTT, WILLIAM C. - Elijah Harbour appointed guardian of Elizabeth Gantt, minor of William C. Gantt.

HARDIN, ALEXANDER M. - Thomas Seaman and George M. Hamilton

appointed administrators of the estate of Alexander M. Hardin.

Pg. 444
HARDIN, ALEXANDER M. - Commissioners appointed to lay off a year's support for the widow and minor orphans of Alexander M. Hardin.

STREET, _____ - J.W. Cantrell appointed guardian of David T. Street, Lucy M. Street, Sarah C. Street, and John T. Street, minors.

Pg. 446
McCARN, HUGH - Petition to revoke probate of the will of Hugh McCarn brought by William H. Majors and Martha Majors, his wife. Legatees mentioned: Elizabeth McCarn - widow, John McCarn, William C. McCarn, Cornelius McCarn, Pamelia C. McCarn, Nancy Manerva McCarn, and Sarah Isabella McCarn. The matter was forwarded to the Circuit Court.

BEASLEY, D.B. - Enos Rose appointed guardian for the minor heirs of D.B. Beasley.

STRICKLIN, JOHN - Last will and testament of John Stricklin presented for probate. Proven by Robert S. Church and Wilkinson Mills, subscribing witnesses. William C. Stricklin qualified as executor.

Pg. 448
PETITION - Petition for the incorporation of the Town of Savannah. Signed by: M.L.P. Pool, W.B. Shields, L.H. Broyles Jr., James Irwin, B.D. Butler, R.B. Barwell, G. Miles Hamilton, John D. Donohoo, H.W. Peeples, E.W. Porter, J.H. Herring, E.H. Shelton, D.A. Street, W.W. Thornton, J.W. Cantrell, W. Russell, J.J. Williams, Lewis H. Broyles, J.S. Winburn, N.G. Parrish, Jesse G. Williams, T.A. Jones, Thomas Maxwell, J.D. Sutton, M.J. Swiney, J.H. Martin, A.P. Pool, A.B. Campbell, and Thomas A. Kerr.

COUNTY COURT MINUTES

BOOK F: 1850 - 1856

6 May 1850

Pg. 7
ROBINSON, _____ - William H. Cherry appointed guardian for Aaron Robinson.

Pg. 8
McCARNS, HUGH - Petition to revoke the probate of the will of Hugh McCarns again presented. Petition brought by William H. Majors and Martha Majors against Daniel McCarns, executor of the estate of Hugh McCarns. Cornelius McCarns and Martha Majors named as two of the heirs of Hugh McCarns.

CHERRY, SARAH S. - William H. Cherry appointed administrator of the estate of Sarah S. Cherry.

Pg. 9
POLK, _____ - Guardian settlement with George Polk, guardian for Marian Polk, minor.

LEE, _____ - Guardian Report filed by A.B. Campbell, guardian for Emily C. Lee, minor.

 McWHORTER, GEORGE - Settlement with Matilda White, administrator of the estate of George McWhorter.

 ROBINSON, DAVID - Additional inventory reported by Elias W. Porter, administrator of the estate of David Robinson.

 HARDIN, ALEXANDER M. - Inventory returned by George Hamilton.

3 June 1850

Pg. 10
 BOSTWICK, G.L. - W.C. Whitlow and R. Bostwick appointed administrators of the estate of G.L. Bostwick.

 JOHNSON, SARAH A. - T.J. Johnson appointed administrator of the estate of Sarah A. Johnson.

 WOLF, _____ - J.P. Wolf appointed guardian of George W. Wolf.

 JOHNSON, SALLY - James S. Hatley renounced executorship of the estate of Sally Johnson.

Pg. 11
 RUSSELL, ROBERT - Alexander Russell and Michael Worley renounced executorship of the estate of Robert Russell.

 GAMMILL, LEWIS - Manuel McClain returned inventory of the estate of Lewis Gammill.

 ABELL, _____ - L.B. Grogan purchased a horse for J.W. Abell for whom he is guardian.

 NICHOLS, G.H. - J.G. Nichols appointed administrator of the estate of G.H. Nichols.

Pg. 12
 BOSTWICK, G.G. - Inquest. Found that G.G. Bostwick died by accidental drowning on 9 April 1850.

 PAYNE, T.P. - Inventory returned by George D. Morrow, administrator of the estate of T.P. Payne.

1 July 1850

Pg. 13
 POOL, J.C. - J.C. Roberts and James Haggard, administrators reported that the estate of J.C. Pool was insolvent.

 MORRISS, SARAH - Sarah Morriss, mother of the infant pauper T.J. Morriss, gave consent to the said pauper being bound out to C.M. Morriss.

Pg. 14
 GARNER, HENRY - Guardian report by Henry G. Garner, guardian of the minor heirs of Henry Garner.

 HAWKINS, P.B. - Settlement made with the administrators of the estate of P.B. Hawkins.

GANTT, JESSE B. - Newton Thornton resigned as guardian of the minor heirs of Jesse B. Gantt. Silas Thornton appointed as guardian.

ABELS, _____ - L.B. Grogan appointed as guardian of the minor heirs.

Pg. 15
MBOYSE - Inquest. Negro boy named MBoyse died of drowning on the 22 December 1849.

GRESHAM, ROBERT - Larkin F. Bell appointed administrator of the estate of Robert Gresham.

Pg. 17
THORNTON, ISAAC - Daniel Smith appointed administrator of the estate of Isaac Thornton.

THORNTON, ISAAC - Commissioners appointed to lay off a year's support for Nancy Thornton, widow, and family of Isaac Thornton.

Pg. 18
RUSSELL, ROBERT - Will of Robert Russell probated and contested by Robert R. Russell and Robertson Winchester.

Pg. 19
FISHER, ELIZABETH - Petition to sale and partition land belonging to the estate of Elizabeth Fisher. Brought by: Paul H. Fisher, Lewis Kindle and Lucy Ann Kindle, his wife and formerly Lucy Ann Fisher, Jonathan H. Fisher, Wm. H. Johnson and Mary Jane Johnson, his wife formerly Mary Jane Fisher, Lydia M. Fisher by her statutory guardian Martin J. Fisher, Martin J.L. Fisher, and Caroline Fisher his wife, all the heirs of Elizabeth Fisher.

Pg. 20
RUSSELL, ROBERT - Transcript of the proceedings on contesting the will of Robert Russell. Brought by Joab Russell against Robertson Winchester, et. al.

Pg. 21
RUSSELL, ROBERT - Joab Russell appointed administrator of the estate of Robert Russell.

Pg. 22
UNKNOWN STRANGER - Inquest. Unidentified man found drowned on 10 July 1850.

HARDIN, A.M. - Robert Hardin appointed guardian for Margaret and Robert Hardin, minors of A.M. Hardin.

GANTT, JESSE B. - Guardian report by N.M. Thornton, guardian for Elijah Gantt, David P. Gantt, and Robert W. Gantt, minors of Jesse B. Gantt.

Pg. 23
GANTT, JESSE B. - Guardian report by James L. Gantt, guardian for A.B. Gantt and A.T. Gantt minors of Jesse B. Gantt.

Pg. 24
AUSTIN, DAVID - James W. Moore appointed administrator of the estate of David Austin.

FLEMMING, _____ - Phebe Flemming appointed guardian of Elizabeth Flemming, minor.

Pg. 25
ALEXANDER, EZEKIEL - W.A. Robinson appointed administrator of the estate of Ezekiel Alexander.

AUSTIN, DAVID - Commissioners appointed to lay off a year's support for the widow and orphans of David Austin.

RUSSELL, ROBERT - Joab Russell, administrator of the estate of Robert Russell, returned an inventory of the estate.

THORNTON, ISAAC - Inventory returned by Daniel Smith, the administrator of the estate of Isaac Thornton.

Pg. 26
REA, JOHN C. - Jincy Rea appointed guardian for Joanna, Thomas T., Elizabeth M., and Lydia Jane Rea, minors of John C. Rea.

McCARN, HUGH - Alexander Doran and G.M. Hamilton appointed administrators of the estate of Hugh McCarn.

THORNTON, ISAAC - Commissioners made their report concerning the year's support laid off for the widow and orphans of Isaac Thornton.

Pg. 27
HARDIN, A.M. - G.M. Hamilton, administrator of the estate of A.M. Hardin, returned an inventory of the estate.

2 September 1850

Pg. 27
BEARD, JAMES - Dispute between George Ross, administrator of the estate of James Beard, and the widow over the sale of certain items belonging to the estate.

Pg. 28
TUCKER, MARGARET SILVANIA - Inquest. Found by the jury that Margaret Silvania Tucker died by drowning on 8 August 1850.

HAWKINS, P.B. - Extra inventory returned by Bowen Davy, the administrator of the estate of P.B. Hawkins.

Pg. 29
UNKNOWN - Inquest. Found by the jury that an unidentified man died by drowning in the Tennessee River at a date and time unknown.

Pg. 30
AUSTIN, DAVID - James W. Moore, administrator of the estate of David Austin, returned the inventory of the estate.

BAIN, WILLIAM - William C. Hughes appointed guardian for Sarah A. and Mary E. Bain, minor orphans of William Bain.

RUSSELL, ROBERT - Daniel Smith appointed guardian of Nancy

J. White, minor heir of Robert Russell.

RUSSELL, ROBERT - J.Y. Nichols appointed guardian of Robert P. Russell, minor heir of Robert Russell.

ALEXANDER, EZEKIEL - Commissioners appointed to lay off a year's support for widow of Ezekiel Alexander.

HURLEY, THOS. - Guardian report by Allan Temples, guardian of the minor heirs of Thos. Hurley.

Pg. 31
GANTT, JONATHAN - Edmund Basye appointed guardian for the minor heirs of Jonathan Gantt.

MITCHELL, ABIGAIL - A colored woman, named Abigail Mitchell, petitioned for and was granted certificates of freedom. Her description was: 30 years old, 5'7", and 195 pounds.

RATTLE, LIBBY JANE - A colored woman, named Libby Jane Rattle, petitioned for and was granted certificates of freedom. Her description was: 28 years old, copper-colored, 5'4", and 115 pounds.

7 October 1850

Pg. 32
THORNTON, ISAAC - Petition for dower by Nancy Thornton, widow of Isaac Thornton, versus Daniel Smith, administrator. James W. Cantrell appointed guardian of Isaac B. Thornton and Thursday M. Thornton, minors of Isaac Thornton.

BRYANT, JOSIAH - Share of land belonging to the estate of Josiah Bryant allotted to G.B. Winningham and his wife, Esperana, formerly Esperana Bryant.

Pg. 33
RUSSELL, ROBERT - Petition to divide land presented by Joab Russell.

Pg. 34
HARDIN, ELIZABETH - Thomas Seaman and George M. Hamilton appointed administrators of the estate of Elizabeth Hardin.

REA, JOHN C. - Guardian report by Jacob Wolf, guardian of the minor heirs of John C. Rea.

BRYANT, JOSIAH H. - Guardian report by W.H. Bryant, guardian of the minor heirs of Josiah H. Bryant.

Pg. 37
HARDIN, A.M. AND ELIZABETH J. - William H. Cherry appointed guardian for the minor heirs of A.M. Hardin and Elizabeth J. Hardin.

ALEXANDER, EZEKIEL - Estate report by W.A. Robinson, administrator of the estate of Ezekiel Alexander.

4 November 1850

Pg. 42
RUSSELL, ROBERT - Partition of land from estate to the following heirs of Robert Russell: Joab A. Russell, Benjamin

P. Russell, Robert P. Russell, and Nancy J. White.

Pg. 45
ROSS, THEODORE - James G. Willough and Thomas A. Nail appointed administrators of the estate of Theodore Ross.

KING, THOMAS R. - Thomas Orr appointed administrator of the estate of Thomas R. King.

Pg. 46
BEARD, _____ - Commissioners appointed to lay off a year's support for Cynthia Beard.

CHURCHWILL, CANDACE - Last will and testament presented for probate and proven by W.T. Blanton.

ROSS, THEODORE - Commissioners appointed to lay off a year's support for the widow of Theodore Ross.

KING, THOMAS R. - Commissioners appointed to lay off a year's support for widow and orphans of Thomas R. King.

Pg. 47
BASYE, _____ - Alexander Doran assigned as guardian to Susannah Basye, she being married to Geo. M. Hamilton.

SHANNON, _____ - N.E. Shannon appointed guardian for William G. Shannon.

Pg. 48
KIRBY, JOHN - Petition by the administrator of the estate of John Kirby to sell the Negro girl Dinah.

Pg. 49
WOLF, JACOB - Petition to sell land from the estate of Jacob Wolf. Petition brought by: Jonathan Wolf, Jincy Rea, Wm. Wolf, Jacob J. Wolf, and G.W. Wolf, the surviving children of Jacob Wolf. Also: A.H. Wolf, J.P. Wolf, Charles Wolf, Richard Wolf, and Washington Wolf, the children of Peter Wolf dec'd and grandchildren of Jacob Wolf. Also: Jacob Wolf, Wm. C. Wolf, Charles H. Wolf, and James Alvis Wolf, the children of John Wolf dec'd and grandchildren of Jacob Wolf.

2 December 1850

Pg. 50
OWEN, JACOB H. - Joseph Smith released as guardian of the minor heirs of Jacob H. Owen.

Pg. 51
GANTT, JESSE B. - Guardian report by Alfred Kimmsey, guardian for L.H. Gantt minor heir of Jesse B. Gantt.

REYNOLDS, _____ and HAM, JACOB - Guardian reports by Daniel Smith, guardian for R.W. Reynolds and Joseph Smith, guardian for the heir of Jacob Ham.

WHITE, _____ - Marshall White appointed guardian for Henry White, Isaac N. White, Martha A. White, Emily C. White, Margaret White, and Dallas White.

Pg. 53
REYNOLDS, JOHN - Petition to sell land and slave from the

estate of John Reynolds. Brought by John D. Reynolds and William
G. Shannon, by his guardian Nathan E. Shannon. The widow of John
Reynolds, Elizabeth Reynolds, has married William Wells. John D.
Reynolds is listed as the son of John Reynolds. Mary Shannon,
wife of Robert Shannon, is listed as the daughter of John Reynolds.
William G. Shannon, grandson of the deceased, is the son of Gharky
Reynolds, who married Nathan E. Shannon. The slave to be sold -
Moses.

6 January 1851

Pg. 56
   KEMP, SOLOMON - Isaac Finch appointed guardian for Daniel,
William Jefferson, John Joseph, and Elizabeth French, minors who
are entitled to a share of Solomon Kemp's estate.

   BAIN, WILLIAM - Stirling L. Fowler appointed guardian for
Sarah Adeline and Mary Elizabeth Bain, minors of William Bain.

   McCARN, HUGH - Morgan H. Ross appointed guardian for Pormelia
Catharine McCarn, minor heir of Hugh McCarn.

   PONELLO(?), GEORGE - David Roach appointed guardian for
Matilda Ann, Emily, and William Henry Roach, minors who are entitled to a share of George Ponello's(?) estate.

Pg. 57
   BAIN, WILLIAM - W.C. Hughes released as guardian for the minor
heirs of William Bain.

Pg. 58
   PERKINS, JOHN G. - H.B. Wade and E.M. Perkins appointed as
administrators of the estate of John G. Perkins.

   MILLIGAN, ELINOR - James S. Milligan appointed administrator
of the estate of Elinor Milligan.

Pg. 59
   DONAHOO, WILLIAM - John J. Donohoo and Lewis B. Parrish
appointed administrators of the estate of William Donahoo.

Pg. 60
   DONAHOO, WILLIAM - Commissioners appointed to lay off a year's
support for the widow and minors of William Donahoo.

   HARDIN, A.M. - Petition to sell land from the estate of A.M.
Hardin. Brought by M.H. Cherry, George F. Benton, and W.H. Cherry,
guardian of Margaret E. Hardin and Robert Hardin, minors of A.M.
Hardin.

Pg. 61
   ROSS, THEODORE - James Willoughby requested that he be re-
placed as administrator of the estate of Theodore Ross.

   ROSS, THEODORE - Isabella Ross and Thos. A. Niel appointed
administrators of the estate of Theodore Ross.

3 February 1851

Pg. 62
   McCARN, HUGH - G.M. Hamilton presented an inventory of the
estate of Hugh McCarn.

HARDIN, ELIZABETH - G.M. Hamilton presented an inventory of the estate of Elizabeth Hardin.

AUSTIN, DAVID - Commissioners appointed to lay off a year's support for Nancy Austin, the widow of David Austin.

Pg. 63
PERKINS, J.G. - Commissioners appointed to lay off a year's support for the widow and orphans of J.G. Perkins.

PERKINS, J.G. - H.B. Wade presented an inventory of the estate of J.G. Perkins.

CASTLEBERRY, ODOM - Giles Holt, guardian of the minor heirs of Odom Castleberry, presented his report.

BRYANT, JOSIAH - Guardian report by Giles Holt, guardian of the minor heirs of Josiah Bryant.

DONAHOO, WILLIAM - John D. Donahoo and Lewis B. Parrish returned an inventory of the estate of William Donahoo.

Pg. 64
DAMERELL, ZACHARIAH - An orphan boy, Zachariah Damerell, was ordered bound out to Mark Rushing as an apprentice.

BRYANT, JOSIAH - Willis Bryant resigned as the guardian of the minor heirs of Josiah Bryant.

POLK, ____ - Guardian Report by George H. Polk, guardian of William H. Polk.

ROBINSON, DAVID - Elias W. Porter reported as the only surviving administrator of the estate of David Robinson.

MEEK, WILLIAM - Commissioners appointed to lay off the widow's dowry for Mary Meek, widow of William Meek.

Pg. 66
THORNTON, ISAAC - Petition for dower brought by Nancy Thornton the widow of Isaac Thornton.

Pg. 67
DONOHOO, WILLIAM - B.B. Alexander appointed guardian for the minors of William Donohoo.

DONOHOO, WILLIAM - Commissioners appointed to lay off the widow's dower for Polly Donohoo, widow of William Donohoo.

ROBINSON, ALEXANDER F. - Report by T.A. Jones, guardian for Sarah A. Robinson, minor of Alexander F. Robinson.

3 March 1851

Pg. 68
RATCLIFF, WILLIAM R. - A colored man, William R. Ratcliff, petitioned the court for certificates of freedom. His description was given as: about 20 years of age, copper colored, 5'5", scar on right cheek under the right ear, and one of the left cheek under the left ear.

Pg. 69
NICHOLS, G.H. - J.Y. Nichols, administrator of the estate of

G.H. Nichols, made a report.

　　AUSTIN, DAVID - Petition to lay off a dowry for Nancy Austin, the widow of David Austin.

Pg. 70
　　WORLEY, _____ - James W. Cantrell appointed guardian for Anna Worley, Stephen S. Worley, and Elizabeth Worley, minor orphans.

　　ROBINSON, _____ - William H. Cherry appointed guardian for David V. Robinson, minor.

Pg. 71
　　KIRBY, JOHN - Petition by Josiah Dodds and Richard P. Kirby to sell a slave girl named Dinah from the estate of John Kirby. She was sold on 25 December 1850 to William H. Cherry for $485.00.

Pg. 73
　　BAIN, WILLIAM - Petition for a dower of land by Martha Jackson formerly Martha Bain, relict of William Bain, versus Sterling S. Fowler, guardian of Sarah A. Bain.

　　FLEMING, _____ - Petition to sell land and a slave, named Eliza, brought by Benj. Hardin, guardian of Rebecca Fleming, Margaret Fleming, and Phebe Fleming.

7 April 1851

Pg. 75
　　BRYANT, JOSIAH - Willis A. Bryant resigned as guardian of the heirs of Josiah Bryant.

Pg. 76
　　SEAMAN, THOMAS - Commissioners appointed to lay off a year's support for the widow and orphans of Thomas Seaman.

　　OGLESBY, JOSEPH - Commissioners appointed to lay off a year's support for the widow and orphans of Joseph Oglesby.

　　BIVENS, AVORY - Commissioners appointed to lay off a year's support for the widow and orphans of Avory Bivens.

　　McCAMES, _____ - Morgan H. Ross resigned as the guardian of Pomelia McCames.

Pg. 79
　　BRYANT, JOSIAH H. - W.H. Duckworth appointed guardian of the minor heirs of Josiah H. Bryant.

　　SEAMAN, THOMAS - James W. Cantrell appointed administrator of the estate of Thomas Seaman.

　　JACKSON, JOSIAH - John Barham appointed administrator of the estate of Josiah Jackson.

　　BIVENS, AVORY - James M. Creel appointed administrator of the estate of Avory Bivens.

Pg. 80
　　OGLESBY, JOSEPH - Alexander Doran and William H. Franks appointed administrators of the estate of Joseph Oglesby.

SEAMAN, THOMAS - Elias W. Porter appointed guardian of William H.H. Seaman, minor of Thomas Seaman.

5 May 1851

Pg. 83
BIVINS, AVORY - James M. Creel, administrator of the estate of Avory Bivins, made his report.

WILLIAMSON, JOHN W. - J.M. Williamson appointed guardian of the minor heirs of John W. Williamson.

BAKER, WILLIAM - Harrison Christian, administrator of the estate of William Baker, was ordered to report to the county court no later than the next term.

Pg. 85
BAIN, WILLIAM - Petition for a dower of land granted to Martha Jackson, formerly Martha Bain.

Pg. 86
McMAHON, JOSEPH - J.H. McConnell and Green H. Polk appointed administrators of the estate of Joseph McMahon.

WORLEY, JOHN - Guardian Report by James Cantrell, guardian of the minor heirs of John Worley.

2 June 1851

Pg. 88
MEEK, WILLIAM C. - Petition for dowery by Mary Meek, widow of William C. Meek, versus W.T. Gibbs and wife, et. al.

RUSSELL, ROBERT P. - Joab A. Russell appointed administrator of the estate of Robert P. Russell.

Pg. 89
BIVINS, AVORY - Petition for dowery by Izza R.S. Bivins, widow of Avory Bivins, versus James M. Creel, administrator. Mentions the following children: Margaret E., Mary L., Joseph W., Rebecca, Lydia S., Julia A., John B., Martha A., and Amanda J. Bivins.

7 July 1851

Pg. 91
HODGE, THOMAS - A pauper, Thomas Hodge, was let out to William Arundell, the lowest bidder, for twelve months.

Pg. 92
WHITSON, HARRIET - Last will and testament of Harriet Whitson presented for probate by Francis Witherspoon, executor.

BROYLES, MARY - Last will and testament of Mary Broyles presented for probate by Mary Guinn, executrix. Proven by Arthur B. Campbell, a subscribing witness.

Pg. 93
HAGDEN, THOMAS - Holley A. Hagden appointed guardian of Ephraim, Nancy Jane, Martha, Thomas, and Elbert Hagden, minors of Thomas Hagden.

SCOTT, WINFIELD B. - A.B. Cowan appointed administrator of the estate of Winfield B. Scott.

NUMBER OF FREE WHITE MALES BY DISTRICT - 1st Dist. 119, 2nd Dist. 167, 3rd Dist. 158, 4th Dist. 123, 5th Dist. 99, 6th Dist. 158, 7th Dist. 97, 8th Dist. 150, 9th Dist. 93, 10th Dist. 157, 11th Dist. 112, 12th Dist. 121, and 13th Dist. 172. Total for the county - 1,720.

11 August 1851

Pg. 96
BROYLES, MARY - Hugh Tarbett, one of the subscribing witnesses, proved the last will and testament of Mary Broyles.

Pg. 98
RUSSELL, JAMES - Mary A. Jenkins, formerly Mary A. Russell, released as guardian of Sarah A.E. and Susan C.T. Russell, minors of James Russell.

RUSSELL, JAMES - David Roberts appointed guardian of the minor heirs of James Russell.

BERRY, WILEY - Settlement with R.C. Hemphill, administrator of the estate of Wiley Berry.

1 September 1851

Pg. 101
WOODBIN, THOMAS - Commissioners appointed to lay off a year's support for the widow and orphans of Thomas Woodbin.

WOODBIN, THOMAS - S.B. Hargrove and Isaac L. Lindsey were appointed administrators of the estate of Thomas Woodbin.

Pg. 102
WELLS, LEWIS K. - Noncupative will of Lewis K. Wells presented for probate by Alfred H. Kindel and Lucinda G. Wells, executors. Lewis K. Wells died on 4 August 1851. Will sworn to by N.S. Wells, M.H. Payne, and A.H. Kindel. James D. Martin appointed guardian of the minor heirs of Lewis K. Wells.

6 October 1851

Pg. 106
LOWRY, I.T. - Last will and testament of I.T. Lowry presented for probate and proven by A.H. Kindle and F.A. Cochran, the subscribing witnesses.

PARRIS, WILLIAM - Commissioners appointed to lay off a year's support for the widow and minor orphans of William Parris.

MADDOX, N. - Commissioners appointed to lay off a year's support for the widow and orphans of N. Maddox.

BARNETT, JOHN - Commissioners appointed to lay off a year's support for the widow and orphans of John Barnett.

REDDING, NELLY - Noted that Nelly Redding, a pauper, was kept for a year by John Redding.

PIGG, PRISTER - Noted that Prister Pigg, a pauper, was kept

for the year by Jonathan Hinkle.

Pg. 107
LOWRY, J.T. - F.A. Cochran was appointed executor of the estate of J.T. Lowry.

PARRIS, WILLIAM - W.C. Porterfield and John Martin appointed administrators of the estate of William Parris.

ARNETT, MARY E.M. - J.B. Winn appointed administrator of the estate of Mary E.M. Arnett.

BARNETT, JOHN - W.B. Barnett appointed administrator of the estate of John Barnett.

ABELL, SILAS - William M. Pickins appointed administrator of the estate of Silas Abell.

Pg. 108
GARRARD, WILLIAM - Elizabeth Garrard appointed administratrix of the estate of William Garrard.

HARGROVE, VALENTINE - S.B. Hargrove appointed administrator of the estate of Valentine Hargrove.

Pg. 109
BROOKS, BENNETT - Petition to divide land from the estate of Bennett Brooks. Brought by Levi Shelby versus the minor daughters of Bennett Brooks, Charity and Celest Brooks. James W. Cantrell appointed guardian of the minors. Maria Brooks mentioned as the widow of Bennett Brooks. William C. Strickland and his wife, and A.P. Downing and his wife listed as formerly having an interest in the estate.

3 November 1851

Pg. 112
EARBY, WILLIAM M. - Commissioners appointed to lay off a year's support for the widow and orphans of William M. Earby.

ARUNDELL, ERASTUS - Battis Hinkle appointed guardian for the heirs of Erastus Arundell.

Pg. 113
MADDOX, J.N. - Jesse Dobbin appointed administrator of the estate of J.N. Maddox.

MADDOX, JOHN N. - Petition for dower by Susannah Maddox, the widow of John N. Maddox. Mentions one child of John N. Maddox for whom Ephraim Maddox is guardian.

Pg. 115
LEE, SIMPSON - Division of land belonging to the estate of Simpson Lee. Brought by Felix G. Lee, Alfred Lee, Emily Lee, and Elizabeth Lee.

ARUNDELL, _____ - Battis Hinkle appointed guardian for Jane Arundell.

MEEK, _____ - Thomas Orr appointed guardian for Mary A. Meek, W.M.B. Meek, Josiah D. Meek, and Nancy E. Meek.

LEE, _____ - Josiah Dodd appointed guardian of Elizabeth Lee who is non compos mentis.

STREET, DANIEL A. - James W. Cantrell made guardian's report.

Pg. 117
HAND, J.W. - A pauper, J.W. Hand, aged twelve years to be apprenticed to Thomas Stand.

McCANDLESS, WILLIAM - William K. Hardin and Amos Hardin appointed administrators of the estate of William McCandless.

SCOTT, WINFIELD - James L. Smith appointed administrator of the estate of James G. Barnett.

BARNETT, JAMES G. - William B. Barnett appointed administrator of the estate of James G. Barnett.

Pg. 118
HURLEY, _____ - A.W. Temples, guardian of James Hurley presented petition to sell land.

Pg. 119
ROSS, T.A. - Thomas A. Niel appointed administrator of the estate of T.A. Ross.

DORAN, JOSEPH - Thompson Hurst appointed administrator of the estate of Joseph Doran.

1 December 1851

Pg. 121
PERRY, _____ - Joel Perry appointed guardian of Suvis Perry, Marion Perry, Sarah Perry, and Margaret Perry minor orphans.

WILLIAMSON, J.W. - James H. Simmons appointed guardian of Elizabeth Williamson, Josephus Williamson, and John M. Williamson, minors of J.W. Williamson.

PERKINS, DAVID - Elizabeth B. Perkins and James M. Smith appointed administrators of the estate of David Perkins.

CHERRY, MARGARET - Samuel Wilson appointed administrator of the estate of Margaret Cherry.

WELLS, MARGARET - Woodson Wells appointed administrator of the estate of Margaret Wells.

Pg. 122
WILLIAMSON, JAMES M. - James H. Simmons appointed administrator of the estate of James M. Williamson.

HARRISON, MARY - A.R. England appointed administrator of the estate of Mary Harrison.

Pg. 123
TYSEN, WILLIAM - Petition to sell land from the estate of William Tysen. Brought by D.A. Street, next friend of Elizabeth Ann, John M., and Martha Jane Tyson versus Andrew M. South, guardian.

GARNER, HENRY AND PEGGY - Petition to sell land from the estate of Henry Garner and Peggy Garner. Brought by John F. Garner, Robert McMahon, Sally Brown, Leah Eades, and Harriet Garner daughter of Peggy Garner dec'd. versus David Garner, Gabriel D. Garner, Polly Duller formerly Garner, Nancy Garner, daughter of Peggy Garner and Henry G. Garner in his own right and as guardian of Joshua and James Garner.

Pg. 124
HATTON, CHARLES - John McRoss and Martha A. Hatton, administrators of the estate of Charles Hatton versus Willis Hancock, administrator of the estate of Priscilla Hutton. A dispute between the two estates.

5 January 1852

Pg. 127
BARNETT, JESSE SR. - L.W. Barnett appointed administrator of the estate of Jesse Barnett, Sr.

Pg. 128
BRYANT, JOSIAH - Allen W. Temples appointed guardian for Bersheba and Mahala Bryant minors of Josiah Bryant.

Pg. 129
PERKINS, EBENEZER - An apprentice, Ebenezer Perkins, released from indenture bond to William A. Bromley all obligation under the bond having been met.

Pg. 130
McQUEEN, _____ - Thomas and John McQueen released from indenture bond to Joseph Carroll.

BRYANT, JOSIAH H. - W.H. Duckworth resigned as guardian of the minor heirs of Josiah H. Bryant.

Pg. 136
MEMORIAL - A memorial from the county court to the state legislature protesting the proposed erection of Taylor County which would consist of parts of Wayne and Hardin counties.

Pg. 137
CANTRELL, LENOIR - Last will and testament presented for probate by Lenoir W. Cantrell, executor and proven by E.H. Shelton and James W. Cantrell, the subscribing witnesses.

2 February 1852

Pg. 139
POOL, JOHN C. - Prorata division of John C. Pool's estate.

Pg. 140
ALLISON, _____ - Thomas A. Kerr appointed guardian of Jane A. Allison.

ALLISON, _____ - William Allison appointed guardian of Rosannah Allison.

ALLISON, _____ - Theophilus Allison appointed guardian of Esther Allison.

PARKER, _____ - Guardian report by William H. Franks, guardian of Aldridge Parker.

Pg. 143
BEASLEY, D.B. - Report by Enos Rose, guardian of the minor heirs of D.B. Beasley.

PACE, _____ - Dempsey Pace appointed guardian of the minor heirs of _____ Pace.

GANTT, JESSE - Elisha Harbour appointed guardian of the minor heirs of Jesse Gantt.

SIMPSON, WILLIAM - Jacob Luther appointed administrator of the estate of William Simpson.

MILLER, J.O. - Thomas W. Luther appointed administrator of the estate of J.O. Miller.

Pg. 146
MEEK, WILLIAM - Petition to sell land by Thomas P. Meek, administrator of William Meek versus Thomas Orr and wife, Harriet N. Miles, and T. Gibbs and wife.

1 March 1852

Pg. 147
BELL, JOHN - Commission appointed to lay off a year's support for the widow of John Bell.

Pg. 148
BELL, JOHN J. - James M. Creel appointed administrator of the estate of John J. Bell.

SMITH, LEVI - Peyton Smith and J.M. Smith appointed administrators of the estate of Levi Smith.

LACEFIELD, THOMAS - J.H. Lacefield and Susan Lacefield appointed administrators of the estate of Thomas Lacefield.

HINKLE, MARY - R.P. Bailey appointed administrator of the estate of Mary Hinkle.

LACEFIELD, THOMAS - Commission appointed to lay off a year's support for the widow of Thomas Lacefield.

HINKLE, MARY - Commission appointed to lay off a year's support for the minor children of Mary Hinkle.

Pg. 150
GANTT, J.B. - S.R. Thornton, guardian of Elijah Gantt, Daniel Gantt, and Robert Gantt, minor heirs of J.B. Gantt, made his report.

5 April 1852

Pg. 154
WHITE, JOHN - Green H. Polk appointed guardian of Martha, Emily, Margarette, and Dallas White minors of John White.

MILLER, J.D. - Jacob Luther appointed guardian of James, Allen, Louis H., and _____ Miller minors of J.D. Miller.

STEPHENSON, _____ - E.H. Stephenson appointed guardian of Mary Ann, William, James, Elihu, and Hardin Stephenson.

HINKLE, MARY - William Hinkle appointed administrator of the estate of Mary Hinkle in place of R.P. Bailey.

TERRY, T.S. - Thomas Davy appointed administrator of the estate of T.S. Terry.

LANTON, JESSE - A minor, Jesse Lanton, ordered bound out to Joseph Shull until he reaches age 21.

Pg. 155
LANAN, MARY E. - A minor orphan, Mary E. Lanan, was apprenticed to Joseph Shull until she reaches 18 years of age.

LANSON, LUCY C. - A minor orphan, Lucy C. Lanson, was apprenticed to Thomas F. Milam until she reaches 18 years of age.

Pg. 157
ARNETT, MARY E.M. - Division of slaves belonging to the estate of Mary E.M. Arnett, dec'd. Original petition brought by J.B. Winn, administrator versus M. Binion, Ann Robertson, and Mary Crockett. Division was as follows: Lot #1 - consisting of Billy, valued at $700, and Handy, valued at $150, drawn by Mary Crockett; Lot #2 - consisting of Antionette and child, valued at $700, and George valued at $150 drawn by Ann Robertson; Lot #3 - consisting of Jemima and child, valued at $350, and Almeda, valued at $200, drawn by Martin Binion; and Lot $4 - consisting of John, valued at $350, Jerry, valued at $250, and Charles, valued at $250, drawn by J.B. Winn.

3 May 1852

Pg. 175
FLEMMING, W.D. - Settlement with John Hardin, administrator of the estate of W.D. Flemming.

7 June 1852

Pg. 178
REA, JOHN - Accusation of mismanagement of funds by L.F. Bell against Jincy Rea, guardian of Joanna, Hanna, Elizabeth M., and Lydia Jane Rea, minors of John Rea.

Pg. 179
PACE, DEMPSEY - Accusation of mismanagement of funds by James Russell and John F. Pitts against Dempsey Pace, guardian of his minor children Jonathan, James A., Thomas G., William A., and Margaret L. Pace.

5 July 1852

Pg. 182
MATHIS, ALSEY - James D. Mathis appointed guardian of John W. Mathis, Thomas W., and Alsy Mathis, minor orphans of Alsey Mathis.

WHITE, JOHN - Green H. Polk resigned as guardian of the minor heirs of John White.

Pg. 186
RUSSELL, MATILDA - Robert R. Russell appointed guardian of Delilah J. and Elizabeth Jane Russell minor heirs of Matilda Russell.

2 August 1852

Pg. 189
   AUSTIN, DAVID - James W. Moore appointed guardian of the minor heirs of David Austin.

   POLK, THOMAS A. - Thomas D. Shelby appointed administrator of the estate of Thomas A. Polk.

   GREEN, ANDREW - Nancy Green appointed administrator of the estate of Andrew Green.

Pg. 190
   POLK, THOMAS A. - Commission appointed to lay off a year's support for the widow and orphans of Thomas A. Polk.

   GREEN, ANDREW - Commissioners appointed to lay off a year's support for the widow and orphans of Andrew Green.

   MONDAY, SILAS - W.H. Cherry appointed administrator of the estate of Silas Monday.

   ABLE, JAMES H. - L.B. Grogan appointed guardian of the minor heirs of James H. Able.

   ROBERTS, STEPHEN - Last will and testament presented for probate by R.H. and D.A. Roberts, executors. Proven by M.H. Byrd and R.E. Bonds, subscribing witnesses.

Pg. 193
   MOORE, JESSE - A freeman of color, Jesse Moore, appeared in court in order to be registered with the county as a free man of color in accordance with Act of 1806, Chapter 32, Section 1. He was vouched for by W.T. Garrett. He was born in Maury County, Tennessee and was about 24 years old. His mother and grandmother were both free white women. His description was copper-colored, 6'0", 180 pounds, and a scar over his right eye.

6 September 1852

Pg. 196
   ROWSEY, THOMAS - James H. Rowsey appointed administrator of the estate of Thomas Rowsey.

   MULLINS, ELISA - Abell Blankenship appointed administrator of the estate of Elisa Mullins.

   BURKS, B.H. - G.W. Pratt appointed administrator of the estate of B.H. Burks.

Pg. 198
   WOLF, PETER - J.P. Wolf appointed as guardian of G.W. Wolf, minor of Peter Wolf.

   REA, JOHN C. - J.T. Morris appointed as guardian of the minor heirs of John C. Rea.

   COOPER, JONATHAN - Petition for dower by Patience Cooper, widow, versus Moses Lingo, et al.

Pg. 199
   HAYNES, DARLING - Noncupative will presented for probate

by W. Haynes and H. Coffey. Witnessed by Henry and Hiram Haynes.

Pg. 200
BIVINS, AVORY - Petition to sell land belonging to the estate of Avory Bivins. Brought by James M. Creel, administrator versus the heirs at law of Avory Bivins. R.J. Williams appointed guardian of Margaret E., Mary L., Joseph W., Rebecca, Lydia S., Julia A., John B., Martha A., and Amanda J. Bivins heirs of Avory Bivins.

4 October 1852

Pg. 201
GANTT, JOHN - David Cook resigned as guardian of the minor heirs of John Gantt. Nancy Gantt appointed as new guardian.

ALLEN, M.G. - Thomas Davy appointed administrator of the estate of M.G. Allen.

Pg. 202
ALLEN, M.G. - Commissioners appointed to lay off a year's support for the widow and minors of M.G. Allen.

ANDREWS, A.A. - John M. Andrews appointed administrator of the estate of A.A. Andrews.

DAVY, W.T. - R.D. Davy and E.M. Perkins appointed administrators of the estate of W.T. Davy.

KING, EDMUND - James McClaren appointed administrator of the estate of Edmund King.

Pg. 194
MULLINS, ELIZA - Inquest. Found that Eliza Mullins did on the 26th of August 1852 kill herself by drowning.

Pg. 202
KING, EDMUND - W.H. Porter appointed guardian for Thomas King, minor heir of Edmund King.

Pg. 203 (Misnumbered)
GREEN, JAMES C. - License issued by the county court to James C. Green to practice law. States that he is twenty-one years of age.

MILAN, A.G. - Thomas F. Milan appointed administrator of the estate of A.G. Milan.

UNKNOWN - Inquest. Unknown man drowned in the Tennessee River. Description: Hair light, between 25 and 30 years old, sandy beard, scar under chin, 6'0", coat of "Blue Kentucky," waistcoat dark. Found on 13 June 1852.

Pg. 205
MURPHY, A. - John McRoss and J.O. Monday appointed administrators of the estate of A. Murphy.

MURPHY, A. - Commission appointed to lay off a year's support to the widow and minors of A. Murphy.

Pg. 206
GILCHRIST, JOHN - Last will and testament presented for probate by Cornelius Gilchrist and Woods Hassell, executors.

Proven by Geo. D. Morrow and L.H. Broyles, subscribing witnesses.

4 November 1852

Pg. 206

BROWN, WILLIAM - A free boy of color, named William Brown, petitioned for and was granted a certificate of freedom. His description was: copper color, age 22, 150 lbs., 5'10".

Pg. 207

LARKIN, EDMOND - Noncupative will of Edmond Larkin produced for probate by James C. Green. Witnesses to testator's statement were Joseph Stephens and Thomas J. Bray. Edmond Larkin died on or about 12 October 1852. Left no widow and his next of kin resided out of state. James C. Green appointed administrator of the estate.

Pg. 208

MURPHY, ARCHIBALD - Mary L. Murphy, widow of Archibald Murphy, petitioned for her dower. Suit brought against John W. Murphy and others. Mentions the following heirs: Caroline married to Samuel J. Pollick, Elmira B. Shorts, Caledonia married to W.B. Roach, Malinda F. married to William J. Copeland, John W. Murphy, Jas. W.M. Murphy, Berilla J. Murphy, and Wm. H. Murphy. The last two heirs, Berilla J. and Wm. H., were minors.

Pg. 209

MURPHY, ARCHIBALD - Noncupative will of Archibald Murphy produced for probate by Mary L. Murphy. Witnesses to testator's statement were Gideon Blackwood and Ranin Baker. The will was accepted as authentic.

MURPHY, ARCHIBALD - Commissioners appointed to lay off a year's support for Mary L. Murphy, widow of Archibald Murphy, and minors.

ALLEN, M.G. - Report from commissioners charged with laying off a year's support for Elizabeth Allen, widow of M.G. Allen.

Pg. 210

BYNAM, MARY - Jesse Hatley appointed administrator of the estate of Mary Bynam.

JONES, WILLIAM - Josiah Jones appointed administrator of the estate of William Jones.

BAKER, MILTON - Wm. F. Hodge appointed administrator of the estate of Milton Baker.

WOLVERTON, _____ - Laura Jane Wolverton, age 14, and Wiley Green Wolverton, age 12, bound out to John Wolverton.

Pg. 211

MURPHY, ARCHIBALD - James W. Cantrell appointed guardian for Barilla J. Murphy and Wm. H. Murphy, minor heirs of Archibald Murphy.

BARNHILL, JAMES - Last will and testament of James Barnhill presented for probate by Giles Holt and Mary Barnhill, executors. Proven by A.B. Campbell and Samuel Gammill, subscribing witnesses.

6 December 1852

Pg. 212
BROOKS, BENNETT - W.H. Cherry appointed guardian for the minor heirs of Bennett Brooks.

Pg. 214
HUTTON, CHARLY - W.S. Bivens appointed guardian for the minor heirs of Charly Hutton.

SMITH, WILEY - Thos. Orr appointed administrator of the estate of Wiley Smith.

SMITH, WILEY - Commissioners appointed to lay off a year's support for the widow and minors of Wiley Smith.

Pg. 216
POLK, THOMAS A. - Petition for dower by Margaret Polk, widow versus Thos. D. Shelby, et al.

4 January 1853

Pg. 219
BERRY, W.H. - S.H. Baker, guardian for the minor heirs of W.H. Berry, resigned.

Pg. 220
BAIN, WILLIAM - S.L. Fowler appointed guardian of the minor heirs of William Bain.

Pg. 223
OUTLAW, LEWIS - Petition to divide land from the estate of Lewis Outlaw. Brought by Alexander Outlaw versus F.M. Outlaw, Joseph Outlaw, guardian for Emeline and Richard Outlaw minors of Lewis Outlaw, dec'd.

7 February 1853

Pg. 228
WHITSETT, WILLIAM G. - Noncupative will presented for probate by Frances M. Fisher. Testator died at the dwelling of Thomas Carroll on 23 September 1852. Dr. John H. Logan and Francis M. Fisher witnessed testator's statement. Testator bequeathed everything he possessed to his sister Martha P. Carroll and her husband, Thomas Carroll.

Pg. 232
WHITE, ARCHIBALD - Eli Cherry appointed guardian of Elizabeth White, a minor heir of Archibald White.

DILL, JAMES - Robert Forbes appointed guardian of J.A., D.M., Susan, Patsy, and James Dill, minor heirs of James Dill.

DILL, JAMES - Commissioners appointed to lay off a year's support for the minor children of James Dill.

Pg. 233
McCALL, JOHN - James G. Hamilton appointed administrator of the estate of John McCall.

ABELS, J.H. - R.W. Tucker appointed guardian of the minor heirs of J.H. Abels.

WHITE, JOHN - B.B. Alexander appointed guardian of the minor heirs of John White.

AUSTIN, _____ - G.A., A.J., D.J., and J.W. Austin bound out to S.A. Austin until they reach the age of 21.

ROBINSON, _____ - J.W. and Wily G. Robinson, minors, bound out to M.C. Weatherspoon until they reach the age of 21.

Pg. 234
DAVY, KATHERINE - H. Perkins appointed administrator of the estate of Katherine Davy.

Pg. 235
MONTGOMERY, JAMES - Alfred Montgomery appointed administrator of the estate of James Montgomery.

Pg. 236
MONTGOMERY, JAMES - Commissioners appointed to lay off a year's support for the widow and orphans.

7 March 1853

Pg. 237
ABELLS, J.L. - R.W. Tucker appointed guardian for the minor heirs of J.L. Abells.

4 April 1853

Pg. 253
BROOKS, BENNETT - W.J. Counce appointed guardian for Charity Trease, formerly Charity Brooks, a minor heir of Bennett Brooks.

2 May 1853

Pg. 255
WHITE, RIDER M. - C.H. Almond appointed administrator of the estate of Rider M. White.

Pg. 256
KERR, A.D. - George F. Davidson appointed administrator of the estate of A.D. Kerr.

6 June 1853

Pg. 257
HAYS, JESSE - W.S. Petty appointed administrator of the estate of Jesse Hays.

DAVY, MOSS - Last will and testament of Moss Davy presented for probate by W.M. Perkins, executor. Proven by Robert Forbes and William Philips.

Pg. 259
McCONNELL, JOSHUA - Last will and testament of Joshua McConnell presented for probate by J.H. McConnell.

WHITE, RECISK(?) - Commissioners appointed to lay off a year's support for the widow of Recisk(?) White.

Pg. 260
TINSLEY, _____ - An 8 year old orphan, named James T. Tinsley, bound out to Green H. Polk.

TINSLEY, ____ - An orphan, named Emily F. Tinsley, bound out to Lucious B. Parrish.

MAY, ____ - An orphan, named Frances May, bound out to William Loyd.

Pg. 262
  McCONNELL, MARY - John H. McConnell appointed administrator of the estate of Mary McConnell.

4 July 1853

Pg. 266
  TINSLEY, JAMES T. - Green H. Polk released from the indenture bond he had put up for James T. Tinsley.

  ABELS, JAMES H. - Guardian report by R.W. Tucker, guardian for James L. and M. Abels, minor heirs of James H. Abels.

  WHITE, REDNICK - Commission appointed to lay off a year's support for the widow.

Pg. 267
  MOORE, STEPHEN - Inquest. Found that Stephen Moore died on 19 February 1853 on the public road near the Wayne County line as a result of being chilled to death by the cold rain.

  MURPHY, MARY - Last will and testament presented by W.H. Murphy for probate. Proven by John L. Smith and Will Murphy. John O. Munday and John McRoss appointed administrators.

Pg. 268
  MURPHY, A. - Dempsey White appointed guardian of William H.H. Murphy and Burwell Murphy minor heirs of A. Murphy.

  BERRY, ____ - Nathan Dungan appointed guardian of Cynthia Jane, Samuel Jefferson, James Madison, Eliza P., and John W. Berry, minor orphans.

  CASSEY, JOHN - Elizabeth and Hubbard Cassey appointed administrators of the estate of John Cassey.

  LESTER, GERMAN - R.W. Tucker appointed administrator of the estate of German Lester.

Pg. 275
  HOUSTON, ____ - Division of land for James H. Houston, Wm. A. Houston, and J.W.A. Kerr. J.W.A. Kerr is a heir of A.D. Kerr.

1 August 1853

Pg. 278
  GARNER, WILLIAM - Commission appointed to lay off a year's support for the widow.

Pg. 279
  CASEY, JOEL - Last will and testament presented for probate by Conway Broyles. Proven by John A. Smith and Stirling C. Evans. Conway S. Broyles is the executor.

  GARNER, WILLIAM - John H. McConnell appointed administrator of the estate of William Garner.

Pg. 280
BARNETT, WILLIAM - Last will and testament presented for probate by Elisha Pack. Proven by J.W. Jenkins. Elisha Pack appointed administrator.

Pg. 282
BERRY, WILEY - Rebecca Berry's petition for dower filed.

5 September 1853

Pg. 286
SHANNON, E.E. - Commission appointed to lay off a year's support for the widow and orphans.

Pg. 287
GARNER, HENRY - Order for the county surveyor to run and mark out the lines of tract of land belonging to the estate of Henry Garner, dec'd. Mentions a deed between James Hardin and Henry Garner for the said tract of land dated 5 April 1824.

OUTLAW, MARY J. - A minor orphan, named Mary J. Outlaw, bound out to Charles R. Morris.

Pg. 288
SANDERS, _____ - An orphan, named Adeline Sanders, bound out to Lorenz Hitchcock.

Pg. 289
PERKINS, SAMUEL - Last will and testament presented for probate by Ebenezer M. Perkins and Hardeman Perkins, executors. Proven by W.T. Blanton and William H. Wilson.

Pg. 290
SPAIN, JOHN D. - Last will and testament presented for probate by W.G. Campbell, executor. Proven by C.W. Taliaferro and C.J. Campbell. (See Loose Wills)

BAILEY, GEORGE W. - Moses Bailey appointed administrator of the estate of George W. Bailey.

GARNER, WILLIAM - Year's support laid off for Mary Ann Garner, widow, and children, of William Garner.

3 October 1853

Pg. 295
BLAKELY, J.C. - Commissioners appointed to lay off a year's support for the widow of J.C. Blakely.

NICHOLS, J.A. - Commissioners appointed to lay off a year's support for the widow and minors of J.A. Nichols.

PERKINS, SAMUEL - R.W. Crump appointed guardian for Simion and Eliza Perkins, minor children of Samuel Perkins.

DAVY, _____ - H.B. Wade appointed guardian of Richard S. Davy, minor.

Pg. 296
NICHOLS, JAMES A. - J.L. Nichols appointed administrator of the estate of James A. Nichols.

Pg. 299
BURKS, R.H. - Petition for a dower by Mary T. Burks, widow of R.H. Burks.

7 November 1853

Pg. 301
BAILEY, GEORGE W. - Commissioners appointed to lay off a year's support for the widow and orphans of George W. Bailey.

AUSTIN, DAVID - S.A. Austin released of his indenture bond for the minor heirs of David Austin.

ELLIOT, WILLIAM - Commissioners appointed to lay off a year's support for the widow and orphans of William Elliot.

Pg. 303
OWEN, DAVID - Petition by John Seal, guardian of Alexander and Mary Owen who are minor orphans of David Owen. Both minors are under the age of 14. The petition is to sell land from the estate. The said minors, Alexander and Mary, reside in Madison County, Missouri.

Pg. 306
GILDCHRIST, JOHN - J.W. Hassell resigned as an executor of the estate of John Gildchrist. Mention made of notifying heirs of the estate who do not live in Hardin County.

Pg. 307
OUTLAW, _____ - A minor, Martha A. Outlaw, bound out to D.W. Blankenship.

AUSTIN, _____ - Two minors, Andrew J. Austin and George A. Austin, bound out to W.H. Franks until they become of age.

AUSTIN, _____ - A minor, J.W. Austin, bound out to Larkin Yount until he becomes of age.

McCANDLESS, G.B. - G.G. Hardin appointed guardian of the minor heirs of G.B. McCandless.

GREARNER, _____ - Washington Wells appointed guardian of James Grearner, minor.

Pg. 308
ELLIOTT, WILLIAM - T.W. Poindexter appointed administrator of the estate of William Elliott.

5 December 1853

Pg. 313
JIM - A negro boy, named Jim, came into court as a free person of color. William Thornton appointed to see to his business affairs and manage his dealings. This was to prevent him from becoming chargeable to the county. Since Jim was born in Tennessee, he was permitted to reside in Hardin County without bond or other security.

Pg. 314
OUTLAW, _____ - Joseph Outlaw appointed guardian of Mary J. Outlaw, Sarah Outlaw, Martha E. Outlaw, and Lewis Outlaw, minors and orphans.

COVEY, SARAH - Noble W. Covey appointed administrator of the estate of Sarah Covey.

HASSELL, J.W. - R.D. Davey and J.D. Hassell appointed as the administrators of the estate of J.W. Hassell.

2 January 1854

Pg. 321
FLEMING, W.D. - Woodson Wells appointed guardian of Elizabeth W. Fleming, minor of W.D. Fleming.

Pg. 323
SPAIN, JOHN D. - Commissioners appointed to lay off a year's support for the widow and minor orphans of John D. Spain.

Pg. 325
PHILIPS, JAMES - Petition to divide land by James Philips, and his wife Beersheba, and Mahala Bryant, by her guardian Allen A. Temples.

GARNER, WILLIAM - Petition for dower by Mary Ann Garner, the widow of William Garner.

6 February 1854

Pg. 329
ARUNDELL, ERASTUS - Bollis Hinkle appointed guardian for Jane Arundell, minor of Erastus Arundell.

HASSELL, J.W. - R.D. Davy resigned as administrator for the estate of J.W. Hassell.

Pg. 330
GANT, _____ - Elisha Harbour resigned as guardian for Daniel P. Gant.

GANT, _____ - James L. Gant appointed guardian for Daniel P. Gant.

HASSELL, J.W. - J.D. Hassell and R.W. Crump appointed as the administrators of the estate of J.W. Hassell.

6 March 1854

Pg. 345
BARNETT, _____ - W.B. Barnett appointed guardian for F. Barnett, W.A. Barnett, Jas. A. Barnett, Burton Barnett, Elizabeth Barnett, and Sarah J. Barnett, minor orphans.

BARNES, WRIGHT - William Childers appointed administrator of the estate of Wright Barnes.

FLATT, JAMES - Last will and testament of James Flatt presented and proven by A. Barham and Alfred Ross.

3 April 1854

Pg. 364
STRANGER - Inquest. Found by the jury that the unknown man died at a time unknown by accidentally drowning in the Tennessee river.

Pg. 366
CASSEY, JOHN - Petition for a dowery by Elizabeth Cassey, the widow of John Cassey.

GILCHRIST, JOHN - Cornelius Gilchrist resigned as executor of the estate of John Gilchrist. He was ordered to publish a notice in the McNairy County Gazette in order to notify all heirs not living in Hardin County.

1 May 1854

Pg. 368
HAWKINS, ELIZABETH - John Bourland appointed administrator of the estate of Elizabeth Hawkins.

PITTS, C. - Alfred Pitts appointed administrator of the estate of C. Pitts.

FLATT, JAMES - Tolbert Willis appointed administrator of the estate of James Flatt.

Pg. 369
FLATT, JAMES - Commissioners appointed to lay off a year's support for the widow and minors of James Flatt.

CRENSHAW, JACKSON - A pauper, named Jackson Crenshaw, let out to the lowest bidder, J. Frie.

HODGE, _____ - A pauper, named Hodge, let out to the lowest bidder.

GILCHRIST, JOHN - Nicholas Gilchrist appointed administrator of the estate of John Gilchrist.

Pg. 370
LAKEY, _____ - A minor, named James M. Lakey, apprenticed to John Mc. Ross until age 21.

5 June 1854

Pg. 373
BENTON, GEORGE F. - A.H. Kindel appointed administrator of the estate of George F. Benton.

Pg. 374
BENTON, GEORGE F. - Commissioners appointed to lay off a year's support for the widow and minors of George F. Benton.

3 July 1854

Pg. 380
TAYLOR, SARAH L. - An infant, named Sarah L. Taylor, with no means of support, bound out to William Huling.

McWHORTER, TABITHA - Narcissa McWhorter appointed administratrix of the estate of Tabitha McWhorter.

Pg. 382
HOBBS, BARNABAS - Last will and testament of Barnabas Hobbs presented for probate and proven by John Bundy and Benajah Peacock, the subscribing witnesses. John Hardin named as executor, but he appeared in court and renounced it. John Bundy appointed as the administrator of the estate.

7 August 1854

Pg. 388
GLOVER, JAMES D. - Last will and testament of James D. Glover presented for probate by Archilans Walker. Proven by James B. Britton and W.M. Britton. Archilans Walker named as executor of the estate.

Pg. 389
BAIRD, JAMES - Felix G. Harlan appointed guardian of Margaret, Rachel, and William Hamilton Baird, infants of James Baird.

4 September 1854

Pg. 390
PORTERFIELD, C.L. - John Martin appointed administrator of the estate of C.L. Porterfield.

Pg. 391
REED, D.K. - W.D. Reed appointed administrator of the estate of D.K. Reed.

BROWN, L.Y. - R.W. Tucker appointed administrator of the estate of L.Y. Brown.

GROGAN, L.B. - L.F. Booker appointed administrator of the estate of L.B. Grogan.

LARKIN, EDMUND - James C. Green ordered relieved as the administrator of the estate of Edmund Larkin.

WILLIAMS, _____ - An orphan, named John Williams age 16, apprenticed to Robert Hames.

Pg. 392
BROWN, L.Y. - Commissioners appointed to lay off a year's support to the widow and children of L.Y. Brown.

GROGAN, L.B. - Commissioners appointed to lay off a year's support to the widow and children of L.B. Grogan.

PORTERFIELD, CHARLES - Commissioners appointed to lay off a year's support to the widow of Charles Porterfield.

REED, D.K. - Commissioners appointed to lay off a year's support to the widow and orphans of D.K. Reed.

ROWSEY, _____ - J.C. Steely released from the indenture bond for H. Rowsey.

Pg. 397
ROBISON, JOHN W. AND WILEY G. - George M. Hamilton, attorney for Wm. McMahan, informed the court that Moses Witherspoon, the indented master of John W. and Wiley G. Robison, plans to leave the county. Court decided to ascertain whether Witherspoon intends to remove the said apprenticed orphans from the jurisdiction of the county.

ORPHANS - Sheriff ordered to bring Watkins Ratliff and Maranda Mitchell, orphan children of color, to the court to be apprenticed out.

2 October 1854

Pg. 400

FISHER, ABRAHAM - Commissioners appointed to lay off a year's support to the widow and minors of Abraham Fisher.

ROBERTSON, J.W. AND W.G. - Moses Witherspoon released of his indenture bond for J.W. and W.G. Robertson.

Pg. 402

McCRARY, SOPHIA - Inquest. Found by the jury that Sophia McCrary was killed by James McCrary. About six weeks prior to the report, James McCrary "gave her a round in the heat of blood that caused her death on the 7th of July 1854 against the peace and dignity of the state." Report signed 8 July 1854.

REED, DAVID K. - Inventory returned by W.D. Reed and E.R. Reed, administrators of the estate of David K. Reed.

HARDIN, GIBSON G. - Last will and testament of Gibson G. Hardin presented for probate by executors Mark Hardin and John Hardin. Proven by Woodson Wells and Benjamin Hardin.

Pg. 403

BARNETT, _____ - A.H. Kindle appointed guardian for Frances Barnett, W.A. Barnett, James Barnett, S.V. Barnett, Elizabeth Barnett, and Sarah T. Barnett.

CROCKETT, _____ - J.B. Winn appointed guardian for Mary E. Crockett.

BENTON, GEORGE F. - John W. Kendel appointed guardian for John and Jerusha Benton, minor heirs of George F. Benton.

BARNETT, _____ - E.H. Autry appointed guardian of Sarah F. Barnett, W.S. Barnett, and Elizabeth Barnett.

McMILLAN, JOHN - Moses Glenn appointed administrator of the estate of John McMillan.

CARROLL, JAMES - T.M. Russell appointed administrator of the estate of James Carroll.

Pg. 404

FISHER, ABRAHAM - F.M. Fisher appointed administrator of the estate of Abraham Fisher.

KINCANNON, FRANCIS - Last will and testament presented for probate by Andrew Kincannon, executor of the estate of Francis Kincannon. Proven by Joab A. Russell and Stephen S. Dove, the subscribing witnesses.

KINCANNON, FRANCIS - Petition for dower by Sarah Kincannon, the widow and relict of Francis Kincannon.

REED, D.K. - Petition for dower by Mary Reed, the widow and relict of D.K. Reed.

6 November 1854

Pg. 407

KINCANNON, FRANCIS - Commissioners appointed to lay off a year's support for the widow and orphans of Francis Kincannon.

Pg. 408
DAY, _____ - H.B. Wade appointed guardian for Richard S. Day, minor.

Pg. 409
REA, JINCY - C.W. Morris appointed administrator of the estate of Jincy Rea.

HOWELL, BENJAMIN - Levi Howell appointed administrator of the estate of Benjamin Howell.

KINCANNON, FRANCES - Joseph Dillon appointed administrator of the estate of Frances Kincannon.

Pg. 412
SIMPSON, MACLEAN - Petition to sell land by Eliza Sparkman versus the heirs of Maclean Simpson. Eliza Sparkman's place of residence given as Williamson County, Tennessee. Heirs of said Maclean Simpson are Mathew K., John P., Eliza, Margarett, Rebecca Jane (all age 21 or above), Thomas, Sarah M., Mary E., James M., Martha, Susan, George W., and Mathew A., minors. W.R. Simpson is the guardian of the minors.

Pg. 413
REED, DAVID K. - Inquest. Found by the jury that he died on 10 August 1854 as a result of being struck by lightning while at his son's near his own residence.

WELCH, JOHN J. - Inquest. Found that he died on the night of 27 October 1854. He was hunting with some other people and was caught under a tree which they had cut down to get at a raccoon.

4 December 1854

Pg. 415
MORRIS, THOMAS - C.W. Morris released from his indenture bond for Thomas Morris.

Pg. 416
WILLIS, _____ - A. Willis, guardian of Mary and David Willis, made his report.

TURNER, JOHN - James Turner appointed administrator of the estate of John Turner.

1 January 1855

Pg. 422
POLK, THOMAS A. - Thos. D. Shelby appointed guardian for William H., Robert M., and Mary A. Polk, minor heirs of Thomas A. Polk.

WHITE, _____ - B.F. Guinn appointed guardian of Martha Guinn, his wife, formerly Martha White.

WOODBURN, _____ - J.L. Lindsey appointed guardian of William K., Sarah C., Alonzo A., Ranzo(?), and Patience Woodburn.

Pg. 423
VINCENT, JORDAN - Catherine Vincent, widow of Jordan Vincent, appointed as administratrix of his estate.

SHELBY, ELI - Archibald C. Shelby and George H. Polk named as executors of the estate of Eli Shelby.

Pg. 426
PEA, THOMAS J. - Petition to divide negroes by Thomas J. Pea and his wife, Margaret E. Pea. Slaves mentioned: Lot #1 to Thomas J. Pea and his wife - Tom, Minerva, and Edd; Lot #2 to Robert Hardin - King and Rutter and their two children, and Sam.

Pg. 427
MURPHY, ARCHIBALD - Petition to sell slave girl named Mary who had been willed to Mary Murphy, the widow.

5 February 1855

Pg. 431
BLANKENSHIP, THOMAS - Commission appointed to lay off a year's support to the widow and orphans of Thomas Blankenship.

COUCH, MOSES W. - James Bennett appointed administrator of the estate of Moses W. Couch.

COUCH, MOSES W. - Commission appointed to lay off a year's support to the widow and orphans of Moses W. Couch.

BIVENS, BARNEY - A.G. Pickens appointed administrator of the estate of Barney Bivens.

Pg. 432
BIVENS, BARNEY - Commission appointed to lay off a year's support to the widow and orphans of Barney Bivens.

BLANKENSHIP, THOMAS - Abel Blankenship appointed administrator of the estate of Thomas Blankenship.

BAIN, _____ - S.L. Fowler appointed guardian of Sarah A. and Mary E. Bain.

5 March 1855

Pg. 437
HARDIN, _____ - A.S. Hardin appointed guardian for Gideon, Grace, and Mary Hardin, minors.

McCANDLESS, _____ - Mark Hardin appointed guardian for Gideon and William McCandless.

2 April 1855

Pg. 447
SPAIN, MARSHALL D. - James F. Bell appointed administrator of the estate of Marshall D. Spain.

EDWARDS, SUSAN - An orphan, named Susan Edwards, bound out to Jesse Jones.

SPAIN, MARSHALL D. - Commissioners appointed to lay off a years support to the widow of Marshall D. Spain.

WINNINGHAM, G.B. - Commissioners appointed to lay off a year's support to the widow of G.B. Winningham.

Pg. 449
PEARCE, HENRY - Inquest. Found that he died on 17 March 1855 by falling into Snake Creek and drowning.

WHITLOW, JOSHUA - Inquest. Found that he died on or about 7 March 1855 as a result of being stabbed with a knife by James Clifton.

7 May 1855

Pg. 455
AUSTIN, _____ - Larkin Yount released from his indenture bond for James Austin.

HODGES, THOS. - A pauper, named Thos. Hodge, let out for twelve months to Margaret Black.

HARDIN, JOHN - Last will and testament presented for probate by Benjamin Hardin, executor.

Pg. 456
BRADFORD, GEORGE W. - A pauper of 13, named George W. Bradford, with no mother, father, or legal guardian bound out to William Counts.

4 June 1855

Pg. 457
LOWRY, ISAAC T. - F.A. Cochran resigned as executor. A.H. Kindel appointed administrator of the estate of Isaac T. Lowry.

2 July 1855

Pg. 460
GAMMILL, JAMES - Manuel McLain and W.S. Gammill appointed administrators of the estate of James Gammill.

ABEL, J.L. - R.W. Tucker appointed administrator of the estate of J.L. Abel.

GAMMILL, JAS. - Commissioners appointed to lay off a year's support to the widow.

Pg. 461
UNKNOWN - Inquest. An unknown male was found in the Tennessee River on 18 April 1855. Among personal effects were: a pocketbook with $7.55, a trunk key, a $5.00 note on NW Bank of Virginia.

Pg. 462
SCHARF, JOHN - Inquest. Found that he died on 30 May 1855 by accidental drowning.

TAYLOR, CASWELL - Inquest. Found that he was killed on 7 June 1855 by rifle shot inflicted by John George.

6 August 1855

Pg. 464
HOWELL, _____ - Commissioners appointed to lay off a year's support to the widow.

OUTLAW, _____ - Commissioners appointed to lay off a

year's support for the widow.

Pg. 465
HARBOUR, S.B. - Elijah Harbour appointed administrator of the estate of S.B. Harbour.

BOURLAND, JOHN - W.G. Campbell appointed administrator of the estate of John Bourland.

OUTLAW, JAMES - James Stemmill appointed administrator of the estate of James Outlaw.

WARD, JANE - James Ward, husband, appointed administrator of the estate of Jane Ward.

ANDERSON, _____ - William Anderson appointed guardian of William Anderson and T.P.W. Anderson.

COOPER, _____ - B.B. Alexander appointed guardian of J.B. Cooper.

Pg. 466
PRESTON, JOHN - P.B. Preston appointed guardian of J.A. Preston, J.L. Preston, M.E. Preston, W.J. Preston, minor heirs of John Preston.

JONES, SARAH - A fourteen year old orphan, named Sarah Jones, bound out to James Cassool.

Pg. 467
BAIRD, JAMES - Probate of will contested by James Ward, husband of Jane Ward, dec'd heir of James Baird versus George S. Ross, administrator, Cynthia Baird, Rachel M. Baird, and William H. Baird.

Pg. 468
HOWELL, BENJAMIN - Petition for dower by Mary Howell, widow of Benjamin Howell. Noted that Benjamin Howell died on 2 October 1854. Only surviving children and heirs: Levi J. Howell, David P. Howell, Benj. F. Howell, Doctor Riley Howell, Mary A. Howell, and Jonathan Howell.

Pg. 471
HELTON, JAMES - Noncupative will presented for probate by James Russell and John F. Pitts.

3 September 1855

Pg. 472
ALEXANDER, W.R. - J.H. Alexander appointed administrator of the estate of W.R. Alexander.

COPELAND, SOLOMON - John Copeland appointed administrator of the estate of Solomon Copeland.

HELTON, JAMES - John F. Pitts appointed administrator of the estate of James Helton.

Pg. 473
MEADOW, M.G. - A.B. Anderson appointed administrator of the estate of M.G. Meadow.

Pg. 475
BENTON, GEORGE F. - John N. Kindel appointed guardian of George F. Benton minor heir of George F. Benton.

COOPER, DRUSSINA - John Cooper appointed administrator of the estate of Drussina Cooper.

1 October 1855

Pg. 476
HELTON, JAMES - Commissioners appointed to lay off a year's support for the widow and orphans of James Helton.

BOURLAND, JOHN - Commissioners appointed to lay off a year's support for the widow and orphans of John Bourland.

Pg. 477
ALEXANDER, _____ - R.W. Crump appointed guardian for W.H.T. Alexander.

GANT, _____ - A.J. Gant appointed guardian for Robert W. Gant.

Pg. 478
PICKENS, JOHN G. - John Pickens appointed guardian for the minor heirs of John G. Pickens.

TACKER, _____ - William Pickens appointed guardian for Delice Tacker and Homer(?) Tacker.

LONG, LYDIA - Seamore Long appointed administrator of the estate of Lydia Long.

DANIEL, WATSON - Jason Paulk appointed administrator of the estate of Watson Daniel.

HOPPER, CHARLES - Jacob Johnson appointed administrator of the estate of Charles Hopper.

Pg. 479
HOPPER, CHARLES - Inquest. Found that he was thrown or fell from his horse in the lane near Saltillo on 24 September 1855 which resulted in his death.

5 November 1855

Pg. 481
HUGHLITS, W.T.A. - Commissioners appointed to lay off a year's support for the widow and orphans of W.T.A. Hughlits.

MEEK, WILLIAM - Thomas Meek appointed guardian of the minor heirs of William Meek.

Pg. 482
McCALL, DAVID - E.C. Welch appointed administrator of the estate of David McCall.

HEWLITT, W.T.A. - Eli C. Hewlitt and Thomas Davy appointed administrators of the estate of W.T.A. Hewlitt.

LOWRY, ISAAC T. - A.H. Kindel appointed administrator of the estate of Isaac T. Lowry in the place of F.A. Cochran.

QUICK, M.K. - Last will and testament presented for probate by A.H. Kindell, executor. Proven by F.A. Cochran and Frank Cherry, subscribing witnesses.

Pg. 483
POOL, ARCHIBALD - Last will and testament presented for probate by Catherine Pool. Proven by Henry Garrard and J.T. Thompson, subscribing witnesses.

SPAIN, MARSHALL D. - James F. Bell resigned as administrator of the estaet of Marshall D. Spain. Thomas Maxwell and P.M. Tucker appointed administrators in his place.

3 December 1855

Pg. 486
BIVENS, BARNEY - Petition for dower by Mary Bivens, widow versus A.G. Pickens and F.C. Bivens.

Pg. 487
STEPHENSON, _____ - E.H. Stephenson appointed guardian of William, Mary A., James, Elihu, and Hardin Stephenson.

BARNETT, B.N. - Robert S. Church appointed administrator of the estate of B.N. Barnett.

Pg. 488
McCALL, DANIEL - Commissioners appointed to lay off a year's support for the widow and children of Daniel McCall.

YOUNG, WILLIAM N. - David Young appointed guardian for James W., Margaret J., and Isaac R. Young minor heirs of William N. Young. (These individuals had evidently just moved into Hardin County.)

7 January 1856

Pg. 491
BRADY, FREDERICK - Charles Brady paid for keeping his father, Frederick Brady, a pauper, for the year.

Pg. 494
DANIEL, J.W. - Petition for dower by Nancy Daniel, widow versus Jason Paulk.

Pg. 496
SCOTT, MARTHA A. - James L. Watson appointed administrator of the estate of Martha A. Scott.

4 February 1856

Pg. 503
HAGGY, HENRY - Lewis Haggy appointed administrator of the estate of Henry Haggy.

MAY, MITCHEL - Last will and testament presented for probate and proven by William A. and John Austin.

3 March 1856

Pg. 515
WOODS, JAMES - Commissioners appointed to lay off a year's support for the widow and minors of James Woods.

WORLEY, _____ - William Russell appointed guardian for Stephen Worley, a minor.

Pg. 529
WOODS, JAMES - John H. Wood appointed administrator of the estate of James Woods.

MAY, MICHAEL- F.A. Cockran appointed administrator of the estate of Michael May.

7 April 1856

Pg. 538
McCARN, WILLIAM - Last will and testament presented for probate. James G. Hamilton appointed executor.

OLDS, WILLIAM - Benjamin Johnson appointed guardian for the minor heirs of William Olds.

GAMMILL, _____ - Alfred Gammill appointed guardian for F.G. Gammill.

Pg. 539
WOODS, JAMES - Petition for dower by Sarah Woods, widow of James Woods.

COUNTY COURT MINUTES

BOOK G: 1857 - 1860

5 January 1857

Pg. 3
HODGE, THOMAS - A pauper, Thomas Hodge, was kept for one year by Mrs. Marianne Baker.

Pg. 4
GRIFFIN, KIZZIAH - A pauper, Kizziah Griffin, kept for one year by E.P. Blount.

RUSSELL, HUGH - A pauper, Hugh Russell, kept by his mother Nancy Russell for one year.

Pg. 5
McCOLLUM, SUSANNAH - P.M. Tucker appointed guardian for Sarah A., Martha A., Nancy A., James Stephens, and Thomas McCollum, minor heirs of Susannah McCollum, formerly Susannah Howard.

6 April 1857

Pg. 7
LAMB, NANCY - A pauper, Nancy Lamb, let out to the lowest bidder, John Gross.

6 July 1857

Pg. 14
NEWMAN, NUBY(?) - An indigent orphan, Nuby(?) Newman, apprenticed out to Henry Newman.

3 August 1857

Pg. 17
   WOODS, SARAH - Last will and testament proven in open court and ardered to be recorded.

   DILL, _____ - Robert Forbish, guardian of James Dill and Patsy A. Dill, made his settlement and resigned. J.H. Rowsey appointed in his place.

   HASSELL, _____ - Joseph Hassell appointed guardian of Elizabeth and Mak(?) Hassell.

7 September 1857

Pg. 18
   HOPPER, E.S. - Commissioners appointed to lay off a year's support for the widow of E.S. Hopper.

   KYLE, GILBERT - Commissioners appointed to lay off a year's support for the widow of Gilbert Kyle.

   COVEY, ROENA - Alfred K. Covey appointed administrator of the estate of Roena Covey.

Pg. 19
   KYLE, GILBERT - William Kyle appointed administrator of the estate of Gilbert Kyle.

   HOPPER, E.S. - James M. Creel appointed administrator of the estate of E.S. Hopper.

   ALLEN, E.J. - Last will and testament presented for probate. Proven by the two subscribing witnesses.

   ALLEN, E.J. - Morgan H. Ross and Thomas Poindexter qualified as the executor of the will of E.J. Allen.

5 October 1857

Pg. 21
   DUCKWORTH, W.H. - Special election held for county court clerk occasioned by the death of W.H. Duckworth. William Baker was elected.

6 October 1857

Pg. 22
   COCKBURN, CANNY(?) - Wallace Hays appointed guardian of Canny(?) Cockburn, minor heir of Canny(?) Cockburn.

   MITCHELL, _____ - Ordered that Sarah J. Mitchell, aged 6, Henry T. Mitchell, aged 5, and Martha E. Mitchell, aged 4, be bound as apprentices to T.J. Campbell.

   LAMB, JAMES - John Austin appointed administrator of the estate of James Lamb.

Pg.23
   BOLLIN, JOHN - James H. Simmons appointed guardian of J. B. Bollin, minor heir of John Bollin.

   BARNES, MALINDA - L.B. Parrish appointed administrator

of the estate of Malinda Barnes.

9 October 1857

Pg. 30
    DUCKWORTH, W.H. - C.S. Robertson appointed administrator of the estate of W.H. Duckworth.

3 November 1857

Pg. 31
    BARNES, J.L. - Commissioners appointed to lay off a year's support for Elizabeth Barnes, widow of J.L. Barnes. (This entry was crossed out in the book.)

4 January 1858

Pg. 34
    MONTGOMERY, _____ - Petition to partition or divide land. Brought by Alfred Montgomery, et al, versus Mary Montgomery, et al. Other defendants are: Katharine Montgomery, Joseph Montgomery, Emily Montgomery, Caroline Montgomery, and Thomas F. Montgomery, all infants.

Pg. 35
    BOURLAND, _____ - Petition to sell land brought by Washington G. Campbell versus the infant defendants John B. Bourland, Samuel R. Bourland, and Susan A. Bourland.

    GANT, JOHN - William Strayhon appointed guardian of the minor heirs of John Gant.

    REA, JOHN C. - Thomas Maxwell appointed guardian of E.M. Rea and T.F. Rea, minors of John C. Rea.

5 January 1858

Pg. 37
    COLBERT, STEPHEN - Commissioners appointed to lay off a year's support for Mrs. Colbert.

Pg. 38
    ASHWORTH, G.H. - James W. Ashworth appointed administrator of the estate of G.H. Ashworth.

Pg. 39
    BINGHAM, ALEXANDER - Commissioners appointed to lay off a year's support for Mary Bingham and children.

    PARRISH, ABEL - Irvin Parrish appointed administrator of the will annexed of the estate of Abel Parrish.

    BASYE, DAVID - Geo. M. Hamilton appointed administrator of the estate of David Basye.

    BINGHAM, ALEXANDER - Alfred Pitts appointed administrator of the estate of Alexander Bingham.

Pg. 44
    BARNES, JOHN L. - Petition for dower by Elizabeth Barnes, widow of John L. Barnes.

Pg. 45
PARRISH, ABEL L. - Noncupative will presented for probate by Thomas Davy and James Russell, the witnesses. Will was made on 2 November 1857 at the house of Irvin Parrish, testator's son.

YOUNT, LARKIN - Commissioners appointed to lay off a year's support for Eliza Yount widow of Larkin Yount.

Pg. 47
PETITION - Petition presented by the residents of the 7th Civil District. It requested that they be redistricted so that they fall in the 8th District. Signed by C.Y. Hudson, Peter Hudson, F.G. Harlan, J.B. Harlan, J.W. Smith, H.M. Hudson, J. Gibson, Jos. Duncan Jr., J.G. Pickens, John Irwin, H.N. Covey. Petition was granted.

Pg. 50
HAMILTON, _____ - Petition to divide Negroes by James G. Hamilton, George M. Hamilton, Abraham Baughman, and J.A.R. Hamilton. Slaves mentioned: Jim and Amelia.

1 February 1858

Pg. 54
BRATTON, PAUL - Commissioners appointed to lay off a year's support for Pulsy Bratton, widow of Paul Bratton.

BAUGHMAN, E.A. - Abraham Baughman appointed administrator of the estate of E.A. Baughman.

BRATTON, PAUL - Paul Bratton appointed administrator of the estate of Paul Bratton.

BOURLAND, _____ - Robert Bourland, a minor orphan age 15, bound to J.M. Cunningham.

Pg. 55
HARDIN, _____ - William Hardin, a minor age 16, bound to Washington Wells.

SOUTH, _____ - John South, a minor of 13 years, bound to Levi South.

EOFF, SQUIRE - Alfred Pitts appointed administrator of the estate of Squire Eoff.

Pg. 56
EOFF, SQUIRE - Commissioners appointed to lay off a year's support to Senah Eoff, widow of Squire Eoff.

1 March 1858

Pg. 58
BAUGHMAN, ELIZABETH A. - Inventory returned by Abraham Baughman, administrator of the estate of Elizabeth A. Baughman.

HINKLE, JONATHAN - Inventory returned by James Harman, administrator of the estate of Jonathan Hinkle.

TANKESLEY, FOUNTAIN - Thomas Maxwell appointed guardian of Caledonia Tankesly, minor of Fountain Tankesley.

Pg. 59
PARSONS, NANCY L. - Samuel H. Parsons appointed guardian of Nancy L. Parsons, his wife.

BARNETT, _____ - A.D. Harrison appointed guardian of Mary Barnett and Sarah Barnett, minor orphans of his wife Mary Jane Harrison.

Pg. 62
DUCKWORTH, W.H. - Petition to sell slaves to pay off the estate debt. Brought by C.S. Robertson, administrator versus the Heirs of W.H. Duckworth. Heirs named: Mary A. Duckworth widow, Sarah J., Wm. S., Elizabeth, John W., Harriet, and Anna Duckworth, minor children. J.N. Baker appointed guardian of the said minors.

5 April 1858

Pg. 69
JORRELL(?), R.A. - Commissioners appointed to lay off a year's support to Mary Jane Jorrell, widow of R.A. Jorrell.

Pg. 70
JOEL, R.B. - Ephraim Maddox appointed administrator of the estate of R.B. Joel.

HELTON, JAMES - James W. Ashworth gave bond as guardian of the minor heirs of James Helton.

Pg. 71
HAGY, WILLIAM - Robert J. Williams appointed guardian for Robert Hagy, minor heir of William Hagy.

ROBINSON, MARY A. - Lewis Hagy appointed guardian of the minor heirs of Mary A. Robinson.

SHEILD(?), W.B. - Thomas Maxwell appointed administrator of the estate of W.B. Sheild.

BRIM, JOSEPH - Last will and testament presented for probate by James J. Davis and N.J. Brim. Proven by James R. Bridges and James Perkins, subscribing witnesses. James J. Davis and Newton J. Brim qualified as executors.

Pg. 90
REA, JOHN C. - Petition to divide land belonging to the estate of John C. Rea. Heirs named: Levi J. Horrell and his wife Joanna Horrell formerly Joanna Rea, Thomas T. Rea, Elizabeth M. Rea, and Lidia Jane Rea.

6 April 1858

Pg. 97
BAYSE, JAMES - Petition to sell slaves. Heirs of James Bayse named: Thomas D. Shelby and wife Virginia A., Archibald Pool and wife Caroline M., James E. Blount, Edmund Basye, G.M. Hamilton and wife Susannah, Elijah Basye, Joseph T. Basye, and Lydia Basye.

Pg. 98
HAWKINS, R.T. - William Davis appointe guardian of William J. Hawkins, minor of R.T. Hawkins, in Tishomingo County, Mississippi. Money was owed to the estate of said minor by W.G.

Campbell.

3 May 1858

Pg. 106

HALEMAN, W.W. - N.M.D. Kemp appointed administrator of the estate of W.W. Haleman.

HAMILTON, ELIZABETH - Petition ex parte to sell land from the estate of Elizabeth Hamilton. Brought by George M. Hamilton, James G. Hamilton, J.A.R. Hamilton, James A. Baughman, George M. Baughman, John H. Baughman, Elizabeth A. Baughman, Malecia Baughman, who are the only surviving heirs of Elizabeth Hamilton. She received land warrant No. 72069 on 25 August 1857 as the widow of Andrew Hamilton a veteran of the War of 1812. She died intestate on 15 November 1857.

Pg. 109

CANTRELL, JAMES W. - Last will and testament presented for probate by Lenore Cantrell. No subscribing witnesses. Document was found among valuable papers of the deceased. John N. Cantrell, who was appointed executor in the will, has removed to Texas. Lenore Cantrell appointed administrator. (Following this entry is a copy of the will. It is abstracted here.) Testator desires that his body be buried at his brother Lenore Cantrell's place where hhis wife Therza and daughter Eleanor are buried. Heirs: Wife - Eunice Cantrell; children - John N., Calisto L., Lenoir W., Theresa E., Levi L., James K.P., Aaron V.B., Olenor H.P., Minerva R., and Harry Cantrell. Slaves: Washington. Executor: John N. Cantrell. Dated: 18 November 1855.

7 June 1858

Pg. 112

YOUNG, R.G. - Last will and testament presented and proven for probate by Isaac H. Young.

MULLINS, SILAS - Commissioners appointed to lay off a year's support for the widow of Silas Mullins.

YOUNG, R.G. - Isaac H. Young issued executor's letters on the estate of R.G. Young.

PICKENS, JONATHAN R. - Last will and testament presented for probate by John H. Meek, executor. Proven by common form.

Pg. 113

BAKER, WM. - Last will and testament presented for probate by G.M. Hamilton, executor. Proven in common form.

MULLINS, SILAS - Thos. S. Spencer appointed administrator of the estate of Silas Mullins.

Pg. 115

HAMILTON, ANDREW - A further record of the petition to sell land from the estate of Elizabeth Hamilton. Statement that Andrew Hamilton, dec'd husband of Elizabeth, served in Captain Ellis' Company of the Tennessee Militia in the War of 1812.

5 July 1858

Pg. 123
CANTRELL, JAMES W. - Eunice Cantrell dissented from the will of her husband and asked that commissioners be appointed to lay off a year's support.

CANTRELL, JAMES W. - Eunice Cantrell appointed guardian of Manerva R. Cantrell and William H. Cantrell, minor heirs of James W. Cantrell.

HAYS, C.L. - Lawson Hays appointed guardian of James Hays, Dudly Hays, and Calista Hays, the minor heirs of C.L. Hays.

CANTRELL, JAMES W. - A.H. Kindell appointed guardian for James K.P. Cantrell, Aaron V.B. Cantrell, and Olivia H.P. Cantrell, the minor heirs of James W. Cantrell.

OLD, WILLIAM - Benjamin Johnson appointed guardian of Isaac Old and George Old, minor orphans of William Old.

6 July 1858

Pg. 124
IRWIN, JAMES - Noncupative will presented for probate. Widow and next of kin of James Irwin being Nancy Irwin, Sim E. Irwin, Hattie L. Irwin, Juliette S. Irwin, Mary D. Irwin, Cornelia L.B. Irwin, John S. Irwin, Linis B. Irwin, James W. Irwin, W.H. Cherry, and Annie M. Cherry were ordered to appear at the present term of court to contest the will if they chose to do so. Proven by Joseph F. Matley and William F. Hodge. Will was made in the presence of Lewis H. Broyles Sr., William F. Hodge, and Joseph F. Matley on 26 May 1858.

Pg. 126
SPAIN, MARSHALL D. - Petition to sell land from the estate of Marshall D. Spain. Brought by Thomas Maxwell and Petser M. Tucker, administrators. Mentions Hannah D. Spain as widow and John M.D. Spain and James W.D. Spain as the only heirs.

7 July 1858

Pg. 128
BAUGHMAN, E.A. - George M. Hamilton appointed guardian of James A. Baughman, G.M. Baughman, John H. Baughman, Elizabeth Baughman, and Malicia Baughman, minor children of E.A. Baughman. Hamilton is to take charge of a fund coming to them from a sale of a land warrant which descended to them from their grandmother, Elizabeth Hamilton, dec'd.

2 August 1858

Pg. 135
BLOUNT, AMERICA - Daniel Smith appointed administrator of the estate of America Blount.

BLOUNT, JAMES J. - Daniel Smith appointed administrator of the estate of James J. Blount.

BLOUNT, FLORIA - Daniel Smith appointed administrator of the estate of Floria Blount.

Pg. 136
CAMPBELL, A.G. - Last will and testament presented for probate by W.G. Campbell. Proven in common form.

IRWIN, JAMES - Nancy Irwin and James W. Irwin appointed administrators of the estate of James Irwin.

IRWIN, JAMES - J.S. Irwin appointed guardian of Susannah Irwin, Hettie L. Irwin, Juliet S. Irwin, Mary D. Irwin, and Cornelia L.B. Irwin, minor orphans of James Irwin.

Pg. 138
CAMPBELL, ARTHUR B. - Archibald McDougal and James D. Martin proved the last will and testament and a codicil.

Pg. 139
RAY, JOHN C. - Elizabeth Ray, a minor heir of John C. Ray, attained the age of 14 and chose Charles W. Morris as her guardian.

6 September 1858

Pg. 141
ROSS, JOHN M. - Isaac W. Ross and C.C. Williams appointed administrators of the estate of John M. Ross.

LEE, _____ - James M. Hooks appointed guardian for Elizabeth Lee.

PORTERFIELD, CHARLES L. - John Martin, guardian for the minor heirs of Charles L. Porterfield, ordered to pay Nancy Porterfield, widow, $65.00 for the support of the youngest children.

Pg. 144
BRASTFIELD, ASA - John Wolverton appointed administrator of the estate of Asa Brastfield.

Pg. 146
WORLEY, _____ - Final settlement made with William Russell, guardian of Stephen Worley.

BLANKENSHIP, _____ - D.W. Blankenship appointed guardian for Mary Blankenship.

4 October 1858

Pg. 148
JENKINS, J.W. - D.A. Roberts appointed administrator of the estate of J.W. Jenkins.

GILBERT, JOSEPH W. - Henry H. Smith appointed administrator of the estate of Joseph W. Gilbert.

GILBERT, J.W. - Eliza Gilbert, minor heir of J.W. Gilbert, asked the court to appoint James M. Smith her guardian.

WHITE, ABRAHAM - John D. White appointed administrator of the estate of Abraham White.

Pg. 149
JENKINS, J.W. - Commissioners appointed to lay off a year's support for Mary A. Jenkins, widow and children of J.W. Jenkins.

Pg. 150
   WINCHESTER, R.R. - Commissioners appointed to lay off a year's support for the widow and children of R.R. Winchester.

   WINCHESTER, R.R. - Commissioners appointed to lay off a dower's interest to Sarah Winchester, widow.

Pg. 152
   KINCANNON, _____ - William Mosier asked that the following minor children be bound to him: Nancy E. Kincannon born 17 June 1843, Thomas W.P. Kincannon born 15 June 1845, Rebecca J. Kincannon born 20 July 1847, and James F. Kincannon born 11 June 1849. The request was granted.

Pg. 155
   ALEXANDER, CYRUS - W.T. Alexander received payment for keeping Cyrus Alexander, a pauper.

1 November 1858

Pg. 162
   POOL, AARON - Henry H. Smith appointed administrator of the estate of Aaron Pool.

   McDANIEL, JAMES - C.W. Taliaferro appointed administrator of the estate of James McDaniel.

   DAVIDSON, _____ - John Davidson, an orphan aged 16, bound to S.S. Davidson until age 21.

   MILLER, _____ - James Miller, an orphan, bound to Jacob Luther until age 21.

Pg. 163
   KOGER, WILLIAM - Copy of the last will and testament of William Koger, late of Lauderdale County, Alabama, presented and authenticated. Jesse Koger qualified as executor.

6 December 1858

Pg. 165
   EOFF, SQUIRE - Petition for dower by Sena Eoff, widow. Heirs under 21 years of age are: George W. Anderson and his wife Mary E.W.J., Winny R., Eliza J., James D., Nancy L., Sena H., and Elijah Eoff.

Pg. 168
   DEARIN, JAMES - N.P. Dearin appointed administrator of the estate of James Dearin.

Pg. 169
   SCOTT, WINFIELD - M.M. Dickson appointed guardian of James Scott, minor heir of Winfield Scott.

3 January 1859

Pg. 171
   LEWIS, POLLY - Jesse Power paid for keeping Polly Lewis, a pauper, for eight months.

   MILLIGAN, GEORGE M. - James W. Bennett received payment for keeping George M. Milligan, a pauper.

Pg. 177
BOURLAND, JOHN - J.B. Bourland, minor heir of John Bourland, asked that J.W. Cunningham be appointed his guardian.

7 February 1859

Pg. 180
THOMPSON, WILLIAM - M.H. Ross appointed administrator of the estate of William Thompson.

BARNETT, WILLIAM - John Martin appointed administrator of the estate of William Barnett.

THOMPSON, WILLIAM - Commissioners appointed to lay off a year's support for Mary J. Thompson, widow, and children of William Thompson.

McCULLEN, D.G. - C.W. Taliaferro appointed administrator of the estate of D.G. McCullen.

McCULLEN, D.G. - Commissioners appointed to lay off a year's support for the widow and children of D.G. McCullen.

RAY, _____ - C.W. Morris, guardian for Elizabeth Campbell formerly Elizabeth Ray, resigned.

RAY, _____ - John A. Campbell appointed guardian for Elizabeth Campbell, his wife, formerly Elizabeth Ray.

Pg. 181
BINGHAM, MARTHA - Alfred Pitts appointed guardian of Mary Bingham, minor heir of Martha Bingham dec'd formerly Martha Sumner.

SUMNER, BENJAMIN - Alfred Pitts appointed guardian of J.B., W.P., and Sarah E. pitts, minor heirs of Mary Pitts formerly Mary Sumner.

BAIN, WILLIAM - Pythias Blankenship appointed guardian of his wife, Sarah A. Blankenship, formerly Sarah A. Bain, minor child of William Bain.

PICKENS, ANDREW J. - Last will and testament presented for probate by Jesse B. Walker and Martha Pickens. Proven by James D. Martin and A.G. McDougal, subscribing witnesses.

Pg. 182
PICKENS, ANDREW J. - Jesse B. Walker and Martha Pickens gave bond as executors.

Pg. 185
JONES, T.A. - Mrs. E.J. Jones appointed guardian of her son, N.T. Jones, minor heir of T.A. Jones.

7 March 1859

Pg. 187
HOOKS, HARRY - A free person of color, Harry Hooks, asked that Josiah Dodds by appointed to act as his agent.

Pg.188
SMITH, HIRAM - P.M. Smith appointed administrator of the estate of Hiram Smith.

McCANLESS, A.J. - William K. Hardin appointed administrator of the estate of A.J. McCanless.

McCARN, DANIEL G. - E.J. Gillis appointed guardian of John D. McCarn, minor heir of Daniel G. McCarn. Mother of the child was present and consented.

SMITH, HIRAM - Commissioners appointed to lay off a year's support for Mrs. Sarah Smith, widow of Hiram Smith.

Pg. 190
McDOUGAL, JOHN - John McDougal gave bond so that his slave Jerry could carry a gun on his premises.

4 April 1859

Pg. 195
UNKNOWN - Coroner's Jury paid for holding an inquest over the body of a strange white man found floating in the Tennessee River.

UNKNOWN - Coroner's Jury paid for holding an inquest over the body of a strange Negro man found floating in the Tennessee River.

UNKNOWN - Coroner's Jury paid for holding an inquest over the body of a white man found in the Tennessee River.

Pg. 196
PICKENS, ANDREW J. - Coroner's Jury paid for holding an inquest over the body of Andrew J. Pickens.

Pg. 200
MANGUM, JOHN E. - Harwell Mangum appointed administrator of the estate of John E. Mangum.

2 May 1859

Pg. 209
CULLINS, JOHN G. - William H. Franks appointed administrator of the estate of John G. Cullins.

FISHER, F.M. - Thomas Davy appointed administrator of the estate of F.M. Fisher.

FISHER, F.M. - Commissioners appointed to lay off a year's support for Mary Jane Fisher, widow and children of F.M. Fisher.

FARRIS, _____ - John Huggins appointed guardian for his wife, L.E. Huggins, formerly L.E. Farris.

CULLINS, JOHN G. - Commissioners appointed to lay off a widow's portion to Mrs. Mary Cullins, widow, and family of John G. Cullins.

Pg. 210
FRIE, JONATHAN - W.G. Frie appointed administrator of the estate of Jonathan Frie.

Pg. 211
MANGUM, _____ - Petition to sell land by Harwell Mangum. Thomas C. Mangum, Jefferson Hitchcock and wife Elizabeth, Joseph Smith and wife Lucy and Isaac Lucas named in petition and listed

as non-residents of the state. Lucy Smith, formerly Lucy Mangum, William W. Mangum, James Mangum, and Issac Mangum listed as minors.

6 June 1859

Pg. 214
McINTOSH, THOMAS L. - Thomas Maxwell appointed administrator of the estate of Thomas L. McIntosh.

TANKERSLEY, _____ - Thomas Maxwell resigned as guardian of Caledonia Wood, formerly Caledonia Tankersley. John C. Wood, her husband, appointed guardian.

4 July 1859

Pg. 219
OUTLAW, LEWIS - John Copeland appointed administrator of the estate of Lewis Outlaw.

OUTLAW, LEWIS - Commissioners appointed to lay off a year's support for Mrs. Outlaw, widow of Lewis Outlaw.

1 August 1859

Pg. 228
KING, CARROLL - R.J. Wilkinson appointed guardian of Rebecca C. King, minor heir of Carroll King.

Pg. 229
FRANK, FREDERIC - W.N. Ross appointed administrator of the estate of Frederic Frank.

Pg. 232
RICE, HENRY - Thomas S. Spencer appointed administrator of the estate of Henry Rice.

5 September 1859

Pg. 234
COLE, WILLIAM - John Cole appointed administrator of the estate of William Cole.

YOUNG, ISAAC H. - James L. Smith appointed administrator of the estate of Isaac H. Young.

Pg. 235
YOUNG, ISAAC H. - Commissioners appointed to lay off a year's support for Mrs. Young, widow of Isaac H. Young.

Pg. 236
CHILDRESS, WILLIAM - Petition for dower brought by Washington Campbell versus Sarah Childress, et al. Allotment for Harriet McAfee, formerly Harriet Childress, widow of William Childress.

3 October 1859

Pg. 244
LOVE, JOHN - E.S. Tidwell appointed administrator of the estate of John Love.

BOOKER, L.F. - Eliza and William Booker appointed administrators of the estate of L.F. Booker.

Pg. 245
FRANK, FREDERIC - Commissioners appointed to lay off a year's support for Nancy Frank, widow of Frederic Frank, and family.

Pg. 247
SHELBY, LEVI - Commissioners appointed to lay off a year's support for Mrs. Shelby, widow of Levi Shelby.

SHELBY, LEVI - Last will and testament of Levi Shelby was presented for probate by B.F. Shelby, E.J. Gillis, and Edward Tatum. Proven by Alfred H. Kindel and Samuel H. Parsons, the subscribing witnesses.

WEATHERFORD, HILL K. - Last will and testament of Hill K. Weatherford presented for probate by William Frank. Proven by John C. Welch and William Nichols.

Pg. 248
YOUNG, R.G. - James L. Smith appointed administrator of the estate of R.G. Young.

McCALL, JOHN B. - Inquest. Found by the jury that John B. McCall died on or about 15 August 1859. He accidentally drowned at Lot's Landing in the Tennessee River.

NEIL, ALFRED - Inquest. Found by the jury that Alfred Neil shot himself at the graveyard near his residence on 8 August 1859.

7 November 1859

Pg. 251
NEWMAN, GARRETT - James Hanna and Clark Newman appointed as the administrators of the estate of Garrett Newman.

ROBERTSON, JOHN W. - James H. Rowsey appointed administrator of the estate of John W. Robertson.

Pg. 252
FRANK, FREDERIC - John Frank appointed administrator of the estate of Frederic Frank.

Pg. 253
NEWMAN, GARRETT - Commissioners appointed to lay off a year's support for Mary Ann Newman, widow of Garrett Newman, and children.

WHITSON, HARRIET - J.L. Davy appointed guardian for James Whitson, minor heir of Harriet Whitson.

HOPPER, E.S. - Avis Hopper appointed guardian of T.E. Hopper, Minda Hopper, and Emily Hopper, minor heirs of E.S. Hopper.

Pg. 254
WEATHERFORD, HILL K. - William G. Frank gave bond as the executor of the estate of Hill K. Weatherford.

Pg. 255
LAMB, JAMES - Benjamin Watkins, of Carroll County, Arkansas, presented his appointment as guardian of the minor heirs of James Lamb. Minors named: Levicy E. Lamb age 14, James H. Lamb under 14, M.A. Lamb under 14, Benjamin Lamb under 14, Jeremiah Lamb over 14, and Sarah E. Lamb over 14. James Lamb was late of Hardin

County.

Pg. 257
  NEIL, ALFRED - Thomas A. Neil appointed administrator of the estate of Alfred Neil.

  SPARKS, ____ - W.J. Sparks appointed guardian of S.E. Sparks, J.F. Sparks, J.L. Sparks, J.N. Sparks, and Mary Hughlin, formerly Mary Sparks.

  WHITLOW, GRANDVILLE - Milton Whitlow appointed guardian of the minor heirs of Grandville Whitlow.

5 December 1859

Pg. 261
  MITCHELL, JACK - A free man of color, Jack Mitchell, who was born in Hardin County in 1834 and was born of a free woman of color, petitioned for certificates of freedom. Description: Black color, 175 lbs., scar just above left eye and the nail off the third finger of the right hand, scar on the right arm above the wrist, about 34 years of age. He served an apprenticeship or was bound to one A.B. Campbell, late of Hardin County. Ordered that Jack Mitchell is a free man.

Pg. 266
  TUCKER, R.W. - Certified to practice law.

Pg. 270
  BOOKER, L.F. - Commissioners appointed to lay off a widow's dower for Mrs. Booker, widow of L.F. Booker.

2 January 1860

Pg. 274
  COSSEY, ____ - Petition to sell land by William Cossey, et al. Mary Cossey, Sarah Cossey, Herbert Cossey Jr., Lucretia Cossey, and W.H.D. Cossey named in the petition and listed as non-residents of the state.

Pg. 277
  MAXWELL, THOMAS - Certified to practice law.

  WHITLOW, HENDERSON - Milton Whitlow appointed guardian for Sarah Whitlow, minor heir of Henderson Whitlow.

6 February 1860

Pg. 280
  SIMMONS, WILLIAM - J.B. Britton appointed administrator of the estate of William Simmons.

  SIMMONS, WILLIAM - Commissioners appointed to lay off a year's support to M.L. Simmons, widow.

  SOWELL, JOHN - Commissioners appointed to lay off a year's support to Susannah Sowell, widow.

Pg. 282
  PICKENS, JAMES G. - A.K. Covey appointed administrator of the estate of James G. Pickens.

  PICKENS, JAMES G. - Commissioners appointed to lay off

a year's support for Mrs. Pickens, widow.

BURTON, JOHN JR. - John Burton appointed administrator of the estate of John Burton, Jr.

HESTER, J.K. - Alfred Pitts appointed administrator of the estate of J.K. Hester.

Pg. 283
BAIRD, JAMES - Last will and testament presented for probate by A.G. McDougal. Proven by John J. Welborn.

KENDRICK, ALLAN - Last will and testament presented for probate by Nancy H. Kendrick. The will was not witnessed. Handwriting proven genuine by Cary A. Armstrong, James T. Fraley, and Jacob Luther.

Pg. 284
BAIN, GEORGE - Noncupative will presented for probate by Daniel Bain and Sarah Bain, witnesses. Will made on 4 December 1859. Wife - Sally Bain.

Pg. 287
MITCHELL, JAMES - Petition for papers of freedom by James Mitchell, a free man of color, for himself, his wife Linda Mitchell, and his children George Washington and James Jackson Mitchell. All were born in Tennessee. Descriptions: James, 44 yrs. old, dark, scar on right leg 3" below knee, another scar on nose below the eyes, 5'8", stout; Linda, 6'0", mulatto, small ears and black hair; Children, mulatto.

Pg. 288
MITCHELL, CYNTHA - Petition for papers of freedom by Cyntha Mitchell, a free female of color. She was born and always lived in Tennessee. Description: 14 years old, deep black color, 4'6", and heavy in form and size.

Pg. 289
SEATON, GEORGE - Last will and testament presented for probate by William Carter and James W. Moore. Proven by same.

5 March 1860

Pg. 290
WINCHESTER, RUSSELL - John A. Smith appointed administrator of the estate of Russell Winchester.

PARTLE, SAMUEL S. - J.R. Laden appointed administrator of the estate of Samuel S. Partle.

HARGROVE, E.C. - O.H. Hargrove appointed guardian of John H. Hargrove and Samuel D. Hargrove, minor heirs of E.C. Hargrove, formerly E.C. Garrard.

Pg. 295
CALLINS, JOHN G. - Petition for dower by Mary Callins, widow, versus W.H. Franks and others. Mentions the following heirs under the age of 21: William Callins, James Callins, Lewis Callins, Josephine Callins, and Green Callins.

2 April 1860

Pg. 320
UNKNOWN - Inquest. Unknown came to his death by drowning in the Tennessee River near Hamburg.

Pg. 321
UNKNOWN - Inquest. Found that a black boy belonging to J.L. Nichols came to his death by falling off J.R. Laden's mill house into Indian Creek and drowned on 22 December 1859.

Pg. 322
UNKNOWN - Inquest. Found that an unknown man, thought to be a deckhand on a steamboat, drowned near the Flat Bluff.

Pg. 323
PACK, ELISHA - Last will and testament presented for probate by Peter Pack. Proven by Elijah Harbour and Ashley G. Blount, subscribing witnesses. Also presented a codicil proven by J.M. Cunningham.

Pg. 325
SOWELL, JOHN - Susannah Sowell appointed administratrix of the estate of John Sowell.

7 May 1860

Pg. 336
BOURLAND, JOHN - J.M. Cunningham appointed guardian of S.A. Bourland, minor heir of John Bourland.

Pg. 337
BLANKENSHIP, THOMAS - Abel Blankenship appointed guardian of the minor heirs of Thomas Blankenship.

BARNETT, JOHN - Settlement made with Anna Barnett, guardian of the minor heirs of John Barnett.

ARMSTRONG, CARY A. - Last will and testament presented for probate by Hugh White Armstrong and D.D. Brotherton. Proven by B.W. Linn and J.J. McMullins.

9 May 1860

Pg. 347
COLE, WILLIAM - Stephen Cole appointed guardian of Mary Cole, minor heir of William Cole.

4 June 1860

Pg. 349
WOOD, JOSIAH - John H. Wood, brother of Josiah Wood, asked that M.T. Emmerson be appointed administrator of the estate of Josiah Wood.

SHANNON, GEORGE - Last will and testament presented for probate by James M. Hook. Proven by Henry B. Alexander and James M. Hook, subscribing witnesses.

2 July 1860

Pg. 354
HORTON, LEMUEL - R.J. Williams appointed administrator of the estate of Lemuel Horton.

Pg. 356
UNKNOWN - Inquest. Found that an unknown man drowned at Kemp's Landing on or about 25 June 1860.

OWEN, JOHN W. - Inquest. Stated that the deceased was found sitting on his plow on 7 June 1860 with the lines in his hands, face upon the ground, on the land of William Robinson. Found by William Robinson, D.R. Lee and Mrs. Owen. There were no signs of violence. Death was ruled by natural causes.

6 August 1860

Pg. 365
GARNER, WILLIAM - Mrs. Garner asked that Joab A. Russell be appointed guardian of the minor heirs of William Garner.

ACULLBERGER, DAVID - R.J. Williams appointed administrator of the estate of David Acullberger.

Pg. 366
STEPHENSON, E.H. - John Stephenson appointed administrator of the estate of E.H. Stephenson.

Pg. 369
BLACK, JOHN - Jane Meek, daughter of said John Black, who was a revolutionary pensioner and who died in York District, South Carolina on 18 June 1842, asked that as his only surviving heir that she receive the pension.

3 September 1860

Pg. 372
ACABERGER, DAVID - Robert J. Williams administrator of David Acaberger, a pensioner of the United States who died in Hardin County on 25 June 1860, swore that David Acaberger left no widow and no children.

ALLEN, E.J. - M.M. Dickson appointed guardian of E.J. Allen, minor heir of E.J. Allen.

JONES, J. - D.M. Jones appointed guardian of L.A. Jones, minor heir of J. Jones.

Pg. 373
GILBERT, _____ - J.N. Peacock appointed guardian of his wife E.A. Peacock, formerly E.A. Gilbert.

Pg. 374
WHITE, JOHN - G.H.G. Penn appointed guardian for his wife Margaret Penn, formerly Margaret White, minor heir of John White.

WHITE, JOHN - J.S. Perry appointed guardian for his wife Emily Perry, formerly Emily White, minor heir of John White.

1 October 1860

Pg. 377
COFFEE, NATHAN - Morgan H. Ross tendered his bond as trustee for Lucinda Ross, Margaret Davis and Caroline Todd, daughters and legatees of the last will and testament of Nathan Coffey, late of Maury County. Isaac N. Coffee and William M. Coffee refused to become involved.

Pg. 381
WILLIAMS, H.D. - Jane Williams and James M. Forest appointed administrators of the estate of H.D. Williams.

MORRIS, CHARLES R. - William B. Morris appointed administrator of the estate of Charles R. Morris.

DAVEY, SARAH A. - J.L. Davey appointed guardian of S.E. Davey, minor orphan of Sarah A. Davey, formerly Sarah A. Patton.

Pg. 384
McGEE, JOHN - Joel Kilburn and E.T. McGee appointed administrators of the estate of John McGee.

5 November 1860

Pg. 388
McGEE, JOHN - Commissioners appointed to lay off a year's support for Sarah McGee, widow.

SMITHWICK, MARY - Cathahill Robinson appointed administrator of the estate of Mary Smithwick.

MONTGOMERY, ELIZABETH - William B. Montgomery appointed administrator of the estate of Elizabeth Montgomery.

MONTGOMERY, JAMES - William B. Montgomery appointed guardian of Cyntha Montgomery and Thomas F. Montgomery, minor orphans of James Montgomery.

Pg. 389
MONTGOMERY, JAMES - John Montgomery appointed guardian of Joseph Montgomery and E.E. Montgomery, minor orphans of James Montgomery.

JONES, JERIMIAH - Daniel M. Jones appointed guardian of Melissa Ann Jones, heir of Jerimiah Jones.

Pg. 394
BIVENS, B.S. - Petition to divide land for the heirs. Heirs mentioned: Delilah Jane Bivens, Franklin C. Bivens, Arisbell Stevens formerly Arisbel Bivens, Susan A. Tucker formerly Susan A. Bivens, Nancy J. Steele formerly Nancy J. Bivens, James P. Bivens, Martha A. Bivens, Evan P. Bivins, George M.D. Bivens, and Harriet A. Bivens. Sons-in-law: W.R. Stevens, J.R. Tucker, and W.J. Steele.

3 December 1860

Pg. 408
SHANNON, GEORGE - Jane K. Shannon, widow, dissented from the will of George Shannon.

THE TAX LISTS

This section encompasses lists of individual who, for a variety of reasons, were either excused from paying taxes for a particular year or were unable to pay. The only tax records extant for the subject period are those for the years 1833 - 1837. This makes these lists even more important. In a limited way, these releasements, insolvencies, and removals are a record of the deaths, financial situation, and immigration of the people of Hardin County.

There were approximately three ways to get out of paying one's taxes during the nineteenth century - death, being released for some reason, and removing from the county. Another method, and by far the most prevalent, was to be financially unable to pay the stated tax. Some of these lists specify the reason that the tax was unpaid. Others do not. Some lists are arranged by civil district. Others are not. These lists were included in the county court minutes but have been included separately here. It is felt that they merited their own section. For a few years, there are no lists. The reason for this is unclear. In some cases, one can trace a particular individual on a year-to-year basis. In other situations, these lists can be used to determine what year a certain person left the county. One note of caution: Since Hardin County sat directly above both Alabama and Mississippi, it is not unusual to see the same person listed as removed from the county in, say, 1843, and removed from the county in 1845 again. A good many people moved back and forth between these states.

Below are the explanation of abbreviations used in this section. Some lists did not specify the reason that the person had not paid his/her taxes. Some did and it is these which are the most valuable.

```
C     ------------ Crippled
D     ------------ Dead
DF    ----------- Doubtful entry
DT    ----------- Double taxed or Down Twice
G     ------------ Gone
GI    ----------- Gone and Insolvent
I     ------------ Insolvent
ITD   ---------- In Two Districts
ISD   ---------- In Second District
IIF   ---------- Insolvent in the Fifth District
ITP   ---------- In Two Places
I2D   ---------- In Second District
IPUL  --------- In Pick-up List
LID   ---------- Lives in Decatur
LT    ----------- Listed Twice
NF    ----------- Not Found
NT    ----------- Not Found
NSM   ---------- No Such Man
NSP   ---------- No Such Person
M     ------------ Mistake
NTBF  --------- Not to be Found
NSL   ---------- No Such Land
O     ------------ Old
OA    ----------- Overage
OAG   ---------- Overage and Gone
OSD   ---------- On Second District
P     ------------ Prison
R     ------------ Removed (same as Gone)
```

```
RD  ----------- Released
RAW ----------- Run-a-way
RO  ----------- Road Overseer
THD ----------- Thirteenth District
TI  ----------- Twice Interred
TO  ----------- Too Old
TT  ----------- Taxed Twice
TY  ----------- Too Young
UA  ----------- Underage
```

Some of these explanations are very straighforward and some are very ambiguous. There are a few people listed as dead in the tax records for whom there is no corresponding entry in the body of the county court minutes. Whether these people had no estate property to justify the appointment of an administrator is unclear. However, these lists do supplement the county court minutes in this regard.

In addition to the lists described above, occasionally there appears lists of individuals who paid their taxes but were omitted from the tax rolls. These lists are included as well and are noted as such. While the number of such individuals was small, it was deemed worthy of inclusion.

REMOVALS AND INSOLVENCIES
FROM THE TAX ROLLS
As Listed in the County Court Minutes

April Term 1823. "Owners or claimants on whose tracts of land the collector has been unable to collect the said tax." Pg. 124 Book A.

John Armstrong
William C. Aiken
William Anderson
John L. Baird
John Chrisholm
George Cathey and William Campbell
William Fawls
John Garland (for the President and trustees)
Daniel Gillespie
Thomas Gardner
Malcom Gilchrist
John Greer and Vance
Robert Hibbits
William Hughlett
Henderson and Calvin Jones
William Howell
Thomas Harris
David Joiner's heirs
James David's heirs
John Kirkpatrick
Alex. McCall
John McNairy
Richard C. Napier
John Owens
Thomas Polk
Samuel Polk
John Purdy
Hubbert Petty
Philip Philips and Michel Cambell
John Rice
Felix Robinson
Thomas Shute
Thomas Shute and Beal Bosley
John Simington
Richard Smith
Samuel Spraggins
John Scott
Samuel Williams
David Wilson

The following list is of land that was not reported for taxes for the year 1822.

8th District

    Graham, James
    Paul H. Neely
    Robert Walker
    Henry Mosely's Heirs
    David McGavock and Alex. McDougall
    Henson Grove
    Rosamond P. Scott

7th District

    John Manley
    McGavock and McDonald
    Alex. McDonald
    Peter Buram
    Alex. McDonald and
    Alex. McClintock
    Fountain Lester
    David C. Mitchell

January Term 1824. Removals and Insolvencies for the year 1823. Book A Pg. 174.

Buram, Peter
Barr, Silas heirs of
Garland, John
Harris, Richard C.
Kelton, William
Lester, Fountain
Williams, Samuel H.
Taylor, John P.
Scott, Rosamond
Anderson, William
Brahan, Thos. G.
Brasfield, Wiley and Samuel Dickey
Carron, John H.
Cathy, George and W. Campbell
Pinkerey, D. and P. Cavenaugh
Doty, Nathaniel
Dickens, Samuel
Goodloe, John M.
Goodman, Samuel
Hilberts, Robt. H.
Jones, Henderson and Calvin
Harris, Thomas
McCall, Alexander
McNairy, John
Killer, Andrew
Napier, Richard C.
Omens, John
Polk, Samuel
Petty, Hubbard
Philips, Joseph
Polk, Joseph
Polk, S. and Peter Sanson
Reed, John
Robertson, Felix
Shute, Thomas
Thompson, Robert
Washington, Thomas
Wilson, David
Williams, Sampson
Wilson, William
Williams, Thomas H.
Donaven, Andras
Higgins, Powell
Lacefield, Jesse

McLemore, John C.
Mitchell, George
Mitchell, David
Shurley, Lake
Wasson, Abner
Woods, William
Neely, Paul H.
Walker, Robert
Wilson, James
Armstrong, John
Baird, John L.
Brown, Harry H.
Chambers, John
Devereas, Thomas
Davis, Isaiah heirs
Falls, William
Gardner, Thomas
Hughlett, William
Howell, William
Kirkpatrick, John
McIver, John
McCollum, David
Mud, Joseph
Orr, John
Penson, Joel
Polk, Thomas
Philips, Philip
Pillow, Abner
Read, William
Shepherd, William
Simington, John
Smith, Richard
Spraggins, Samuel
Spencer, Charles
Shannon, Robt.
Tatum, H. and H. Wiggins
Trustees-Cumberland Coll.
Trustees-North Carolina
Williams, Samuel
Whitehed, William
Williams, Clayburn
Whiteside, Jenkin
Williams, Thomas J.
Williams, Maria

25 March 1825. "A list of taxable property omitted to be given in and owner or claimant has no goods, chattel, or other property from which to collect the tax for 1824." Pg. 284 Book A.

Cathey, George and W. Campbell
Brown, Hamilton
Brown, Henry H.
Beard, John L.
Green, Andrew
Groves, Henson
Hulett, William
McNairy, John
Mickel, George
Mickel, David C.
McCall, Alexander

McIves, John
Neely, Paul H.
Shurley, Luke
Spencer, Charles
Scott, John
Taylor, John
Whitehead, William
Wilson, Samuel
Woods, William
Walker, Robert

"Taxes omitted to be paid for the year 1824." Pg. 286 Book A.

Jones, John
Manley, John
McIver, John
Goodloe, John M.
McCall, Alexander

Owens, John
Sorrells, David
Spraggins, Samuel
Shute, Thomas
Bosley, Beal

3 April 1837. "Persons who have removed from the county or are insolvent." Pg. 168 Book C.

1st Dist.	David McCall(R)	6th Dist.	James Garson(R)
	Morgan Rinkle(I)		Francis F. McGassock
	Jonathan Helms(I)		William Watt(R)
	James Lezer(R)	7th Dist.	John Buie(R)
	S.G.R. Romines(R)	8th Dist.	David Berry(R)
	George Williams(R)		Joel Dyer(R)
2nd Dist.	John M. Clifton(R)		Andrew Fielder(R)
	David Hall(R)		Witherbe Hanes(R)
	Hugh McCall(R)		John Parret(R)
	William Newson(R)	9th Dist.	Enoch Autrey(R)
3rd Dist.	A.L. Greenwood(R)		Richard Ray(R)
	William Hall(R)		David Read(R)
2nd Dist.	Dennis O'Neal(R)		John Thomas(R)
	H.A. Freeman(R)		James Thomas(R)
	John Freeman(R)		William Thomas(R)
3rd Dist.	William Burge(I)		Richard Thomas(R)
	David Hughling(I)		Bannister Wyan(R)
	William Henkin(NF)		Abel Walker(R)
	George Lemmon(R)	10th Dist.	Liberty Byrd(R)
4th Dist.	John D. Porterfield(R)		John S. Eberton(R)
	F.W. Ross(R)		William Harrison(R)
	David L. Ross(I)		George Taylor(R)
	Samuel Johns(I)		James Williams(R)
	R.C. Hale(R)	11th Dist.	Hezekiah Childress
	A.S. Brown(I)		Alfred Griggs(R)
5th Dist.	William Hendrix(I)		James W. Hawks(R)
	Mr. Wright	12th Dist.	Thomas Hutchinson(R)
	Isaac Hendrix(I)		James Rodes(R)
6th Dist.	William Morris(R)		Abner Rodes(R)

1 July 1839. "Insolvent and removed from the county." For the year 1838. Pg. 271 Book C.

William M. Atton
John Dillian
Abraham Dixon
John Day
Robert Gray
Joseph Hammons
Joshua Haldin
John King
Obadiah Musgrove
Sterting Morris
Daniel McCall
John M. Morgan
Elijah Powell
Samuel Turnbo
Carson Ashworth
William Cunningham

James Hale
Isaac Hix
N.A. Piper
Isaac Wells
William Whitworth
Anderson West
Francis A. Bradley
Stephen Houge
L.P. Kirk
Elisha Harwon
James McLin
Newton Wallis
Andrew Boyd
M.D. Bookout
Samuel Gammill
Joel Martin

William Oglesby
Wm. Parrish
Samuel Smiddy
Abner Blevin
J.M. Church
Isaac Jones
John Norton
George White
John Ashcraft
Cornelius Buie
Joel Childers
John Matthews
James Jewell
Peter Tumbleston
Joseph Woody
Nathaniel Bivens
Solomen Copelen
Orville Harrison
Wade M. Marris
D.L. Ross
James Winburn
John Adams
Jesse Bigs
William Eelliot
Thomas Henly
Joseph McMillin
Nimrod Pigg
George W. Terry
Jacob Franks
John Gay
George Martin
A.M. Parrish
James Spearman
Jeremiah Scott

R.S. Church
Andrew Hood
J.C. Nichols
John Welch
William L. Hollis
John Brichen
Washington Bowlin
Rbert Childers
James Matthews
Robert Thrasher
Hiram Tumbleston
H.M. Austin
F.W. Carothers
R.T. Day
John Morris
R.S. Nelson
Thomas Slone
Drew Za(?)
William Braton
J.C. Cook
Samuel Hanes
Canst. McCaig
Robert Mitchell
John A. Stoop
Tilman Haley
Thomas Hodge
John McDaniel
John Utley
William Givin
Nathan Philip
Elijah Loderdale
Drewrey Smith
Jonathan Douglas
John H. Lowry

4 January 1841. "Being insolvent and removed out of the county."
For the year 1840. Pg. 370 Book C.

Warson, William
Horton, Henry(G)
Byrd, Lewis(I)
Casey, Riley
Dellian, Jessee
Eoff, Squire
Forester, Robert
Northcut, John H.
Turner, John
Winborn, James
Allen, William
Bookout, Mormon
Duncan, Jesse
Gammill, Samuel
James, Daniel
Matthews, David
Morris, William
Smith, John Jr.
Scott, Jeremiah
Brechin, R.S.
Clarke, Dickson
Monks, Jessee
Nolen, Thomas
Robinson, Richard

Toriee, Wm.
Wolf, Nicholas
Downing, Josiah
Dillian, John
Emmerson, Isaac
McSwain, Edmond
Strawn, Richard
White, Thomas B.
Allen, Wilson
Ashcraft, James
Brewer, Thomas
Frields, Thomas
Hodges, William
Jernigan, Henry
Martin, Joel
Oglesby, William
Adams, John
Brown, Sampson
Ledbetter, J.P.
Nolen, David
Robertson, Thomas
Smith, William
Trusty, James
Boon, Watson

Julius, Seasor
Huton, Taswell
Pitty, Joel
Woods, George
Irwin, Alexander
Meek, Moses
Neely, Hugh
Banks, John
Dames, Delphia
Dicus, William
Godwin, Jacob
Humphreys, Machael
Kounce, Redding
Lingo, Michael
Murry, Silas
Overton, Miles
Powell, Hardin
Reaves, Drewry
Walker, G.M.
Martin, Polly
Brunch, Isaac
Buris, Jonathan
Case, Chacy
Falkner, John
Hall, James
Hundley, J.Y.
McMahan, Wm.
Adams, Samuel
Jewell, William
Owen, Daniel
Wallace, Thomas
William, Isaac
Lemons, John
Sherley, E.S.
Bunck, Richard
Franks, Joseph
Kerr, George
Cossey, John
Dickson, Thos.
Hames, Weatherly
Laxten, James
Green, John
Johnson, Wm.
Rodney, Dorton
Brown, George

King, Hezekiah
Charles, Richard
Brook, Richard
Darnes, Merideth
Dudley, Guilford
Fleming, John
Hasey, James
Helms, Jonathan
Lewis, John
Murrey, Philip
McMillan, Neal
Daniel, Lewis
Purley, Green
Sutherland, Cantin
Woodward, John
Brunch, Eli
Bigs, Ezekiel
Courtney, James
Cagle, John
Gerard, Daniel
Hundley, Edmund
Hundly, Freeman
Miller, Abraham
Edward, Levi
Jackson, J.B.
Thompson, Jesse
Wallace, William
Hogden, James
Slone, Thomas
Buie, John
Franks, William
Franks, John
Williams, Eli
Christian, Harrison
Howell, William
Huggins, Thomas
Middleton, Perry
Woodwy, Joseph
Woodey, Robert
Combs, Thomas
Pike, Elisha
Woody, William
Woodward, -----
Long, David

6 December 1841. "Insolvent and Removed out of the county."
For the year 1841. Pg. 247 Book C.

Brooks, Richard
Brooks, John
Grayham, -----
Howard, George
Kounce, Redding
McCanless, Isaac
Nance, Allen
Powell, Hardin
Wallis, John
Branch, Eli
Burris, Jonathan
Case, Chancy
Falkner, John

Brooks, Jeremiah
Churchwill, William
Humphreys, Michaiel
Humphreys, Thomas
Lingo, Pernell
McMillen, Neal
Powell, Lewis
Pollg, Martin
Webster, Levi
Branch, Isaac
Courtney, James
Clayton, W.D.
Garrard, D.M.

Garrard, W.B.
James, William
Miller, Abraham D.
Stander, John S.
White, Elijah
White, Perry
Winchester, Robirson
Dobbins, Jesse B.
Lee, M.B.
Massey, W.H.
Thompson, J.T.
Brim, Walter
Boyd, Andrew R.
Dameril, Joseph
Graves, Jacob
Harner, Philip
Morris, W.H.
Nelson, Robt. S.
Polk, Thomas
Talley, William
Bratton, Sterling
Collins, John H.
Downing, Josiah
Duleen, John
Henry, Jesse
Northcutt, Anderson
Owein, Daniel
Wade, John
White, Samuel
Ashcraft, James
Bookout, Marman
Barnett, Daniel
Ducan, Jesse
Jarnagan, Hery
Mathews, David
Morris, William
Massey, Lewis
Pollard, John B.
Spencer, Hiram
Sego, Seaman
Tankerely, Thornton
Haggard, James
McMillon, Joseph
Satterfield, R.S.
Trure, William
White, Noel
Winchester, Maden
Brown, A.S.
Huling, James
Martin, L.D.
Massey, John
Brewer, Mark
Boyd, R.H.
Conner, Thomas
Eaks, Zachariah
Graves, John
Hampton, Isaiah
Morris, James C.
Newell, H.F.
Pain, Thos. P.
Bratton, Thomas
Byrd, Lewis
Casey, Riley

Dulion, Jesse
Dorcas, James
Johnson, Larkin
Nix, Joseph
Snow, William
Wade, Wm. H.
Allen, William
Bookout, Charles
Butler, Lemul
Deshago, Miles
Gammill, William
Mitchel, Zachariah
Martin, George
Morris, John
Oglesby, William
Pollard, George
Spenser, James
Scott, Martin
Smithwick, Jordan
Berry, John
Duke, William B.
Franks, William
House, Mark
Pain, George
Bunch, Richard L.
Cossey, John
Childers, Robert
Hancock, William
McKisick, Archibald
Ray, Robert
Woody, Joseph
Hawkins, M.T.
Kilough, Hezekiah
Shurley, E.S.
Austin, John
Clark, Dickson
Trusty, James
Burn, Shepherd
Boon, Watson
James, Jones H.
Riddle, John
Waldrup, John
Ater, George
Majors, Nelson
Outlaw, Joseph
Sewell, William
Buler, John
Combs, Thomas
Brooks, William
Edwards, William
Franks, John
McMullin, William
Williams, Eli
Busely, Amor
Childress, Joel
Crunk, George
Lopp, Jacob
Middleton, Thomas
Redin, Ezekiel
Emerson, Thomas
James, William
Smith, Lem
Ashcraft, James

Bird, David
Henley, Thomas
Anderson, Reuben
Baity, Ezekiel
Heaton, William
McMillon, John
Tilley, Samuel

Wheat, Wyley
Bailey, Absalom
Orr, George W.
Rowsey, Morgan
Austin, Willis
Malley, Joseph

5 December 1842.   Insolvencies and removals for the year 1842.
Pg. 519 Book C.

Abraham Baitman
Thomas S. Brewer
William J. Brewer
John Banks
T.K. Cash
Ezekiel Conley
John Copeland
Meridd Davi(?)
Daniel Green
Matthewes Groves
Josiah Groves
Adam Greenfield
George W. Gill
James C. Gill
H.N. Graham
Thomas Humphreys
Alex. Hicks
John Hicks
George Howard
John Johnson
Richard Lane
Charles McKirley
Isaac McCanles
Thomas McElry
Piter Morehead
William Moten
Neal McMullin
Henry Oaks
Polly Martin
Hardin Smith
Thomas W. Smith
John Stuart
Robert Shaw
Joseph Sutton
James West
John Wallis
Nelson Wilson
Josiah Duke
Philip Broaden
Eli Branch
William Caldwell
Chancy Case
Joseph Dillian
John Falkner
Henry Garner
George Hamilton
John Harris
Jackson Hall
John Stander
R.S. Satterfield

William Truse
John Vasser
Elijah White
James Winchester
John Winchester
James T. Ward
Robinson Winchester
William Winchester
Alex. Wilson
James Cash
William Clark
Jesse B. Dobbins
Thomas Frulds
M.B. Fowler
Wm. Kizer
M.B. Lee
S.T. Martin
John Massey
James A. Reni
Jesse T. Thompson
W.R. Brim
R.H. Boyd
John Graves
Isaiah Hampton
Harbet Thom
Wm. T. Alexander
Sterling Burton
Elijah Blevins
James Brown
H.B. Bailes
Samuel Bougsster
Washington Bartee
Joseph Dowing
James Davis
Joseph Frand
Daniel Greer
William Holland
Jesse H-----
Wm. H. Johnson
Larkin Johnson
James Linsey
James C. McLin
William Montgomery
Daniel Owen
Joseph S. Gatt
Hardeman Stone
William Thompson
James White
William Allen
James Allen

Joseph Bivens
Thomas Brooks
Joseph P. Church
Levi Edwards
John Tuer
John Wetherford
John Brooks
Samuel Clem
Eli Loyd
Ed McSwain
William Mitchell
Robert Rey
John Williams
John Welch
Moses Bachelor
A.I. Clark
Matthew Dickerson
Stephen Hester
Jesse Monk
Joseph Sweney
Willis Arnold
George W. Bashears
Ezekiel Baitey
John Cook
Lewis Fowler
Eli Lucas
Linis Robinson
Miles A. Thomas
A.B. Anderson
Stephen P. Crumsey
William Ferrel
William Hefton
James Hogden
James Laxton
William McClain
Lewis Massey
John B. Pollard
Leonidas Parrish
James Shearman
Jordan Smithwick
Siamon Sego
James Wills
Terril Brooks
William Edwards
William Franks
Eli Williams
Richard Brooks
Luke Cossey
Isham P. Gibbs

William McMullins
Mitchel McCrow
Samuel McCrow
Ezekiel Roden
Thomas Wisdom
David E. Byrd
John Beard
Hiram Clark
R.L. Figjerrol
Jacob Ham
Elmarine Stephenson
Jacob Truce
Lee Arnold
Stephen Burris
Andrew Boyd
William Cook
Josiah Fowler
William Murdock
Matthew Lea
Williamson Walker
Ambrose Crusey
James A. Clack
John W. Delaney
Jackson Gun
M.T. Hawkins
M.G. Meadow
John B. Ross
E.S. Shearley
Matthew Weaver
Thomas Wilkerson
Absalem Baitiy
George Bailey
Jacob Mills
Richard Rowsey
William Shelley
Robertson King
Richard Garner
C.H. Gardner
Martin House
William Redding
John Redding
E.W. Shearley
Washington Herrod
John Ater
James Brumley
Hail Irwin
Thomas Orr
Morgan Rowsey
Alexander Irwin

December 1843. Insolvencies and Removals for the year 1843.
Pg. 36 Book D.

Thomas Brewer
Edwin Cole
William F. Gray
Thomas Humphreys
George Howard
Mark Hutchens
Theoden Johnson
Neal McMillan
G.B. McCanlis

James F. McCall
Jackson Porter
Wm. J. Polk
Edward Y. Spaar
Thomas D. Wiseman
William Wiseman
William Powell
Philip Branden
William G. Berry

Chancy Case
Elijah White
John Winchester, Jr.
William Winchester, Jr.
Wm. Winchester, Sr.
Thos. Frulds
Robert Jackson
William Loyd
Jackson Matthews
Richard Strawn
Abraham Vincent
Russell Winchester
R.H. Boyd
Calvin Morris
Harbert Thorn
W.T. Alexander
Madison Brooks
Ezekiel Conley
Jacob Godwin
John Hicks
John Huddleston
John Harris
Ridding Counce
William Moten
J.G. McCanlis
Peter Morehead
Martin Polley
John Standers
Thomas W. Smith
Elias Wright
Michael Lingo
Joseph Laden
Isaac Branch
Samuel Boothe
Joseph Dillon
James Winchester
William Williams
Felix West
A.S. Brown
Wm. Jewell
M.B. Lee
S.W. Maddox
F.A. Rorie
Jesse T. Thompson
Daniel Winchester
W.A. Barrie
Michael Conroy
A.E. Shull
James S. Winburn
Sterling Burton
William Brumley
Samuel Conner
Josiah Downing
James Davis
Davis Eaves
William Eaves
Daniel Green
Josiah Hodges
Obediah Lanxten
J.C. McGuin
Wm. Montgomery
L.W. Peru
Wm. Allen

Jackson Carter
David Cherry
Wm. Gilbert
James Hogden
George Key
Wm. McMullin
John B. Massey
George Moore
Leonidas Parrish
Jordan Smithwick
Martin Shoults
Wm. Franks
Squire Eoff
Edward Shipman
Eli Williams
John Cossey
Lenard Cossey
Isham P. Gibbs
William Howell
Owen Loyd
T.J. Middleton
William Qualls
Stephen Roden
Wm. Simmons
Anderson Williams
David E. Byrd
Hiram Clark
Matthew Dickson
Peter Bryant
Miles M. Conner
John Devaney
Wm. Eaton
Isaac Emerson
Burtwell Greer
Jesse Henry
Larkin Johnson
James Lee
Samuel Musgrove
Daniel Owen
Wm. Liley
James Allen
Wm. Coldwell
Wm. Terrell
Wm. O. Harris
Hamilton Jarnagan
James Laxton
Lewis Massey
Wm. Moore
John B. Pollard
Hiram R. Smith
Simon Seago
Joseph P. Church
Eli Halley
Anquist Patterson
John Ticer
John Weatherford
Luke Cossey, Jr.
L.D. Frie
George Gray
Amos Hutchison
Samuel McCrow
William Nolen
Thos. Robertson

Nathan Roden
John Williams
Thomas Milam
Moses Bachelor
John Dunaway
Wm. Fisher
John Green
William Lackey
Israeil Payne
Richard Robinson
George W. Terry
Wm. Wolf
Gabriel Washburn
Daniel Arnsworthy
Ezekiel Rustiy
Nelson Deal
Wm. Murdock
Irise Reynolds
John Shelby
Allen Tucker
Wm. Williams
Absalom Burley
George W. Burley
Robert Finger
A.H. Graham
Yancey Harper
James Prewit
Hugh Wallis

A.J. Campbell
Stephen Crusey
Andrew Jones
John Smith
John P. Herrod
Nimrod Morris
Wm. N. Phelps
John Smith
James Teague
Alexander West
John Arnold
Perry Armstrong
Liberty Byrd
Terenze Fowler
Henry Pelly
J.H.D. Spain
George Shelby
Thomas Teague
John Birden
James Brumley
Willis Dunn
George W. Herrod
Wm. P. Moore
Morgan Rowsey
William Bird
Curtis Cody
Daniel Jones
Wm. C. Scott

2 December 1844. Insolvencies and Removals for the year 1844.
Pg. 100 Book D.

J.C. Allison
Abraham Bartmant
Thomas S. Brewer
Madison Brooks
Ezekiel Conley
Meredith Davis
Jacob Godwin
William F. Gray
Thomas Humphries
George Howard
Mark Hutchens
Isaac McCandless
Martin Pollsy
William Powell
Joel Smith
John Standen
Thomas Hurtt
Edbine Griffin
Phillip Brandon
Isaac Branch
Peter Bryant
Chauncy Case
Joseph Dillon
John Goldsmith
Jesse Turner
William Winchester
S.A. Duckworth
Thomas Fruliy
Francis Lee
Sterling Burton

Josiah Downing
John Downing
William Evans
Jesse Henry
Ruben Huling
Jourdan Smithwick
Madison H. Smith
James Tankersley
Abraham Vincent
James Allen
Jesse Allen
Joseph Cherry
Daniel Cathey
William Gammill
Archibald Gammill
Mark Hatley
Daniel Jones
James B. Smith
George Moore
Hiram Smith
Joseph Mohair
Richard Shaw
Aaron Shannon
Daniel Winchester
Alfred Wisdom
John Brumley
William Barnhill
R.H. Boyd
Wm. D. Johnson
John Lemores

W.H. Morris
Thomas P. Payne
A.E. Shull
John Pollard
James E. Wallis
Thomas Boswell
William Coleson
Elbert Clark
C.C. Gibbs
Larkin John
William Johnson
Daniel W. Knox
Tarltno H. Lee
Daniel Owens
Pendleton Church
Mark House
John Autry
David G. Barnett
Levi Busby
Thomas Chrisney
William Doran
Siminon King
Jesse Mark
William Murdock
John McGuire
James Richards
Joseph M. Shinon

Rany Jones
John G. Braden
John Pace
Miles Thomas
Asa Hactnick
Jackson Hurt
Robert Jackson
M.B. Lee
Eli Loyd
Owen Loyd
James H. Loyd
Samuel McCraw
N.W. Saunders
John Williams
Thomas Wisdom
R.M. DeNison
William Green
Daniel Jones
Samuel Phillips
Thomas Saunders
John B. Pollard
William Brim
James Pruit
Hugh Wallace
Micky Frules
Thomas Stevens

1 December 1845.   Insolvencies and Removals for the year 1845.
Pg. 165 Book D.

Thomas Brewer
William Brewer
Ezekiel Conelly
Madison Brooks
Wm. F. Gray
George Howard
Thomas Humphries
Isaac McCandless
James F. McCall
Hampton Stroud
Edmund Spear
Jesse T. Thompson
Robert Wiggs
Benjamin Yarbrey
William Winchester
John Winchester
William West
Green S. Covey
Austin Cook
A.W. Campbell
James Cash
James Deloach
Edmund Franks
Joseph Mahair
A.J. Tarkington
David Maddin
----- Brown
George Brandt
R.H. Boyd
J.M. Downing
James Hogden

Andrew Limerick
John Lemons
William Maim
Ezekiel Polk
Thos. P. Payne
James Rudle
Wilson Tucker
R.J. Talley
Wm. G. Alexander
John Byrd
William Eaves
Jesse Henry
William Huling
Josiah Head
John Jones
James Allen
William Broadaway
James Gilbert
Mark Hatley, Jr.
James Matthews
Jesse Monk
James C. Richards
John A. Smith
Sidney Tines
Malsiah Toliver
Jesse Harvey
Jiremiah Dial
Washington Norwood
John Pale
Thomas Miles
Daniel Vail

David McCullom
Joseph Burden
Barrack Jones
Amaziah Meek
Hugh Wallace
Peter Bryant
Burgess Childers
Joseph Matthews
James M. Milam
Joseph Martin
J.B. Pollard
George Pollard
Joseph Schwarts
Robert Thompson
Levi Busby
David E. Byrd
Matthew Dickson
William Fisher
Irwin Hitchcock
James Henley
Collins Herron

Joseph Landrum
John McGuin
Frederick McGuin
William Mason
James Cooper
Stephen P. Crucy
Champen Guinn
William Griffin
T.J. Kemp
Riley Pope
Thos. Sanders
W.C. Scott
William Sanderson
Hedley Shannon
John Roane
Browder Brooks
Jackson Hurt
M.B. Lee
William Simmons
David Smith

7 December 1846. Insolvencies and Removals for the year 1846.
Pg. 224 Book D.

1st Dist.   Blaringin, J.H.
            Brown, Wm.
            Conley, Ezekiel(TI)
            Coldwell, Wm.(TI)
            Courtney, Amos(G)
            Godwin, Alfred(I)
            Howard, George(I)
            Hatley, Sherrod(I)
            Counce, Reddon(I)
            Lingo, G.W.(G)
            McKey, Robertson(I)
            McCandless, Isaac(GI)
            Pool, William(NSM)
            Stroud, Hampton(I)
            Turtow, Joseph(G)
            Thompson, Jesse(I)
            McWallace, Alex.(G)
            Wort, Jones(NSM)
            Arnott, Christian(I)
            Wiggs, Probate(I)
2nd Dist.   Booth, Samuel(I)
            Booth, Andrew(I)
            Gray, Franis(I)
            Hamilton, George(DT)
            Love, Joseph(I)
            Lanxton, A.(I)
            McCurdy, James(I)
            Mathews, Andrew(I)
            Mathews, Benjamin(I)
            Mires, James(I)
            Newton, Henry G.(NSM)
            Solomon, John(I)
            Winchester, Thomas(RAW)
            West, Felix(G)
            White, Elijah(I)
            Winchester, John(I)
3rd Dist.   Covey, John T.(G)

3rd Dist.   Cash, James(I)
            Campbell, S.P.(G)
            Dickey, S.G.(ITP)
            King, Bolen(ITP)
            Mosley, Wm.(ITP)
            McQueen, Daniel(RAW)
            Moon, Templeton(I)
            Plummer, E.B.(G)
            Roard, Henikiah(I)
            Strawn, Richrd
            Taylor, Denis(G)
            Wallace, Wesley(ITD)
5th Dist.   Burton, Sterling(G)
            Byrd, Lewis(I)
            Byrd, John(O)
            Eads, William(I)
            Henry, Jesse(I)
            Northcutt, Adrian(I)
            Sutton, John(ITD)
4th, 6th,   Jno. Shull(ITD)
7th & 8th   Joseph Abells
            Robt. H. Boyd
            Carson, Henry
            Solomon, Saml.
            Metters, G.W.
            Allen, James
            Allen, Jesse
            Duncan, Robt.
            Hopkins, E.L.
            Martin, Joseph
            Stroud, Aaron
            Tucker, Thomas
            Green, James C.
            Hargerson, Parris
            Lanxten, Obediah
            Childers, Joel
            Jackson, Robt.

136

	Rea, John		Pace, John
	Sherfield, Ephraim		Belcher, Berry
	Simmons, Wm.		Bookout, M.D.
	Simmons, Lemuel		Hunter, Daniel
9th Dist.	Ashcraft, Ichabod		Kizer, Julian
	Branes, Wm.		Seay, Leven
	Dearing, Larkin	11th Dist.	Brown, G.H.
	Day, L.F.		Hale, James
	Gordan, Nicholas		Rousey, Richardson
	McKindley, L.E.		Rousey, Morgan
	Monk, Jesse		Wallace, Hughes
	Mosses, John		Wimms, Wm.
	Rodgers, A.J.		Gilchrist, Daniel
	Stephenson, W.H.		Flat, Madison
	Trees, Jacob		Taylor, John
	Wyatt, Ephraim		Moore, Wm. P.
	Willer, Logan	12th Dist.	Brawley, Thomas G.
10th Dist.	Byrd, D.E.		Brawley, C.W.
	Crouch, Willis		Byrd, Wm.
	Estus, John B.		Bryant, Peter
	Holdin, Archibald		Carter, G.W.
	Hichcock, Edwin		Creasy, A.R.
	Monk, Briant		Creasy, Stephen P.
	Pack, Carroll		Flat, L.W.
	Willett, R.H.		Guinn, Champion
	Tackett, George		Guinn, W.C.
	Huckaby, Isaac		Garrard, Richard
	Jones, Wm.		Howell, E.
	Chardin A. McWhorter		Jones, Charles
	Nelson, Robt.		Jones, Andrew
	Norvil, Wm. C.		Kelly, Kinchen
	Norvil, David J.		Poole, Riddley
	Ross, James		Reddon, George
	Thomas, Miles A.		Ross, James

6 December 1847. Insolvencies and Removals for the year 1847.
Pg. 287 Book D.

1st District
    Leroy Brit
    Wm. P. Caldwell
    Merideth Davis
    D.H. Downey(G)
    Lee Guttery(G)
    Thos. Humphries(I)
    John Hanks(G)
    Riding Koonce(OA)
    James F. McCall(I)
    Wiley C. Perry(G)
    James Wirt(I)
    Beverly Gordon(I)
3rd District
    Joseph Branch(I)
    Templeton Moon(G)
    Wesley Wallace(G)
    Joseph Branch(IIF)
    Jesse Henry(I)
    Eli Rose(OA)
    John James(G)
    William Eaves(I)
9th District
    Cannon Semore(G)

9th District
    Clark, Deacan(G)
    Clark, Riley(D)
    Dearin, Larkin(I)
    Sloan, James(NSM)
    Henly, Janes(I)
    Holdin, Archibald(G)
    Kilpatrick, Presly(NSM)
    Parmly, John(G)
    Richard, William(I)
    Stephenson, Emerine(I)
    Thompson, David(G)
    Willitt, R.H.(G)
    Yoakham, David(G)
10th District
    Acook, James(I)
    Bradly, Charles(NSM)
    Cacks, Isaac(I)
2nd District
    Thos. England(I)
    Andrew Booth(I)
    E.C. Branch(IIF)
    William Denham(I)
    Andrew Mathews(I)

James McCaslin(UA)
Carroll McCaslin(G)
Benjamin Mathews(I)
John Winchester(I)
Probate Wiggs(I)
J.G. Vasler(UA)
6th District
John Rice(NTBF)
John Smith(NTBF)
7th District
James Bishop(G)
Jerry Hinds(G)
8th District
H.P. Baswell(G)
James Cline(G)
Samuel Cline(G)
Jonathan Baker(G)
James Hood(G)
William Qualls(G)
Robert Hood(G)
John Sanders(G)
Henry Simmons(G)
William Stout(G)
Eli J. Martin(G)
John Gibbs(G)

Davis, William(NSM)
Hunter, Danil(I)
Kerr, Caswell(NSM)
Manuels, John A.(NSM)
Neilson, Robert(G)
Reynolds, W.N.(G)
Lewis, C.
10th District
Tisiley, Abbert(G)
Norwood, G.W.
White, Jonathan(NSM)
11th District
Brown, G.H.(I)
Copeland, W.C.(I)
Lane, John(G)
Mills, Jacob(OA)
Rasberry, Joseph(G)
Ransey, Richard(I)
Tuton, Benjamin(G)
12th District
S.P. Creasy
James Andrews(G)
William Wonburn(G)
Yarbrough(G)

1 January 1849. Insolvencies and Removals for the year 1848.
Pg. 357 Book D.

1st District
Robert Anders
Thos. Brewer
---- Brile
Thos. B. Garrard
Alfred Godwin
John Hicks
George Howard
N.G. Rirdin
W. Main Cook
James Cork
Henry Kemp
Jason Laun
Robert Miky
Henry Manes
Lewis Paul
Andrew Scott
Silas Topper
I.T. Thompson
Thomas Humphres
Benjamin Yarbrough
Thos. Coldwell
2nd District
Andrei Booth
Eli Branch
Ezekiel Conley
G.W. Campbell
Henry Garner
Joseph Love
Wm. Mathews
Andru Mathews
Benjamin Mathews
Pinckney J. Nichols

Jefferson J. Nichols
James Wirt
William Winchester
John Winchester
Probate Wiggs
Thomas Anglin
Joseph Branch
James Cash
John C. Jenl
Wm. Tarkinton
A.T. Tarkinton
James Walker
John Lett
R.D. Allen
5th District
W.T. Alexander
Richard Manas
C. Toodman
J.W. Northcutt, Sr.
Daniel Owen
J. Ray
A. Campbell
Thos. Langh
J.D. Murphy
C. Bishop
4th District
D.D. Crook
Nicholas Choat
Jesse Duberry
James Laxton
John McMullin
Hugh McMullin
Lewis Massey(OSD)

C.B. Neilson
Larkin Parish
G.W. Shields
William Thornton
Moses Wood
Erastus Arendell
6th District
   Milas Gammill
   Calvin Morris(ISD)
   Lewis Massey(ISD)
   ----- Price
   John Shull(ISD)
   Robert Shull(D)
   Mark Vanhoose
7th District
   John Laky
   Isaac Smith
   Isaac Boggs
   William Gadson
8th District
   William Baggs
   Joseph Baggs
   John Laky
   James Slider
   William Welch
9th District
   William Simpson
   Moses Bacheldor
   Joseph Wood
   M.P. Simpson
   James Petty
   Josiah Petty
10th District
   Jason Carr

Jonathan White
Larthan Dornel
William Phillips(ISD)
Morgan Rowsey(TO)
11th District
   Mark Nolen
   William Oldham(TD)
   W.C. Hughes(ITD)
   J.H. Hughes(TY)
   Washington Woods(TY)
   Ralph Berdon(TY)
12th District
   William Baker
   Richard Garner
   James Holt
   Richard Redic
   William F. Vires
   Isaac Wright
   J.D. Cooper
   John Ashworth
   Charles Austin
   R.J. Malcoks

7 January 1850. Insolvencies and Removals for the year 1849.
Pg. 419 Book D.

1st District
   James Griffin
   James Garrard
   Benjamin Housey
   G. Howard
   C. Humpheys
   T. Humphrys
   H. Kemp
   J.H. Lucas
   Jacob Tepper
   Thos. Coldwell
   William Tepper
2nd District
   James Eddings
   Thos. Anglin
   W. Campbell
   Jas. Emerson
   H. Garner
   W. Matthews
   M. Parisans
   W. Durman
   G. Vasser
   B. Winchester
   John Winchester

5th District
   T. Law
   John Umborgo
   A. Campbell
4th District
   Churchwell, Wm.
   Copeland, Wm.
   Carter, William
   Dameril, Joseph
   Eakes, Hovey
   G.V. Gantt
   Hudiburgh, Thos.
   Hannah, Robt.
   Lemmons, John
   McCall, W.P.
   McKay, -----
   Mayful, N.J.
   Neilson, C.B.
   Payne, T.P.
   Russell, William
   Roan, Hastin
6th District
   Bedwill, A.W.
   Bramly, James

    Gammill, Lewis
    Hagarty, Wm. Jr.
    Harris, Jn. Sr.
    Keyton, Wm.
    Milam, W.A.
    Tankersly, George
8th District
    Dishaga, Miles
    Harris, John
    Wingo, Josiah
3rd District
    Covy, S.G.W.
    Wisdom, J.R.
9th District
    Adams, L.(G)
    Emmerson, T.(G)
    Hunt, Jonathan
    Green, J.M.(I)
    McManas, Wm.(G)
    Monk, Jessee(G)
    Speare, Isaiah
    Wallace, Lawron
    Hales, John
    Ashcraft, J.
    Petty, James
    Russell, Mary Ann(I2D)
    Brown, Daniel
    Clark, Hiram
    McMullin, Wm.
    McMullen, J.H.

    Nolen, Robert
    Nolen, Mack
    Stell, J.J.
    Tims, Thomas
    Brown, John(TO)
    Cloud, J.P.(TO)
    Norwood, W.P.(D)
    Roberson, W.E.(D)
10th District
    Woods, George(I)
    Parmly, Samuel
    Seay, Lewis(TO)
    Tenneson, W.H.
    Ramsey, Zadach
    Hughs, J.M.(I2D)
    Harper, Yancy
12th District
    Bass, Solomon
13th District
    Acook, James
    Mullins, Eli
    Scott, James A.
    Starr, Wm.
    Bingham, Riding
    Shirley, E.W.
    Stratton, Henry
    Creasy, S.P.
    Gray, Jackson
    Gray, John
    Gray, Thos. P.

7 April 1851. Removals, Insolvencies, and Mistakes in the Tax List for the year 1850. Pg. 81 Book F.

1st District
    John B. Cobb(G)
    William Johnson(G)
    J.F. Rose(D)
2nd District
    Peter Bias(G)
    John Crowder(D)
    Gabriel D. Gaines(G)
    Wm. F. Gray(G)
    L.D. Millis(D)
    Wm. F. Morier(G)
    M.G. Newton(G)
    S.G. Newton(G)
    Henley Sneed(G)
    Berry Smith(M)
3rd District
    A.B. Frie(G)
    James G. Frie(G)
    Alfred Frie(M)
    James J. Freeman(M)
    B.M. Hardin(M)
    A.J. Tarkington(G)
    A. Conway(OAG)
4th District
    Joseph Birdsong(G)
    Wm. Churchwill(G)
    Joseph Dameril(D)
    Jonathan Gantt's Heirs(M)

    R.B. Jones(G)
    Hannah Abraham(G)
    Saml. Long(G)
    James E. Blount(G)
    George McNarnard(P)
    D.M. Morris(D)
    John Nichols(G)
    A.P. Pool(G)
    Ann Robinson(M)
    A. Roane(G)
    John Stamis(G)
    H.A. Barry(G)
    Elias Warren(M)
    Joshua Warren(M)
    Anderson Kerr(M)
    John J. Williams(M)
5th District
    Vincent Ferrell(G)
    John Bryant(G)
    S.W. Cook(G)
    John Coats(G)
    Henderson Gifford(G)
    Larkin Johnson(G)
    Moses Perkins(G)
6th District
    Jesse Allen(G)
    Madison Barnes(G)
    James H. Bennett(G)

----- Champion(G)
James H. Gilbert(G)
James D. Mathews(G)
Wm. A. Milam(G)
John B. Martin(G)
M. Worley(M)
George Ross(M)

7th District
    Josiah Blair(G)
    John Blair(G)
    Columbus Haslin(G)
    H. Pennington(G)
    Lodwick Quick(G)
    Lewis Wallace(G)

8th District
    Luke Cossey(M)
    J. Sibzinger(G)
    Sion Pickins(G)
    Philip Welsh(G)

9th District
    John Autry
    Danl. Brown
    D.E. Byrd
    Hiram Clark
    J.R. Case
    J.M. Green
    Jesse Monk
    Wm. McMullin
    A.W. Petty
    George Taliaferro
    Mary Jane Russell
    J.B. Slaughter
    A.J. Thompson
    A.M. Lombs
    James Wallace
    Walter Wallace
    John Gatis

10th District
    Wm. Ashcraft
    James Britton
    Hiram Brown
    W.P. Bourland
    G.G. Bostwick
    J.L. McIntosh
    James Moses
    Wm. Nowell
    Patrick Pratt
    L.C. Pool

George Wood
Washington Wyatt
Z. Wolf
G.K. Smith
J.D. Shaw

11th District
    John Carry
    John Terrell
    John Milton
    Saml. Pickins
    L.C. Rogers
    G.W. Rowsey
    Franklin Rowsey
    C.C. Rushing
    J.T. Stoveall
    E. Slaymaker
    Benj. Perkins
    John Hunter

12th District
    ----- McAlexander
    Thomas Byrd
    N.B. Burden
    Thomas Caldwell
    Jas. Robertson
    J.L. Raspberry
    A. Turnbaugh

13th District
    C. Ashcraft
    C.N. Bausby
    D.L. Cooper
    J.P. Graham
    John Gray
    A. Hutchings
    James Williams
    Pleasant Kelby
    Danl. Jones
    A. Montgomery
    M. McBride
    Wm. Newsome
    H. Patrick
    H. Redden
    F.T. Reaves
    M. Robins
    John Rickets
    G.W. Stamford
    E.D. Smith
    Wright's Heirs

5 April 1852. Releasements and Insolvencies for the year 1851.
Pg. 168 Book F.

1st District
    J.S. Allison
    John Cole
    J.B. Eddings
    Abner Johnson
    Wm. Morgan
    Wm. Snodgrass
    Silas Tippa
    Levi Tore
    W. Wetherford

    Jno. Wellbunk
    Allen Quilley
    Jacob Davidson
    Dewson Holden
    James Martin
    Jno. McCall

2nd District
    Thomas A. Booth
    Elias Bird
    Abram Branch

Champin Gwinn
Bird Hardin
Lawrence Harrison
Grant A. McCaslin
Benjamin Matthews
Wiley Solomon
John Solomon
Wm. Solomon
John Sloan

3rd District
S.A. Duckworth
John Freeman
J. Hamilton's heirs
----- Polk
Joshua Polk
J.B. Stewart
William Morris

4th District
A.S. King
R.P. McBride
---- McReynolds
Wm. Arundell
Wm. H.H. Seaman
Jesse D. Sutton
John Sutton
John Wells
J.D. Patterson
Alfred Kinnery

5th District
Lewis Bird
Thos. Bratton
Jno. Bryant
James Cox
W. Downing
E.T. Edmiston
E. Hobbs
S. Kellogg
J.S. Mullun
L. McLin
Eli Teninnor
Wm. Welbanks

6th District
Isaac Brooks
Moses Gammill, Jr.
William T. Gammill
John James
George W. James
Andrew I. James
Kerr & Porterfield
Lewis Crotts
Harry Lucus
Samuel Mangrano
William Spearman
Elias Warren
John Williams
Joseph Oblesby

7th District
Alfred Duff
Wm. Franks
G. Harlun
S. Cherry
Mary Gwin

8th District
Henderson Baswell
Wm. Davis
Jas. G. Pickens
W.B. Smith
Jacob Sorrels
C.W. Tidwell
Robinson Williams

9th District
D. Bugg
Geo. Bugg
A.J. Clark
Hiram Clark
H.H. Davis
Bufield Lett
Bryant Monk
Felix G. Monk
Mark Nolen

10th District
W.P. Borland
A.J. Colbert
Wm. Daniel
Z.G. Fowler
G.W. Fraley
J.C. Fraley
T.P. Hain
Jesse Hodges
W.D. Hiniman
J.P. Lemberson
L.H. Sonden
R.H. Millikein
C.D. McCrary
John Moses
John Smithwick
L.B. Wood
Geo. Wood
Jas. Britain

11th District
Elez. Brassfield
Jacob Berdor
Jno. Bowman
W.G. Combs
Martin Copeland
Thos. Clary
John Oldham
Z. Rowsey
A.A. Rylie
L.J. Cunningham

12th District
Q.P. Caldwell
B.B. Hughes
Andrew Kincannon
Irvin Moore
Jas. W. Wallace
Harriet Whitson
W.J. Weems
Geo. M. Francis

13th District
J.W. Burns
Thos. S. Burns
J.C. Bell
L. Creasy

T.E.L.M. Dickerson
John F. Fisher
John Gray
Thos. P. Gray
Josiah S. Gullin
Jackson Gray
J.H. Harrison
William C. Hooks
James M. Hooks
Wm. B. Hill

John E. Settle
James Loggins
James McCurdy
John R. Patton
John Rickets
F.F. Rives
G.W. Stanfield
J.B. Vancleave
Daniel Wyatts

4 April 1853. Insolvencies and Releasements for the year 1852. Pg. 248 Book F.

1st District

Perry S. Allison
Mathew Allen
Robert Bond
J.H. Blackshue
Richd. Coupland
Alexd. Coupland
Jerry M. Crutchfield
William Calends
Masion Clifton
Jesse Carter
John Davy
John Gallion
William Garner
Alfred Godwin
Caloway Hardin
Thomas Humphreys
William Henry
Abner Johnson
William P. Johnson
Jesse Lassiter
William H. Leak
Andrew McMahan
William Morgan
George McDaniel
Z. Owens
R.B. Owens
Levi Pettigru
Jesse Paget
William Page
Calvin M. Prince
Jacob Keesling
Larkin Snodgrass
John Snodgrass
Robert Stanton
David Thomas
William Thornton
Richd. G. Ticer
James Ticer
James Wirt
William Woodward
Probate Wiggs
James Walker
John E. Wright
Christopher Robinson

2nd District

James W. Ashworth
J.C. Alduron

William Adams
John Black
Elias Byrd
Hezekiah Bryant
Abraham Branch
William Churchwell
------- Denham
John Hargrove
Byrd Hardin
James Jackson
----- Keith
Isaac S. Lindsey
Thomas Love
Andrw Mathews
Abraham Miller
Francis McGaws(?)
M.F. Newton
John D. Newton
W.H. Polk
Robt. Russell
Wylie Solomon
John Sloan
James Wallace
Peter Wallace

3rd District

Saml. Crowder
John Crowder
W.A. Freeman
J.R. Kerr
Jessee Robertson
Charles Smith
Hugh Sutton
John Ledwill
J.B. Thornton

4th District

B.B. Alexander
J.W. Coupland
A.W. Dinson
D.D. Crook
Saml. Day
G.M. Hulery
A.S. Green
J.S. Irwin
T.J. McCorkle
Thomas Owen
W. Parrish
W.P. Palmer

J.R. Shader
James R. Straton
H.W. Peeples
5th District
　Saml. Beasely
　W.F. Duncan
　A.S. McClain
　T.B. White
6th District
　Daniel Robertson
　William Brown
　William Brooks
　John Bryant
　Saml. Easeley
　James Franks
　Christopher Emmet
　John James
　Andrw. Kelley
　James Milam
　William Sherman
　George S. Ross
　George Rinck
　Alexd. Stout
　Saml. Vermillion
　John Williams
　Jacob Warren
7th District
　J.D. Emberson
　Kindrick Castiel
　John Franks
　Mark House
　Mrs. Alice House
　M. Murphy
8th District
　W.H.R. Kellison
　Marion Childress
　Temple Johnson
　F. Mitchell
　Biven Swanford(?)
　Henry Tumbleston
　A. Williams
　Daniel J. Hutton
　James G. McGee
9th District
　Robt. E. Bond
　Peter Bullard
　Henry Hays, Jr.
　Henry Hays, Sr.

Meredith Stone
G.M. Wisdom
11th District
　John Barnes
　James H. Terry
　Jacob Ridden
12th District
　Newton Alexander
　Andrw. T. Green
　William F. Viars
　William Barnes
13th District
　T.J. Aydlett
　J.W. Ashworth
　John Ashworth
　Henry Ashworth
　Dizzert Blackwell
　William Bennington
　David Cox
　Willis Crooker
　Stephen P. Creasy
　John Creasy
　William B. Creasy
　T.E.S.M. Dickerson
　Green G. Ellis
　W.M. Edwards
　John F. Fisher
　Stephen W. Flatt
　W.C. Guinn
　Alexd. Welburn
　Thomas P. Gray
　Jackson Gray
　John Henderson
　Smith H. Harrison
　W.B. Hill
　George Higgins
　James Suggins
　W.C. McFerrin
　William Newsom
　William Parker
　J.C. Ross
　M.C. Redding
　F.J. Spencr
　J.T. Trevillian
　J.B. Vanclave
　Calvin Webb
　Nowell White

3 April 1854. Releasements and Insolvencies for the year 1853.
Pg. 357 Book F.

1st District
　James Braine(R)
　Joseph Braine(R)
　E.M. Blackshere
　Stephen Boatwright(R)
　Jerry Goforth(I)
　J.B. Garrard(R)
　Richd. Hedgepath(D)
　Amos Holt(I)
　W.G. Morgan(R)

Hugh McCall(NSP)
Wm. Powell(R)
Jno. Powell(NSM)
Isaac Perry(R)
C.A. Prince(R)
Jno. Sloan(D)
Will Snodgrass(D)
Danl. Snodgrass(R)
Jessee Thompson(R)
Jacob Thomas(R)

Jno. Wellbanks(R)
2nd District
    Jno. Black(R)
    Peter Bryant(I)
    Abraham Branch(OA)
    W. Churchwill(I)
    E. Connelly(R)
    Lewis Duncan(R)
    James Jackson(NSM)
    Geo. Z. Saton(R)
    Jef Loving(R)
    T.C. Loving(R)
    Thos. Love(R)
    Andrew Mathews(I)
    Abraham Miller(R)
    James Miller(R)
    John Miller(R)
    R.R. McMahan(RD)
    F. McGavoc(RD)
    M.F. Newton(RD)
    G.A. Polk, Guardian(RD)
    R.P. Russell(R)
    Robt. Russell(NSM)
    Robt. Russell(R)
    Thos. F. Sewell(NSL)
    Noah Wade(RAW)
    Thos. Winchester(R)
    Robt. Winchester(R)
3rd District
    M.W. Bunch(RD)
    Jas. Donavan(R)
    G.M. Fry(R)
    W.W. Faulkner(TT)
    E.M. Powers(NSM)
    Jessee Robinson(NSM)
    Hugh Sutton(R)
    Jno. Tidwell(R)
4th District
    Jno. R. Helton(OA)
    Amos Lawson, Sr.(RD)
    McDaniel & McGavock(RD)
    James H. Smith(R)
    Jacob Warren(R)
5th District
    Thos. R. Calwell(I)
    Thos. Eves(R)
    Jno. Henry(R)
    W.E. Manuel(R)
    R. Lilley(R)
6th District
    W.J. Anderson(R)
    James Brumley
    W.C. Binum(D)
    W. Brown(NSM)
    W. Brooks(R)
    Jno. Bryant(R)
    Jno. Brady(R)
    Jos. Brady(R)
    Thos. Durham(D)
    Wm. Elliott(D)
    Jas. Franks(I)
    Geo. Ross(R)
    Geo. R---(R)

Saml. Snellgrove(R)
A.B. Scott
Stephen Smith(RAW)
Saml. Vermillion(R)
Jno. Williams(NSM)
Jno. B. White
W.J. Warren
7th District
    Anderson Cole(RAW)
    Wm. Mathis
    Wm. Nolen
    H.K. Robins
    W.J. Robins
8th District
    J.T. Baker
    Wm. Simmons
    H.C. Stewell
    Jno. Schubert
    Thos. Wisdom
    Green D. Williams
    Danl. G. Woods
    Anderson Williams
9th District
    W.B. Byrd
    W.H. Cherry(RD)
    Hiram Clark
    Jno. McClean
    E.F. Stone
    W.J. Rose
    W.J. Bivins
    C.W. Taliaferro(W)
10th District
    A.C. Anderson(R)
    John E. Anderson(R)
    James Anderson
    L.H. Cunningham
    Simon Camron(NSM)
    Larkin Dearing(W)
    John C. Garner(R)
    J.C. Graves
    Jacob Luther(OA)
    J.F. McMullin
    C.B. McCreasy
    J.P. Norvill
    David Norvill
    Wm. Simmons(W)
    M.A. Thomas
    Geo. Wood
    Wm. J. Wills(THD)
    Calvin Webb(THD)
11th District
    James Hurley, Jr.
    D. Robinson's Heirs(RD)
    Harris(I)
    Simion Perkins(RD)
    Z. Rowsey
    James H. Terry(R)
    Jack Haynes(R)
    Jacob Ellis(NSM)
12th District
    Thos. Byrd
    W. Barnes
    W.C. Coupland

W.A. Clark
W.C. Kincannon
M. Perkins
James R. Pond
C. Stobuck
James N. Hughes
13th District
  Jno. Ashworth
  H. Ashworth
  Jas. W. Ashworth
  B.F. Allen
  Jno. Allen
  S. Bivins
  R. Bingham
  John Creasy
  W.R. Creasy
  Jno. Cooper
  T.E.S.M. Dickson
  G.G. Ellis

J.S. Flatt
T.P. Gray
W.W. Herrell
John Henderson
Saml. Henderson
J.H. Harrison
W.B. Hill
W. Jones(OA)
C. Hendricks
W.D. Johnson
Jas. Logan
Jno. Lowry
W.C. McFerren
James C. Rose
J.D. Stanfield
W.R. Robinson

Tax Collected for the year 1853, but omitted from the tax lists.

1st District
  Wm. Snow
  Wylie H. Berry's heirs
  Enos Rose
  T.J. Owen
  A.M. Counts
  R.B. McMahan
2nd District
  A.M. Prim
  Enos Rose
  D.E.G. Garner
  D.M. Smith
  J.W. Lindsey
  Jno. Cagle
3rd District
  Saml. Adams
  Jno. Pickens
  O.W. Wingo
  Andrew Clark
  Joel Casey
  Wm. Doran
  B.R. Freeman
  L.W. Deberry
  James Sherling
  C.S. Broyles
  E. Baysee
  Lydia Bayse
  J.J. Freeman
  A.J. Pickens
  J.H. Young
4th District
  James Neil
  W.P. Caldwell

5th District
  Mary Parris
  O.W. Wingo
  W.S. Meadows
  Jno. Gifford
  J.W. Northcut
6th District
  Jessee Duncan
  R. Martin
7th District
  W.C. Godwin
  J.M. Cooper
  T. Petty
  J.M. Murphy
  B.F. Shelby
8th District
  Wm. Westly
  H.W. Harris
9th District
  Allen Kendrick
10th District
  Jno. Simpson, Jr.
  J.M. Martin
  A. McFalls
11th District
  J.M. Pickens
  Wylie Luten
12th District
  Abel Blankenship
  W. Henry
13th District
  Geo. Fisher
  Jos. Hollingsworth
  S.R.D. Dollerson

2 April 1855. Insolvencies, Removals, and Releasements for the year 1854. Pg. 451 Book F.

1st District
  James Adams(R)
  Larkin Allen(R)

Jno. Adams, Jr.(R)
H. Abels(R)
James Abels(R)

E.M. Blackshear(R)
F.M. Burns(R)
J.A. Burden(R)
Thomas Clifton(R)
J.H. Clancey(NF)
H. Cooper(R)
E.H. CooperNSM)
Robt. Donohoo(R)
James Eldridge(R)
Elihu Forchand(I)
Alfred Godwin(I)
Jerry Goforth(R)
Calloway Hardin(R)
Wm. Insevy(R)
Wylie M. Kemp(R)
Morrison Koonce(R)
James Lackey(I)
John Loyd(I)
Hugh McCall(R)
Andrew Machians(I)
Zach Owens(I)
Jno. Prince(R)
Francis Paggit(R)
Jessee Paggit(R)
D.F. Snodgrass(R)
George Thomas(I)
Jno. Wilbanks(R)
Jno. Woodward(R)

2nd District
Peter Bryant(R)
Wm. Churchwill(I)
Cahpman & Molletklel
Wm. Clark(R)
Alex. K. Dickey(OA)
H.W. Davis(OA)
B.M. Garner(R)
Thos. Muse(R)
Jackson Austin(NF)
Thos. F. Sewell(NSL)
Robt. Shannon(RD)
Martin Stillgil(NF)
Wm. Turner(RD)
Geo. Poll(R)
W.C. Wills(R)
Benjn. Winchester(R)
Jno. Worley's heirs
T.P. Wilson(R)
T.J. Welch(R)

3rd District
Mark Massey(R)
W.T. Nolen(R)
W.R. Sielis(R)

4th District
Robt. Franks
W.T. Shelton(R)
Jessee Abernithy(R)
Amos Lawson(OA)
N.M. Thornton(RD)

5th District
Jno. Bryant(R)
Thos. Coupland(I)
Dudley Lee(I)

D.S. Duncan(OA)
Jas. Dudley(R)
Jackson Dudley(R)
P.P. Darven(I)
A.J. Darven(R)
James Nichols(R)

6th District
Jas. Brumley(R)
W.R. Bachelor(I)
John Brady(R)
Jas. Bodny(R)
Jas. Milligan(NF)
V. Crotts(R)
C. Emmitt(NN)
W.C. Gilbert(R)
H. Harris(R)
Wm. Jones(R)
Saml. Murphy(R)
Rutledge heirs(RD)
Rinch, Geo.(R)
Rinch, Elisha(R)
Snellgrove, Saml.(R)
Shull, W.W.(R)
Shields, Jessee(R)
Sego, S.(I)
Tankersley, F.(R)

7th District
Beckham, G.(R)
Cook, Geo.(R)
Castell, K.(R)
Davis, B.A.(NF)
Mills, Adam(OA)
James, John(R)
Parrons, Saml.(R)
Pennington, H.(R)
Robbins, C.(R)
Wade, W.B.S.(R)

8th District
Sanders, Austin(R)
J.T. Baker(R)
P. Branon(R)
W.K. Casteel(R)
Jno. Casteel(RD)
J.L. Cooper(R)
H. Heathcock(R)
Eli Loyd(R)
Jno. Ray(R)
S. Simmons(R)
J.W. Smith(I)
H.C. Stillwill(NF)
W.R. Tacker(R)
A. Williams(R)

9th District
Bowen, E.P.(R)
Bowlis, J.P.(I)
Clark, H.(R)
Cherry, W.H.(RD)
Froler, H.
Fisher, J.M.(R)
Elliott, Jos.(I)
Finch, Wm.(R)
Frazier, W.S.(R)

    Bryant & Co.
    McAllen(R)
    Davis Piggs(R)
    J.B. Hise(R)
    Jas. Rose(NF)
    Jas. Reaves(R)
    Stephen Reaves(R)
    Swannen, Lacy G.(RD)
    Wilds, Jas. S.(R)
    Williams, J.S.(R)
10th District
    Brown, W.(R)
    Blackard, C.(R)
    Baswell, B.(RD)
    Britton, Jas.(R)
    Coffman, J.D.(R)
    Col Egar(R)
    Elliott, Jos.(I)
    Flake, R.K.(I)
    Hundley, Jas.(D)
    Horam, S.P.
    Novel, J.P.(R)
    Novel, D.(R)
    Spain, J.D.(NSL)
    Jno. Sewell(RD)
    Jas. M. Morton
    Wm. McManus(OA)
    M.A. Thomas(I)
    W.E. Varick(R)
    Geo. Wood(I)
    R.G. Wicker(R)
    J.J. Williams(RD)
11th District
    Bailey, M.(OA)
    Kemp, P.C.(R)
    Terry, J.C.(R)
12th District
    Bivins, Wm.(I)
    Hughes, Vistal(R)
13th District
    Bingham, R.(I)
    Creasey, S.P.(R)
    Colbert, Owen(I)
    Childs, A.T.(R)
    Fisher, J.F.(R)
    Higgins, Geo.(R)
    Riley, Jas.(I)
    Loggins, Jas.(I)
    Lowry, J.(I)
    McNatt, F.M.(R)
    Mayfield, J.(R)
    Pressley, C.(R)
    Readen, M.C.(R)
    Ross, J.C.(R)
    Sanders, W.R.(R)
    Stanfield, G.W.(I)
    Thompson, J.C.(I)
    Trevillian, H.(I)
    Webbs, C.(I)
    White, M.(I)
14th District
    Stanfield, H.D.(RD)
    Creasy, Jno.(I)
    Shannon, T.S.(RD)
    Dulaney, J.(OA)
    Holland, T.A.(I)
    Kelley, G.(RD)

The following persons were omitted from the tax list by mistake.
For the year 1854.

1st District
    Alexd. Russell
    W.B. Gill
    Jas. Gore
    C.H.T. Briscoe
2nd District
    Gwin, B.F.
    Prim, A.M.
    Starn, Jack A.
3rd District
    Shirling, M.
    Wingo, C.W.
    Basye, L.
    Basye, Edmd.
    Spann, M.
    Bivins, J.S.
    Freeman, B.R.
    Freeman, J.J.
    Worley, Jacob
    Dickey, Alexd.
4th District
    Robinson, S.A.
    Daniels, Mrs.
    Daniels, J.
    Scheaber, Mo.
    Seaman, W.H.H.
6th District
    Holt, A.J.
    Duncan, J.J.
    Kendrick, Allen
7th District
    Nolen, J.H.
    Mills, Adam
    Brannon, C.C.
    Hunts, H.
10th District
    Turner, Thos.
    Williams, M.
    Hagey, Jno.
    Clounce, J.F.
    Kindrick, Allen
    McIntoch, T.S.
    Britton, J.B.
    Watkins, A.
    Swinson, Wm.
    Terry, M.C.
    Duncan, Jos.
    Rea, William
    Whorton, S.
11th District
    Stack, Jno.
    Scott, Jas.

11th District
    S.A. Robinson
    Tuten, W.
    Ausley, W.
12th District
    Parker, J.G.
    Pristow, P.V.
    Boyd, Alfred
    Blankenship, P.

13th District
    Shannon, W.R.
    Shirley, Thos.
    Flatt, G.W.
    Perkins, J.S.
    Montgomery, J.
14th District
    Holland, -----
    White, Jas.

7 April 1856. Releasements and Insolvencies for the year 1855.
Pg. 540 Book F.

1st District
    Eli Bunes
    R.N. Church
    James Por
    Sherrod Hattley(R)
    Robt. Harden(R)
    W.A. Henry(R)
    David McEads(RD)
    A. Mathews(I)
    Patton Kincaid
    J. Price
    L. Snodgrass
    W. Spraks
    W.W. Thomas
2nd District
    Elias Byrd(R)
    Peter Bryant
    J. Buroghs
    L.S. Booths
    W. Churchwell
    James Courtney(R)
    Conall Courtny
    Chapman & ----(RD)
    A.K. Dicky(RD)
    W. Donhau
    Denis Gold---
    E.W. Green
    John Gollain
    Samul Gullur
    Betty Goad(NSP)
    J.L. Lindsy
    G----Laden(RD)
    J.W. McNealey
    A. Pool(OA)
    R. Patrick
    Peacock
    John M. Sloan
    J.W. Snague
    Jesse Shittan
    William Steel
    Connall Smith
    B. Winchester
    Williamson Heirs
    Calvin G. Woodbun
    T.P. Welborn
    Cabert
    W. Dallun
3rd District

    O. Bourland
    Joseph Welch
    Wiley Guin
    W. Pickens
    J.T. Phillips
    R. Hualess
    M. Smith
    Williams(NF)
4th District
    T.P. Bay
    Samel. Day
    James C. Green
    D.A. Gant
    A.B. Helton
    J.W. Jinkins
    Isabela Ross
    John Shive(RD)
    George W. Shields
    N.M. Tarnton
    J.G. William
5th District
    Thomas Copland
    W.S.D. Duncan
    Mathew Feril
    J.G. Harbour
    J.T. Hames(R)
    J.J. Lumpkins(R)
    James M. Neal(R)
    W.J. White(R)
    John Patton(R)
6th District
    W.R. Bachelor(R)
    Wm. I. Anderson(R)
    H.J. Burds(NF)
    Richard Burnes
    John Brown
    J.J. Dudley
    S.S. Dudly(R)
    W.C. Gilbert(R)
    Pleasant Gilbert(R)
    T.R. Gant(R)
    Mark Hatley, Jr.(R)
    Hugh Haris(R)
    Joseph Hardin(I)
    William James(R)
    Sarner Long(R)
    P. Massey(I)
    John Massey(R)

John Matus(R)
R.J. Porter
Samuel Sego(I)
J.D. Tankesley(R)
J.H. Vermillion(R)

7th District
Green Beckham
Wm. Ferill(R)
Kinith Casteel
Wm. Franks(RD)
Houston(R)
John Mahan(R)
Josiah Perry(R)
Wm. Austin
J.J. Steely(RO)
A.C. Shelby(R)
J.M. Weatherford
J.W. Weatherford
Wm. Wingo(R)

8th District
W.T. Austin(R)
John Austin(RO)
E.K. Bivens(R)
W.M.K. Casteel(R)
J.W. Casey(RD)
Daniel Belshazer(R)
S.S. Dudley
A.L. Dudley(I)
D.W.N. Gillis(NF)
H. Hithcock(R)
Wiatherby Haynes(NF)
Andrew Haris(R)
William H. Haris
Wm. Robins(R)
W.G. Robins(R)
Philip South(D)
John Sharp(R)
W.R. Tacker(R)
Eli Loid(R)
J.G. Martin(RD)
Benjmin Morris(R)
J.R. Pickens(R)

9th District
Stephen Brown(RD)
George Courtis(R)
Moses Curtis(R)
Helory Courtis(R)
W.F. Courtis(R)
W.H. Cherry(RD)
T.A. Fissher(I)
M. Faultenberry(R)
M.H. Gresham(R)
Samuel C. Hunter(R)
H. Helmack(RD)
Wm. King(NF)
J.N. Outen
Johnathan Short(R)
Geo. Tackett(R)
E.W. Ward(R)
L. Winn(R)
T.F. Wilis(R)
Jacob Bivens(R)
Samuel Bell (TT)

B. Boswell(RD)
James Bean(R)
Birton Park(I)
Moses Barnes
W.P. Bolan(I)
F.D. Barefoot(R)
Daniel Coffman(I)
James Childres(R)
Josep Eliot(R)
D. Fraley(R)
J.L. Flake(R)
Robert Flake(R)
James Allen(NF)
S.P. Hardin(R)
James Martin(RD)
E.W. McGowen(I)
J.D. Spain's heirs(RD)
J.D. Spain(R)
A.J. Terley(R)
John Trice(R)
George Woods(I)
L.B. Woods(I)
J.E. Woods(I)

11th District
W. McDaniel(RO)
Pleasat Parker(R)
H. Pierce(D)
Thomas Raynes(I)
J.H. Tevery(R)
E. Towry(R)
George M. Hamilton(TT)
A.P. Chammes(D)
James Beard(I)
Samuel South(R)
Robt. Gamal(NF)
Crump & Hassel(RD)
William Layton(R)
M. Layton(I)
James Crumwell(NT)
John Maxwell(NT)
B.F. Perkins(R)
William Griffin(RD)
Thos. Adams(NF)

12th District
J.N. Alexander(R)
J.B. Arundell(R)
Wm. Broadaway(RD)
Wm. Banes(I)
T.G. Brawley(R)
H. Cromby(R)
Sal Copeland(D)
John George(R)
John A. Harbet(UA)
S.M. Huling(R)
John Jackson(D)
J.C. King(D)
R.P. Kerby(D)
Robert Newal(R)
M. Standfield
C. Taylor(D)
George Thompson(NF)
A.J. Yancy(R)
Wm. Yarberry(R)

J. Aldman(NF)
Bowen Davy(RD)
13th District
   Joel Finley(I)
   Samuel Howell(R)
   George W. Hicks(R)
   Charles Harpour(I)
   Samuel Henderson(I)
   John Henderson(I)
   Riley Jones(R)
   James Logan(I)
   J. Lowery(I)
   F.M. McNatt(R)
   R.P. Newman(R)

Richard McNatt(RD)
J.D. McBride(I)
Prsley Cob(R)
A.G. Pickins(RD)
W.R. Robinson(RD)
George W. Standfield(R)
Calvin Webb(I)
Nicholas Woolf(R)
14th District
   Joseph Delaney(R)
   T.J. Holland(R)
   Alford Batts(R)
   Jeremiah Creesy(I)

6 October 1857. Releasements, Insolvencies, and Removals for the year 1856. Pg. 25 Book G.

1st District
   Robert Cole(I)
   Pilmone Cole(D)
   M.W. Davis(R)
   Alfred Godwin(I)
   John Gowers(R)
   Henry Kemp(I)
   W.M. Kenedy(R)
   Hu. McCall(R)
   Isham Power(R)
   Henry Rose(DT)
   W.H. Sparkes(D)
   Anthony Strawn(R)
   Bennett Thomas(R)
   Jacob Thomas(R)
   John Thomas(R)
   Wm. Willbanks(R)
2nd District
   Jonathan Burrys(R)
   Andrew Booth(R)
   Wm. Churchwill(I)
   W.M. Cairns(R)
   Jerimiah Fergison(R)
   Henry Haggard(I)
   J.H. McConnell(RD)
   Jackson Austin(R)
   Geo. Pool(I)
   Robt. Russell(RO)
   Peter Southion(R)
   Jacob Southiorn(RO
   Geo. White(R)
   W. Williams(R)
   John Wallace(R)
   Franklin Young(R)
3rd District
   D.R. Buie(RD)
   H.G. Black(RD)
   L.W. Deberry(RD)
   James Freeman(R)
   Matthew Fenio(R)
   Arthur Garrison(R)
   Anderson Holt(R)
   H---- Kerr(RD)

W. Moses(RD)
J.T. Phillips(R)
4th District
   Z. Carpenter(R)
   Danl. Bain(OA)
   Saml. Day(R)
   R.H. Day(R)
   J.C. Green(R)
   G. Falls(R)
   J.R. Kerr(DT)
   J.L. Neill(R)
   L. Parrish(D)
5th District
   Paul Braunt(R)
   Lucius Brown(R)
   Wallace Brown(R)
   Francis Downing(R)
   Henry Daniels(R)
   John Davis(R)
   Waldrip Duckworth(R)
   Jas. McNeill(R)
   Obidiah Lucas(I)
   Geo. Potts(R)
   C.R. White(R)
6th District
   Wm. Bachilor(I)
   H.I. Beoke(I)
   Pleast. Gilbert(R)
   J.C. Martin(RO)
   John Matthews(R)
   Simeon Seago(R)
   Saml. Scott(R)
   John Smith, Jr.(R)
   Abrahm White(RD)
   Alex. Harrison(RD)
   J.H. Vermillion(RD)
   Kenitre Cashstue(RD)
7th District
   John Austin(RO)
   Browder Brooks(RD)
   James W. Cossey(R)
   D.B. Conaway(R)
   Saml. Craig(I)

Benj. Cook
William Dunham
Jas. D. Estus
A.J. Lindsey(R)
8th District
  Quimby Lewis(R)
  Wm. Martin(R)
  Merdo Martin(R)
  J.W. Nolen(R)
  John Palmer(R)
  W.M. Vandergrift(R)
  Jas. J. Austin(R)
9th District
  A.L. Adams(R)
  Martha Elkins(RD)
  E.H. Autry(RD)
  A.Y. Barnett(RD)
  John Cobb(RD)
  W.H. Cherry(RD)
  Edmund Cobb(RD)
  Wm. Dunham(D)
  John Dorman(RD)
  J.J. Gibon(RD)
  Thos. Griffin(RD)
  Wm. Johnson(I)
  Griffin Jones(I)
  Presly Johnson(R)
  Henry Kiddy(R)
  James Rose(R)
  Thos. Smith(R)
  Saml. Smith(R)
  John E. Smith(R)
  Henry Suttill(R)
  M.I. Williams(RD)
10th District
  H.A. Brown(R)
  Parker Britton(I)
  Willoughby Blackard(I)
  J.W. Barnes(R)
  W.C. Barnes(R)
  Cassell Counce(R)
  Robt. Slake(R)
  Martin Highman(R)
  T.W. Lucas(I)
  Danl. McDonold(OA)
  E.W. McGowen(R)
  A.W. Pickins(I)
  David Pickins(I)
  J.C. Robinson(R)
  Robt. Cornhill(R)
  John Frise(R)
  W.J. Warden(R)
  Saml. Wood(R)
  E.J. Wood(R)
  Peter Wood(OA)
  L.B. Wood(I)
  J.J. Williams(RD)
  J.D. Hussell(RD)
11th District
  Thos. Field(RD)
  David McColum(RD)
  B.F. Perkins(R)
  A.J. Romines(R)

G.W. Rushing(R)
J.H.T. Stephens(RD)
Wm. Seratt(RD)
R.W. Street(RD)
12th District
  Josiah Alexander(I)
  R.W. Burton(I)
  Wm. Barnes(D)
  John Huckabee(I)
  Shamet Huckabee(I)
  Benj. Hill(I)
  David Hamilton(I)
  S.G. Hardin(I)
  Richd. Meyeris(I)
  Geo. W. Orr(I)
  Alex. Outlaw(I)
  Wm. Parrish(R)
  C.R. Parrish(R)
  P.V. Priston(R)
  Caswell Smith(R)
  B.F. Wallace(R)
  Simeon Tidwell(R)
  William Yarbrough(I)
  John N. Brown(R)
  Redman Bingham(R)
  Joseph Little(R)
  Geo. Huggins(R)
  Oliver Rice(R)
  Joseph Hollinsworth(RD)
13th District
  Wm. Austin(R)
  Sm. Boswell(R)
  Joseph Broyles(R)
  S.G. Brogel(R)
  John Allen(I)
  Owen Colbert(I)
  Joel Finlay(R)
  Saml. Howell(I)
  Jonih Jones(R)
  Charles Hopper, Jr.(R)
  J.M. Carr(RD)
  J.D. McBride(R)
  W.G. Perkins(R)
  Geo. Phillips(I)
  E.F. Shurley(RO)
  John Starn(R)
  J.P. Wolfe(R)
14th District
  Alfred Bolts(R)
  Allen Barber(R)
  John Creasy(R)
  Jeremiah Creasy(R)
  John Gorvere(R)
  James Martin(R)
  T.R. Parker(R)
  T.S. Shannon(RD)
  John Henderson(I)
  Saml. Henderson(I)
  S.P. Creasy(I)
15th District
  J.W. Ashworth(OA)
  Wm. Adamson(D)
  Wm. Byrd(R)

Saml. Byrd(R)
Wm. Bankham(R)
Jonathan Hamilton(R)

James Moses(R)
John Moses(R)
Wm. Turner(RO)

The following taxes were collected but not entered on the books for the year 1856.

1st District
   John Watson
   J.S. Allison
2nd District
   C. Weaks
   Williams Pool
   Sharp & Kelley
   John Austin
   Robt. Shannon
   J.W. Lindsey
   Mr. Tubbs
3rd District
   J.R. Kerr
   William Bain's heirs
   J.B. McCowen
   H. Cockburn
   John Pickens
   Washington Shelley
   James Simmons
   W.P. McDaniel
4th District
   S.M. Palmer
   J.M. Cooper
   C.M. Morris
   W.M. Ross
   D. Bohannon
   J.T. Palmer
   A. Bickner
6th District
   Joshua Warren
7th District
   Tatum Edwards
   James Welch

8th District
   J.W. Carson
   H. Cossey
   Eli Cherry
9th District
   J.B. Britton
10th District
   M.J. McCrary
   A.J. Kincaid
   L.B. Grogan
   John Hagy
   Calvin Wicker
   Geo. Sewell
11th District
   Thomas A. Osley
   James Perry
   J.C. Towry
12th District
   Joseph Pratt
13th District
   William Perkins
   J.D. Davis
   Mary Bill
   James S. McClinton
   Lewis Goff
   William Jones
   Mr. Bishop
14th District
   L.P. Nowell
   A. Wyatte
   W.V. Akin

4 April 1859. Releasements and Insolvencies for the year 1858. Pg. 200 Book G.

1st District
   Robert Cole(GI)
   Wyle Keep(G)
   William Snow(LID)
   Jessee Keep(NTY)
2nd District
   Michal Branch(I)
   Ezekel Connelly(G)
   Hunton, Geo.(NSM)
   Campbell, Hutton(NSM)
   John Harris(TY)
   Charles Morrison(NSM)
   S. Marsh(G)
   James Martin(NSM)
   Thomas Medcalf(G)
   Geo. Pool(I)
   John Rose(I)
   W. Stout(G)
   James Shannon(G)

   John Shannon(G)
   Peter Southerland(I)
   Isaac Vicer(NSM)
   B. Winchester(G)
   Wm. Winchester(G)
   Calvin Whitlow(I)
   Henry White(I)
   J.M. Wisdom(I)
   S. Winchester(NSM)
   Franklin Young(TY)
   D. Young(DF)
3rd District
   L. B. Arendell(LT)
   E.P. Blount(RO)
   Elizabeth Barnes(LT)
   James Cash(DF)
   Thomas Freeze(G)
   Richard Joel(I)
   William Nolen(G)

T.G. Rentfrow(G)
J.N. Rentfrow(G)
Geo. Rentfrow(G)
Mark Vanhoose(DF)
J.G. Worley(NSM)
4th District
    Lawson Blund(DF)
    W.C. Boyd(RO)
    Wm. Brady(DF)
    James Brown(DF)
    D. Clingham(I)
    T. Caldwell(G)
    Clayton, S.H.(G)
    Calvin Hunt(G)
    Robt. Hodge(G)
    Frank Jones(G)
    Kerr, J.R.(TO)
    Kiddy, ---- (I)
    William Mills(I)
    J.K. Pollock(I)
    M.H. Palmer(DF)
    Linn Parrish(I)
    Richard Rice(I)
    Joseph Ray(DF)
    Isaac Roane(DF)
    William Snelgrove(G)
    W.B. Shields(D)
    M.M. Smoot(RO)
    S.S. Steadman(G)
5th District
    Charles Brady(DF)
    J.H. Dolton(G)
    Fielder S. Holt(G)
    Alexander Harvil(G)
    Allen McGee(DF)
    B.M. Northcut(G)
    Wm. Person(G)
    J.H. Robinson(TY)
    O.P. Wade(RO)
    Wilie Waldo(DF)
6th District
    W.P. Couch(G)
    Eli Frank(G)
    Bryant Francam(I)
    H.J. Holt(RO)
    D.E. Harrison(NF)
    Geo. Haynes(I)
    J.D. Ferris(G)
    M.G. Lucas(G)
    Nevil, T.E.(G)
    Millom, L.C.(I)
    Terry, David(I)
    Tucker, ----(NF)
    Reuben Walls(DF)
7th District
    John Benson(NF)
    Denneth Corttile(G)
    G.B. Milam(G)
    Geo. Stephens(G)
8th District
    John Austin(RO)
    Daniel Burny(G)
    James Clausewell(G)

Samuel Craig(G)
W.C. Cross(G)
G.W. Davis(I)
Thomas Evis(I)
John Guunin(I)
Godwin, W.A.(I)
Miles Green(I)
H.M. Hudson(NSM)
G.G. Hudson(NSM)
Jo. Harling(I)
Henry Lamb(DF)
Stephen Lamb(DF)
Murdock Martin(I)
Henry Morris(I)
Thomas McKee(I)
J.S. Mathews(G)
W.E. Martin(I)
Fred Martin(I)
J.M. Nicks(I)
J.G.W. Richards(G)
Samuel Russell(I)
J.S. Stout(TO)
J.W. Smith(G)
Jno. Shull(G)
John Tycer(G)
R.P. Turpens(G)
9th District
    A.M. Adams(RO)
    Jasper Brown(G)
    W.C. Byrd(G)
    N.C. Byrd(TY)
    John Brown(LT)
    W.J. -----(D)
    Mat Dickerson(D)
    Wm. Edwards(DF)
    G.W. Fedrick(G)
    Jno. Orne(G)
    Julius Poindexter(G)
    Isham Pulum(G)
    John Saner(G)
    R.C. Short(G)
    James Williams(G)
10th District
    W.P. Bourland(G)
    Wilson Buchler(G)
    Robert Flake(I)
    John Keeland(G)
    McCrary, T.B.(G)
    R.W. Preston(G)
    David Shean(G)
    Thomas Taylor(G)
    J.R. Thacker(G)
    Thomas F. Wood(I)
    L.B. Wood(I)
    Samuel Wood(I)
11th District
    Henry Barnes(G)
    Robert Bailey(G)
    James Bivens(NF)
    William Clemmons(G)
    Samuel Curtis(DF)
    Woodson Curtis(G)
    W.C. Guy(NF)

Henry Hurley(TY)
John Pool(G)
J.H. Rousey(RO)
Joseph Rousy(G)
Geo. Stephens(G)
Jesse Stinnet(G)
Bynum Tutor(DF)
12th District
Josiah Alexander(G)
J.D. Alexander(G)
William Ausly(G)
Ed Brown(G)
Henry Brown(G)
T.P. Boyd(DF)
Isaac Cronk(TO)
John Emmerson(NF)
Eoff, Wm.(TY)
Cull Gowen(I)
Benjamin Floyd(G)
M. Floyd(G)
A. Leftwick(LT)
D.L. Loud(NF)
Thomas Little(G)
Meek, A.(NSM)
Meek, J.H.(NSM)
Morris, R.G.J.(NSM)
Mathews, Thomas(NSM)
Mathews, James(IPUL)
Norwood, Fletcher(G)
Orr, Richard(TY)
Outlaw, A.(DF)
T.M. ----(I)
Thomas Polk(G)

Puckett, Robt.(DF)
Robinson, W.(DF)
Rice, Richard(LT)
Rickets, John(G)
Rickets, A.(NF)
Rice, C.O.(I)
Swinney, Gyle(I)
Shull, A.M.(DF)
Tacket, Thos.(G)
White, Jno.(DF)
Yarboro, W.(DF)
Yocum, Dan(G)
13th District
Britt, W.C.(RO)
Baker, Joseph(NF)
Copeland, James(G)
Goff, Lewis(NF)
Hollingsworth, J,B,(G)
Lancaster, Jesse(LID)
Montgomery, Alf(G)
Meadows, J.S.(I)
O'Neal, Thomas(RO)
Phillips, Green(I)
Phillips, J.J.(NF)
-------- J.S.(NF)
Reeves, W.H.(G)
14th District
Cole, W.(NF)
Davidson, Robt.(D)
Davidson, Jackson(I)
Low, Thomas(I)
Smith, J.P.(G)

5 March 1860. Insolvencies, Releasements, and Removals for the year 1859. Pg. 298 Book G.

William M. Talley(R)
E. Ashcraft(R)
B. Bradley(R)
John Bourton(R)
Crawford(R)
Thomas Fisher
J.R. Houghton
Robert Hammock
William Poindexter
John Stephenson
Robert Flake
Thomas Fisher
Wellis Gray
A. Mayse
William Nelson
David Pickins(OA)
James Stephenson(UA)
C. Wyatt
Colley Harrison(OA)
Calvin King(D)
Thomas Love
Richard Orr
Lewis Outlaw(D)
F.M. Outlaw
Dock Phillips

Oliver Rice
Wilson Ridley
William Robinson
J.W. Stumph(G)
John Winchester
Henry Kidel
Alexander Hames(UA)
Colbert Hughes
Andrew Courtney(D)
George Crocket(R)
Dock Frazier
A.L. McLin
W.F. Mozier
Joseph Pool
Joseph Ridden
J.H. Wisdom
John Diffey
George Renfrore
James W. Renfroe
Thomas J. Renfroe
Washington Niel(D)
William Pinckston(R)
Jasper Hale
R.C. Kincannon(NF)
Edward M. Smith

M.C. Whitson
James Brown
James Crouch(R)
W.P. Couch(R)
Paul Corbley
James Franks(R)
Isaac Gross
R.K. Martin(RO)
Joel Penney(G)
Henry Poindexter(R)
W.H. Dove
Joseph Franks
J.W. Franks(NF)
Thomas McDaniel
Allen McGee
G.A. Merchirson
William Roberson
George Ward
C.C. Brannum
P.F. Burrow
Thomas Dickson(OA)
G.W. Davis
Michel Gray(OA)
George Haynes
Franklin Hutton
Charles Hutson(C)
William Mathews

M.L. Martin
J.G. Martin
T.J. Price
Levi Wicker(OA)
Alsey Brastfield(NSM)
John Laton
Lewis Graves
J.R. Allen
Joseph Crowder
J.T. Gotilly
W.R. Parrsons
Isaac Vincent
William Lakey(R)
Akins, J.T.
Thomas Dugan
J.F. Sharp
S. Clayton
Andrew Broun
J.P. Gidding(R)
Robert Hodge(R)
C.S. Stay(R)
W.M. Tidwell
J.W. Dudley
James Cash(D)
George Burton(R)
John Essory

THE WILL & INVENTORY BOOKS

Will and Inventory Books B and D, 1836 -1848, are abstracted in their entirety. There is, as a result, some overlap between these books and the county court minutes of the same period. However, these different records supplement each other more often than not. For example, the will and inventory books will provide an abstract of a will while the county court minutes provide the date it was presented for probate. Also, an executor, appointed in the will, may have been unable to serve and this would be noted in the county court minutes.

Unfortunately, the other will and inventory books for the period 1820 - 1860 have not survived. There are some loose wills and other documents for this period and these have been abstracted and added to the end of this section. The entries are arranged just as they were found in the books. Generally speaking, they are in chronological order. Intermingled with the estate records are the registration records of stock marks. Why these were put in with the wills and inventories is anyone's guess.

These books contain guardian settlements and reports as well as the estate records. Information in these entries can be very valuable. Every effort has been made to provide any information of value in these entries. Sometimes money received by the guardian is noted as having come from another state. This, of course, indicates that the children either had relatives in the state mentioned or that the estate, to which they had fallen heir, had business interests in that state. Any such relationship mentioned is included in the abstracts.

By following the successive guardian settlements, the age of some of the children can be determined. As the names of children disappear from the settlements, it can be deduced that the child in question had either died or reached legal age. At times, as a child did reach the legal age, a special guardian settlement is listed as a final settlement.

One added bonus is the inclusion of the names of all slaves mentioned in these books. This should assist anyone working in black genealogy in Hardin County. Often slaves were mentioned in wills and guardian settlements. It was not uncommon for the ages of slaves to be given, and sometimes relationships between slaves were noted.

WILLS, INVENTORIES, AND SETTLEMENTS

BOOK B: 1836 - 1842

BRATTENBOUCHER, JOHN J. - Sale. Held on 10 May 1836. (Pg. 1-20)

ROBINSON, SAMUEL - Inventory and Sale. 2 July 1836. (Pg. 21-22)

RUSSELL, J. T. - Inventory and Sale. Returned by James Scott, administrator. No Date. (Pg. 22-23)

RUSSELL, JOHN T. - Inventory. Returned by James Scott, administrator. No Date. (Pg. 23-24)

NEWMAN, THOMAS - Inventory and Sale. Returned by Samuel Newman and Perry B. Hawkins, administrators. January 1836. (Pg. 24-25)

HANNAH, ALEXANDER - Sale. Returned by John Houston, administrator. 5 August 1836. (Pg. 25-27)

BOOKOUT, JESSE - Inventory and Sale. Returned by Henry M. Bookout, administrator. 16 September 1836. (Pg. 29-30) Sale on 15 November 1836. (Pg. 27-29)

COX, MEREDITH - Inventory of perishable property. Returned by Joseph and William Cox, administrators. 30 September 1836. (Pg. 31-32)

POLK, JOHN - Extra amount of property sold. Returned by Thomas Blakely, administrator. 7 November 1836. (Pg. 32)

CHERRY, ISHAM - Account of property sold from the estate since 1 January 1836. Returned by Eli and Jesse Cherry, executors. (Pg. 33)

CHERRY, NOAL - Expenses paid to Eli Cherry, guardian of the minor heirs of Noal Cherry in getting back a Negro woman and child that were taken to Benton in Mississippi. 5 April 1836. (Pg. 33)

JEFFERS, JOHN A. - Settlement with John Davy and P.B. Hawkins, administrators. 23 July 1836. (Pg. 34)

KINCANNON, DAVID - Settlement with David Robinson, administrator. 5 September 1836. (Pg. 34)

JAMES, THOMAS - Settlement with John Scott, administrator. 5 December 1836. (Pg. 35)

CHERRY, ISHAM - Settlement with Eli Cherry, administrator. 5 September 1836. (Pg. 35)

NORVILLE, JAMES - Claim against estate based on a judgement obtained in McNairy County presented by Nathaniel Erwin, administrator. No Date. (Pg. 36)

REYNOLDS, HENRY - Settlement with Jesse B. Gantt and Elisha Pack administrators. 5 September 1836. (Pg. 36-37)

BRATTENBOUCHER, JOHN JACOB - List of notes in favor of the estate in the possession of James Robinson and James Irwin, administrators. No Date. (Pg. 37-39)

BRATTENBOUCHER, JOHN J. - List of accounts remaining in the ledger of the deceased. 4 July 1836. (Pg. 40-43)

REYNOLDS, HENRY - Additional settlement information presented by Jesse Gant and Elisha Pack, administrators. 7 February 1837. (Pg. 44)

KERR, JANE - Settlement with William Wells and Thomas Gray, administrators. 3 February 1837. (Pg. 44)

HANNAH, JOHN - Settlement with John Houston and John D. Porterfield, administrators. 6 February 1837. (Pg. 45)

CHERRY, ISHAM - Report from Eli Cherry, administrator, of sale of land from estate on 17 January 1837. (Pg. 45)

CHERRY, NOEL - Expenses paid by Eli Cherry, guardian of the minor heirs of Noel Cherry. For the year 1836. (Pg. 45)

CHERRY, NOEL - Eli Cherry, guardian of the minor heirs of Noel Cherry, purchased a life-time estate in the Negro woman Sally from James G. Walker. Sally had been left to Nancy, wife of Isham Cherry and after her death to the heirs of Noel Cherry. She had come into the possession of Walker and Eli Cherry was afraid she would be lost. No Date. (Pg. 46)

COOPER, JONATHAN - Notes found among deceased's papers at death. Reported by James Graham, administrator. 6 February 1837. (Pg. 46-47)

GARNER, HENRY - Widow's dowry laid off. 15 December 1836. (Pg. 47)

COOPER, MRS. - Dowry laid off for Mrs. Cooper. No Date. (Pg. 48)

WRIGHT, JAMES SR. - Settlement with Wm. Wright and James Wright, administrators. 15 December 1836. (Pg. 48)

COOPER, JONATHAN - Sale. Returned by James B. Graham. 6 and 7 October 1836. (Pg. 49-55)

MILLIGAN, WILLIAM - Sale. Returned by J.S.G. Milligan, administrator. 25 February 1837. (Pg. 56-60)

HOUSTON, _____ - Settlement with H. Tarbit, administrator. 6 March 1837. (Pg. 60)

ORR, _____ - Dowry laid off for the Widow Orr. 16 February 1837. (Pg. 60)

POLK, JOHN - Report of rent due for 1836 for rent of land belonging to the estate. Reported by Thos. Blakely, administrator. No Date. (Pg. 60)

REYNOLDS, JOHN - Guardian Report by William and Elizabeth Wells, guardians for the minor heirs of John Reynolds. March 1837. (Pg. 61)

JEFFERS, JOHN A. - Report of accounts paid by Jehu Davy and P.B. Hawkins, administrators. No Date. (Pg. 61)

COOPER, JONATHAN - Additional Inventory. Reported by James B.

Graham, administrator. 1 April 1837. (Pg. 62)

PORTER, WM. - Inventory and Sale. Returned by Eleanor Porter, administrator. 5 August 1837. (Pg. 63-64)

McMAHAN, JAMES F. - Will. Dated: 29 October 1832. Heirs: Brothers - John D. McMahan and Robert B. McMahan, Sisters - Sirzy Coatny, and Minerva Hartgroves, Wife - Nelly McMahan. Executors: Nelly McMahan and Alexander Russell. Witnesses: Thomas Davy, John Davy, and Solomon Hudiburg. (Pg. 64)

McMAHAN, JAMES F. - Sale. 31 August ----. (Pg. 65-66)

REYNOLDS, HENRY - Inventory of property left to wife Matilda Reynolds and her four children. Returned by Jesse B. Gantt and E. Pack, administrators. No Date. (Pg. 66-67)

REYNOLDS, HENRY - Settlement with administrators. September 1837. (Pg. 67)

GARNER, HENRY - Guardian Return by Daniel Beasley, guardian for the two minor heirs of Henry Garner. 2 October 1837. (Pg. 68)

LEE, SIMPSON - Guardian Return by James Robinson, guardian for Felix, Alfred C., and Emily C. Lee minor heirs of Simpson Lee. 2 October 1837. (Pg. 68-69)

WAGGONER, DANIEL - Division of land for widow Martha Waggoner in accordance with the will of Daniel Waggoner. 21 September 1837. (Pg. 69-70)

RUSSELL, DELILAH - Extra Return by Alexander Russell, administrator. October Term 1837. (Pg. 70)

WAGGONER, DANIEL - Settlement with J.J. Williams and Martha Waggoner, administrators. 30 September 1837. (Pg. 70-71)

WILLIAMS, WILLIAM L. - Inventory. Returned by Jas. Warren, administrator. No Date. (Pg. 71)

RUSSELL, JAMES - Widow's portion laid off. 14 October 1837. (Pg. 71)

LEE, SIMPSON - Guardian Return by Fanny Lee, guardian for Elizabeth Lee minor heir of Simpson Lee. 6 November 1837. (Pg. 72)

CHERRY, ISHAM - Report of sale of land from estate by Eli Cherry, executor. 12 August 1837. (Pg. 72)

POLK, JOHN - Settlement with Thomas Blakely, administrator. 6 November 1837. (Pg. 72)

WINDSOR, JONATHAN - Inventory. Returned by Jonathan Wellborn, administrator. 15 July 1837. (Pg. 73)

POLK, JOHN - Guardian Return by Thomas Blakely, guardian for Polly Ann Polk one of the minor heirs of John Polk. 4 December 1837. (Pg. 73-74)

POLK, JOHN - Guardian Statement by Thomas Blakely, guardian of Cassander Polk child of John Polk. 4 December 1837. (Pg. 74)

POLK, JOHN - Guardian Return by Thomas Polk, guardian for Ezekiel Polk child and heir of John Polk. 4 December 1837. (Pg. 74-75)

POLK, JOHN - Guardian Return by Thomas Polk, guardian for Elizabeth Jane Polk child and heir of John Polk. 4 December 1837. (Pg. 75)

VIARS, REBECCA - Settlement with John Kirby, administrator. 25 November 1837. (Pg. 76-77)

GARNER, HENRY - Extra Inventory reported by George Johnson and Elizabeth Garner, administrators. 4 December 1837. (Pg. 77)

WINDSOR, JONATHAN - Sale. Return by Jon. Wellborn, administrator. 1 September 1837. (Pg. 77-79)

REYNOLDS, HENRY - Report of sale of all property upon the death of Matilda, wife of Henry Reynolds. Submitted by executors Elisha Pack and Jesse B. Gantt. No Date. (Pg. 80-83)

RUSSELL, JAMES - Inventory. Returned by Thomas Tucker, administrator. 30 November 1837. (Pg. 83)

McCLAIN, JAMES - Inventory. Returned by John Martin and Manuel McClain, administrators. February Term 18--. (Pg. 84-85)

McCLAIN, JAMES - Year's support laid off for widow McClain and minor orphans. 16 January 1838. (Pg. 85)

GARNER, HENRY SR. - Settlement with George Johnson and Elizabeth Garner, administrators. 3 February 1838. (Pg. 85-86)

REYNOLDS, JOHN - Guardian Return by William and Elizabeth Wells, guardians for the minor heirs of John Reynolds. 23 March 18--. (Pg. 86)

WILLIAMS, WILLIAM L. - Sale. Return by James Warr, administrator. April Term 1838. (Pg. 87)

GARNER, HENRY G. - Settlement with George Johnson, administrator. 31 May 1838. (Pg. 87)

SATTERFIELD, JEREMIAH - Settlement with George Johnson, administrator. 31 May 1838. (Pg. 88)

NEWMAN, THOS. - Settlement with Samuel Newman and Parry B. Hawkins, administrators. 17 March 1838. (Pg. 88-89)

ORR, JAMES - Sale. Returned by John White, administrator. 2 July 1838. (Pg. 90-91)

STEVENS, HENRY - Will. Dated: 28 ---- 1838. Heirs: Wife - Elizabeth and children property to be divided when youngest reaches 21. Slaves mentioned by name: Eve, Henrita, Ezekiel, Harry, Wesley, Robert, Riley, Dulcina, Willie, Abraham, Julius, Martha, Luiza, and Manerva.

GARNER, _____ - Guardian Return by Daniel Beasley, guardian for Joshua and James Garner. October 1838. (Pg. 93)

RUSSELL, ALEXANDER - Extra settlement information for unnamed estate Russell is executor of. No Date. (Pg. 93)

WINDSOR, JONATHAN - Inventory. Returned by Martha Windsor, administratrix. 1 October 1838. (Pg. 93-94)

EMMERSON, ELI - Widow's allowance. 13 September 1838. (Pg. 95)

EMMERSON, ELI - Sale. Returned by Terence Emmerson and John Hawk, administrators. 1 October 1838. (Pg. 95-97)

OWEN, THOS. - List of property in estate. Returned by David Owen, administrator. 3 September 1838. (Pg. 97)

HANNAH, ALEX. - Inventory. Returned by George D. Morrow, administrator. No Date. (Pg. 97-98)

FREEMAN, WILLIAM P. - Sale. 11 October 1838. (Pg. 98-102)

BUIE, CORNELIUS - Sale. Returned by John Buie, administrator. 20 October 1838. (Pg. 103-104)

ROBERTSON, SAMUEL - Settlement with Samuel Robertson, administrator. 5 October 1838. (Pg. 105)

CHERRY, NOEL - Guardian Return by Samuel Watson, guardian of the minor heirs of Noel Cherry. Included are the names of slaves who formed part of inheritance. Slaves named: Sarah, Minny, Sally, Carolin, Jos., Peter, Henderson, Matilda (2 yrs. old), and Rachel (2 yrs. old). No Date. (Pg. 106-107)

LEE, SIMPSON - Guardian Return by James Robinson, guardian for Felix, Emily, and Alfred Lee minor heirs of Simpson Lee. 1 October 1838. (Pg. 107)

LEE, SIMPSON - Guardian Return by Fanny Lee, guardian for Elizabeth Lee minor heir of Simpson Lee. 1 October 1838. (Pg. 108)

COOPER, JONATHAN - Settlement with James B. Graham, administrator. 5 November 1838. (Pg. 108-110)

KINCANNON, FRANCIS - Will. Dated: 12 February 1838. Heirs: Wife - Frances, Children - David, Mary Wright, Heirs of Elizabeth Rambo, Margaret Elliot, Martha Waggoner, Nancy Ketron, James, Ann Wright, Francis, and Sally Fuller. Executors: David Cook and Daniel Smith. Witnesses: David Garner and Nancy Ashworth. (Pg. 110)

DICKSON, JOHN M. - Sale. Returned by William Dickson, administrator. 25 October 1838. (Pg. 110-113)

WINDSOR, JONATHAN - List of Estate. Returned by Jonathan Wellborn, administrator. 1 September 1838. (Pg. 113-115)

COOPER, JONATHAN - Guardian Report by James B. Graham, guardian of the minor heirs of Jonathan Cooper. 4 February 1839. (Pg. 115)

FRALEY, HENDERSON G. - Will. Dated: 7 December 1838. Heirs: Wife - Lucinda Fraley (pregnant), Son - William Jackson Fraley, Mother - Sarah Fraley (father deceased). Witnesses: John L. Abell, and E.H. Stephenson. (Pg. 115-116)

LADEN, GEORGE - Will. Dated: 28 July 1838. Heirs: Wife - Cady Laden, Children - Elizabeth Anderson wife of J.S.M.

Anderson, J.L.W. Laden, Tabitha Cane Laden, Richard Laden, Lewis Laden, George W. Laden, Jackson Laden, Alexander Laden, and Henry Laden. Executrix: Cady Laden. Witnesses: Henry Garrard, Thomas Callen and Archibald Pool. (Pg. 116-117)

KINCANNON, FRANCIS - Sale and Inventory. Returned by Daniel Smith, administrator. 22 December 1838. (Pg. 118-119)

McDANIEL, JOEL - Sale and Inventory. Returned by John McDaniel, administrator. 29 October 1838. (Pg. 119-120)

WAGGONER, DANIEL - Guardian Report by guardian of Matthias Waggoner, Nancy Waggoner, adn Francis Waggoner, minor heirs of Daniel Waggoner. 1 October 1838. (Pg. 121)

JAMES, THOMAS - Guardian Return by John Scott, guardian of the minor heirs of Thomas James. 1 March 1839. (Pg. 121)

JAMES, THOMAS - Settlement with John Scott, administrator. 1 March 1839. (Pg. 121-122)

MILLIGAN, WM. - Settlement with Geo. M. Milligan, administrator. 2 March 1839. (Pg. 123-124)

COOPER, JONATHAN - Widow's allowance laid off. 1 February 1839.

COOPER, JONATHAN - Sale. Returned by Wm. C. McFerrin, administrator. No Date. (Pg. 124-126)

FRALEY, MARTIN - Widow's allowance for Sarah Fraley and minor heirs. 8 December 1838. (Pg. 127)

FRALEY, MARTIN - Inventory. Submitted by John L. Abell, Giles McBride, and E.H. Stephenson, appraisers. Followed by notes on hand belonging to the estate. Submitted by Andrew J. Fraley and Sarah Fraley, administrators. 7 January 1839. (Pg. 127-129)

FRALEY, MARTIN - Sale. Returned by A.J. Fraley and Sary Fraley, administrators. 7 January 1839. (Pg. 129-135)

FRALEY, HENDERSON - Estate Appraisal by John L. Abell, Levi Cunningham, and T. Tucker, appraisers. 26 January 1839. (Pg. 135-136)

FRALEY, HENDERSON G. - Sale. Returned by Sary Fraley, executrix. 28 January 1839. (Pg. 136-137)

GOLDSMITH, WM. - Sale. Returned by C.H. Eads, administrator. 23 February 1839. (Pg. 137)

WELLS, JAMES - Settlement with Samuel Wells, administrator. December Session 1835. (Pg. 138)

WELLS, JAMES - Guardian Return by James Duff, guardian of Sarah Jane Wells and husband of the widow of James Wells. 21 March 1839. (Pg. 138-139)

CHERRY, NOEL - Guardian Return by Samuel Watson, guardian of the minor heirs of Noel Cherry. 30 March 1839. (Pg. 139-140)

BRATTENBOUCHER, JOHN JACOB - Settlement with James Robinson, and James Irwin, administrators. 6 August 1838. (Pg. 140-147)

WINSLOW, JOSEPH - Settlement with Joseph W. Ellis and Joshua Reams, administrators. 10 October 1834. (Pg. 148)

WINSLOW, JOSEPH - Additional settlement with Joseph W. Ellis and Joshua Reams, administrators. 1 June 1839. (Pg. 148-150)

JOHNSON, HUGH - Inventory. Returned by Lucinda Johnson, administrator. 8 November 1836. (Pg. 150)

JOHNSON, HUGH - Sale. 8 November 1836. (Pg. 150-152)

JOHNSON, HUGH - Settlement with administratrix. 12 June 1839. (Pg. 152-153)

ABELL, JAMES H. - Will. Dated: 13 March 1839. Heirs: Wife - Sarah H. Abell, Children - Laura, John, James, and Minerva. Mentions Mills owned by himself and John L. Abell on Chamber's Creek. Executrix: Sarah H. Abell. Witnesses: James G. Carlisle and Richard Thompson. (Pg. 153-154)

KINCANNON, FRANCIS - Sale. 30 April 1839. (Pg. 154)

POLK, CHARLES T. - Widow and minor heirs portion allotted. 26 May 1839. (Pg. 154-155)

POLK, CHARLES T. - Inventory. Taken by Green M. Polk and C.H. McGinnis, administrators. 24 May 1839. (Pg. 155-156)

POLK, CHARLES T. - Sale. Held Thursday, 27 June 1839. (Pg. 156-161)

HAWKINS, JNO. T. - Settlement with James O. Hawkins, administrator. 2 September 1839. (Pg. 161-163)

SHANNON, _____ - Guardian Return by James O. Hawkins, guardian for Sarah A. Shannon. Has been guardian for five years. 2 September 1839. (Pg. 163-164)

LEE, SIMPSON - Guardian Return by James Robinson, guardian for Alfred, Emily, and Felix Lee minor heirs of Simpson Lee. 1 October 1839. (Pg. 165)

DAVEY, RICHARD - Will. Dated: 28 August 1839. Heirs: Sons - William T. Davey and Richard D. Davey, Daughters - Nancy wife of George D. Morrow and the wife of James W. Hassel. Indicates that his Negro man, Masse and his mother be emancipated. Testator also mentions property in Hickman County. Executors: George D. Morrow and John Barham. Witnesses: Samuel Perkins, P.B. Hawkins, and Thomas Davy. (Pg. 165-167)

STEVENS, HENRY - Inventory. Returned by Elizabeth Stevens and Willis Lucas, executors. 10 December 1838. (Pg. 168-169)

POLK, CHARLES T. - Additional sale. 11 October 1839. (Pg. 170)

ROBINSON, ALEXANDER F. - Inventory. Returned by Dorson H. Robinson, administrator. Slaves mentioned: Sam - 17 yrs. old, Philli - 14 yrs. old, and Jo - 7 yrs. old. 4 November 1839. (Pg. 171)

DAVY, RICHARD - Inventory. Returned by George D. Morrow and John Barham, executors. Slaves mentioned: one boy David - 15 yrs. old and one boy Wesley - 17 yrs. old. No Date. (Pg. 171-173)

GARNER, HENRY - Guardian Report by Daniel Beasley, guardian for Joshua and James Garner minor heirs of Henry Garner. No Date. (Pg. 174)

LEE, SIMPSON - Guardian Report by Fanny Lee, guardian for Elizabeth Lee minor heir of Simpson Lee. 1 October 1839. (Pg. 174)

OWEN, DANIEL - Noncupative Will. Daniel Owen died on Thursday evening at 10:30pm 10 October 1839. This will was given on the Monday previous. He willed all his estate to his mother, Mary Owen. Witnesses: Caroline Battle and Sarah Ann Gray. (Pg. 174-175)

OWEN, DANIEL - Oath administered to Caroline Battle and Sarah Ann Gray to verify their presence when Daniel Owen gave his noncupative will. Oath given by Fielder Woodard, J.P. 24 October 1839. (Pg. 175)

WILLIAMS, J.J. - Guardian Report by John J. Williams, guardian of Susan, Daniel, Elizabeth, and Julia Williams grandchildren of Daniel Waggoner. 2 December 1839. (Pg. 175-176)

WILLIAMS, J.J. - Guardian Report for 1839 by John J. Williams, guardian. 2 December 1839. (Pg. 176-177)

WAGGONER, DANIEL - Guardian Report by James Graham, guardian of the minor heirs of Daniel Waggoner. 25 November 1839. (Pg. 177)

REYNOLDS, HENRY - Settlement with Elisha Pack and Jesse B. Gantt. 4 November 1839. (Pg. 178-179)

REYNOLDS, JOHN - Guardian settlement with William Wells, late guardian of Joseph and John D. Reynolds, the minor heirs of John Reynolds. Joseph Reynolds is the present guardian. 2 December 1839. (Pg. 179-181)

POLK, JOHN - Guardian settlement with Thomas Blakely, guardian of Polly Ann and Cassander Polk minor heirs of John Polk. 29 November 1839. (Pg. 181-182)

POLK, JOHN - Guardian settlement with Thomas Polk, guardian of Ezekiel and Elizabeth Jane Polk minor heirs of John Polk. 2 December 1839. (Pg. 182)

HATLEY, SHERROD - Widow's dowry laid off for Elizabeth Hatley. 19 November 1839. (Pg. 183)

HATLEY, SHERROD - Sale. Returned by James Hatley, administrator. 19 November 1839. (Pg. 183-185)

POLLARD, JAMES - Guardian Report for four years by Swain Ward, guardian of minor heirs of James Pollard. 23 December 1839. (Pg. 185)

POLK, CHARLES T. - Division of land for widow Catherine Polk. No Date. (Pg. 186-187)

POLLARD, JAMES - Settlement with Swain Ward, guardian for the minor heirs of James Pollard. Heirs appear to be Nancy and Louisa Pollard. 25 December 1839. (Pg. 187-189)

ROBINSON, ALEXANDER F. - Sale. 6 January 1840. (Pg. 189)

ASHWORTH, JOSEPH - Settlement with James W. Ashworth, executor of the estate of Joseph Ashworth. 3 December 1838. (Pg. 190-191)

McCLAIN, JAMES - Settlement with John Martin and Manuel McClain, administrators of the estate of James McClain. 10 January 1840. (Pg. 191-192)

PORTER, WILLIAM - Settlement with Eleanor Porter, administratrix of the estate of William Porter. 11 January 1840. (Pg. 192-193)

WILLIAMS, SAMUEL - Will. Dated: 7 January 1840. Codicil dated 8 January 1840. Heirs: Wife - Nancy Williams, Son - Lewis Williams, Daughters - Nancy Wood, Mary Wood and "the heirs of her body," Jane Tankersley, the heirs of dec'd daughter Elizabeth Pyburn. Executors: Charles Wood and Lewis Williams. Slaves mentioned: Harriet, Margaret, Mary, Lucy and her infant child named Green. Witnesses: Elisha Pack and William Pyburn. (Pg. 194)

ORR, JAMES - Settlement with John White, administrator of the estate of James Orr. 23 November 1838. (Pg. 195-196)

BRATTENBOUCHER, JOHN J. - Extra return of the sale. 1 June 1836. (Pg. 197)

HAMBLETON, JOSEPH - Sale. Reported by Stephen Hosey, administrator of the estate of Joseph Hambleton. 31 May 1839. (Pg. 197 carried to 203-204)

WILLIAMS, SAMUEL - Widow and minor heirs portion laid off. 5 February 1840. (Pg. 198-202)

WILLIAMS, SAMUEL - Sale. 24 February 1840. (Pg. 198-202)

COOPER, JONATHAN - Settlement with James B. Graham, guardian of the minor heirs of Jonathan Cooper. 4 February 1840. (Pg. 204-205)

ASHWORTH, JOHN - Settlement with Solomon Hudiburgh, guardian of Joseph and John Ashworth, minor heirs of John Ashworth. No Date. (Pg. 205)

ROBINSON, ALEXANDER F. - Additional inventory and sale. 21 March 1840. (Pg. 206)

ABELL, JAMES H. - Inventory. Taken 18 January 1840. (Pg. 207)

NICHOLLS, NANCY - Sale. Returned by William Nichols, administrator of the estate of Nancy Nicholls. -- March 1840. (Pg. 208-209)

RUSSELL, DELILAH - Settlement with Alexander Russell, administrator of the estate of Delilah Russell. 2 October 1837. (Pg. 210)

THAXTON, WILLIAM W. - Will. Dated: 6 January 1830. Heirs: Wife - Martha S. Thaxton, Son - W.B. Thaxton, and "other children." Witnesses: Archibald Davis, Jesse C. Kincannon, Daniel Owen, and D. Robinson. (Pg. 210)

RUSSELL, JAMES - Settlement with Thomas Tucker, administrator of the estate of James Russell. No Date. (Pg. 211)

CHERRY, NOELL - Guardian settlement with Samuel Watson, guardian of Mary, Harry Bell, and Isham B. Cherry, minor heirs of Noel Cherry. 4 May 1840. (Pg. 212)

ROBINSON, THOMAS - Widow and minor heirs' years provisions laid off. 25 April 1840. (Pg. 213)

ROBINSON, THOMAS - Sale. Returned by Elisha Pack, administrator of the estate of Thomas Robinson. 4 May 1840. (Pg. 213-216)

CRENSHAW, _____ - Settlement with Joseph W. Ellis, guardian of Jackson Crenshaw. 30 May 1840. (Pg. 217-218)

STOCKTON, THOMAS - Inventory. Returned by Daniel L. Stockton, administrator of the estate of Thomas Stockton. 5 May 1840. (Pg. 218)

KINCANNON, DAVID - Additional Inventory. Returned by David Robinson, administrator of the estate of David Kincannon. July Court 1840. (Pg. 219)

CASEY, RILEY - Sale. Returned by John Hollandsworth, administrator of the estate of Riley Casey. 6 July 1840. (Pg. 219-220)

STOCKTON, THOMAS - Widow and minor heirs' years provisions laid off. 12 June 1840. (Pg. 220)

McMAHAN, JAMES F. - Settlement with Eleanor McMahan and Alexander Russell, executors of the estate of James F. McMahan. 23 July 1840. (Pg. 220-221)

BASEY, JAMES T. - Widow and minor heirs' portion laid off. 9 July 1840. (Pg. 221-222)

BASEY, JAMES T. - Sale and Inventory. Returned by Samuel Wells and Thomas D. Shelby, administrators of the estate of James T. Basey. Slaves mentioned: Alfred 30, Washington 31, Malinda 28, Sintha 28, Mary 15, Lissa 10, Henry 12, Low 12, Manuel 8, Windd 7, Isaac 7, Amra 4, Eli 3, George, Delilah 24, Aelsey 7, Isaiah 3, and Zichariah 1. 3 August 1840. (Pg. 222-224)

BASEY, JAMES T. - Sale. 28 July 1840. (Pg. 225-229)

HUNLEY, J.Y. - Inventory and Sale. Returned by C.H. Eads, administrator of the estate of J.Y. Hunley. 5 September 1840. (Pg. 230-232)

OWENS, MARY - Will. Dated: 3 June 1840. Heirs: Sons - Thomas I. Owens, David Owens, and William H. Owens. Daughters - Virginia Roach and Caroline Battles. Grandchild: Daniel Roach. Executor: Joel C. Hancock. Witnesses: Sarah A. Gray and H. Morton. (Pg. 232)

BYRD, WILLIAM - Settlement with John R. Byrd, administrator of the estate of William Byrd. 19 August 1840. (Pg. 233-234)

WILBORN, JONATHAN - Settlement with William and Martha Brim, the administrators of the estate of Jonathan Wilborn. 4 September 1840. (Pg. 234-235)

WILLIAMS, JOHN J. - Settlement with John J. Williams, guardian of the minor heirs of John J. Williams and grandchildren of Daniel Waggoner. 5 September 1840. (Pg. 236)

STOCKTON, THOMAS - Sale. 14 June 1840. (Pg. 237-239)

WILLIAMS, WILLIAM L. - Settlement with James Warr, administrator of the estate of William L. Williams. 29 September 1840. (Pg. 239-240)

DICKSON, JOHN M. - Settlement with William Dickson, administrator of the estate of John M. Dickson. 26 September 1840. (Pg. 240-241)

MOORE, JOSEPH - Widow's and minor heirs' portion laid off. Dated during the September Term 1840. (Pg. 241-242)

MOORE, JOSEPH - Sale. Returned by James A. Nichols, administrator of the estate of Joseph Moore. 25 September 1840. (Pg. 242-243)

LEE, SIMPSON - Settlement with James Robinson, guardian of the minor heirs of Simpson Lee. No Date. (Pg. 243-244)

STEPHENS, HENRY - Settlement with Willis Lucas and Elizabeth Stephens, executors of Henry Stephens' estate. 29 September 1840. (Pg. 244-247)

FREEMAN, WILLIAM P. - Settlement with James Robinson, administrator of the estate of William P. Freeman. 25 September 1840. (Pg. 247-248)

EMMERSON, ELI - Settlement with John Hawk and Terence Emmerson, administrators of the estate of Eli Emmerson. 7 September 1840. (Pg. 249-250)

FREEMAN, WILLIAM P. - Report by Isaac Thornton, guardian of Elizabeth Freeman, one of the minor heirs of William P. Freeman. 5 October 1840. (Pg. 250)

LEE, SIMPSON - Settlement with Fanny Lee, guardian of Elizabeth Lee, minor heirs of Simpson Lee. 1 October 1840. (Pg. 251)

WINDSOR, JONATHAN - Settlement with William Brim, guardian of William B. Windsor, minor heir of Jonathan Windsor. 2 November 1840. (Pg. 252)

OWEN, DAVID - Will. Dated: 21 May 1840. Heirs: Wife and two children. Witnesses: H. Mortin, Caroline Battles, and James West. (Pg. 252)

WARD, SWAIN - Year's provisions laid off for the widow. 24 October 1840. (Pg. 253)

WARD, SWAIN - Inventory. 20 October 1840. (Pg. 253)

WARD, SWAIN - Sale. Returned by James Warr, administrator of the estate of Swain Ward. 24 October 1840. (Pg. 254-256)

LAYTON, THOMAS - Will. Dated: 17 July 1838. Heirs: Wife - Priscilla. Daughters - Martha Angeline Layton and the children of Mary Ann James. Sons - William Lawcy Layton, Thomas Layton, George Zachariah Layton. Executors: William and Thomas Layton. Witnesses: King White and Nancy White. (Pg. 256-257)

OWEN, MARY - Inventory and division of estate. 7 December 1840. (Pg. 258)

ROACH, JOHN - Inventory. Returned by J.C. Hancock, administrator of the estate of John Roach. 7 December 1840. (Pg. 259-261)

DOREN, JAMES G. - Inventory. Returned by Alexander Doren and John M. Andrews, administrators of the estate of James G. Doren. 7 December 1840. (Pg. 261-263)

DOREN, JAMES G. - Widow's and minor heirs' portion laid off. 28 November 1840. (Pg. 264)

GOLDSMITH, WILLIAM - Settlement with Charles H. Eads, administrator of the estate of William Goldsmith. 15 November 1840. (Pg. 264-265)

GARNER, HENRY - Settlement with Daniel B. Beasley, guardian of Joshua and James Garner, minor heirs of Henry Garner. 1 October 1840. (Pg. 265-266)

REYNOLDS, HENRY _ Settlement with Daniel Smith, guardian of Sarah Ann, Tabitha J., Henry, and Redding W. Reynolds, minor heirs of Henry Reynolds. 5 March 1840. (Pg. 266-267)

WAGGONER, DANIEL - Settlement with James Graham, guardian of Nancy, Mathias, and Francis Waggoner, minor heirs of Daniel Waggoner. 1 October 1840. (Pg. 268)

BLOUNT, REDDING - Settlement with Jesse B. Gantt, guardian of Susan, Henry, James, Ensley, John, and Rebecca Blount, minor heirs of Redding Blount and grandchildren of Henry Reynolds, dec'd. 30 November 1840. (Pg. 269)

PICKINS, JONATHAN R. - Settlement with Jonathan R. Pickins, guardian of Sion R. Pickins, James G. Pickins, Mary J. Pickins, Elizabeth B. Pickins, and Archibald G. Pickins, minor heirs of Jonathan R. Pickins and grandchildren of Sion Record, dec'd. 1 January 1840. (Pg. 269-270)

KINCANNON, FRANCIS - Settlement with Daniel Smith, administrator of the estate of Francis Kincannon. 4 January 1841. (Pg. 270-271)

OWEN, THOMAS - Inventory and sale. Returned by William H. Owen, administrator of the estate of Thomas Owen. 4 January 1841. (Pg. 272)

OWEN, _____ - Widow's dowry laid off for Ann Owen, widow. 4 November 1840. (Pg. 272)

OWEN, DAVID - Inventory and sale. 23 November 1840. (Pg. 273-275)

RICE, JOHN A. - Widow's and minor heirs' portion laid off. 17 December 1840. (Pg. 275)

RICE, JOHN A. - Inventory and sale. Returned by Richard Parks, administrator of the estate of John A. Rice. 5 January 1841. (Pg. 276-277)

OWEN, MARY - Return of the sale of property which had been willed to Daniel Roach by Mary Owen, dec'd. January Term 1841. (Pg. 277)

HATLY, SHERROD - Extra return by Stephen Hatly, administrator of the estate of Sherrod Hatly. No Date. (Pg. 277)

STOCKTON, THOMAS - Extra return by Daniel Stockton, administrator of the estate of Thomas Stockton. 3 December 1841. (Pg. 278)

BASEY, JAMES T. - Additional return of sale. No Date. (Pg. 278-280)

REYNOLDS, HENRY - Settlement with Francis Coburn, guardian of Tabitha J. Reynolds and Henry Reynolds, minor heirs of Henry Reynolds. 5 December 1840. (Pg. 280-281)

JAMES, THOMAS - Settlement with John Scott, guardian of Priscilla, Elizabeth, Samuel, and Dalitha James, minor heirs of Thomas James. 1 March 1840. (Pg. 281)

ASHWORTH, JOHN C. - Settlement with Solomon Hudiburgh, guardian of Joseph and John C. Ashworth, minor orphans of John C. Ashworth and grandchildren of Joseph Ashworth. 1 February 1841. (Pg. 282)

RUSSELL, WYATT - Widow's and minor heirs' portion laid off. 23 February 1841. (Pg. 283-284)

RUSSELL, WYATT - Inventory and sale. Returned by Alexander Russell, administrator of the estate of Wyatt Russell. 26 February 1841. (Pg. 284)

BLOUNT, REDDING - Settlement with Samuel Harbour, guardian of Ashley Blount, minor orphan of Redding Blount. 1 December 1840. (Pg. 285)

REYNOLDS, HENRY - Settlement with Samuel Harbour, guardian of Sarah Ann Reynolds, minor orphan of Henry Reynolds. 1 December 1840. (Pg. 285-286)

FRALEY, MARTIN - Settlement with Sarah Fraley and A.J. Fraley, administrators of the estate of Martin Fraley. 22 January 1841. (Pg. 286-288)

FRALEY, HENDERSON G. - Settlement with Sarah Perry (formerly Sarah Fraley), executrix of the estate of Henderson G. Fraley. 25 February 1841. (Pg. 288-289)

McDANIEL, JOHN - Inventory. Returned by Murdock McDaniel, the administrator of the estate of John McDaniel. 22 February 1841. (Pg. 290)

WATSON, JOHN - Inventory and sale. Returned by Samuel and James L. Watson, executors of the estate of John Watson. 28 January 1841. (Pg. 291-295)

WHITE, JOHN - Inventory and sale. Returned by Samuel White and Levi Shelby, administrators of the estate of John White. 20 March 1841. (Pg. 296-298)

WATSON, JOHN - Will. Dated: 21 August 1837. Heirs: Sons-in-law Rosseman P. Scott, John Scott, Elisha Smith, Martin Forehand, and Thomas L. Pain. Sons - James L. Watson and Samuel Watson. Others: Mary (no relation given). Witnesses: R.A. Randolph, Thomas I. Owen, and N.G. Murphy. (Pg. 298-299)

WHITLOW, HENDERSON - Will. No Date. Heirs: Sons - Ezra Forrest Whitlow, Milton Whitlow, and Paschal Whitlow. Daughters -

Permelia Whitlow and Antiwithe Whitlow. Wife - Sally Whitlow. Executors: Milton Whitlow and Daniel Beasley. Witnesses: Thomas Blakely and William Turner. (Pg. 300)

MOORE, JOSEPH - Inventory of notes. Returned by James A. Nicholds, administrator of the estate of Joseph Moore. 3 April 1841. (Pg. 301)

BASEY, JAMES T. - Extra return of sale. Returned by Samuel Wells and Thomas D. Shelby, administrators of the estate of James T. Basey. 1 March 1841. (Pg. 301)

COOPER, JONATHAN - Settlement with William McFerrin, administrator of the estate of Jonathan Cooper. 1 May 1841. (Pg. 302-303)

ROBINSON, ALEXANDER F. - Settlement with Dorson H. Robinson, the administrator of the estate of Alexander F. Robinson. 28 April 1841. (Pg. 303-304)

REYNOLDS, JOSEPH - Inventory and sale. Returned by Nathan E. Shannon, administrator of the estate of Joseph Reynolds. 30 April 1841. (Pg. 305-306)

POLK, JOHN - Settlement with Thomas Polk, guardian of Ezekiel and Elizabeth J. Polk, minor orphans of John Polk. 2 December 1840. (Pg. 307)

RIDDLE, NATHANIEL - Inventory. Returned by Evin Beachamp, the administrator of the estate of Nathaniel Riddle. 3 May 1841. (Pg. 308)

OWENS, DAVID - Additional return of sale. 1 March 1841. (Pg. 309)

OUTLAW, LEWIS - Widow's portion laid off for Matilda Outlaw. 3 May 1841. (Pg. 312)

OUTLAW, LEWIS - Inventory and sale. Returned by John Kirby, the administrator of the estate of Lewis Outlaw. 7 June 1841. (Pg. 309-312)

ADAMS, SAMUEL - Inventory and sale. Returned by Rix A. Randolph, administrator of the estate of Samuel Adams. 14 May 1841. (Pg. 313-314)

ADAMS, SAMUEL - Widow's and minor orphans' portion laid off. 5 May 1841. (Pg. 315)

MOORE, REBECCA - Inventory and sale. Returned by S. Hudiburgh, administrator of the estate of Rebecca Moore. 17 April 1841. (Pg. 315-316)

LAYTON, THOMAS - Inventory and sale. 7 June 1841. (Pg. 317)

FRALEY, MARTIN - Dower of land allotted and set apart for Sarah Fraley, widow of Martin Fraley. 21 May 1841. (Pg. 318)

EMMERSON, ELI - Settlement with John Hawk and Terence Emmerson, administrators of the estate of Eli Emmerson. 15 May 1841. (Pg. 319)

BRYANT, ELISHA - Widow and minor orphans' dowery laid off for Peggy Bryant, widow of Elisha Bryant. 17 May 1841. (Pg. 320)

WHITLOW, HENDERSON - Inventory. Returned by Milton Whitlow, the executor of the estate of Henderson Whitlow. 7 June 1841. (Pg. 320)

CHERRY, NOEL - Settlement with Samuel Watson, guardian of the minor orphans of Noel Cherry. 30 March 1841. (Pg. 321)

CRENSHAW, _____ - Settlement with Joseph W. Ellis, guardian of Jackson Crenshaw. 21 May 1841. (Pg. 322-323)

COOPER, JONATHAN - Settlement with James B. Graham, guardian of Elizabeth, John, and Vachel Cooper, minors of Jonathan Cooper. 4 February 1841. (Pg. 323-324)

JAMES, THOMAS - Settlement with John Scott, guardian of the minor orphans of Thomas James. 1 March 1841. (Pg. 325)

HAMILTON, JOSEPH - Settlement with Stephen Hosey, administrator of the estate of Joseph Hamilton. 21 May 1841. (Pg. 325-326)

REYNOLDS, HENRY - Settlement with Daniel Smith, guardian of Redding W. Reynolds, minor orphan of Henry Reynolds. 5 March 1841. (Pg. 327)

NIX, JOSEPH - Inventory and sale. Returned by Thomas White, the administrator of the estate of Joseph Nix. 5 July 1841. (Pg. 328)

NIX, JOSEPH - Widow's dowry laid off for Elizabeth Nix, widow of Joseph Nix. 19 June 1841. (Pg. 328)

FILLOWS, T.J.C. - Widow's portion laid off for Sarah Fillows, the widow of T.J.C. Fillows. 7 June 1841. (Pg. 329)

FELOWS, THOMAS J.G. - Inventory and sale. Returned by William Adams, administrator of the estate of Thomas J.G. Felows. 5 July 1841. (Pg. 330-332)

WHITLOW, HENDERSON - Widow's portion laid off for Sarah Whitlow, widow of Henderson Whitlow. No Date. (Pg. 332)

HURLEY, THOMAS - Will. Dated: 13 February 1841. Heirs: Wife - Rebecca Hurley. Son - John R. Hurley and "other children." Executors: Rebecca Hurley and Samuel Perkins. Witnesses: Allan Temples and Henry Hagy. (Pg. 333)

HAWKINS, JAMES O. - Will. Dated: 18 January 1840. Heirs: Brothers - Martin Hawkins and his children Lucy and James, Parry B. Hawkins, and Roland T. Hawkins. Sister - Elizabeth T. Hawkins. Half-Sister - Mary. Niece - Mary. Witnesses: H.G. Bodes, Bowen Davy, and John Davy. Codicil dated 6 October 1840. Mary, the niece, had died, and half-sister, Mary, able to live without a bequest from the testator. Both individuals dropped from the will. (Pg. 334-336)

HOLT, JOHN W. - Widow's portion set off for Sarah Holt, widow of John W. Holt. No Date. (Pg. 336)

HOLT, JOHN W. - Inventory and sale. Returned by Giles Holt, the administrator of the estate of John W. Holt. 21 July 1841. (Pg. 337-338)

ATER, GEORGE - Widow's portion set apart for Sarah Ater, widow of George Ater. 26 July 1841. (Pg. 339)

ATER, GEORGE - Inventory and sale. Returned by Sarah Ater, the administrator of the estate of George Ater. 2 August 1841. (Pg. 339-340)

BRYANT, ELISHA - Inventory and sale. Returned by John White, the administrator of the estate of Elisha Bryant. No Date. (Pg. 341-342)

STOCKTON, THOMAS - Settlement with Daniel Stockton, administrator of the estate of Thomas Stockton. 12 August 1841. (Pg. 343-344)

HURLEY, THOMAS - Inventory. Returned by Rebecca Hurley, the administratrix of the estate of Thomas Hurley. 6 September 1841. (Pg. 344-345)

WARD, SWAIN - Extra return of sale. 27 September 1841. (Pg. 345-346)

SHELBY, MOSES A. - Guardian return by Thomas Shelby, guardian of M.W. Shelby, Sarah Ann Shelby, Mary M. Shelby, and Elizabeth J. Shelby, minor heirs of Moses A. Shelby. 4 October 1841. (Pg. 346)

BAIN, WILLIAM - Inventory and sale. Returned by George Bain and Daniel Smith. 2 October 1841. (Pg. 347-349)

LEE, SIMPSON - Guardian settlement with James Robinson, guardian of Alfred, Emily, and Felix Lee, minors of Simpson Lee. 4 October 1841. (Pg. 349-350)

POLK, CHARLES T. - Settlement with Green H. Polk and Christopher H. McGinnis, administrators of the estate of Charles T. Polk. 20 September 1841. (Pg. 351-352)

GARNER, HENRY - Settlement with Daniel B. Beasley, guardian of the minor heirs of Henry Garner. 1 October 1841. (Pg. 352-353)

RIDDLE, BRITTON - Sale. Returned by Delila Riddle, administratrix of the estate of Britton Riddle. 24 September 1841. (Pg. 353-355)

GAMMILL, ELISHA - Widow's portion laid off for Rebecca Gammill, widow of Elisha Gammill. 1 November 1841. (Pg. 355)

WILLIAMS, J.J. - Settlement with John J. Williams, guardian of the minor heirs of J.J. Williams and grandchildren of Daniel Waggoner. 5 September 1841. (Pg. 356-357)

WINDSOR, JONATHAN - Settlement with William Brim, guardian of William B. Windsor, minor orphan of Jonathan Windsor. 2 November 1841. (Pg. 357)

BAIN, _____ - Widow's portion laid off for Patsy Bain, widow. 20 September 1841. (Pg. 358)

LEE, SIMPSON - Settlement with Fanny Lee, guardian of Elizabeth Lee, minor orphan of Simpson Lee. 1 October 1841. (Pg. 358)

FREEMAN, WILLIAM P. - Settlement with Isaac Thornton, guardian of the minor heirs of William P. Freeman. No Date. (Pg. 359)

WAGGONER, DANIEL - Settlement with James Graham, guardian of the minor heirs of Daniel Waggoner. 1 October 1841. (Pg. 359-360)

BASEY, JAMES T. - Dower of land set off for Lydia Basey, widow of James T. Basey. 22 November 1841. (Pg. 360-361)

HATLEY, SHERROD - Settlement with James Hatley, administrator of the estate of Sherrod Hatley. 26 November 1841. (Pg. 361-362)

BRYANT, ELISHA - Inventory. Returned by John White, administrator of the estate of Elisha Bryant. 6 December 1841. (Pg. 362-364)

HAWKINS, JAMES O. - Inventory and sale. Returned by P.B. Hawkins, executor of the estate of James O. Hawkins. 24 September 1841. (Pg. 364-377)

ROBINSON, ABSALOM L. - Will. Not Dated. Heirs: Wife - Rebecca; Son - David V. Robinson. Executor: David Robinson (Testator's Father.) Others mentioned: Zachariah Eaks (noted as having died in 1841); Riley Sawyers. Slaves mentioned - Dorcas and her child Molly, Manerva, Henry, Anthony, Mabe, Milly and her child Nancy, "mulatto" Ann and her child Mary, and Dilcey. Witnesses: Reuben Day and Garland Day. (Pg. 377-379)

WORLEY, GEORGE - Will. Dated: 1 February 1840. Heirs: Wife - Elizabeth; Children - Anna Worley, Juranner Worley, Abraham Worley, and other children. Executors: Abraham Worley and Jacob Vanhoose. Witnesses: Jonathan W. Martin and John Worley. (Pg. 379-380)

ABELL, JAMES H. - Sale. Returned by Sarah Grogan, executrix of the estate of James H. Abell. 2 September 1841. (Pg. 380-381)

TRENTHAM, ZACHARIAH - Widow's portion laid off for Sarah Trentham, widow of Zachariah Trentham. 4 December 1841. (Pg. 381-382)

WALLACE, _____ - Dowery laid off for the widow Wallace. 10 December 1841. (Pg. 382)

LOWRY, JOHN - Widow's and minor orphans' portion laid off. 30 December 1841. (Pg. 383-385)

LOWRY, JOHN - Inventory and sale. Returned by Kiziah Lowry, the administratrix of the estate of John Lowry. 3 January 1842. (Pg. 385)

BAIN, WILLIAM - Widow's dowry of land laid off for Martha Bain, widow of William Bain. 29 December 1841. (Pg. 386)

BLOUNT, RIDDING - Settlement with Jesse B. Gantt, guardian of the minor heirs of Ridding Blount and grandchildren of Henry Reynolds. 30 November 1841. (Pg. 387)

WHITE, JOHN - Extra return of sale. 25 January 1842. (Pg. 387)

REYNOLDS, HENRY - Settlement with Francis Coburn, guardian of Tabitha Reynolds and Henry Reynolds, minor orphans of Henry Reynolds. 5 December 1841. (Pg. 388-389)

COOPER, JONATHAN - Settlement with James B. Graham, guardian of the minor orphans of Jonathan Cooper. 4 February 1842. (Pg. 389-390)

LEE, SIMPSON - Guardian Report by Arthur B. Campbell, guardian of Emily, Felix, and Alfred Lee, minor heirs of Simpson Lee. 7 February 1842. (Pg. 390-392)

WORLEY, GEORGE - Inventory. Returned by Abraham Worley and Jacob Vanhoose, executors of the estate of George Worley. 26 January 1842. (Pg. 392-393)

WORLEY, GEORGE - Sale. Recorded 7 March 1842. (Pg. 393-395)

PARKS, RICHARD - Will. Dated: 25 October 1834. Heirs: Wife - Susan; Others - Richard Parks Kirby (son of John and Nancy Kirby), and Mary Susan Vawney (daughter of Joel and Mary Vawney). Executors: John Kirby and Isaac Vawney. Witnesses: John Barham and Bowen Davy. (Pg. 396)

RIDDLE, NATHANIEL - Sale. Recorded 4 April 1842. Submitted by Evin Beachamp, administrator of the estate of Nathaniel Riddle. (Pg. 397-399)

MOORE, JOSEPH - Administrator's return by James Nicholls. 4 April 1842. (Pg. 399)

HARBOUR, SAMUEL - Guardian Report by Samuel Harbour, guardian of Ashley Blount and Sarah Reynolds. 5 January 1842. (Pg. 400)

GAMMILL, ELISHA - Inventory and sale. Returned by James Gammill, administrator of the estate of Elisha Gammill. Recorded 2 May 1842. (Pg. 401-402)

ROBINSON, THOS. - Settlement with Elisha Pack, administrator of the estate of Thos. Robinson. 2 April 1842. (Pg. 403)

BURGESS, ELIAS - Inventory and sale. Returned by John Cooper, the administrator of the estate of Elias Burgess. 21 March 1842. (Pg. 404-405)

BURGESS, ELIAS - Widow's portion laid off for Rachel Burgess, widow of Elias Burgess. No Date. (Pg. 405)

DAVEY, RICHARD - Settlement with George D. Morrow and John Barham, administrators of the estate of Richard Davey. 21 January 1842. (Pg. 405-407)

CHERRY, NOEL - Settlement with Eli Cherry, guardian of the minor heirs of Noel Cherry. 1 January 1842. (Pg. 408-409)

POLK, GREEN W. - Guardian settlement with Green W. Polk. 1 February 1842. (Pg. 409)

BASEY, JAMES T. - Settlement with Alex. Doren, guardian of America, James, Susannah, Joseph T., Elijah, and David Basey, minor heirs of James T. Basey. 28 February 1842. (Pg. 410-411)

LEE, SIMPSON - Settlement with Arthur B. Campbell, guardian for Felix, Alfred, and Emily Lee, minor orphans of Simpson Lee. 1 April 1842. (Pg. 411-413)

ROBINSON, ABSALOM - Inventory. Returned by David Robinson, the executor of the estate of Absalom Robinson. 4 April 1842. (Pg. 414-415)

WALLACE, WILLIAM - Inventory and sale. Returned by Rachel Wallace, administratrix of the estate of William Wallace. 4 April 1842. (Pg. 416-417)

NICHOLS, MARY - Settlement with William Nichols, administrator of the estate of Mary Nichols. 28 April 1842. (Pg. 418)

CHERRY, NOEL - Settlement with Samuel Watson, former guardian of the minor orphans of Noel Cherry. 1 April 1842. (Pg. 419)

WILLIAMS, SAMUEL - Settlement with Lewis Williams and Charles Wood, executors of the estate of Samuel Williams. 2 March 1842. (Pg. 420-421)

DICKSON, ELIZABETH - Will. Dated: 20 May 1842. Heirs: Daughters-Jane and "others"; Sons - William N. Dickson, John H. Dickson, and Alexander R. Dickson. Slaves: Samuel. Executors: John H. and William N. Dickson. Witnesses: Jas. Robinson and R.B. Boswell. (Pg. 421-422)

WHITE, KING - Widow's portion laid off for the widow of King White. 23 May 1842. (Pg. 422-423)

WHITE, KING - Inventory and sale. Returned by N. White, administrator of the estate of King White. Nancy White noted as the widow of King White. 4 June 1842. (Pg. 423-424)

POLK, JOHN - Settlement with Thomas Blakely, guardian of Polly Ann Polk and Cassander Polk, minor orphans of John Polk. 29 November 1841. (Pg. 425)

ATOR, GEORGE - Settlement with Sarah Ator, administratrix of the estate of George Ator. 24 May 1842. (Pg. 426)

McDANIEL, JOHN - Settlement with Murdock McDaniel, administrator of the estate of John McDaniel. 7 May 1842. (Pg. 427)

HUNDLEY, J.Y. - Settlement with Charles H. Eads, administrator of the estate of J.Y. Hundley. 29 June 1842. (Pg. 428-430)

DOREN, JAMES G. - Settlement (Prorata Distribution) of the insolvent estate of James G. Doren. Returned by Alexander Doren and John M. Andrews, administrators. 2 July 1842. (Pg. 431-432)

DICKSON, ELIZABETH - Inventory. Returned by John H. Dickson and William N. Dickson, executors of the estate of Elizabeth Dickson. 4 July 1842. (Pg. 433)

BURGESS, ELIAS - Extra return of sale. Returned by John Cooper, administrator of the estate of Elias Burgess. -- October 1842. (Pg. 433-434)

OWEN, MARY - Sale. Returned by J.C. Hancock, executor of the estate of Mary Owen. No Date. (Pg. 434)

ROACH, JOHN - Sale. Returned by Joel C. Hancock, administrator of the estate of John Roach. No Date. (Pg. 435-438)

POLK, JOHN - Settlement with Thomas Polk, guardian for Ezekiel and Elizabeth J. Polk, minor orphans of John Polk. 2 December 1841. (Pg. 438-439)

FRALEY, MARTIN - Settlement with Joseph Perry, guardian of Nancy, David, James, Caleb, and Thomas Fraley, children and heirs-at-law of Martin Fraley. 1 August 1842. (Pg. 439-441)

ALLISON, ADAM B. - Inventory. Returned by Thomas A. Kerr and

William Alison, administrators of the estate of Adam B. Alison. 3 October 1842. (Pg. 442)

ALISON, ADAM B. - Sale. December 1842. (Pg. 443-445)

THORNTON, ISAAC - Settlement with Isaac Thornton, guardian. No other information given. 3 December 1842. (Pg. 445)

REYNOLDS, HENRY - Settlement with Daniel Smith, guardian for Redding W. Reynolds, minor orphan of Henry Reynolds. 5 March 1842. (Pg. 446)

COVEY, LEVEN L. - Will. Dated: 21 September 1842. Heirs: Wife-Sarah; Daughter - Mary; Son - Lewis G.W. Covey; and Grandson - Leven Edwards Covey. Executors: Joshua Jones and Noble H. Covey. Witnesses: Jesse Plummer, Andrew White, and Wm. O. Flemming. (Pg. 447-448)

FREEMAN, WILLIAM P. - Settlement with Isaac Thornton, guardian of the minor orphans of William P. Freeman. 5 October 1842. (Pg. 448)

WILLIAMS, JOHN J. - Settlement with John J. Williams, guardian of the minor heirs of John J. Williams and grandchildren of Daniel Waggoner. 5 September 1842. (Pg. 449-450)

ROBINSON, ABSALOM L. - Settlement with David Robinson, executor of the estate of Absalom L. Robinson. 2 September 1842. (Pg. 450-451)

WAGGONER, DANIEL - Settlement with James Graham, guardian of the minor heirs of Daniel Waggoner. 1 October 1842. (Pg. 452)

POLK, CHARLES T. - Settlement with Green H. Polk, guardian of Marian A. Polk, minor orphan of Charles T. Polk. 1 October 1842. (Pg. 452-453)

SHELBY, MOSES A. - Settlement with Thomas D. Shelby, guardian of the minor heirs of Moses A. Shelby. 4 October 1842. (Pg. 453-454)

GARNER, HENRY G. - Settlement with Daniel B. Beasley, guardian of Joshua and James Garner, minor heirs of Henry G. Garner. 1 October 1842. (Pg. 454-455)

COVEY, LEVEN L. - Inventory and sale. Returned by Noble W. Covey. 3 December 1842. (Pg. 455-456)

WARD, SWAIN - Settlement with James Ward, administrator of the estate of Swain Ward. 18 October 1842. (Pg. 457-458)

MARTIN, JANE - Inventory and sale. Returned by John Martin and Robert K. Martin, administrators of the estate of Jane Martin. 7 November 1842. (Pg. 459-460)

WINDSOR, JONATHAN - Settlement with William Brim, guardian for William B. Windsor, minor orphan of Jonathan Windsor. 2 November 1842. (Pg. 461)

OWEN, MARY - Settlement with Joel C. Hancock, executor of the estate of Mary Owen. 5 November 1842. (Pg. 462)

ROACH, JOHN - Settlement with Joel C. Hancock, administrator of the estate of John Roach. 5 November 1842. (Pg. 463-464)

CHERRY, NOEL - Eli Cherry received the guardianship of the minor heirs of Noel Cherry from Samuel Watson, former guardian. No Date. (Pg. 465)

RUSSELL, MARY A. - Guardian Report by Mary A. Russell. No other information given. 1 December 1842. (Pg. 465)

CHERRY, ELI - Guardian Report by Eli Cherry. No other information given. 1 February 1843. (Pg. 465)

BLOUNT, REDDING - Settlement with Jesse B. Gantt, guardian of the minor orphans of Redding Blount and grandchildren of Henry Reynolds. 31 November 1842. (Pg. 466)

SMITH, JOHN - Noncupative Will. Statement given by James Gammill, Aaron Anderson, and William McClain that they heard the statement of John Smith on Monday, 24 October 1842, and that he died on Tuesday morning, 25 October 1842. Heirs: Wife - Elizabeth; Son - Jarrod. Slaves: Anthony, Sophia and her child Marion, John Jackson, and Letha Ann. All of testator's children were of age. Witness to oath: James Scott. Sworn to by: James Gammill, Aaron Anderson, and William McLane. (Pg. 467-468)

WILLS, INVENTORIES, AND SETTLEMENTS

BOOK D: 1842 - 1848

GRIMES, JAMES B. - Will. Dated: 27 May 1842. Heirs: Wife - Rebecca, and "all my children." Executrix: Rebecca Grimes. Witnesses: Fielder Woodward and Samuel Watson. (Pg. 1)

OWEN, DAVID - Inventory. Returned by Fielder Woodward, adminisrator of the estate of David Owen. 28 November 1842. (Pg. 1-2)

CASEY, RILEY - Settlement with John Hollingsworth, administrator of the estate of Riley Casey. 27 January 1843. (Pg. 3)

LAYTON, THOMAS - Settlement with John White, executor of the estate of Thomas Layton. 19 December 1842. (Pg. 4)

BASEY, JAMES T. - Settlement with Samuel Wells and Thomas D. Shelby administrators of the estate of James T. Basey. 8 July 1842. (Pg. 5-7)

SOWELL, NEWTON - Inventory. Returned by John Sowell, administrator of the estate of Newton Sowell. 27 May 1843. (Pg. 7)

McDANIEL, JOHN - Settlement with Murdock McDaniel, administrator of the estate of John McDaniel. 11 February 1843. (Pg. 8)

RICE, JOHN A. - Settlement with William T. Blanton, administrator of the estate of John A. Rice. Richard Parks noted as the former administrator. 5 December 1842. (Pg. 8-9)

ROBINSON, A.L. - Additional inventory. Returned by David Robinson, executor of the estate of A.L. Robinson. 3 January 1843. (Pg. 10-14)

WRIGHT, JAMES - Widow's dower set apart for Nancy Wright, widow of James Wright. 19 January 1843. (Pg. 14)

WRIGHT, JAMES - Inventory and sale. Returned by Isaac Wright and Alex. Barham. 7 February 1843. (Pg. 15-18)

ROBINSON, ABSALOM L. - Additional inventory. Returned by David Robinson. 7 February 1843. (Pg. 18-23)

RUSSELL, WYATTE - Settlement with Alexander Russell, administrator of the estate of Wyatte Russell. 3 March 1843. (Pg. 24-25)

WHITE, JOHN - Settlement with Samuel White and Levi Shelby, the administrators of the estate of John White. 6 March 1843. (Pg. 25-26)

RIDDLE, NATHANIEL - Settlement with Evan Beachamp, administrator of the estate of Nathaniel Riddle. 1 May 1843. (Pg. 27)

WATSON, JOHN - Settlement with Samuel and James Watson, the executors of the estate of John Watson. 27 April 1843. (Pg. 28-29)

ATOR, GEORGE - Settlement with Sarah Ator, administratrix of the estate of George Ator. 26 February 1843. (Pg. 29)

POLK, JOHN - Settlement with Thomas Polk, guardian of Ezekiel and Cassander Polk, minor heirs of John Polk. 2 December 1842. (Pg. 30)

JAMES, WILLIAM R. - Settlement with Prissila Layton, guardian of Mary A. James, minor heir of William R. James. 3 December 1842. (Pg. 30)

REYNOLDS, HENRY - Settlement with Francis Coburn, guardian of Tabitha J. Reynolds, minor orphan of Henry Reynolds. 5 December 1842. (Pg. 31)

REYNOLDS, HENRY - Settlement with Samuel Harbour, guardian of Sarah Reynolds, minor orphan of Henry Reynolds. 3 January 1843. (Pg. 32)

COOPER, JONATHAN - Settlement with Isaac Thornton, guardian for the minor orphans of Jonathan Cooper. 4 February 1843. (Pg.32-33)

FRALEY, MARTIN - Settlement with Joseph Perry, guardian of the minor heirs of Martin Fraley. 7 February 1843. (Pg. 33-34)

BASEY, JAMES T. - Guardian Report for 1843 by Alexander Doren, guardian for Caroline M., James, Susannah, Joseph T., Elijah, and David Basey, minor heirs of James T. Basey. -- March 1843. (Pg. 35-36)

LEE, SIMPSON - Guardian Report for 1143 by Arthur B. Campbell, guardian for Felix, Emily, and Alfred Lee, minor heirs of Simpson Lee. 6 April 1843. (Pg. 37-38)

ROACH, JOHN - Settlement with Daniel Smith, guardian of Daniel Roach, minor orphan of John Roach. 7 March 1843. (Pg. 39)

CHERRY, NOWELL - Settlement with Eli Cherry, guardian of Mary Ann, H.L., and J.B. Cherry, minor heirs of Nowell Cherry. 1 April 1843. (Pg. 39-40)

MOORE, REBECCA - Settlement with Solomon Hudiburgh, administrator of the estate of Rebecca Moore. 28 April 1843. (Pg. 40-41)

MOORE, JOSEPH - Settlement with James A. Nichols, administrator of the estate of Joseph Moore. 23 January 1843. (Pg. 41-42)

BAIN, WILLIAM - Extra return by Daniel Smith and George Bain, the administrators of the estate of William Bain. 1 January 1843. (Pg. 43)

SMITH, JOHN - Inventory and sale. Returned by Alexander Doren and Hu. Tarbet, administrators of the estate of John Smith. 1 May 1843. (Pg. 43-45)

HOLT, JOHN W. - Prorata division(insolvent estate) by Giles Holt, administrator of the estate of John W. Holt. 24 June 1843. (Pg. 45-46)

BRYANT, ELISHA - Prorata division(insolvent estate) by John White, administrator of the estate of Elisha Bryant. 14 July 1843. (Pg. 47-48)

FELLOWS, THOMAS J.G. - Settlement with William Adams, administrator of the estate of Thomas J.G. Fellows. 28 June 1843. (Pg. 49-50)

ADAMS, SAMUEL - Prorata division(insolvent estate) by Rix A. Randolph, administrator of the estate of Samuel Adams. 27 July 1843. (Pg. 50-51)

McCLAIN, KIZIAH - Sale. Returned by Manuel McClain, administrator of the estate of Kiziah McClain. 3 July 1843. (Pg. 51-52)

OUTLAW, LEWIS - Settlement with John Kirby, administrator of the estate of Lewis Outlaw. 4 August 1843. (Pg. 52-53)

EMMERSON, ELI - Settlement with John Hawk and Terrine Emmerson, administrators of the estate of Eli Emmerson. 15 July 1843. (Pg. 53-54)

LEE, WILLIAM C. - Inventory and sale. Returned by Bowen Davy, administrator of the estate of William C. Lee. 7 August 1843. (Pg. 55)

LEE, WILLIAM C. - Extra return by Bowen Davy, administrator. 6 April 1844. (Pg. 56)

MARTIN, JANE - Extra return by John Martin and Robert K. Martin, administrators of the estate of Jane Martin. 30 May 1843. (Pg. 56)

JOHNSON, JOHN - Widow's portion laid off for Sally Johnson, widow of John Johnson. 20 October 1843. (Pg. 56)

JOHNSON, JOHN - Inventory and sale. Returned by J.S. Hatley and Joseph Bivens, administrators of the estate of John Johnson. 6 November 1843. (Pg. 57-59)

POLK, WM. - Inventory and sale. Returned by Daniel Smith and Charles M. Polk, administrators of the estate of Wm. Polk. 2 October 1843. (Pg. 60-63)

POLK, WILLIAM - Year's portion laid off for Feraby Polk, the widow of William Polk, and family. 2 November 1843. (Pg. 63-64)

MARTIN, JONATHAN W. - Inventory. Returned by Chisley Garrison, administrator of the estate of Jonathan W. Martin. 2 October 1843. (Pg. 64)

WINBORN, ELIHU - Year's provisions laid off for Katherine Winborn, widow of Elihu Winborn, and Rebecca and Samuel Winborn, minor children. 11 October 1843. (Pg. 64-65)

HUDSON, JOSEPH G. - Inventory. Returned by Alexander M. Hardin, administrator of the estate of Joseph G. Hudson. 2 October 1843. (Pg. 65)

WAGGONER, DANIEL - Guardian Report by James Graham, guardian for Francis Waggoner, minor orphan of Daniel Waggoner. 1 October 1843. (Pg. 65-66)

SHELBY, MOSES A. - Guardian Report by Thomas D. Shelby, guardian of M.W. Shelby, Mary A. Shelby, and Elizabeth J. Shelby, minor heirs of Moses A. Shelby. 4 October 1843. (Pg. 66-67)

GARNER, HENRY - Guardian Report by Daniel B. Beasley, guardian for Joshua and James Garner, minor heirs of Henry Garner. 1 October 1843. (Pg. 67)

WAGGONER, DANIEL - Guardian report by John J. Williams, guardian for Susan, Daniel, Elizabeth, and July Williams, minor orphans and grandchildren of Daniel Waggoner. 5 September 1843. (Pg. 68)

FREEMAN, WILLIAM P. - Guardian Report by Isaac Thornton, guardian of the heirs of William P. Freeman. 3 October 1843. (Pg. 69)

POLK, _____ - Guardian Report by Green H. Polk, guardian of Marian A. Polk, minor. 1 October 1843. (Pg. 69-70)

WINSOR, JONATHAN - Guardian Report by William Brim, guardian for William B. Windsor, minor orphan of Jonathan Winsor. 2 November 1843. (Pg. 70)

BLOUNT, RIDDING - Guardian Report by Jesse B. Gantt, guardian of the minor heirs of Ridding Blount and grandchildren of Henry Reynolds. 30 November 1843. (Pg. 71)

BRUTON, SAMUEL - Guardian Report by Wright Barnes, guardian of Nancy Bruton, one of the children and heirs-at-law of Samuel Bruton. 4 December 1843. (Pg. 71)

JAMES, _____ - Guardian Report by Prissilla Layton, guardian of Mary A. James. 2 December 1843. (Pg. 72)

GANTT, WILLIAM C. - Inventory and sale. Returned by Jesse Gantt, administrator of the estate of William C. Gantt. 5 August 1844. (Pg. 73-74)

REDDING, SAMUEL - Inventory and sale. Returned by James Redding, administrator of the estate of Samuel Redding. 5 August 1844. (Pg. 74)

WALLACE, WILLIAM - Settlement with Rachel Wallace, administratrix of the estate of William Wallace. 1843. (Pg. 75)

WHORLEY, GEORGE - Settlement with Jacob Vanhoose and Abraham Whorley, executors of the estate of George Whorley. 10 February 1844. (Pg. 76)

FRALEY, MARTIN - Settlement with Joseph Perry, guardian of John C., Caleb, Elizabeth, Sarah A., James, and David Fraley, minor heirs of Martin Fraley. 7 February 1844. (Pg. 77)

MARTIN, JANE - Settlement with John and Robert K. Martin, the administrators of the estate of Jane Martin. 10 February 1844. (Pg. 78)

REYNOLDS, HENRY - Settlement with Francis Coburn, guardian of Tabitha J. Reynolds, minor orphan of Henry Reynolds. 5 December 1843. (Pg. 79)

ROBINSON, ABSOLOM L. - Settlement with David Robinson, executor of the estate of Absolom L. Robinson. 25 December 1843. (Pg. 80-81)

COOPER, JONATHAN - Guardian Report by Isaac Thornton, guardian of the minor heirs of Jonathan Cooper. 4 February 1844. (Pg. 82)

LEE, SIMPSON - Guardian Report by Arthur B. Campbell, guardian of the minor orphans of Simpson Lee. 6 April 1844. (Pg. 83-84)

BAYSE, JAMES T. - Guardian Report by Alexander Doren, guardian of Caroline M., James, Susannah, Joseph T., Elijah, and Daniel Bayse. 1 March 1844. (Pg. 85-86)

CHERRY, NOWEL - Settlement with Eli Cherry, guardian of the minor heirs of Nowel Cherry. 1 April 1844. (Pg. 87)

HAMES, CHARLES - Widow's and minor heirs' portion laid off. 24 February 1844. (Pg. 88)

HAMES, CHARLES - Inventory and sale. Returned by James L. Smith and John Hames, administrators of the estate of Charles Hames. 4 March 1844. (Pg. 88-90)

LOWRY, SAMUEL - Will. Dated: 14 August 1843. Heirs: Wife - Delilah; Daughters - Vianah Kindle, Minerva Lowry, Lucinda Lowry, and Sarah An Lowry; Sons - Isaac T. Lowry; Brother - Squin Lowry. Executors: Delilah Lowry and Alfred H. Kindle. Witnesses: Eli Cherry and Samuel White. Slaves mentioned: Ben, Isaac, Sibby and her child Hannah, and George. (Pg. 90-91)

LOWRY, SAMUEL - Widow's and minor orphans' portion laid off. 15 January 1844. (Pg. 91)

LOWRY, SAMUEL - Inventory. Returned by Delilah Lowry and A.H. Kindle, executors of the estate of Samuel Lowry. 1 January 1844. (Pg. 92-93)

POLK, WILLIAM - Will. Dated: 27 May 1839. Heirs: Wife - Pharily Sons - Thomas A., Michael Lee, Charles M., George H., and William Henry Polk; Daughters - Mary Polk, Martha Polk, and Synthia Matilda Bowls. Executors: Charles M. Polk and Daniel Smith. Slaves mentioned: Lis and Smart. Witnesses: Charles M. Polk, George H. Polk, William Henry Polk, James L. Smith, and Hu. Tarbet. (Note: Testator indicated that at the time of the writing of the will, his sons, George H. and William Henry, had no children.) (Pg. 94-96)

THAXTON, MARTHA - Inventory and sale. Returned by W.C. Kincannon, administrator of the estate of Martha Thaxton. 4 December 1843. (Pg. 96)

KINCANNON, FRANCIS - Inventory and sale. Returned by Daniel Smith, executor of the estate of Francis Kincannon. The inventory included receipts from John White of Virginia. 1 July 1844. (Pg. 97)

JOHNSON, JOHN - Inventory and sale. Returned by Joseph Bivens and James S. Hatley. 1 December 1843. (Pg. 98-99)

WHITLOW, HENDERSON - Inventory and sale. No Date. (Pg. 100-101)

OUTLAW, LEWIS - Extra Inventory. 10 May 1844. (Pg. 102)

OUTLAW, LEWIS - Extra Inventory. 27 April 1844. (Pg. 102)

TOWERY, JOHN - Settlement with Kiziah Towery, administratrix of the estate of John Towery. 24 June 1844. (Pg. 102)

HURLEY, THOMAS - Guardian Report by John Hagy, guardian of the minor heirs of Thomas Hurley. 6 May 1844. (Pg. 103)

POLK, _____ - Guardian Report by Thomas Polk, guardian of Ezekiel and Elizabeth Polk. 2 December 1843. (Pg. 103)

CHERRY, NOEL - Guardian Report by Eli Cherry, guardian for the minor heirs of Noel Cherry. No Date. (Pg. 104)

HURLEY, THOMAS - Settlement with Rebecca Hagy, formerly Rebecca Hurley. Two children are mentioned: Henry and six year old Polly Hurley. 18 March 1844. (Pg. 104-105)

COOPER, _____ - Widow's dowery laid off for Mrs. Cooper. 24 August 1844. (Pg. 105)

COOPER, JOHN - Inventory and sale. Returned by Elisha Pack, the administrator of the estate of John Cooper. 26 August 1844. (Pg. 106-108)

WAGGONER, MARTHA - Inventory and sale. Returned by Matthias and F.G.R. Waggoner. 24 August 1844. (Pg. 108-111)

GAMMILL, JAMES T. - Inventory and sale. Returned by M----- and W.S. Gammill, administrators of the estate of James T. Gammill. 2 September 1844. (Pg. 111-112)

VARNER, ADAM - Inventory and sale. Returned by H.W. Daviss, the administrator of the estate of Adam Varner. 26 September 1844. (Pg. 113-119)

HAGY, WILLIAM - Inventory and sale. Returned by Henry Hagy, the administrator of the estate of William Hagy. Mentions Celina Hagy as the widow of William Hagy. 15 February 1845. (Pg. 119-120)

GIBBS, C.C. - Widow's portion laid off for the widow of C.C. Gibbs. 21 November 1844. (Pg. 120)

HAGY, WILLIAM - Widow's dowery settled on the widow of William Hagy. 15 February 1845. (Pg. 120-121)

ATORS, S. ANDERSON - Sale. Returned by M.D. Ator, administrator of the estate of S. Anderson Ators. 4 November 1844. (Pg. 121-123)

REDDING, SAMUEL - Inventory and sale. Returned by William Jones and Jane Redding. 3 February 1845. (Pg. 123)

LANE, WILLIAM T. - Inventory and sale. Returned by Thompson Hurst, administrator of the estate of William T. Lane. 2 January 1844. (Pg. 124)

FRALEY, MARTIN - Heirs' inventory. Returned by E.H. Stephenson. 3 March 1845. (Pg. 124-125)

WHITE, NANCY - Inventory and sale. Returned by Nowell White, the administrator of the estate of Nancy White. 3 February 1845. (Pg. 125-127)

GANTT, WILLIAM C. - Report of a second sale. Returned by Jesse B. Gantt, administrator of the estate of William C. Gantt. 6 January 1845. (Pg. 128)

LONG, DANIEL - Inventory and sale. Returned by Isaac Long and Rebecca Long. 6 January 1845. (Pg. 128-129)

DAVID, ISAAC - Received of Berry M. David and Alexander Vawn, the administrators of the estate of Isaac David, $617.75. This money was a bequest from the estate of Isaac David to William Brooks for the use of Brooks' mother, Charity Brooks. William Brooks had died by the time of the bequest and the money was received by his administrator, Bennett Brooks. 16 September 1844. (Pg. 129-130)

WAGGONER, DANIEL - Guardian Report by J.J. Williams, guardian of Susan, Daniel, Elizabeth, and Julia Williams, minor orphans and grandchildren of Daniel Waggoner. 5 September 1844. (Pg. 130)

ATOR, SARAH - Inventory. Reported by William Strawn, administrator of the estate of Sarah Ator. 4 November 1844. (Pg. 131)

WILLIAMS, LEWIS - Will. Dated: 26 July 1844. Heirs: heirs of deceased sister Elizabeth Pyburn, heirs of Charles Woods and deceased sister Nancy Woods, sister Mary Woods, sister Jane Tankersley, and William Pyburn, the son of Susan Pyburn. Slaves mentioned: Ben and Isaac. Executor: Elisha Pack. Witnesses: David R. Reeds and John R. Byrd. (Pg. 131-132)

WILLIAMS, LEWIS - Inventory. Returned by Elisha Pack, executor of the estate of Lewis Williams. 3 February 1845. (Pg. 133)

POLK, _____ - Guardian Report by Green H. Polk, guardian of Marian Polk. 1 October 1844. (Pg. 134)

REYNOLDS, HENRY - Settlement with Francis Coburn, guardian of Tabitha J. Reynolds, minor orphan of Henry Reynolds. 5 December 1844. (Pg. 134-135)

JAMES, _____ - Guardian Report by Prisscilla Layton, guardian for Mary A. James. 2 December 1844. (Pg. 135)

STRATTON, JOHN R. - Inventory and sale. Returned by Ezekiel Tennison. 4 November 1844. (Pg. 135-136)

RUSSELL, JAMES - Guardian Report by Mary A. Russell, guardian of Martha and Susan C. Russell, minor heirs of James Russell. 1 October 1844. (Pg. 136-137)

LOWRY, SAMUEL - Settlement with A.H. Kindel, guardian of Lucinda Lowry, minor heir of Samuel Lowry. 2 December 1844. (Pg. 137-138)

RICE, JOHN A. - Settlement with William T. Blanton, guardian of Charles O., Carroll M., and Jonathan T. Rice, minor heirs of John A. Rice. Mary Rice mentioned as the widow. 2 December 1844. (Pg. 138-139)

SHELBY, MOSES - Settlement with Thomas D. Shelby, guardian of Mary A. Shelby, minor heir of Moses Shelby. 4 October 1844. (Pg. 139)

BLOUNT, REDDING - Settlement with Jesse B. Gantt, guardian of the minor heirs of Redding Blount and grandchildren of Henry Reynolds. 30 November 1844. (Pg. 140)

FREEMAN, WILLIAM P. - Guardian Report by Isaac Thornton, guardian of the minor heirs of William P. Freeman. 5 November 1844. (Pg. 140-141)

POLK, JOHN - Guardian Report by Thomas Blakely, guardian of Polly Ann and Cassander Polk, minor heirs of John Polk. 29 November 1844. (Pg. 141-142)

REYNOLDS, HENRY - Guardian Report by Samuel Harbour, guardian of Sarah Reynolds, minor orphan of Henry Reynolds. 5 January 1845. (Pg. 142)

WRIGHT, JAMES - Settlement with Alexander Barham and Isaac Wright, administrators of the estate of James Wright. 12 February 1845. (Pg. 143-145)

ALLISON, ADAM - Settlement with Thomas A. Kerr and William Allison, administrators of the estate of Adam Allison. 28 February 1845. (Pg. 145)

SCOTT, JOHN - Inventory. Returned by Jas. Warr. No Date. (Pg. 145-146)

COOPER, JOHN - Additional inventory. Returned by Elisha Pack, the administrator of the estate of John Cooper. No Date. (Pg. 146)

COVEY, WESLEY - Will. Dated: No Date. Heirs: Wife - Nancy H. Covey; Son - John Marshall Covey. Executor: Russell R. Covey (testator's father). Slaves mentioned: Anny and Manda(age 11). Witnesses: L.H. Broyles and G.D. Morrow. (Pg. 146-147)

CHERRY, NOEL - Hire of Negroes from the estate of Noel Cherry. Slaves mentioned: Joseph, Winn, Henderson, Caroline with two children, Rachel, Sarah (too old to hire), and Matilda, a small girl. No Date. (Pg. 148)

GIBBS, JOHN - Widow's year's support laid off for Delila Gibbs, the widow of John Gibbs. 4 April 1845. (Pg. 148)

LEE, SIMPSON - Guardian Report by Arthur B. Campbell, guardian of Alfred and Emily Lee, minor orphans of Simpson Lee. 5 April 1845. (Pg. 149-150)

CHERRY, NOEL - Guardian Report by Eli Cherry, guardian of Mary Ann Cherry and Harrell Cherry, minor orphans of Noel Cherry. No Date. (Pg. 150-151)

WRIGHT, JAMES SR. - Settlement with Isaac Wright and Alexander Barham, guardians for Rachel Wright, minor heir of James Wright, Sr. 4 March 1845. (Pg. 151-152)

MARTIN, JONATHAN W. - Settlement with Chisley Garrison, the administrator of the estate of Jonathan W. Martin. 28 March 1845. (Pg. 152-153)

GARNER, HENRY SR. - Guardian Report by Daniel B. Beasley, guardian of Joshua and James Garner, minor orphans of Henry Garner, Sr. 2 May 1845. (Pg. 153-154)

COOPER, JONATHAN - Settlement with Isaac Thornton, guardian of the minor heirs of Jonathan Cooper. 4 February 1845. (Pg. 154)

COVEY, WESLEY - Inventory. Returned by Russell Covey, executor of the estate of Wesley Covey. Received by him on 9 April 1845. (Pg. 155)

WHITE, JOHN - Widow's dowery laid off for Margaret S. White. 11 April 1845. (Pg. 156)

GRIMES, JAMES B. - Settlement with Fielder Woodward, administrator of the estate of James B. Grimes. 11 November 1844. Second settlement dated 19 March 1844. (Pg. 156-158)

CARTER, SAML. - Inventory. Returned Wm. Carter, administrator of the estate of Saml. Carter. 2 June 1845. (Pg. 158-159)

SEWEL, NEWTON - Inventory and sale. Returned by John Sewell. 20 May 1843(5?). (Pg. 159)

HAM, JACOB - Guardian Report by Joseph Smith, guardian of the minor heirs of Jacob Ham. 2 June 1845. (Pg. 159)

WHITE, JOHN - Inventory and sale. Returned by Margaret White and George Johnson, administrators of the estate of John White. 30 April 1845. (Pg. 160-168)

KERR, ANDREW - Will. Dated: 2 December 1792. (Recorded in Iredell County, N.C.) Proven by Gilbreath Neil. Heirs: Wife and children. Executors: Andrew Neil (testator's father-in-law) and James Kerr (testator's brother). Witnesses: George Davidson and Gilbreath Neil. (Several documents follow the will. All were issued by Iredell County, N.C. and all attest to the authenticity of the will. The documents are dated 20 May 1845. (Pg. 169-171)

BRIM, WILLIAM - Inventory and sale. Returned by J. Kirby, the administrator of the estate of William Brim. 31 May 1845. (Pg. 171-172)

SCOTT, JOHN - Inventory and sale. No Date. (Pg. 172)

DEBERRY, _____ - Year's provisions laid off for widow Disha Deberry and family. 10 June 1845. (Pg. 172)

FULLER, EMILY - Guardian Report by William W. Covey, guardian of Rebecca E., Joshua J., and Noble W. Covey, heirs-at-law of Emily Fuller. 7 July 1845. (Pg. 173)

MOORE, JOSEPH - Guardian Report by George H. Polk, guardian of the minor heirs of Joseph Moore. 6 August 1845. (Pg. 173)

DEBERRY, BENJAMIN - Inventory and sale. Disha Deberry listed as a buyer. Returned by Henry D. Deberry. 7 July 1845. (Pg. 173-174)

WAGONER, DANIEL - Settlement with James Graham, guardian of Francis Wagoner, minor orphan of Daniel Wagoner. -- October 1844. (Pg. 175)

REYNOLDS, HENRY - Settlement with Francis Coburn, guardian of Tabitha Reynolds, minor orphan of Henry Reynolds. 7 July 1845.

COVEY, LEVIN V. - Settlement with Noble W. Covey, executor of the estate of Levin V. Covey. 29 July 1845. (Pg. 176-177)

BASEY, JAMES T. - Settlement with Alexander Doran, guardian of the minor heirs of James T. Basey. 1 March 1845. (Pg. 177-179)

McLAIN, KIZIAH - Settlement with Emanuel McLain, administrator of the estate of Kiziah McLain. 2 July 1845. (Pg. 180)

LEE, WILLIAM C. - Settlement with Bowen Davy, administrator of the estate of William C. Lee. (Prorata division of the estate) 31 July 1845. (Pg. 181)

WAGONER, DANIEL - Settlement with J.J. Williams, guardian of Susan, Daniel, Elizabeth, and Julia Williams, minor heirs and grandchildren of Daniel Wagoner. 5 September 1845. (Pg. 182)

HUDSON, JOSEPH G. - Settlement with Alexander M. Hardin, the administrator of the estate of Joseph G. Hudson. 20 September 1845. (Pg. 183)

POLK, JOHN - Guardian Report by Thomas Polk, guardian for Ezekiel and Elizabeth Polk, minor orphans of John Polk. No Date. (Pg. 184)

GANTT, JESSE B. - Guardian Report "for his children." 4 October 1845. (Pg. 184)

FRALEY, MARTIN - Settlement with Sarah Perry, wife and agent for Joseph Perry who was guardian for the minor orphans of Martin Fraley. 13 September 1845. (Pg. 185)

HURLEY, THOMAS - Settlement with John Hagy, guardian of the minor children of Thomas Hurley. 6 May 1845. (Pg. 186)

ALLISON, ADAM - Guardian Report by Thomas A. Kerr, guardian for Mary Jane Allison, minor orphan of Adam Allison. 6 October 1845. (Pg. 186-187)

ALLISON, ADAM - Guardian Report by William B. Allison, guardian of Rosanna and Esther Allison, minor orphans of Adam Allison. 6 October 1845. (Pg. 187)

SOWELL, NEWTON - Settlement with John Sowell, administrator of the estate of Newton Sowell. 2 June 1845. (Pg. 187-188)

POLK, _____ - Settlement with Green H. Polk, guardian for Marian Polk. 1 October 1845. (Pg. 188-189)

JOHNSON, JOHN - Settlement with James S. Hatley and Joseph Bivens, administrators of the estate of John Johnson. 3 November 1845. (Pg. 189-190)

COOPER, JOHN - Extra inventory. Returned by Elisha Pack, the administrator of the estate of John Cooper. 1 November 1845. (Pg. 191)

RUSSELL, JAMES - Settlement with Mary A. Russell, guardian for the minor heirs of James Russell. 1 October 1845. (Pg. 191-192)

BLOUNT, REDIN - Settlement with Jesse B. Gantt, guardian of the minor children of Redin Blount and grandchildren of Henry Reynolds. 30 November 1845. (Pg. 192-193)

REA, JOHN A. - Settlement with W.T. Blanton, guardian of the minor children of John A. Rea. 2 December 1845. (Pg. 193)

BROOKS, BENNETT - Widow's and family's portion laid off for Maria Brooks, widow of Bennett Brooks. 3 November 1845. (Pg. 194)

NORWOOD, JOHN P. - Inventory and sale. Returned by Giles McBride, administrator of the estate of John P. Norwood. 1 December 1845. (Pg. 194-198)

HARRISS, RICE AND REBECCA - Inventory and sale. Returned by William Wyatte, administrator of the estate of Rice and Rebecca Harriss. 1 December 1845. (Pg. 198-200)

CUNNINGHAM, AARON - Inventory and sale. Returned by Levi Cunningham, administrator of the estate of Aaron Cunningham. 1 December 1845. (Pg. 201)

SHELBY, THOS. D. - Stock mark registered in the name of Thos. D. Shelby. Swallow fork in the right and cross and half-cross in the left ear. No Date. (Pg. 201)

FREEMAN, WILLIAM P. - Settlement with Isaac Thornton, guardian of the heirs of William P. Freeman. 5 November 1845. (Pg. 202)

SHELBY, MOSES - Settlement with Thomas D. Shelby, guardian of the minor heirs of Moses Shelby. 4 October 1845. (Pg. 203)

OUTLAW, LEWIS - Settlement with William A. Clark, guardian of the minor heirs of Lewis Outlaw. 13 December 1845. (Pg. 203-204)

JAMES, _____ - Settlement with Priscilla Layton, guardian of Mary A. James. 2 December 1845. (Pg. 204)

BRIM, WILLIAM - Administrator's return by John Kirby, administrator of the estate of William Brim. 5 January 1846. (Pg. 205)

TRUSTEES OF SAVANNAH ACADEMY - Settlement by the Trustees. Shows that H.R. Sheilds was paid for teaching. 19 December 1845. (Pg. 205)

LEE, SIMPSON - Settlement between Arthur B. Campbell and Felix Lee, formerly a minor heir of Simpson Lee. 5 April 1845. (Pg. 206)

BROOKS, B. - Sale. Returned by James M. Brooks, administrator of the estate of B. Brooks. 25 November 1845. (Pg. 206-208)

POLK, WILLIAM - Extra return by Daniel Smith and Charles Polk, administrators of the estate of William Polk. 5 January 1846. (Pg. 209-210)

BRIAN, JOSEPH H. - Sale. Returned by Alston Hatley and Mary Brian, administrators of the estate of Joseph H. Brian. 5 January 1846. (Pg. 210-212)

WHITE, JOHN - Dower laid off for Margaret S. White, widow of John White. 3 January 1846. (Pg. 212-213)

LOWRY, SAMUEL - Extra settlement. Returned by Alfred H. Kindel and Delilah Lowry, executors of the estate of Samuel Lowry. 13 December 1845. (Pg. 213-214)

REDDING, SAMUEL - Settlement with William Jones, administrator of the estate of Samuel Redding. 5 January 1846. (Pg. 214-215)

ELLIS, J.J. - Stock mark registered in the name of J.J. Ellis. Swallow fork and underbit in right and underbit in left. 27 January 1846. (Pg. 215)

COOPER, RACHEL R. - Stock mark registered in the name of Rachel R. Cooper. Swallow fork in the right ear and underbit in the left ear. 9 March 1846. (Pg. 215)

BROOKS, BROWDER - Inventory and sale. Returned by Daniel G. Wood, administrator of the estate of Browder Brooks. 30 and 31 January 1846. (Pg. 216-218)

WHITE, JOHN - Extra return by George Johnson and Margaret S. White, administrators of the estate of John White. No Date. (Pg. 218-219)

BROOKS, BROWDER - Widow's dower laid off for the widow of Browder Brooks. 29 January 1846. (Pg. 220)

POLK, WILLIAM - Settlement with C.M. Polk and Daniel Smith, the executors of the estate of William Polk. 22 January 1846. (Pg. 220-222)

BAIN, WILLIAM - Settlement with George Bain and Danl. Smith, administrators of the estate of William Bain. 28 January 1846. (Pg. 223-224)

FRALEY, MARTIN - Settlement with E.H. Stephenson, guardian of the minor heirs of Martin Fraley. 3 March 1845. (Pg. 224-225)

ABELL, JAMES A. - Guardian Report by Lewis B. Grogan, guardian of the minor heirs of James A. Abell. March Term 1846. Guardian settlement with the same. 2 March 1846. (Pg. 225-226)

BRIM, RALIEGH - Inventory. No Date. (Pg. 226-227)

COOPER, JONATHAN - Settlement with Isaac Thornton, guardian of the minor heirs of Jonathan Cooper. 4 February 1846. (Pg. 227)

BROOKS, BENNETT - Inventory. Returned by James M. Brooks, the administrator of the estate of Bennett Brooks. 3 April 1846. (Pg. 228)

REYNOLDS, _____ - Settlement with Saml. Harbour, guardian for Sarah Reynolds. 1 December 1845. (Pg. 228-229)

REYNOLDS, _____ - Change of guardian for Sarah Reynolds from Samuel Harbour to Elijah Harbour. 1 December 1845. (Pg. 229)

WINDSOR, _____ - Guardian Report by Thomas Hail, guardian of W.B. Windsor, minor orphan. 6 April 1846. (Pg. 229)

BASEY, JAMES T. - Settlement with Alex. Doran, guardian for the minor heirs of James T. Basey. 1 March 1846. (Pg. 230-231)

POLK, JOHN - Guardian settlement with Thomas Blakely, guardian of Polly Ann and Cassander Polk minor orphans of John Polk. 29 November 1846. (Pg. 231)

LEE, SIMPSON - Guardian settlement with Arthur B. Campbell, guardian of Alford Lee and Emily C. Lee minor orphans of Simpson Lee. 7 April 1846. (Pg. 232-233)

CHERRY, NOEL - Guardian Report by Eli Cherry concerning the hire of Negroes belonging to the minor heirs of Noel Cherry. 1846. (Pg. 233)

SMITH, JOHN - Settlement with A. Doran and H. Tarbet, administrators of the estate of John Smith. 1 April 1846. (Pg. 234)

CHERRY, NOEL - Guardian settlement with Eli Cherry, guardian of Maryann, Harrell, and Isham B. Cherry minor heirs of Noel Cherry. 1 April 1846. (Pg. 235-236)

HARGROVE, STANLEY M. - Stock Mark. Smooth cross and upperbit in the right ear and split in the left. 4 August 1846. (Pg. 237)

MOORE, JOSEPH - Guardian settlement with George H. Polk, guardian of the minor heirs of Joseph Moore. 9 March 1846. (Pg. 237)

MATTHEWS, ALSA - Inventory and sale. 25 April 1846. (Pg. 238)

BRIM, RALEIGH - Inventory. No Date. (Pg. 239)

ABELL, JOHN L. - Will. Dated: 7 March 1846. Heirs: Wife - Elizabeth B. Abell. Slave mentioned: Ned. To be given at death of Elizabeth to Methodist E. Church South. To be controlled for the church by James Graham, David Thompson, and Thomas W. Poindexter. Can be sold by the "Memphis Conference" but not to be separated from his wife and children except by his consent. Executor: Elizabeth B. Abell. Witnesses: T.W. Poindexter and James Graham. (Pg. 241)

ABELL, J.L. - Inventory. Includes Negro men Ned and Daniel, and one woman Philis. No Date. (Pg. 242)

GARNER, HENRY SR. - Guardian settlement with Daniel B. Beasley, guardian of the minor heirs of Henry Garner, Sr. 23 June 1846. (Pg. 243-244)

HURLEY, THOMAS - Guardian Report by John Haggy, guardian of the minor heirs of Thomas Hurley. No Date. (Pg. 244-245)

KINCANNON, FRANCIS - Settlement with Daniel Smith, executor of the estate of Francis Kincannon. 30 June 1846. (Pg. 245-247)

RUSSELL, J.R. - Inventory and sale. Returned by Thomas M. Russell, administrator of the estate of J.R. Russell. No Date. (Pg. 247-249)

GANTT, WILLIAM C. - Settlement with Jesse B. Gantt, administrator of the estate of William C. Gantt. 23 June 1846. (Pg. 249-250)

HARBOUR, SAMUEL - Will. 28 October 1841. Heirs: Wife - Nancy; Sons - Samuel Belle Harbour(not yet 21) and Elijah Harbour; Daughters - Nancy Emmaline Kiser, Matilda Cro Robinson, and Hannah Roann Kiser. No relation given: Metil Caroline Cro Harbour. Slaves mentioned: Elias, Sampson, Kyer(f), Jonathan, Green, Ester, Orange(m), Daniel, James, Betsy, Philip, Isaac, and John. Executor: Elijah Harbour. Witnesses: John Allen, John Hollis, Arthur Garrison, Elisha Harbour, and Jesse Powers. (Pg. 250-252)

COOPER, JOHN - Settlement with Elisha Pack, administrator of the estate of John Cooper. 28 July 1846. (Pg. 253-254)

HARBOUR, SAMUEL - Inventory. Slaves mentioned and their ages: Ambrose 55, Owen 45, Isaac 22, Sphiah 35, Edeline 22, July 6, Polly Ann 6, Jeremiah 6, Peter 4, and Wm. Gorden 2. August 1846. Returned by Elijah Harbour, administrator of the estate of Samuel Harbour. (Pg. 255-259)

HARBOUR, SAMUEL - Sale. 7 September 1846. (Pg. 260-261)

VANCE, ADAM - Settlement with Henry W. Davis, administrator of the estate of Adam Vance. 4 September 1846. (Pg. 261-262)

ATOR, S.A. - Settlement with M.D. Ator, administrator of the estate of S.A. Ator. 8 September 1846. (Pg. 262-263)

GANTT, J.B. - Inventory. Returned by Daniel Smith. 31 August 1846. (Pg. 264-266)

LILLY, JOHN - Stock mark registered in the name of John Lilly. Swallow fork in right ear and cross and split in left ear. 5 October 1846. (Pg. 266)

GANTT, JESSE B. - Widow's and family's portion allotted for Rachel Gantt, widow of Jesse B. Gantt. 5 September 1846. (Pg. 267)

LANE, WILLIAM T. - Extra return by Thompson Hurst. 1846. (Pg. 267)

DUNCAN, JOSEPH - Stock mark registered in the name of Joseph Duncan. Smooth cross off of each ear. 30 September 1846. (Pg. 267)

GARNER, ELIZABETH - Inventory and sale. Returned by J.H. McCormick administrator of the estate of Elizabeth Garner. 2 September 1846. (Pg. 268)

KINNERY, ALFRED - Stock mark registered in the name of Alfred Kinnery. Cross underbit in left ear and split in the right ear. 14 November 1846. (Pg. 268)

BAKER, J.N. - Stock mark registered in the name of J.N. Baker. Cross and split in right ear. 14 November 1846. (Pg. 268)

NORTHCUTT, JOHN W. - Stock mark registered in the name of John W. Northcutt. Half cross off left ear and split in the right ear. 9 December 1846. (Pg. 268)

FULLER, EMILY - Settlement with W.W. Covey, guardian of Rebecca E., Joshua J., Noble W., and Margaret, heirs of Emily Fuller. 7 July 1846. (Pg. 268) Note: Pages are misnumbered.

McMILLAN, ALFRED - Stock mark registered in the name of Alfred McMillan. Smooth cross off of right ear and split in the left ear.

GANTT, J.B. - Inventory and sale. Returned by Daniel Smith. 5 September 1846. (Pg. 269-274)

POLK, _____ - Settlement with Green H. Polk, guardian of Marian Polk. 1 October 1846. (Pg. 275)

ATOR, SARAH - Extra inventory. Returned by W. Strawn, administrator of the estate of Sarah Ator. 2 November 1846. (Pg. 275)

RUSSELL, JAMES - Settlement with Mary A. Russell, guardian of the minor heirs of James Russell. 1 October 1846. (Pg. 276)

GARNER, ELIZABETH - Extra inventory. 29 October 1846. (Pg. 277)

RICE, JOHN A. - Settlement with Wm. T. Blanton, guardian of the minor heirs of John A. Rice. 2 December 1846. (Pg. 277)

LAIN, WM. T. - Settlement with Thompson Hurst, administrator of the estate of Wm. T. Lain. 7 December 1846. (Pg. 278)

WAGONER, MARTHA - Settlement with Matthias Wagoner, administrator of the estate of Martha Wagoner. 23 December 1846. (Pg. 279)

ATOR, SARAH - Settlement with Wm. Strawn, administrator of the estate of Sarah Ator. 28 November 1846. (Pg. 279-280)

NORWOOD, JOHN - Inventory. Returned by Giles McBride, administrator of the estate of John Norwood. No Date. (Pg. 280)

GARNER, ELIZABETH - Extra inventory. Returned by John H. McConnell, administrator of the estate of Elizabeth Garner. 1846. (Pg. 280)

WATSON, JOHN - Settlement with James Watson, one of the executors of the estate of John Watson. 21 November 1846. (Pg. 281)

JAMES, _____ - Settlement with Priscilla Laton, guardian of Mary A. James. December 1846. (Pg. 281-282)

REYNOLDS, HENRY - Settlement with Elizabeth Harbour, guardian of A. Reynolds, minor orphan of Henry Reynolds. 1 December 1846. (Pg. 282)

ALLISON, ADAM - Settlement with Thomas A. Kerr, guardian of Mary Jane Allison, minor orphan of Adam Allison. 6 October 1846. (Pg. 282-283)

OUTLAW, LEWIS - Settlement with William A. Clark, guardian of the minor heirs of Lewis Outlaw. 13 December 1846. (Pg. 283)

LOWRY, SAMUEL - Guardian Report by A.H. Kindell, guardian of Sarah A. Lowry, minor heir of Samuel Lowry. 2 February 1846. (Pg. 284)

WILLIAMS, LEWIS - Settlement with Elisha Pack, executor of the estate of Lewis Williams. 23 November 1846. (Pg. 284-285)

POLK, WILLIAM - Settlement with Daniel Smith and Charles M. Polk, executors of the estate of William Polk. 15 January 1847. (Pg. 285-287)

POLK, WILLIAM - Settlement with T.A. Polk, guardian of Martha Polk, now Martha Clark, minor heir of William Polk. 16 February

1847. (Pg. 287)

FREEMAN, WILLIAM P. - Settlement with Isaac Thornton, guardian of the minor heirs of William P. Freeman. January 1847. (Pg. 288)

COVEY, WESLEY - Settlement with Russell R. Covey, executor of the estate of Wesley Covey. 7 April 1847. (Pg. 288-289)

BAIN, WM. - Settlement with George Bain, guardian of the minor heirs of Wm. Bain. 4 May 1847. (Pg. 290)

WHITE, JOHN - Settlement with George Johnson, administrator of the estate of John White. 1 April 1847. (Pg. 290-293)

CHERRY, NOEL - Guardian Report by Eli Cherry, guardian of Isham B. Cherry and Harrell Cherry, minor heirs of Noel Cherry for the year 1847. The oldest heir, Mary Ann Cherry, has married George B. Clifton and has petitioned the court for her part of the Negroes. (Pg. 293-294)

GANTT, WM. C. - Guardian Report by Elijah Harbour, guardian of the minor heirs of Wm. C. Gantt. 3 May 1847. (Pg. 294)

CHERRY, NOEL - Settlement with Eli Cherry, guardian of Harrell and Isham B. Cherry, minor heirs of Noel Cherry. 1 April 1847. (Pg. 294-296)

LOWRY, SAMUEL - Settlement with A.H. Kindel, guardian for Sarah H. Lowry, minor heir of Samuel Lowry. 2 February 1847. (Pg. 296-297)

WORLEY, JOHN - Inventory and sale. No Date. (Pg. 297-301)

ABEL, JAMES H. - Settlement with Lewis Grogan, guardian of the minor heirs of James H. Abel. 2 March 1847. (Pg. 301-302)

COOPER, JONATHAN - Settlement with Isaac Thornton, guardian of Elizabeth, John, and Vach Cooper, minor heirs of Jonathan Cooper. 4 February 1847. (Pg. 302)

JONES, WILLIAM - List of property sold. Returned by W.G. Campbell, administrator of the estate of William Jones. 4 January 1847. (Pg. 303)

ABELL, T.L. - Sale. 6 December 1846. (Pg. 303-306)

WHITE, JOHN - Book Accounts. No Date. (Pg. 307-309)

LEE, SIMPSON - Settlement with Arthur B. Campbell, guardian of Alfred Lee and Emelia Lee, minor orphans of Simpson Lee. 7 April 1847. (Pg. 309-310)

WAGGONER, DANL. - Settlement with John J. Williams, guardian of the minor heirs-at-law and grandchildren of Danl. Waggoner. 5 September 1846. (Pg. 310-311)

FRALEY, MARTIN - Settlement with E.H. Stephenson, guardian of the minor heirs of Martin Fraley. No Date. (Pg. 312)

BRIM, WILLIAM - Settlement with John Kirby, administrator of the estate of William Brim. 29 April 1847. (Pg. 312-313)

COOPER, JOHN - Settlement with Elisha Pack, administrator of the estate of John Cooper. No Date. (Pg. 313-314)

McWHERTER, GEORGE - Widow's portion laid off for Matilda McWherter the widow of George McWherter. 1 May 1847. (Pg. 314)

BLOUNT, REDEN - Guardian Report of funds turned over by the former guardian of the minor heirs of Reden Blount to Elijah Harbour, the new guardian. 1 February 1847. (Pg. 314)

McWHERTER, GEORGE - Sale. No Date. (Pg. 315-316)

FREEMAN, WILLIAM - Amount of the estate of William Freeman in the hands of B.R. Freeman - $113.50. 4 January 1847. (Pg. 316)

JONES, JEREMIAH - Will. Dated: 1 October 1846. Heirs: Wife - Easter; Sons - None named but all noted as being under the age of 21; Daughters - Elizabeth "who should take charge of my unfortunate daughter Malecian." Executrix: Easter Jones. Slaves mentioned: Dinah. Witnesses: John Barham and Alexander Hamil. (Pg. 317-318)

ALLISON, WILLIAM - Will. Dated: 16 December 1845. Heirs: Wife - Rosana Allison; Sons - Theophilus and William B. Allison; Daughters - Jane Kerr wife of Thomas A. Kerr, Isabella Baker wife of Solomon Baker, and Polly Watt relict of Dr. Watt dec'd; Granddaughters - Mary Jane Allison, Rosana Matilda Allison, and Esther Allison, the daughters of "my deceased son Adam Allison." Slaves mentioned: Phebe, Malinda, Kizziah, Adam, Mille, and George. Executors: William B. and Theophilus Allison. Witnesses: A.M. Hardin, L.H. Broyles, and J.N. Kindel. (Pg. 318-320)

BEARD, JAMES - Will. Dated: No Date. Heirs: Wife - Cynthia; Children of my last wife Cynthia - Rachel, Margret, and William Hamilton Beard; Daughter - Jane, wife of James Ward; Sons - Anderson H. Beard and James C. Beard; and the children of my son John. Slaves mentioned: Fanny and her youngest child Elihu, Frank, Calvin, Fetney and her child Adaline, Ellis, and R.M. and W.H. infants. Executor: Lewis H. Broyles. Witnesses: G.M. Milligan, Saml. Perkins, and John J. Williams. (Pg. 320-322)

DUCKWORTH, WILSON H. (County Clerk) - Report of Revenues paid to the county court for 1847. Stores; L.H. Briscoe, W.H. Sparks, Wm. Spencer, Jacob Wolf, R.H. Cooper, J. and R.J. Barham, J.J. Williams, A.H. Kindel, W.H. Cherry and Co., Broyles and Johnson, L.H. Broyles, G.G. Bostwick, Broyles and Irwin, and L.H. Wells. 23 September 1847. (Pg. 322-324)

GANTT, JOHN - Sale and accounts. Returned by James L. Smith and Nancy E. Gantt. 24 and 25 September 1847. (Pg. 325-328)

GANTT, JOHN - Year's support laid off for Nancy Gantt, widow of John Gantt, and family. 24 September 1847. (Pg. 328-329)

GANTT, JONATHAN W. - Sale and accounts. Returned by Thomas D. Shelby, administrator of the estate of Jonathan W. Gantt. 18 June 1847. (Pg. 329-331)

HARDIN, GIBSON - Inventory and sale. Returned by David Cook and Benjamin Hardin, administrators of the estate of Gibson Hardin. 5 July 1847. (Pg. 332-335)

HARDIN, GIBSON - Year's support set apart for the widow and family of Gibson Hardin. 25 June 1847. (Pg. 336)

RUSSELL, MARY A. (Guardian) - Report of the hire of two negroes, Gabriel and Louisa, by Mary A. Russell. No other information given. 4 October 1847. (Pg. 336)

WILLIAMS, WRIGHT - Inventory and sale. 12 March 1847. (Pg. 337-340)

WILLIAMS, WRIGHT - Year's support set apart for the widow of Wright Williams. 5 March 1847. (Pg. 341)

MOORE, JOSEPH - Guardian Report and settlement with George H. Polk, guardian of minor hiers of Joseph Moore. 9 March 1847. (Pg. 341-342)

CLARK, KELSO - Inventory and sale. Returned by William Clark, administrator for the estate of Kelso Clark. No Date. (Pg. 342)

DAVIS, SAMUEL - Year's support set apart for Margarett E. Davis, widow, and the family of Samuel Davis. 10 may 1847. (Pg. 343)

DAVIS, SAMUEL - Inventory and sale. Returned by Geo. F. Benton and E.H. Shelton. 17 May 1847. (Pg. 343-346)

BAIN, WILLIAM - Guardian Report by Geo. Bain, guardian for the minor heirs of Wm. Bain. 1 March 1847. (Pg. 346)

RUSSELL, JAMES - Guardian settlement with Mary A. Russell, guardian for Martha E. Russell one of the heirs of James Russell. 1 October 1847. (Pg. 347)

COLE, JOHN - Inventory and sale. No Date. (Pg. 347-348)

HAGY, WILLIAM - Settlement with Henry Hagy, administrator of the estate of William Hagy. 1 May 1847. (Pg. 349)

GANTT, JONATHAN - Year's support laid off for America Gantt, widow and the family of Jonathan Gantt. June Term 1847. (Pg. 349-350)

JONES, JERM. - Inventory. No Date. (Pg. 350)

DEBERRY, BENJAMIN - Settlement with Henry D. Deberry. 22 May 1847. (Pg. 351)

COVEY, WESLEY - Settlement with Russell R. Covey, executor of the estate of Wesley Covey. Shows one receipt on Nancy Covey, guardian for John Covey. 13 August 1847. (Pg. 351)

BASEY, JAMES T. - Guardian settlement with Alexander Doren, guardian of Joseph, Susan, Elijah, and David Basey minor heirs of James T. Basey. 1 March 1847. (Pg. 352)

HURLEY, THOMAS - Guardian settlement with John Hagy, guardian of the minor heirs of Thomas Hurley. 6 May 1847. (Pg. 352-353)

ROBINSON, A.L. - Guardian Report by W.H. Cherry, guardian of David V. Robinson, minor heirs of A.L. Robinson. David Robinson mentioned as former guardian. Slaves mentioned: Mabe(m), Ann, Diley(f), and child. 7 October 1847. (Pg. 353-354)

COVEY, WESLEY - Guardian Report by Lawson Kelly, guardian for John Covey minor heir of Wesley Covey. Nancy H. Kelly is mentioned as former guardian. 6 September 1847. (Pg. 354)

WHITE, REUBEN - Guardian Report by Thomas White, guardian for Henry, Nicy, James, Pernicey, and Milly Francis White minor heirs of Reuben White. $328.63 noted as received in North Carolina. 6 September 1847. (Pg. 354)

ROBINSON, DAVID - Settlement with A.M. Hardin and E.W. Porter, administrators of the estate of David Robinson former guardian for David V. Robinson, minor heir of A.L. Robinson. 6 October 1847. (Pg. 355-356)

ROBINSON, DAVID - Sale. Returned by Elias W. Porter and Alexander M. Hardin, administrators of the estate of David Robinson. 1 October 1847. (Pg. 356-364)

THORNTON, NEWTON M. - Stock Mark. Smooth cross off right ear and under half cross in the left ear. 6 December 1847. (Pg. 364)

ALFORD, ____ - Year's support laid off for the widow Alford. No Date. (Pg. 365)

PARISH, SHERWOOD - Stock Mark. Split in each ear and underbit in the same. 4 February 1848. (Pg. 365)

JAMES, ____ - Guardian Report by Priscilla Laton, guardian for Mary A. James. 17 December 1847. (Pg. 365)

ABELL, JAMES H. - Guardian Report by L.B. Grogan, guardian for the minor heirs of James H. Abell. 2 March 1848. (Pg. 366)

WHITLOW, HENDERSON - Guardian Report by Milton Whitlow, guardian of the minor heirs of Henderson Whitlow. 13 July 1846. (Pg. 366-367)

SHELBY, MOSES- Guardian Report by Thomas D. Shelby, guardian of Mary and Elizabeth Shelby minor heirs of Moses Shelby. 4 October 1847. (Pg. 367)

HAM, JACOB - Guardian Report by Joseph Smith, guardian of the minor heirs of Jacob Ham. 2 June 1847. (Pg. 367-368)

WHITLOW, HENDERSON - Guardian Report by Milton Whitlow, guardian of the minor heirs of Henderson Whitlow. 1 July 1845. (Pg. 368)

ALLISON, ADAM - Guardian Report by Thomas A. Kerr, guardian of Mary Jane Allison minor heir of Adam Allison. 6 October 1847. (Pg. 368-369)

HAIL, THOMAS (Guardian) - Guardian Report by Thomas Hail. 3 October 1847. (Pg. 369)

RICE, JOHN A. - Guardian Report by William T. Blanton, guardian of the minor heirs of John A. Rice. 2 December 1847. (Pg. 369-370)

LOWRY, SAMUEL - Guardian Report by Alfred H. Kindle, guardian of Sarah A. Lowry minor heir of Samuel Lowry. 2 February 1848. (Pg. 370)

REYNOLDS, _____ - Guardian Report by E. Harbour, guardian of Sarah A. Reynolds. James M. Mathis becomes the new guardian. 3 November 1847. (Pg. 370-371)

LEE, SIMPSON - Guardian Report by Arthur B. Campbell, guardian of Alfred Lee minor heir of Simpson Lee. 30 November 1847. (Pg. 371)

WHITLOW, HENDERSON - Guardian Report by Milton Whitlow, guardian of the minor heirs of Henderson Whitlow. 1 July 1847. (Pg. 372)

ALLISON, ADAM - Guardian Report by William Allison, guardian of Rosanna and Esther Allison minor orphans of Adam Allison. Two reports. 6 October 1846 and 6 October 1847. (Pg. 372-373)

HARRIS, RICE AND REBECCA - Guardian Report by Nahom Camron, guardian of Martha Jane and Josephine Harris minor heirs of Rice and Rebecca Harris. 7 February 1848. (Pg. 373)

ROBINSON, _____ - Guardian Report by William H. Cherry, guardian for D.V. Robinson. 7 February 1848. (Pg. 373)

FLATT, WILLIAM - Inventory. Returned by Solomon Flatt. 6 December 1847. (Pg. 374)

ALFORD, J.M. - Extra return of sale. Returned by W.H. Cherry, administrator of the estate of J.M. Alford. 7 February 1848. (Pg. 374)

BRIM, RALEIGH - Settlement with John R. Shell, administrator of the estate of Raleigh Brim. 9 February 1848. (Pg. 374-375)

FREEMAN, WILLIAM - Guardian Report by B.R. Freeman, guardian for minor heirs of William Freeman. 4 January 1848. (Pg. 375)

POLK, _____ - Guardian Report by Green H. Polk, guardian of Marian Polk, orphan. 1 October 1847. (Pg. 375-376)

HARRIS, RICE AND REBECCA - Settlement with William Wyatt, administrator of the estate of Rice and Rebecca Harris. 1 November 1847. (Pg. 376-377)

BROOKS, BENNETT - Settlement with James M. Brooks, administrator of the estate of Bennett Brooks. 4 December 1847. (Pg. 377-378)

BROOKS, BROWDER - Settlement with David G. Wood, administrator of the estate of Browder Brooks. 25 January 1848. (Pg. 378)

CUNNINGHAM, AARON - Settlement with Levi Cunningham, administrator of the estate of Aaron Cunningham. 8 November ----. (Pg. 379-380)

JONES, JEREMIAH - Sale. Returned by W.T. Blanton and Easter Jones, executors of the estate of Jeremiah Jones. 28 October 1847. (Pg. 380)

ALFORD, JOHN N. - Settlement, sale, and inventory. Returned by Wm. H. Cherry and Jas. Couch, administrators of the estate of John N. Alford. 10 November 1847. (Pg. 381-382)

NORWOOD, JOHN - Settlement with Giles McBride, administrator of the estate of John Norwood. 1 November 1847. (Pg. 382-383)

JOHNSON, WILLIAM - Inventory and sale. Returned by Isaac Northcutt and Nancy Johnson, administrators of the estate of William Johnson. No Date. (Pg. 383-384)

STEPHENSON, E.H. (Guardian) - Guardian accounting for 1848. (Pg. 384)

COOPER, JONATHAN - Guardian Report by Isaac Thornton, guardian of the minor heirs of Jonathan Cooper. 4 February 1848. (Pg. 385)

MOORE, _____ - Guardian Report by George H. Polk, guardian of Elizabeth Moore. 4 March 1848. (Pg. 385)

MOORE, _____ - Guardian Report by John R. Laden, guardian of Mary J. Laden formerly Mary J. Moore. No Date. (Pg. 385)

HAGY, JOHN (Guardian) - Guardian Report by John Hagy. 1 May 1848. (Pg. 386)

CHERRY, _____ - Guardian Report by Eli Cherry, guardian of Harrell L. Cherry and Isham B. Cherry, concerning the hire of some negroes for 1848. No Date. (Pg. 386)

COOPER, SMITH D. - Year's support laid off for Susan Cooper, widow of Smith D. Cooper, and family. 8 January 1848. (Pg. 387)

COOPER, SMITH D. - Inventory and sale. No Date. (Pg. 387)

BRYANT, JOSIAH H. - Settlement with Mary Bryant, administratrix of the estate of Josiah H. Bryant. 12 January 1847. (Pg. 388)

LINDSEY, JONAH G. - Report by John W. Lindsey, administrator of the estate of Jonah G. Lindsey. 22 April 1848. (Pg. 388)

COVEY, HULDAH - Guardian Report by Edward S. Covey, guardian of the minor heirs of Huldah Covey. 1 May 1848. (Pg. 389)

HARRIS, RICE - Guardian Report by William Wyatt, guardian of William Z., Julianna, Freedonia A., and Marinda, four of the minor heirs of Rice Harris. Mentions N. Cameron, guardian of two of the minor heirs of Rice Harris. 3 April 1848. (Pg. 389)

ALFORD, JOHN - Widow's portion laid off for the widow of John Alford. 30 November 1847. (Pg. 389)

POLK, WILLIAM - Guardian Report by George M. Polk, guardian of William H. Polk, one of the children and minor heirs-at-law of William Polk. Slaves mentioned: Peter 12, Sam 9, and Patsey 35. 7 March 1848. (Pg. 390)

COOPER, JOHN - Report by Elisha Pack, administrator of the estate of John Cooper. 1 November 1847. (Pg. 390)

LINDSEY, JOSIAH G. - Inventory. Returned by J.W. Lindsey, the administrator of the estate of Josiah G. Lindsey. Mentions a slave named Hugh age 9 or 10. 3 April 1848. (Pg. 391)

BRYANT, JOSIAH - Inventory and sale. No Date. (Pg. 391-392)

HOLLAND, THOMAS - Inventory. Returned by Chisley Holland and S.G. Newton. 6 December 1847. (Pg. 392-393)

FRAILEY, MARTON - Guardian Report by E.H. Shipman, guardian of the minor heirs of Marton Frailey. 2 March 1848. (Pg. 394)

BAINE, WILLIAM - Guardian Report by S.T. Fowler, new guardian of Sarah Adeline and Mary Elizabeth, minor heirs of William Baine. The former guardian was George Baine. 7 June 1848. (Pg. 394)

REA, JOHN C. - Sale, notes, and receipts. Returned by C.W. Morris and Ginsey Rea, administrators of the estate of John C. Rea. 26 June 1848. (Pg. 395-402)

DAVIS, JOSEPH - Stock mark registered in the name of Joseph Davis. Cross and underbit in each ear. 22 January 1849. (Pg. 402)

CALDWELL, W.P. - Stock mark registered in the name of W.P. Caldwell. Cross and split in right ear. Swallow fork and over bit in left ear. 22 January 1849. (Pg. 402)

SCOTT, JOHN - Receipt of money paid by administrator of the estate of John Scott. Scott was the guardian of the minor heirs of Thomas James. 1 August 1848. (Pg. 403)

SEAY, LEWIS - Stock mark registered in the name of Lewis Seay. Swallow fork and cross split in each ear. 27 January 1849. (Pg. 403)

WOODWARD, MOSES - Stock mark registered in the name of Moses Woodward. Cross and split in left ear. 29 January 1849. (Pg. 403)

HODGES, WILLIAM F. - Stock mark registered in the name of William F. Hodges. Cross off right and split in the left ear. This mark was originally registered in the name of Alfred McMillan who has left the county and is not expected to return. 22 March 1849. (Pg. 403)

POLK, T.A. - Stock mark registered in the name of T.A. Polk. Smooth cross off left ear and swallow fork in the right ear. 24 August ----. (Pg. 403)

WALLACE, JENNETTE - Stock mark registered in the name of Jennette Wallace. Cross and split in the right ear. Swallow fork in the left ear. 28 September 1849. (Pg. 403)

LOOSE WILLS

1853 - 1859

The following are a few wills pulled from loose files for the period prior to 1860. These loose files include wills written from 1838 to the 1890's. Some, however, were recorded in either Book B or Book D. The wills abstracted below are the ones which were not included in either of the will books.

NORTHCUTT, ISAAC - Will. Dated: 13 September 1858. Heirs: Wife - Jane Northcutt; Sons - Lewis B. Northcutt, Alford Northcutt Isaac Northcutt, Jefferson Northcutt, and James K.P. Northcutt; Daughters - Nancy Johnson, Jennetta Holt, and Sarah Ann Northcutt. Executor: Jane Northcutt. Witnesses: G.M. Hamilton and James W. Irwin.

PACK, ELISHA - Will. Dated: 3 May 1859. Heirs: Wife and children. Executors: Francis A. Pack and Peter Pack. Witnesses: Elijah Harbour, A.G. Blount, and E----- Blount. Codicil dated 1860: Mentions daughter Nance Pack and wife Harret Pack. John Pack's estate is noted and Elizabeth Huston mentioned as an heir.

PLUMMER, JESSE - Will. Dated: 30 November 1856. Heirs: Wife - Mary A.S. Plummer; Son - Emsley Plummer; Daugher - Elisabeth P. White. Executors: N.W. Covey and Daniel Perkins. Witnesses: Jesse Powers and E.L.M. Perkins.

ROSE, SARAH - Will. Dated: 14 December 1853. Heirs: Daughters - Elizabeth Snow, Martha Benham, and other children. Witnesses: Samuel Watson and Margaret Watson.

SPAIN, JOHN D. - Will. Dated: 1 March 1853. Heirs: Wife - Elizabeth. Grandchildren: John, Green, Charlotte, and America Britton children of William and Patsy Britton; Charlotte and John Belcher children of Alia Belcher; John, Charlotte, and James D. Spain children of Peter D. Spain; all the children of Lotty McIntosh; all the children of Tempy Thompson. Sons - Marshall D. Spain and John D. Spain. Daughter - Sooky Bell. Executor: W.G. Campbell. Witnesses: C.W. Taliaferro and T.J. Campbell.

This will was presented in court on 25 November 1853 for probate by Washington G. Campbell. Larkin F. Bell and wife Susan Bell, John D. Spain, Peter D. Spain, Marshall D. Spain, William Thompson and his wife Tempy Thompson petitioned the court to revoke the probate of the will.

THE LAND SURVEYS

Entry Books 1 and 2 of Hardin County Surveys cover the period 1820 to 1837. The deed entry book for this period exists but none of the deeds do. These records document the survey of land granted through a series of Occupant Claim Acts and military warrants.

The entries are arranged alphabetically and special items of interest are occasionally noted beneath some entries. It may be helpful to consult the microfilm copy of these books at the Tennessee State Library and Archives. Some pages had gotten wet and these were blurred. If there is a discrepancy in spelling or for additional information(i.e. military warrant number, name of person land was transferred from, etc.), consult the microfilm.

Only the person or persons the land was surveyed for are listed. Individuals who transferred property to the persons for whom the survey was made are not. The location of the survey varies from White Oak Creek to East of the Tennessee River. The entries showing the location as "E. Tenn. River" and "W. Tenn. River" mean east of the river or west of the river. Obtaining a map of the county would prove helpful in locating the site of the survey.

LAND SURVEYS
ENTRY BOOKS ONE AND TWO
1820 - 1837

NAME	ACREAGE	LOCATION	DATE	BOOK AND PAGE NO.
ABELL, James & John	25	Chamber's Creek	6 October 1837	2-203
ABLES, Ezekel	143&3/4	Lick Creek	18 October 1828	1-283
ABLES, John L. & James H.	200	" "	----------	1-315
ADAMS, Jacob	121	Tenn. River	4 May 1837	2-150
ADAMS, Samuel	200	" "	1 June 1827	1-274
AKINS, William	52½	----------	22 May 1824	1-192
ALEXANDER, Richard R.	91	Horse Creek	15 April 1837	2-157
ALLEN, Micager	35¼	Turkey Creek	22 November 1837	2-214
ALLEN, Wilson	40	----------	21 May 1823	1-91
ALLISON, Robt.	166	Tenn. River	4 April 1837	2-106
ANDERSON, Rachel	105&1/3	White Oak Creek	30 January 1833	1-319
ASHWORTH, J.	50	----------	13 August 1825	1-165
ASHWORTH, Joseph	27	Indian Creek	27 February 1823	1-66
BAITY, Andrew	50	----------	20 January 1837	2-189
BAKER, Dunning	13	Rain's Creek	15 April 1825	2-39

202

Name	Acres	Creek	Date	Ref
BAKER, Dunning	20	Rain's Creek	15 April 1825	2-39
BAKER, Jacob	200	-------------	30 November 1835	1-205
BANKS, Enoch	30	-------------	10 July 1827	1-256
BANKS, Simon	56	Turkey Creek	19 November 1836	2-74
BARGE, Jeremiah	14¾	Horse Creek	2 October 1826	1-164
BARNES, James & Jas. Huddleston	320	Sassafras Creek	20 February 1821	2-1
" "	50	-------------	20 February 1821	2-3
" "	50	-------------	16 March 1822	2-15
" "	10	Camp Creek	10 February 1825	2-47
BARNES, Right	200	-------------	2 March 1837	2-118
BARNES, Thos. B.	200	-------------	14 February 1828	1-280
BARNETT, James	159	Indian Creek	3 October 1836	2-62
BARNETT, Jessie	115¾	-------------	21 October 1836	2-91
BARNETT, Wm.	140¾	-------------	22 October 1836	2-92
BARNS, James	2	Turkey Creek	1 July 1826	1-156
BARR, Silas	320	-------------	4 January 1823	1-76
" "	32	-------------	26 September 1825	1-151
BASS, Wm. B.	23	-------------	4 January 1826	1-149
" " "	50	Indian Creek	4 January 1826	1-149

Name	Acres	Location	Date	Ref
BASS, Wm. B.	50	Indian Creek	18 January 1826	1-148
BEARD, A.H.	40	E. Tenn. River	14 April 1837	2-116
BEARD, James A.	34	" "	14 April 1837	2-115
BEARD, James C.	33	Tenn. River	13 April 1837	2-115
BEARDE, John L.	640	Tenn. River	8 December 1826	1-251
BELL, James	34	------------	6 July 1826	1-153
" "	40	------------	1 July 1826	1-154
BERRY, Samuel	160	Short Creek	17 February 1821	2-6
BINGHAM, Alex.	185½	White Oak Creek	-- -------- 1833	1-317
BINGHAM, Alexander	25	------------	2 August 1826	1-255
BINONE, Norwood	200	E. Tenn. River	20 August 1837	2-150
BITTLES, James	132	------------	12 June 1837	2-142
BIVINS, Barnabas	166&3/4	------------	12 August 18--	1-316
BLACK, Jessie	95	Short Creek	29 October 1836	2-71
BLACKSHEAR, Elijah	100	------------	9 October 1835	2-58
BLACKWELL, Thos.	15	Turkey Creek	13 July 1837	2-152
BLANTON, William T.	75	------------	1 April 1827	1-279
BLANTON, Wm.	133&3/4	Beason's Creek	9 September 1836	2-60
BLOUNT, Isaac	10	Turkey Creek	23 October 1824	1-133

BLOUNT, William	13	Choat's Creek	2 November 1824	1-133
BOHANNON(?), David	134	Horse Creek	5 September 1836	2-83
BOWLS, Nathan	100	--------	25 February 1837	2-125
BOWYAR(?), Adam	30¼&9poles	Turkey Creek	8 September 1837	2-178
BOYD, James	8	--------	20 February 1823	1-67
BOYD, James Sr. & James Jr.	480	Swift Creek	25 February 1823	1-66
BOYD, John	160	--------	6 January 1822	1-40
" "	40	Horse Creek	1 July 1831	1-170
" "	20	" "	26 May 1835	1-176
BRASFIELD, G.	2560	--------	5 April 1823	1-181
BRAZELTON, Hannah	100	--------	25 July 1821	2-22
BREWER, Sterling	125	--------	15 May 1823	1-64
BREWTON, Samuel	20	--------	7 December 1826	1-247
" "	22	--------	10 December 1826	1-248
BREWTON, Samuel S.	175	--------	30 October 1828	1-287
BRIGGS, Jessie	196	Tenn. River	26 April 1837	2-158
BRITTON, William	200	--------	25 April 1829	1-296
BROOKS, Bailey	160	White's Creek	10 May 1823	1-87
" "	70½	" "	18 September 1837	2-185
BROOKS, Bennett	50	" "	5 October 1824	1-127

BROOKS, Bennett	97	E. Tenn. River	28 March 1837	2-184
BROOKS, Charles	115	-------------	14 April 1837	2-169
BROOKS, Isaac	25	Horse Creek	6 September 1837	2-188
BROOKS, Terrel	125	Tenn. River	28 March 1837	2-109
BROWN, Dickson	150	Beeson's Creek	1 January 1831	1-303
BROWN, Hamilton	250	-------------	1 May 1823	1-182
BROWN, Henry H.	96	-------------	9 March 1825	1-244
BROWN, Jessie	20	-------------	19 May 1826	2-34
" "	10	-------------	19 May 1825(?)	2-35
BROWN, William	200	-------------	10 May 1827	1-273
BROYLES, John	63	Turkey Creek	11 August 1837	2-170
BROYLES, John S.	34	Tenn. River	19 October 1836	2-68
BROYLES, L.H.	15	-------------	20 September 1825	1-147
BROYLES, Lewis H.	45	-------------	25 September 1825	1-148
BRYAN, Phillips	164	Tenn. River	20 August 1827	1-276
BRYANT, Brooks P.	200	-------------	1 August 1827	1-278
BUCKMAN, David	30	Indian Creek	10 May 1825	1-144
BUNDY, John	76&7/8	" "	12 October 1836	2-65
BURAM, Peter	38	Horse Creek	2 October 1826	1-163
BURGE, Richard	8	Turkey Creek	7 May 1825	1-142

Name	Acres	Location	Date	Ref
BURGS, Henry	12	Horse Creek	1 October 1826	1-163
BURTON, John	15	Indian Creek	7 September 1837	2-176
BURTWELL, John T.	150	White's Creek	5 September 1833	1-264
" "	50	------------	10 February 1835	1-265
BUSHER, Thos.	50	------------	26 February 1828	1-169
BUTCHER, Thomas	200	Horse Creek	-- -------- 1827	1-168
" "	20	" "	18 January 1831	1-169
BUTLER, Thos.	50	------------	6 March 1823	1-63
BYRD, D.E.	124½	Tenn. River	24 April 1832	2-194
BYRD, John R.	119&3/4	------------	24 April 1837	2-133
BYRD, Lore(widow)	102	------------	24 April 1837	2-134
BYRUM(?), Peter	10½	------------	20 May 1823	1-94
CAGLE, George	100	Rain's Creek	31 December 1826	2-50
" "	57¼	Swift Creek	6 July 1837	2-185
CAIGLE, Henry	200	E. Tenn. River	3 February 1837	2-104
" "	149	Indian Creek	6 July 1837	2-171
CALDER, Robert	200	------------	6 May 1829	1-300
CAMBELL, Archibald A.	---	------------	4 January 1827	2-51
CAMBLE, Collin	500	Camp Creek	27 November 1820	2-4
" "	500	" "	26 October 1821	2-4

Name	Acres	Location	Date	Ref
CAMBLE, Collin	500	Camp Creek	27 November 1820	2-5
" "	500	" "	27 November 1820	2-6
CAMPBELL, Samuel	200	E. Tenn. River	2 March 1837	2-110
CARLISLE, James	200	-------------	15 August 1831	1-305
CARTER, William	38½	-------------	2 October 1834	1-324
CASTLEMAN, Andrew G.	200	-------------	18 March 1828	1-258
CATHEY, Geo. & Wm. Campbell	115	-------------	7 March 1825	1-245
CHAMBERS, John	200	-------------	-- March 1832	1-307
CHAPELL, Richard	45	W. Tenn. River	18 February 1837	2-113
CHERRY, Daniel	50	English Creek	22 May 1821	1-20
" "	30	" "	-- --- 1821	1-21
" "	100	Roger's Creek	21 April 1821	1-15
" "	44	English's Creek	-------------	1-22
" "	6	" "	22 May 1821	1-23
" "	15	Turkey Creek	23 May 1821	1-26
" "	150	-------------	3 September 1821	1-28
" "	120	-------------	5 September 1821	1-33
" "	70	Stut's Creek	26 December 1822	1-54
" "	10	Indian Creek	2 January 1823	1-55
" "	50	-------------	26 December 1822	1-73

CHERRY, Daniel	90	----------	27 February 1823	1-77
"	20	Indian Creek	27 February 1823	1-77
"	60	Horse Creek	15 March 1823	1-97
"	160	" "	15 March 1823	1-99
"	100	Turkey Creek	9 May 1823	1-98
"	100	Indian Creek	----------	1-100
"	73½	----------	----------	1-99
"	11	Turkey Creek	22 May 1823	1-102
"	40	Indian Creek	11 May 1823	1-102
"	165	" "	16 July 1823	1-107
"	14	Turkey Creek	24 August 1823	1-109
"	71¼	White's Creek	18 August 1823	1-110
"	50	Turkey Creek	15 October 1824	1-129
"	25	" "	26 November 1824	1-131
"	160	" "	21 October 1824	1-132
"	80	----------	20 October 1826	1-161
"	151½	----------	23 July 1823	1-189
"	274	----------	24 July 1823	1-191
"	160	White Oak Creek	27 August 1821	2-10
"	160	----------	9 July 1821	2-10

CHERRY, Daniel	190	----------	9 May 1822	2-19
CHERRY, Darling	40	Horse Creek	21 April 1821	1-73
" "	50	----------	26 December 1822	1-100
" "	100	Indian Creek	7 May 1823	1-107
" "	100	" "	16 July 1823	1-107
CHERRY, David	184	----------	1 November 1825	2-45
" "	122½	----------	11 September 1836	2-63
CHERRY, Eli	154	Horse Creek	4 September 1821	1-31
" "	228	----------	14 November 1826	1-249
CHERRY, Isham	640	Swift Creek	11 February 1821	1-3
" "	80	Horse Creek	20 April 1821	1-6
" "	30	" "	20 April 1821	1-23
" "	640	Tenn. River	20 December 1822	1-32
" "	640	Turkey Creek	6 April 1821	1-46
" "	7	----------	15 April 1821	1-49
" "	228	Turkey Creek	5 April 1821	1-50
" "	14	Swift Creek	5 April 1821	1-51
" "	50	Tenn. River	21 November 1823	1-117
" "	50	" "	23 July 1823	1-189
CHILDERS, Peter	174	----------	12 June 1835	1-331

210

Name	Acres	Location	Date	Ref
CHILDRESS, John	200	----------	8 August 1833	1-213
CHILDRESS, John Sr.	54	Beeson's Creek	24 November 1828	1-286
CHISHOLM, John & James	160	Tenn. River	30 May 1823	1-187
CHISHOLM, John	100	" "	20 June 1823	1-185
" "	100	----------	26 November 1824	1-202
CLARK, Wm.	72	E. Tenn. River	17 March 1837	2-119
CLIFTON, Eldridge	51½	Hardin's Creek	7 July 1837	2-209
CLIFTON, Turner C.	200	----------	8 June 1831	1-232
CLINKENBIRD, Wm.	200	----------	17 October 1836	2-176
CLOUD, Isaac	100	Owl Creek	26 October 1836	2-76
COBLE, William	137½	----------	18 November 1836	2-76
COCKBUN, Headley	50	----------	7 December 1836	2-202
COLDER, Robert	160	Chamber's Creek	27 July 1837	2-173
COLLINS, Thos.	150	----------	1 February 1837	2-202
CONE, John	106	----------	28 August 1827	1-272
CONNELLY, Peter	10	----------	24 April 1825	2-43
" "	7	----------	13 May 1825	2-44
COOK, Christian	80	Horse Creek	9 June 1837	2-149
COOK, Mortin	25	----------	25 November 1824	1-134
COOPER, John	25	Horse Creek	27 January 1827	1-172

COOPER, John	15	Horse Creek	5 August 1836	1-204
COOPER, Jonathan	100	White Oak Creek	3 October 1828	1-293
"	3	Hardin's Creek	10 July 1825	2-36
"	10	"	10 February 1825	2-37
"	80&3/4	Indian Creek	3 June 1837	2-148
COPELAND, Solomon	150	Tenn. River	21 November 1837	2-213
CORTNEY, Jonathan	24	E. Tenn. River	15 November 1836	2-196
CORY, Russell R.	90	Turkey Creek	18 October 1837	2-211
COURTNEY, John	200	E. Tenn. River	12 January 1837	2-98
COURTNEY, Jonathan	26	Indian Creek	8 July 1824	1-124
"	10	"	22 July 1824	1-125
"	5	"	22 July 1824	1-126
"	13	----------	26 January 1826	1-136
COX, Meredith	25	Horse Creek	16 May 1833	1-172
COX, William	200	Lick Creek	1 May 1832	1-308
CRABB, Steven & James Wright	125	----------	-- --- 1833	1-323
CRAMPTON, John	163	Turkey Creek	23 March 1834	1-213
CROSS, Henry	10	Turkey Creek	25 March 1821	1-47
"	60	Swift Creek	25 April 1823	1-60
"	50	Horse Creek	6 June 1827	1-166

CROSS, Henry	100	Horse Creek	7 June 1827	1-175
CROWNOVER, Joseph	200	Owl Creek	22 December 1830	1-313
CRUNK, Wm.	199½	Tenn. River	20 September 1837	2-192
CUMMINS, Christopher N.	135	----------------	23 March 1834	1-323
CUNNINGHAM, Levi	200	----------------	19 April 1837	2-145
" "	199½	----------------	16 December ----	2-216
CUNNINGHAM, Thos.	200	White Oak Creek	1 October 1831	1-262
DALTON, Elishia & Samuel	320	----------------	----------------	1-1
DANIEL, Pompey	38	Turkey Creek	31 August 1824	1-129
" "	25	Horse Creek	12 October 1826	1-158
DANIEL, Robert	74	Lick Creek	11 September 1828	1-285
DARLTON, Davis	200	----------------	5 November 1836	2-143
DARVEN, Andrew	290	----------------	16 January 1823	1-41
DAVIS, Archibald	10	----------------	-- ------- 1824	1-119
DAVIS, H.W.	150	E. Tenn. River	14 September 1837	2-181
DAVY, Bowen	200	Tenn. River	-- October 1828	1-294
DAVY, John	100	Tenn. River	-- ------- 1833	1-322
DEBERRY, L.W.	105	" "	9 October 1836	2-207
DELANY, John	25	----------------	13 November 1828	1-266
DICKEY, Alexander	53	Turkey Creek	11 October 1836	2-64

DICKS, Sampson	200	Tenn. River	30 April 1829	1-297
DILL, Asa	200	" "	18 October 1828	1-304
DILL, James	200	Snake Creek	2 April 1828	1-282
DODDS, Josiah	185	W. Tenn. River	8 August 1837	2-174
DONOVEN, Andrew	71	Turkey Creek	9 May 1823	1-93
"	82	"	12 May 1823	1-94
"	1412	Tenn. River	3 June 1823	1-97
"	40	" "	2 March 1825	1-243
DOWNING, Wm.	131½	Indian Creek	17 August 1837	2-168
DUCKWORTH, W.J.	117½	Turkey Creek	22 November 1837	2-214
DUFF, Robert	50	Indian Creek	26 September 1836	2-97
EMBERSON, Isaac	20	" "	4 January 1823	1-38
"	2	" "	4 January 1823	1-51
EMERSON, Isaac	121	----------	13 December 1836	2-81
EMERSON, Thomas	164	White Oak Creek	2 February 1833	1-318
ENGLISH, James	230	Turkey Creek	1 March 1823	1-54
"	90	" "	20 May 1823	1-96
"	160	" "	20 May 1823	1-104
"	15	Tenn. River	2 March ----	1-242
"	30	" "	1 March 1825	1-245

ENGLISH, James	100	----------	14 December 1826	1-248
" "	69	Tenn. River	16 October 1829	1-302
FALLS, William	640	Raines Creek	-- October 1820	1-1
FALKNER, Lewis N.	160	----------	----------	1-106
" "	25	Turkey Creek	20 November 1825	1-150
FARRAR, Jefferson	176	Horse Creek	4 September 1821	1-27
FARRAR, John	100	E. Tenn. River	25 January 1837	2-89
(This land surveyed by virtue of an act of the legislature for the purpose of building mills.)				
FERRILL, William	50	Tenn. River	12 December 1826	1-252
" "	150	" "	1 April 1827	1-279
FLANNARY, Daniel A.	20	Wayne County	----------	2-29
FORBES, James	200	Tenn. River	29 December 1829	1-303
FORBES, Robert	20	Indian Creek	24 June 1824	1-125
FORD, John	100	Tenn. River	4 March 1829	1-298
FOSTER, Anthony	200	Lick Creek	15 August 1831	1-219
FOSTER, Robert	20	Indian Creek	12 February 1825	2-28
FRALEY, Martin	15	W. Tenn. River	6 January 1837	2-87
" "	15	W. Tenn. River	6 January 1837	2-87
FREEMAN, Tally	162	E. Tenn. River	9 February 1837	2-179
FRILEY, Martin	200	Tenn. River	26 February 1829	1-299

Name	Acres	Location	Date	Ref
FULLER, John	78¼	Rogers' Creek	28 April 1837	2-195
FURGERSON, Regal, Geo. R. Craft, Jas. G. Walker, Evlin Young, & Ada Harris	155&7/8	Moses Branch	16 June 1832	2-53
"	18	Ross Creek	7 April 1834	2-54
"	25	----------	16 June 1834	2-55
GAMMILL, Ebenezer(?)	20	Long Creek	9 June 1824	1-119
GAMMILL, Moses	15	Turkey Creek	27 October 1825	1-147
GAMMILL, Wm.	200	" "	17 August 1836	1-235
GANT, Jesse B.	150	" "	15 October 1824	1-130
GARLAND, John & James Robinson	228	Tenn. River	3 January 1823	1-41
GARNER, Henry	10	Indian Creek	27 June 1825	1-139
"	45	" "	7 December 1836	2-80
GARRARD, Henry	219	" "	7 November 1837	2-215
GARRISON, Ezekiel	6	----------	9 June 1824	1-119
"	14	Horse Creek	10 June 1824	1-120
"	5	" "	10 June 1824	1-120
GARVILL, Elisha	155	E. Tenn. River	5 September 1836	2-136
GIBSON, Jacob	100	Tenn. River	20 June 1826	1-252
GIFFORD, Sitranus	95¼	Indian Creek	4 August 1837	2-156
GILBERT, Jeremiah	25	----------	27 June 1826	1-253

Name	Acres	Location	Date	Ref
GILBERT, Jeremiah	120	White Oak Creek	15 February 1828	1-281
GILLES, John	30	Horse Creek	19 April 1825	1-145
GODWIN, Samuel	195	Hardin's Creek	7 July 1837	2-152
GOLDSMITH, Wesley	156	-------	31 May 1837	2-141
GOODLOE, John M.	640	Tenn. River	29 September ----	1-196
GOODWIN, James	160	Small Creek	25 December 1822	1-82
" "	133&1/3	-------	12 May 1823	1-86
GORDEN, George & Andrew Donoven	166&2/3	Tenn. River	20 May 1832	1-95
" "	83&1/3	" "	20 May 1832	1-95
GOSSETT, Henry	10	-------	17 April 1835	1-176
GRAHAM, Isaac	200	-------	10 June 1827	1-268
GRAHAM, James	36	Horse Creek	4 March 1834	1-177
" "	300	Indian Creek	23 July 1822	2-18
GRAY, Thos.	157	E. Tenn. River	24 February 1837	2-108
GREEN, Andrew	2187½	Tenn. River	26 June 1821	1-178
GRIMES, James	139	Short's Creek	29 October 1836	2-70
GROVES, Henson	50	Indian Creek	20 September 1823	2-23
" "	50	Tenn. River	5 September 1823	2-24
HAGERTY, Wm.	57	Swamp Creek	18 December 1837	2-217

HAGON, Jacob	25	Indian Creek	5 August 1837	2-164
HAGY, Henry	25	----------	10 June 1825	1-144
" "	87½	Tenn. River	1 September 1830	1-209
" "	112½	" "	20 June 1827	1-275
HAIL, Stephen S.	80	Horse Creek	25 September 1837	2-199
HAINES, Charles	121	Turkey Creek	12 August 1837	2-160
HAINES, G.W.	200	Tenn. River	25 April 1837	2-157
HALBERT, William	160	Turkey Creek	15 October 1824	1-131
HALE, G.S.	52½	----------	18 December 1828	1-236
HALE, Richard C.	134½	Tenn. River	11 December 1829	1-299
HALETT, William	57	----------	16 July 1823	1-192
HAMILTON, John	1000	Tenn. River	15 August 1823	1-109
HAMMONS, Thos.	25	Indian Creek	18 February 182-	1-75
" "	25	Hammon Creek	24 November 1821	1-35
HAND, Elkin	20	Horse Creek	13 March 1823	1-69
" "	20	" "	26 December 1822	1-90
" "	20	" "	22 November 1826	1-160
HANLEY, E.Y.	77	E. Tenn. River	18 March 1837	2-107
HANNAH, John	149	Indian Creek	23 May 1837	2-132
HARBOUR, Elijah	100	Turkey Creek	10 June 1826	1-121

HARBOUR, Elijah	15	Turkey Creek	19 August 1824	1-133
" "	30	Indian Creek	11 December 1824	1-137
" "	2	" "	7 July 1826	1-154
HARBOUR, Elisha	11½	" "	7 September 1837	2-175
HARBOUR, Samuel	30	English Creek	22 May 1821	1-8
" "	40	Horse Creek	6 June 1821	1-10
" "	20	----------	30 September 1821	1-29
" "	20	Horse Creek	28 December ----	1-37
" "	80	Turkey Creek	12 April 1821	1-43
" "	75	" "	14 April 1821	1-44
" "	45	" "	12 April 1821	1-45
" "	30	" "	22 March 1821	1-47
" "	12	" "	18 August 1823	1-110
" "	20	Horse Creek	17 August 1823	1-111
" "	160	Harbour's Creek	22 July 1824	1-123
HARDIN, Benjamin	160	----------	8 May 1823	1-69
" "	37	Indian Creek	30 August 1823	1-115
HARDIN, Gibson	160	" "	26 February 1823	1-67
" "	25	Raines Creek	26 February 1823	1-78
" "	160	Indian Creek	26 April 1823	1-88

HARDIN, Gibson	30	Indian Creek	28 June 1825	1-140
" "	15	" "	14 October 1836	2-65
" "	8	E. Tenn. River	22 March 1837	2-103
" "	20	Indian Creek	25 May 1837	2-130
" "	14	" "	25 May 1837	2-131
" "	8	" "	25 May 1837	2-131
HARDIN, Gibson & Amos	320	Camp Creek	25 July 1821	2-13
HARDIN, James	160	----------	26 May 1821	1-53
" "	2	Turkey Creek	17 May 1821	1-58
" "	160	Indian Creek	10 March 182-	1-68
" "	30	" "	18 February 1823	1-76
" "	160	Turkey Creek	9 May 1823	1-83
" "	100	" "	25 June 1823	1-84
" "	160	Indian Creek	-- ---- 1823	1-85
" "	---	Tenn. River	1 August 1823	1-114
" "	332½	Turkey Creek	3 November 1823	1-118
" "	100	----------	-- June 1825	1-139
" "	160	Indian Creek	9 August 1825	1-145
" "	125	Turkey Creek	24 September 1825	1-146
" "	7	----------	6 July 1826	1-153

Name		Acres	Watercourse	Date	Reference
HARDIN, James		15	Raines Creek	28 August 1826	1-157
"	"	50	Horse Creek	3 October 1826	1-171
"	"	160	White's Creek	10 September 1823	1-177
"	"	163	Raines Creek	23 July 1821	2-12
"	"	200	----------	15 March 1822	2-15
HARDIN, Joseph		50	----------	23 March 1825	2-32
HARDIN, William		33	E. Tenn. River	6 April 1837	2-139
HARGROVE, Valentine		77	" " "	23 March 1837	1-105
HARRIS, Richard C.		50	Turkey Creek	9 May 1823	1-92
HARRIS, Nathaniel		200	Beeson's Creek	1 January 1831	1-313
HARRIS, Rich. C.		40	Hardin's Creek	4 September 1823	2-24
HARROD, John		120	Tenn. River	9 December 1824	1-237
"	"	193	----------	20 August 1827	1-272
HART, James W. & E. Whitehurst		2560	----------	15 August 1823	1-198
HASSELL, James W.		182	W. Tenn. River	17 October 1836	2-61
HATLEY, Green		66	Horse Creek	16 June 1837	2-155
HATTY, Austin		200	----------	----------	1-309
HAUGH, Stephen & Daniel Thornton		175	E. Tenn. River	5 April 1837	2-125
"	"	40	Tenn. River	15 July 1837	2-154

HAWKINS, J.C.	45	Tenn. River	15 September 1837	2-182
HENDERSON, Thos. & Calvin Jones	228	" "	9 March 1825	1-244
HENDRICK, Isaac	200	" "	1 May 1829	1-217
HENRY, Wm.	200	W. Tenn. River	12 --- 1836	2-114
HESTER, Wm.	9	Indian Creek	25 November 1824	1-138
HEWLETT, Wm.	300	Tenn. River	11 March 1825	1-242
HIBBARD, Joseph	162	-------------	17 October ----	2-205
HICKEY, Wm. R.	150	Tenn. River	21 July 1829	1-222
HOBBS, Barnabas	117	E. Tenn. River	12 October 1835	2-137
HOLLAN, Chisley	98	" " "	12 January 1837	2-98
HOLT, David	175	Tenn. River	11 May 1827	1-231
HOSEA, James	200	E. Tenn. River	14 October 1836	2-128
HOSEA, Jesse	170	Hardin's Creek	27 October 1836	2-170
" "	45	" "	24 August 1837	2-172
HOWELL, Jourdan	200	Owl Creek	10 August 1831	1-220
HUDDLESTON, James	10	Hardin's Creek	12 July 1835	2-52
HUDIBURGH, Solomon	75	-------------	23 --- 1825	2-27
HUGHES, A.M.	190	Turkey Creek	4 February 1837	2-94
HUGHES, Stephen	24	E. Tenn. River	15 July 1837	2-104

Name	Acres	Location	Date	Ref
HUGHLING, Reuben	200	Tenn. River	11 June 1835	1-206
HUGHS, Wm. C.	20	-------------	1 January 1835	1-326
HUNTER, Malcolm	200	-------------	-- ------- 1830	1-321
HURLEY, John	150½	Tenn. River	20 August 1830	1-209
HURLEY, Josiah	116	" "	7 June 1827	1-229
HUTSON, Eli	50	" "	25 July 1827	1-231
JACKSON, Aaron	200	White Oak Creek	1 May 1831	1-207
JACKSON, John	61	Turkey Creek	4 August 1837	2-160
" "	11&3/4	" "	4 August 1837	2-160
JAY, Isaac (Heirs of)	640	-------------	16 August 1823	1-198
JEFFERS, John	150	Tenn. River	8 March 1828	1-260
JOHNSON, Benjamin	200	-------------	1 June 1837	2-139
JOHNSON, Lewis	53	Turkey Creek	19 May 1823	1-104
JOHNSON, Samuel	274	-------------	25 May 1823	1-105
JOHNSON, Temple C.	27	E. Tenn. River	9 March 1837	2-110
JOINER, David (Heirs of)	300	Tenn. River	8 December 1826	1-249
JONES, Henry	160	Indian Creek	-- ------- 1823	1-86
JONES, Hester	25	Tenn. River	1 April 1827	1-278
JONES, Jeremiah	200	Tenn. River	10 October 1827	1-228
JONES, Jesse	49	-------------	28 May 1835	1-208

Name	Acres	Location	Date	Ref
JONES, Jesse	160	Raines Creek	24 July 1821	2-13
" "	31	Indian Creek	23 September 1836	2-78
JONES, John	11&3/4	----------	13 May 1825	2-34
" "	9	----------	13 May 1825	2-35
JONES, Thomas	160	Tenn. River	10 December 1824	1-237
JONES, Thos.	50	"	19 February 1821	2-1
KARR, Samuel	200	"	5 June 1827	1-230
KEENNAN, John	200	"	30 April 1829	1-297
KELLEY, Elisha	25½	"	22 May 1823	1-185
" "	75	"	19 February 1828	1-227
" "	90&3/4	----------	28 July 1834	1-329
KELLEY, Joseph	200	Tenn. River	20 October 1833	1-329
KELTON, William	1000	Raines Creek	21 February 1821	1-3
KERBY, William	72½	Tenn. River	11 June 1835	1-206
KILLOUGH, Hezekiah	80	"	23 March 1834	1-324
" "	80	"	16 November 1830	1-210
KINCANNON, David	206	Turkey Creek	1 May 1823	1-92
" " (Heirs of)	25	"	23 July 1832	1-170
KINCANNON, James	15	"	18 April 1825	1-139
KINCANNON, Jessie	62	"	8 May 1837	2-135

KINDLE, John	20	-------------	-- July 1826	1-152
KING, James Jr.	200	Tenn. River	5 June 1827	1-229
KIRBY, John	88	-------------	26 May 1834	1-212
KIRKPATRICK, John	250	-------------	14 July 1823	1-200
KIZER, Julan	175	Lick Creek	21 August 1831	1-306
KNIGHT, Jonathan	147½	-------------	11 June 1835	1-330
KOONCE, Ridding	140	Hardin's Creek	19 August 1837	2-194
LACEFIELD, Robert	6	Indian Creek	28 October 1825	1-149
" "	10	" "	6 January 1826	1-150
LACKEY, Eli	40	Tenn. River	20 August 1829	1-312
LAMB, Redding	125	" "	15 November 1828	1-293
LAUDERDALE, Elijah	200	W. Tenn. River	12 December 1836	2-114
LAYTON, Thos.	94	Tenn. River	10 June 1837	2-93
LEETH, George D.	64	-------------	8 October 1828	1-290
LEETH, James S.	50	Tenn. River	8 October 1828	1-288
LEETH, Josiah	116	" "	17 September 1828	1-290
LESTER, Fountaine	58	" "	30 May 1821	1-24
" "	59	-------------	12 May 1821	1-25
" " & German Lester	640	Tenn. River	30 December 1822	1-52
LIGHT, Samuel L.	138½	Hardin's Creek	18 August 1837	2-190

225

LILLEY, Noah	6¼	Horse Creek	30 April 1821	1-13
"	239	Tenn. River	12 May 1821	1-14
"	35	Swift Creek	16 April 1821	1-48
"	25	----------	16 April 1821	1-49
"	46	Swift Creek	16 April 1821	1-49
"	25	Raines Creek	13 July 1821	1-52
"	165	Horse Creek	14 March 1823	1-93
"	105	Indian Creek	15 June 1823	1-108
"	35	" "	-- ---- 1823	1-116
"	237	----------	8 December 1826	1-251
LINDSAY, Isaac	201	Tenn. River	7 August 183-	1-208
LINDSEY, Ezekiel	25	Raines Creek	2 January 1826	2-46
LINGO, John	154½	Tenn. River	27 May 1837	2-168
LINGO, Wm.	200	----------	27 May 1837	2-140
LOVE, Wm. & Francis (Heirs of)	118	Indian Creek	1 July 1837	2-153
LOVELADY, Thos.	160	Tenn. River	11 December 1824	1-238
"	160	" "	11 December 1824	1-241
LOWERY, John	50	Horse Creek	23 November 1836	2-95
LUCAS, John	200	Tenn. River	1 May 1832	1-221

LUCAS, John	200	----------	-- ----- 1827	1-301
LUSTER, Fontaine	7	Tenn. River	5 May 1821	1-7
MACKY, James	200	----------	10 October 1827	1-275
MACLIN, James C.	195	E. Tenn. River	24 November 1836	2-82
MADOX, Leonard	200	Tenn. River	30 April 1829	1-297
MANLEY, John	274	Horse Creek	18 May 1821	1-6
MARTIN, John	20	Turkey Creek	12 June 1825	1-143
" "	166&3/4	Horse Creek	12 September 1837	2-187
MASSEY, Ausburn	8	Turkey Creek	-- -------- 1825	1-143
McCALL, Alexander	65½	Tenn. River	5 March 1825	1-240
McCAN, Joseph R.	125	White Oak Creek	28 December 18--	1-311
McCARN, Hugh	100	Indian Creek	8 April 1823	1-55
McCLAIN, Morris	146	Horse Creek	----------	2-200
McCLENTOCK, Alexander	20	Indian Creek	7 May 1823	1-106
" "	18	----------	25 June 1827	1-166
McCOROSON, Robert	40	Turkey Creek	17 July 1837	2-155
McDANIEL, Hiram	129	----------	11 June 1835	1-330
McDANIEL, Hugh	80	Tenn. River	10 August 1827	1-273
McDONALD, Alex.	100	Turkey Creek	20 January 1821	1-2

McDONALD, Alex.	100	Horse Creek	4 June 1821	1-18
"	160	"	18 May 1821	1-19
" & John McDonald	10	"	5 June 1821	1-20
"	110	Turkey Creek	21 September 1822	1-36
"	15	Swift Creek	9 May 1823	1-64
"	90	Indian Creek	11 August 1823	1-112
"	44&1/3	Horse Creek	20 June 1825	1-152
"	160	Swift Creek	30 August 1823	1-157
"	49	"	28 February 1828	1-174
"	160	----------	16 July 1822	2-20
McDONALD, John G.	80	Horse Creek	----------	1-167
McFERRIN, Samuel	200	Tenn. River	22 July 1834	1-325
McGAVOCK, David & Alex. McDonald	107½	Turkey Creek	1 May 1823	1-108
"	90	Horse Creek	23 April 1821	1-11
"	163	----------	11 December 1823	2-25
McGAVOCK, Francis & Alexander McDonald	148½	Tenn. River	28 December 1821	1-40
"	251½	"	28 December 1822	1-42
"	100	Indian Creek	1 May 1823	1-60
"	50	Tenn. River	17 May 1823	1-61

McGAVOCK, Francis & Alexander McDonald	50	Tenn. River	17 May 1823	1-61
"	50	"	17 May 1823	1-62
"	50	"	17 May 1823	1-62
"	50	"	19 May 1823	1-70
"	91	"	26 September 1828	1-263
"	1000	"	25 June 1833	1-266
McKEY, Wm.	150	E. Tenn. River	6 April 1837	2-136
McLEMORE, John C.	500	Tenn. River	15 May 1823	1-63
McMAHON, James F.	300	"	20 June 182-	1-178
McMAHON, Joseph	160	Raine's Creek	18 August 1823	1-113
McMILLAN, William L.	200	Tenn. River	9 December 1828	1-286
McNAIRY, John	47	"	14 December 1826	1-249
McQUIN, Agnes	192	Turkey Creek	3 October 1836	2-62
McROSE, John	20	Indian Creek	6 May 1823	1-91
MEADOWS, Thos.	200	White Oak Creek	-- February ----	1-318
MERIDETH, Andrew J.	200	"	21 March 1828	1-282
MERIDETH, Jacob	25	Tenn. River	2 May 1827	1-255
"	33	"	8 May 1827	1-269
MERIDETH, Sarah	25	"	2 May 1827	1-254

MERIDETH, Sarah	50	Tenn. River	2 May 1827	1-270
MERIDETH, John	25	"	2 May 1827	1-254
" "	100	"	10 May 1827	1-269
MERIDETH, Samuel	25	"	2 May 1827	1-254
" "	139½	"	10 May 1827	1-269
MILES, Charles	35	"	1 May 1827	1-257
MILES, James	25	"	2 October 1828	1-261
MILES, Margaret	25	"	2 October 1828	1-261
MILLER, Abram	87½	Indian Creek	22 June 1837	2-166
MILLER, Austin & John Williams	86	Tenn. River	8 August 1837	2-206
MILLER, Austin	4	------------	29 June 1825	1-144
" "	4	Tenn. River	1 July 1825	1-156
MILLER, Dan	200	"	31 December 1830	1-312
MILLER, Jacob	140	------------	26 April 1837	2-162
MITCHELL, David C.	174	Tenn. River	2 May 1823	1-71
" "	90	Tenn. River	15 May 1823	1-73
MITCHELL, David R.	28	Indian Creek	8 May 1823	1-71
MITCHELL, George	10	Horse Creek	-- --- 1821	1-29
MITCHELL, Henry	197	E. Tenn. River	13 April 1837	2-145

MONTGOMERY, James	241	White Oak Creek	30 September 1828	1-262
" "	164½	Tenn. River	2 January 1825	1-292
MONTGOMERY, Joseph	161½	" "	3 January 1828	1-292
MONTGOMERY, Thos. J.	200	" "	2 January 1829	1-290
MOORE, Michael	52	" "	20 October 1828	1-284
MORRIS, Charles	40	Lick Creek	20 January 1829	1-305
MORRIS, William	157½	-------------	10 October 1837	2-182
MORRIS, Stephen	37	-------------	24 November 1825	2-47
" "	14	-------------	18 November 1825	2-48
MOSELY, William (Heirs of)	640	Raines Creek	16 July 1822	2-21
MUNDAY, James	25	Tenn. River	18 February 1834	2-53
MURKISON, Kenneth	320	Indian Creek	13 January 1823	1-38
" "	8	" "	12 March 1823	1-81
MUTTON, Robert	2	Haley Creek	5 October 1824	1-127
NANCE, Allen	95	Short Creek	11 July 1837	2-162
NELSON, Charles B.	1&1/3	Tenn. River	10 July 1827	1-257
NICHOLDS, David	45	-------------	28 April 1837	2-161
NICHOLS, James A.	200	E. Tenn. River	10 January 1837	2-100
NISBET, John	22	Hardin's Creek	1 January 1836	2-59

NORTHCUTT, Archibald	10	Indian Creek	7 May 1823	1-90
"	50	"	5 August 1837	2-177
NORWOOD, John	180	W. Tenn. River	18 April 1837	2-106
NORWOOD, Wm. G.	29	Mud Creek	22 December 1836	2-85
NOWLER(?), Rufus	30	Turkey Creek	18 October 1837	2-211
ODOM, Allen	7	Tenn. River	30 November 1835	1-204
OGLESBY, Wm.	200	Mud Creek	1 August 1836	1-233
ONEIL, Elisha	200	Tenn. River	22 July 1834	1-237
ORR, George	50	----------	26 November 1827	1-203
"	100	Tenn. River	16 March 1826	1-246
OSTONE, Asa	10	"	15 January 1825	1-239
OUTLAW, Lewis	80	E. Tenn. River	2 May 1837	2-119
OWEN, John	340	Tenn. River	3 June 1823	1-183
"	187	"	16 July 1823	1-193
OWENS, David	133	"	2 June 1837	2-147
PACK, Elisha	35	Horse Creek	20 June 1821	1-26
PARISH, Wm.	200	----------	27 September 1837	2-208
PARMLEY, John	196	Lick Creek	-- May 1832	1-310
PARRISH, Mimi(?)	200	Tenn. River	21 June 1836	1-235
PARSONS, Henry	200	"	12 June 1827	1-268

Name	Acres	Location	Date	Ref
PATTERSON, Peter	84½	Indian Creek	26 September 1837	2-201
PATTON, Richard T.	28	Tenn. River	17 July 1823	1-201
" "	157	" "	20 December 1830	1-224
PAULLY, Elijah	29	------	12 May 1821	1-15
" "	20	Tenn. River	12 May 1821	1-16
PAYNE, Mason	200	------	-- --- 1832	1-308
PAYNE, Thos. D.	196	Owl Creek	1 October 1833	1-320
PAYTON, R.T.	25	Indian Creek	10 July 1837	2-96
PEACOCK, Benjiah	104	E. Tenn. River	12 October 1836	2-127
PEACOCK, Malachi	140	Indian Creek	------	2-72
PERKINS, David	200	Choat's Fork	17 July 1837	2-197
PEARCE, Mary	194	W. Tenn. River	30 September 1836	2-66
PERKINS(?), Wm. M.	100	Turkey Creek	1 November 1836	2-69
PETTIGREW, Lem	160¼	Hardin's Creek	18 August 1837	2-183
PETTY, Henry Sr.	200	W. Tenn. River	1 October 1836	2-67
PHILIPS, Joseph	300	Tenn. River	14 July 1823	1-194
PHILIPS, Wm. & Nich. McDaniel	156	" "	28 November 1835	1-205
PIBAS(?), John	160	" "	25 March 1827	1-267
PICKENS, Jonathan	105	Horse Creek	21 April 1821	1-10

PICKENS, Jonathan	55	Shoat's Creek	24 May 1821	1-27
PICKENS, Jonathan R.	20	Turkey Creek	23 November 1824	1-130
PICKINS, Gabriel	75	Roger's Creek	20 June 1837	2-146
PICKINS, J.R.	200	Horse Creek	19 July 1837	2-191
PIPER, William	50	Hardin Creek	11 February 1825	2-37
POINDEXTER, T.W.	140	Tenn. River	15 May 1823	1-103
POLLARD, J.B.	200	" "	12 September 1837	2-193
POPLES(?), Jackson	181	-------	31 August 1837	2-190
POTTER, Thos.	118	Lick Creek	9 August 1833	1-327
POTTS, Joshua	3840	Doe(?) River	16 August 1823	1-197
PYBURN, Christopher	40	Horse Creek	12 April 1821	1-12
" "	20	" "	4 June 1821	1-18
PYBURN, William	25	Horse Creek	4 June 1821	1-17
" "	80	" "	12 May 1821	1-21
RANEY, Doctor	200	W. Tenn. River	30 March 1837	2-126
RANDOLPH, Rix A.	200	E. Tenn. River	4 April 1837	2-117
RATTAFF(?), Sarah Ann	200	-------	5 May 1837	2-138
RAYBURNE, John	100	-------	20 October 1827	1-168
REAVES, George	101½	White Oak Creek	15 February 1828	1-223

REDDING, Isaac	25	----------	24 September 1826	1-256
REED, Amzi	3	----------	3 October 1826	1-158
REED, Angie	27½	Horse Creek	5 September 1837	2-186
" "	26¼	" "	5 September 1837	2-187
REED, James	10	Turkey Creek	9 June 1824	1-122
RENFROE, Stephen C.	200	Tenn. River	20 February 1827	1-228
REYNOLDS, Colan	196	" "	20 August 1831	1-219
REYNOLDS, Henry	50	Shoat's Creek	4 January 1821	1-9
" "	40	Turkey Creek	23 July 1824	1-123
" "	70	" "	23 July 1824	1-124
REYNOLDS, Joseph & John	52	E. Tenn. River	14 January 1837	2-88
RHODES, James	25	----------	25 October 1826	1-159
RICE, John A.	200	----------	17 February 1837	2-204
RICHARDS, Clark	122½	Horse Creek	12 September 1837	2-188
RICHERSON, John	77	----------	21 December 1834	1-325
RIDLEY, Britton	200	Snake Creek	15 August 1831	1-310
RIGGINS, Powell	274	Indian Creek	----------	1-116
ROACH, Stephen	160	Tenn. River	16 February 1821	2-3
" "	29½	" "	16 February 1821	2-14
" "	200	" "	15 ----- 1824	2-26

ROBERSON, David	10	----------	16 October 1826	1-161
ROBERSON, John	75	White Oak Creek	7 January 1829	1-291
ROBERSON, Michael	80	Tenn. River	10 May 1825	1-246
ROBERSON, Richard	100	----------	24 July 1823	1-193
ROBERSON, Samuel Jr.	100	Tenn. River	12 December 1824	1-241
ROBERTSON, Christopher	100	"	-- ------ 1832	1-215
"	50	"	-- May 1827	1-267
"	127	White Oak Creek	4 October 182-	1-293
ROBERTSON, David	60	Turkey Creek	23 May 1821	1-24
"	25	"	9 May 1823	1-82
"	25	Holland's Creek	12 May 1823	1-87
"	25	Swift Creek	12 May 1823	1-89
"	40	Englishes Creek	12 August 1823	1-112
ROBERTSON, Wm.	80	Tenn. River	12 December 1824	1-240
ROBINSON, David	25	Harbour's Creek	17 April 1821	1-34
"	10	----------	12 July 1823	1-56
"	25	Turkey Creek	12 July 1821	1-57
ROBINSON, James	23	English's Creek	6 June 1837	2-144
ROBINSON, James W.	20	Tenn. River	17 October 1828	1-295

ROBINSON, Jesse	125	W. Tenn. River	11 May 1837	2-122
ROBINSON, John M.	200	Tenn. River	----------	1-328
ROBINSON, Major (Surveyed as a mill site)	100	W. Tenn. River	9 June 1837	2-147
ROBINSON, Thomas	160	Tenn. River	4 March 1827	1-298
ROGERS, T.H.	63	Horse Creek	22 September 1821	1-30
ROGERS, Thos. H.	100	Lick Creek	25 April 1829	1-319
ROGERS, William E.	9	Horse Creek	27 April 1821	1-13
ROSE, Frederick	30	Indian Creek	17 November 1836	2-79
ROSS, A.B.	100	----------	13 May 1825	2-45
ROSS, Charles & Ambrose H. Williams	100	E. Tenn. River	26 May 1837	2-129
ROSS, Francis	30	Indian Creek	20 March 1825	2-33
ROSS, George	100	" "	8 April 1823	1-81
" "	100	" "	10 November 1824	1-136
" "	135	Horse Creek	27 June 1837	2-198
ROSS, J.M.	28	" "	27 June 1837	2-197
ROSS, Jessie L.	75	Tenn. River	24 January 1827	2-51
ROSS, William B.	20	----------	24 July 1824	1-126
" "	55	Indian Creek	27 January 1825	1-135

Name	Acres	Location	Date	Ref
ROSS, William B.	50	Turkey Creek	15 August 1836	1-232
" "	80	----------	16 February 1825	2-30
" "	25	Hardin's Creek	16 February 1825	2-30
" "	50	----------	12 February 1825	2-31
" "	60	----------	14 December 1826	2-32
" "	5¼	----------	23 March 1828	2-49
ROSS, William T.	23	----------	12 February 1825	2-29
ROWSEY, Morgan	100	Tenn. River	26 August 1828	1-288
" "	140	----------	30 December 1834	1-326
ROWSEY, John	125	Tenn. River	13 December 1824	1-238
RUDD, Rebecca	165	----------	7 December 1836	2-78
RUNNELLS, Hamilton	115½	----------	28 May 1833	1-214
RUSSELL, Alexander	25	----------	10 April 1825	2-40
" "	8	----------	10 April 1825	2-40
" "	2	----------	10 April 1825	2-41
RUSSELL, James	30	----------	25 December 1825	1-238
RUSSELL, Robert	300	----------	15 March 1822	2-16
RUTLEDGE, George & Robt.	1675	Tenn. River	19 May 1823	1-65
SCOTT, Jeremiah	137½	----------	18 November 1836	2-77

SCOTT, John	165½	Short Creek	12 December 1835	2-57
SCOTT, Rosomond P.	23	------------	15 March 1822	2-17
" "	37	------------	15 March 1822	2-17
SHANNON, Benj. F.	200	Tenn. River	17 March 1828	1-259
SHANNON, Wm.	200	" "	17 March 1828	1-258
SHEARS, Robert	22	Hardin's Creek	10 November 1834	2-56
SHELBY, Ely	2	White Creek	2 March 1837	2-123
SHUIN(?), John D.	200	------------	26 October 1836	2-75
SHULL, Enoch	73	Indian Creek	19 August 1837	2-167
SHULL, John	160	Tenn. River	5 August 1836	1-235
SHULL, Joseph	91	Horse Creek	10 October 1837	2-208
SHURLEY, James	197	W. Tenn. River	21 February 1837	2-167
SHUTE, Thomas	6	Tenn. River	28 December 1824	1-239
" " & Beal Basley	436	" "	4 March 1825	1-243
" "	192	" "	14 December 1826	1-247
" "	240	" "	6 December 1826	1-250
" "	274	" "	20 March 182-	1-253
" "	275	" "	25 June 1828	1-260
" "	227½	White Oak Creek	16 November 1830	1-264

SIMPSON, John C.	64	Tenn. River	11 December 1826	1-247
"	87	"	25 September 1828	1-287
SMITH, Absolom	25	Indian Creek	10 April 1825	2-42
"	10	"	6 April 1825	2-43
SMITH, Daniel	39	"	16 December 1837	2-81
"	62	"	27 October 1837	2-209
SMITH, Geo. W.	15	E. Tenn. River	2 February 1837	2-90
SMITH, Isaac	125	Tenn. River	12 November 1827	1-285
SMITH, James	200	"	12 August 1832	1-316
SMITH, James P.	19	Turkey Creek	22 November 1837	2-219
SMITH, Jesse	100	E. Tenn. River	5 November 1836	2-73
SMITH, Joel	188	"	23 February 1837	2-174
SMITH, Jordan	25	----------	1 September 1837	2-172
SMITH, Payton	125	W. Tenn. River	20 February 1837	2-108
SMITH, William	88	Horse Creek	19 August 1836	1-234
SMITH, William H.	111	E. Tenn. River	24 February 1836	2-180
SMITHWICK, Jordan	198	----------	4 May 1837	2-138
SPAIN, John D.	200	----------	11 August 1833	1-321
SPAIN, Marshall D.	200	Lick Creek	13 June 1829	1-309

SPAIN, Peter D.	200	Tenn. River	1 May 1832	1-321
SPAIN, Solomon D.	200	Lick Creek	27 May 1828	1-283
SPEARS, William	25	----------	2 October 1826	2-49
SPRIGGINS, Samuel	25&3/4	Tenn. River	14 December 1826	1-250
STARR, George	123	Beason's Creek	18 August 1830	1-314
STEVENSON, Elbert H.	100	----------	20 May 1837	2-133
" "	111&3/4	Tenn. River	9 --- 1837	2-210
STONE, Pryor	200	----------	27 September 1836	2-72
STOUT, Andrew	84	E. Tenn. River	24 January 1837	2-178
STOUT, John	101	Dry Creek	14 November 1837	2-218
STRAWN, Richard	112	W. Tenn. River	23 December 1836	2-123
STRAWN, Wm.	25	" "	23 December 1836	2-85
STRIVIN, William	200	Tenn. River	29 August 1830	1-302
SULLIVAN, Elijah	50	----------	10 March 1825	2-38
SURRATT, Jacob	200	Short's Creek	10 July 1837	2-156
TAB, John	50	Horse Creek	14 February 1827	1-236
TANKESLEY, J.H.	100&20poles	" "	19 July 1837	2-164
TARKENTON, Isaac	60	E. Tenn. River	18 March 1837	2-117
TAYLOR, George W.	187½	Lick Creek	8 August 1833	1-211
TAYLOR, John	1500	Tenn. River	4 April 1823	1-181

Name	Acres	Location	Date	Ref
TAYLOR, John P.	160	Rains Creek	15 July 1822	2-20
TAYLOR, Wm.	91	Tenn. River	25 August 1827	1-276
TEAGE, Wm.	200	" "	20 May 1827	1-301
TEAGUE, James	82½	------------------	13 October 1836	2-101
TEAGUE, Wm.	120	------------------	12 October 1836	2-102
TEAL, Timothy	200	------------------	10 --- 1831	1-220
TERRY, E.	158¼	Lick Creek	4 May 1837	2-212
THOMPSON, David	198&3/4	Tenn. River	17 May 1837	2-163
THOMPSON, James	92	" "	1 May 1829	1-296
THOMPSON, Jessie	87	Turkey Creek	26 October 1836	2-68
THOMPSON, John	30	Indian Creek	-- August 1824	1-128
THOMPSON, Richard	27	------------------	6 May 1837	2-216
THRASHER, Joseph	10	Dry Creek	29 May 1821	1-9
" "	30	" "	12 May 1821	1-17
TOLBOTT, Ross	200	------------------	26 May 1834	1-212
TOMKINS, Harrison	200	W. Tenn. River	14 December 1836	2-84
TOMLINSON, Peter	25	------------------	6 July 1837	2-93
TOMPKINS, Harrison	134	Tenn. River	20 March 1827	1-277
TOWNY, Isaac	50	White's Creek	5 September 1821	1-33

TRACE, W.L.	179	----------	24 May 1837	2-165
TUCKER, Thos.	160	Chamber's Creek	27 July 1837	2-158
" "	100	" "	26 July 1837	2-159
TURNER, John	127½	Tenn. River	25 August 1827	1-271
USSING, A.W.P.	200	" "	1 March 1827	1-271
WADE, Richard	174	" "	20 June 1827	1-274
WADE, Samuel	56	Indian Creek	12 October 1836	2-127
WAGGONER, John	110	----------	25 July 1823	1-191
WALDRIP, Abel	200	E. Tenn. River	26 May 1837	2-129
WALDRIP, Thos.	200	W. Tenn. River	10 December 1836	2-86
WALKER, George W.	121½	Lick Creek	10 August 1833	1-211
" "	40	Tenn. River	1 May 1829	1-314
WALKER, James	200	" "	15 May 1833	1-214
WALKER, Mark	193½	Lick Creek	20 August 1831	1-305
WALKER, Robert	25	----------	20 June 1821	2-7
" "	100	Tenn. River	23 June 1821	2-8
" "	60	----------	19 June 1821	2-8
" "	50	Rimsey's(?) Creek	21 June 1821	2-9
WALKER, William B.	92	Tenn. River	25 April 1829	1-221
" "	200	" "	29 April 1829	1-295

WALLACE, Thos.	200	Snake Creek	30 --- 1830	1-313
WALLIS, America G.	25	E. Tenn. River	9 February 1837	2-95
WASHINGTON, Thomas	247	Tenn. River	16 July 1823	1-199
WATSON, John	160	Camp Creek	20 February 1821	2-2
WEATHERFORD, John	50	E. Tenn. River	19 January 1837	2-124
WEBB, Jesse	200	Beeson's Creek	29 August 1828	1-289
WEBB, Joseph	200	" "	15 October 1828	1-288
WEBB, William	156	Tenn. River	8 October 1828	1-223
WELCH, John	80	E. Tenn. River	19 January 1837	2-207
WEST, Wm.	115	----------	3 April 1837	2-151
WHITE, Andrew	133	E. Tenn. River	24 January 1837	2-101
WHITE, George	13	White's Creek	13 April 1837	2-112
WHITE, James	54½	Flat Creek	7 September 1837	2-196
WHITE, John	40	Horse Creek	19 January 1837	2-89
" "	198	Tenn. River	20 December 1837	2-217
WILSON, James	200	Raines Creek	21 July 1821	2-11
WINCHESTER, Daniel	200	Indian Creek	26 August 1836	2-191
WINCHESTER, Thos. & Robert Russell	96¼	----------	11 December 1823	2-25
"	121½	E. Tenn. River	27 February 1837	2-111

WINCHESTER, Thos.	50	E. Tenn. River	27 February 1837	2-112
WOLF, John	200	Lick Creek	8 July ----	1-210
" "	76¼	" "	21 June 1832	1-311
WOLFE, Jonathan	43	------------	10 October 1836	2-74
YARBROUGH, Ambrose	72	Horse Creek	14 March 1823	1-59
YOUNG, Isaac	100	Tenn. River	20 August 1828	1-218
YOUNG, James	122½	" "	13 August 1832	1-317

HARDIN COUNTY INDEX

ABEL, J.L.,101
    , James H.,193
ABELL, Elizabeth B.,190
    , Elizabeth,065
    , J.L.,190
    , J.S.,065
    , J.W.,072

    , James H.,164,166,174,196
    , James S.,063
    , James,164,202
    , John L.,163 ,164,190
    , John W.,063
    , John,162,164,202
    , Laura,164
    , Manerva A.,063
    , Minerva,164
    , Sarah H.,164
    , Silas,082
    , T.L.,193
    , Thornton T.,058
ABELLS, Elizabeth,057
    , J.L.,091
    , John L.,057
    , Joseph,136
ABELS, H.,146
    , J.H.,090
    , James H.,092
    , James L.,092
    , James,146
    , M.,092
ABERNITHY, Jessee,147
ABLE, James H.,043 ,087
ABLES, Charles,045
    , Ezekel,202
    , James H.,043
    , James L.,043
    , John W.,043
    , Joseph T.,045
    , Laura A.,043
    , Manervy A.,043
    , Margarett Ann,045
    , Sarah H.,043
    , Sarah,045
    , Silas,045
ACABERGER, David,121
ACOOK, James,137,140
ACULLBERGER, David,121
ADAM, Varner,051
ADAMS, A.L.,152
    , Jacob,202
    , James,146
    , Jno.Jr.,146
    , John,128
    , L.,140
    , Leroy,040
    , Saml.,146
    , Samuel,059 ,129,171,180
    , Thos.,150
    , William,040 ,143,172,180
ADAMSON, Wm.,152
AIKEN, Parthenia,022
    , Patsy,022
    , William C.,125
    , William,022 ,033
AKIN, Lot (N-Free),051
    , Newton E.,024
    , W.V.,153
    , Willm.,024
AKINS, J.T.,156
    , Samuel,202
ALDMAN, J.,151
ALDURON, J.C.,143
ALEXANDER, B.B.,078,091,102,143
    , Cyrus,113
    , Ezekiel,074 ,075
    , Henry B.,120
    , J.D.,155
    , J.H.,102
    , J.N.,150
    , James H.,062
    , Josiah,065 ,152,155
    , Newton,144
    , Richard R.,202
    , Sarah F.,062
    , W.H.T.,103
    , W.R.,102
    , W.T.,113,133,138
    , Wm.G.,135
    , Wm.T.,131
ALFORD, (Wid),196
    , J.M.,197
    , J.N.,062
    , John N.,197
    , John,198
ALISON, Adam R.,044
    , Rosanah,015
    , William,015,044
ALLEN, B.F.,146
    , E.J. (Minor),121
    , E.J.,106,121
    , Elizabeth,089
    , J.R.,156
    , James,131,133,134,135,136
        ,150
    , Jarod S.,004
    , Jesse,134,136,140
    , Jno.,146
    , John,057,152,191
    , Larkin,146
    , M.G.,088,089
    , Mathew,143
    , Micager,202
    , R.D.,138
    , William,128 ,130,131
    , Wilson,128 ,202
    , Wm.,133
ALLISON, Adam B.,176,177
    , Adam,185 ,187,192,194,
        ,196,197
    , Esther,054,069,084,187,
        194,197

ALLISON, J.C.,134
    , J.S.,141 ,153
    , Jane A.,084
    , John,006
    , Mary Jane,054 ,069,187,
        192,194,196
    , Perry S.,143
    , Robt.,202
    , Rosana M.,194
    , Rosana,194
    , Rosanna,005,054,069,187
        ,197
    , Rosannah,084
    , Theophilus,059,069,084,
        194
    , Thomas,005
    , William B.,059,187,194
    , William Jr.,054
    , William,005,059,069,084
        ,177,185,194,197
ALMOND, C.H.,091
ALTEM, Wm.M.,022
ANDERS, Robert,138
ANDERSON, A.B.,102 ,132
    , A.C.,145
    , Aaron,045,178
    , Elizabeth,162
    , George W.,113
    , J.S.M.,162,163
    , James,145
    , John E.,145
    , Mary E.W.J.,113
    , Rachel,202
    , Reuben,131
    , T.P.W.,102
    , W.J.,145
    , William,102 ,125,126
    , Wm.I.,149
ANDREWS, A.A.,088
    , James,138
    , John M.,037,088,169,176
ANGLIN, Thomas,138
    , Thos.,139
ARENDELL, Erasmus,065
    , Erastus,139
    , L.B.,153
    , William,065
ARMSTRONG, Cary A.,119 ,120
    , Hugh White,120
    , John,125,126
    , Perry,134
ARNETT, Mary E.M.,082 ,086
ARNOLD, John,134
    , Lee,132
    , Willis,132
ARNOTT, Christian,136
ARNSWORTHY, Daniel,134
ARUNDELL, Erastus,082 ,095
    , J.B.,150
    , Jane,082 ,095
    , William,080
    , Wm.,142
ASHCRAFT, C.,141
    , E.,155
    , Ichabod,137
    , J.,140
    , James,128,130
    , John,128
    , Wm.,141
ASHWORTH, Carson,127
    , G.H.,107
    , H.,146
    , Henry,144
    , J.,202
    , J.W.,144 ,152
    , James W.,023 ,026,060,
        107,109,143,166
    , Jas.W.,146
    , Jno.,146
    , John C.,038 ,039,170
    , John,139 ,144,166
    , Joseph S.,002
    , Joseph,023,038,039,166
        ,170,202
    , Nancy,033,162
    , Sarah,060
ATER, George,041,130,172,173
    , John,132
    , Sarah,041,172,173
ATOR, A.D.,191
    , Anderson,051
    , George,176,179
    , John,044
    , Matthia D.,051
    , S.A.,191
    , Sarah,051,176,179,184,192
ATORS, M.D.,183
    , S.Anderson,183
ATTON, William M.,127
AUSLEY, W.,149
AUSLY, William,155
AUSTIN, A.J.,091
    , Andrew J.,094
    , Charles,139
    , D.J.,091
    , David,074 ,078,079,094
    , G.A.,091
    , George A.,094
    , H.M.,128
    , J.W.,091,094
    , Jackson,147,151
    , James,101
    , Jas.J.,152
    , John,104,106,130,150,151
        ,153
    , Nancy,078 ,079
    , S.A.,091,094
    , W.T.,150
    , William A.,104
    , Willis,131
    , Wm.,150,152
AUTREY, Enoch,127

AUTRY, E.H.,098,152
    , John,135,141
AYDLETT, T.J.,144
BACHELDOR, Moses,139
BACHELOR, Moses,132,134
    , W.R.,147 ,149
BACHILOR, Wm.,151
BAGGS, Joseph,139
    , William,139
BAILES, H.B.,131
BAILEY, Absalom,131
    , George W.,093 ,094
    , George,132
    , M.,148
    , Moses,093
    , R.P.,085,086
    , Robert P.,062
    , Robert,153
BAIN, Daniel,025,119
    , Danl.,151
    , Geo.,195
    , George,041,119,173,180,189
        ,193
    , Martha,042,079,080,174
    , Mary E.,053 ,062,074,100
    , Mary Eliz.,077
    , Patsy,041,173
    , Sally,119
    , Sarah A.,053 ,062,074,079,
        100,114
    , Sarah Adeline,077
    , Sarah,119
    , William(Heirs),153
    , William,041 ,042,053,062,
        074,077,079,080,090,
        114,173,174,180,189,
        195
    , Wm.,193
BAINE, Daniel,024
    , George,024 ,199
    , Mary Eliz.,199
    , Sarah A.,199
    , William,199
BAIRD, A.H.,023
    , Cynthia,102
    , James,064,097,102,119
    , Jane,102
    , Jno.,023
    , John L.,125 ,126
    , Margaret,097
    , Rachel M.,102
    , Rachel,097
    , William H.,102
    , Wm.Hamilton,097
BAITEY, Ezekiel,132
BAITIY, Absalom,132
BAITMAN, Abraham,131
BAITY, Andrew,202
    , Ezekiel,131
BAKER, Dunning,202 ,203
    , Isabella,194
    , J.N.,109,191
    , J.T.,145,147
    , Jacob,203
    , Jerman,062
    , Jonathan,138
    , Joseph N.,023
    , Josephine,155
    , Marianne(Mrs),105
    , Martha,062
    , Milton,089
    , Ranin,089
    , S.H.,090
    , Seth,014
    , Solomon H.,045
    , Solomon,194
    , William,067 ,080,106,139
    , Wm.,110
BANES,Wm.,150
BANKHAM, Wm.,153
BANKS, Enoch,203
    , John,129,131
    , Simon,203
BARBER, Allen,152
BAREFOOT, F.D.,150
BARGE, Jeremiah,203
BARHAM, A.,095
    , Alex.,179
    , Alexander,046 ,185
    , Alx.,063
    , J.,194
    , John,034,059,063,079,164
        ,165,175,194
    , R.J.,194
BARKS, Patsey,014
BARNES, Elizabeth,107 ,153
    , Henry,153
    , J.C.,070
    , J.L.,107
    , J.W.,152
    , James,003 ,004,009,010,
        029,200,203
    , Jas.H.,203
    , John L.,009,016,107
    , John,144
    , Madison,150
    , Malinda,106,107
    , Moses,150
    , Right,203
    , Thos.B.,203
    , W.,145
    , W.C.,152
    , William,144
    , Wm.,152
    , Wright,095 ,181
BARNETT, A.Y.,152
    , Anna,120
    , B.N.,104
    , Burton,095
    , Daniel,130
    , David G.,135
    , Delila(N-Free),042
    , Elizabeth,095 ,098

BARNETT, F.,095
       , Frances,098
       , James G.,083
       , James,014 ,017,098,203
       , Jas.A.,095
       , Jesse Sr.,084
       , Jessie,203
       , John D.,018
       , John,081 ,082,120
       , L.W.,084
       , Mary J.,114
       , Mary,109
       , S.V.,098
       , Sarah F.,098
       , Sarah J.,095
       , Sarah T.,098
       , Sarah,109
       , W.A.,095 ,098
       , W.B.,082 ,095
       , W.S.,098
       , William B.,083
       , William,093,114
       , Wm.,203
BARNHILL, James,089
       , Mary,089
       , William,051
       , Wm.,134
BARNS, James,203
       , Wright,048
BARR, Silas(Heirs),126
       , Silas,203
BARREY, Daniel F.,010
BARRIE, W.A.,133
BARRY, H.A.,140
BARTEE, Washington,131
BARTMANT, Abraham,134
BARWELL, R.B.,071
BASEY, America,040 ,175
       , Caroline M.,040 ,060 ,179
       , David,040,175,179,195
       , Edmund,040
       , Elijah,040 ,175,179,195
       , J.T.,065
       , James T.,036,040,042,060,
              167,170,171,174,175,
              178,179,187,189,190,
              195
       , James,040,175,179
       , Joseph T.,040,065,175,179
       , Joseph,195
       , Lydia,042,174
       , Susan,195
       , Susannah,040,175,179
BASHEARS, George W.,132
BASLEY, Beal,239
BASS, Solomon,140
       , Wm.B.,203,204
BASWELL, B.,148
       , H.P.,138
       , Henderson,142
BASYE, David,107
       , Edmd.,148
       , Edmund,016 ,075,109
       , Elijah,109
       , Joseph T.,109
       , L.,148
       , Lydia,109
       , Susannah,076
BATTLE, Caroline,165
BATTLES, Caroline,034 ,167,168
BATTS, Alford,151
BATY, Thomas,024
BAUGHMAN, Abraham,108
       , E.A.,108 ,111
       , Eliz.A.,110
       , Elizabeth A.,108
       , Elizabeth,111
       , G.M.,111
       , George M.,110
       , James A.,110 ,111
       , John H.,104 ,111
       , Malecia,110
       , Malicia,111
BAUSBY, C.N.,141
BAY, T.P.,149
BAYSE, Caroline M.,182
       , Daniel,182
       , Edmund,070
       , Elijah,182
       , James M.,070
       , James T.,182
       , James,109,182
       , Joseph T.,182
       , Lydia,146
       , Susannah,182
BAYSEE, E.,146
BEACHAMP, Evan,179
       , Evin,039 ,171,175
BEAME, Jacob,052
BEAN, James,150
BEAR, Samuel,004
BEARD, A.H.,204
       , Anderson H.,194
       , Cynthia,076 ,194
       , James A.,204
       , James C.,194,204
       , James,060,074,150,194
       , John L.,126
       , John,132,194
       , Margret,194
       , Rachel,194
       , Wm.Hamilton,194
BEARDE, John L.,204
BEASELY, Saml.,144
BEASLEY, D.B.,066 ,071,085
       , Daniel B.,016 ,026,039,
              065,066,169,173,177,
              181,186,190
       , Daniel,160,161,165,171
BEATY, Thomas,019
BECKHAM, David,005
       , G.,147

BECKHAM, Green,150
BEDWILL, A.W.,139
BELCHER, Alia,200
       , Berry,137
       , Charlotte,200
       , John,200
BELL, J.C.,142
       , James F.,100 ,104
       , James,023,204
       , John,085
       , L.F.,086
       , Larkin F.,048,073,200
       , Samuel,150
       , Sooky,200
       , Susan,200
BELSHAZER, Daniel,150
BENHAM, Martha,200
BENNETT, James H.,140
       , James W.,113
       , James,100
BENNINGTON, William,144
BENSON, John,153
BENTLEY, Robert,051
BENTON, Geo.F.,060 ,195
       , George F.,077 ,096,098,
              103
       , Jerusha,098
       , John,098
BEOKE, H.I.,151
BERDON, Ralph,139
BERDON, Jacob,142
HERRIS, Andrew,004
BERRY, Betsy,002
       , Cynthia Jane,092
       , David,127
       , Eliza P.,092
       , James Madison,092
       , John W.,092
       , John,130
       , Mary,002
       , Michael,002
       , Rebecca,093
       , Samuel Jefferson,092
       , Samuel,204
       , W.H.,090
       , Wiley H.,066
       , Wiley,066,081,093
       , William G.,132
       , Wylie H.(Heirs),146
BIAS, Peter,140
BICKNER, A.,153
BIGS, Ezekiel,129
       , Jesse,128
BILL, Mary,153
BINGHAM, Alex.,204
       , Alexander,107
       , Martha,114
       , Mary,107 ,114
       , R.,146,148
       , Redman,152
       , Ridding,140
BINION, M.,086
       , Martin,086
BINONE, Norwood,204
BINUM, W.C.,145
BIRD, David,131
       , Elias,141
       , Lewis,142
       , William,134
BIRDEN, John,134
BIRDSONG, Joseph,140
BISHOP, (Mr.),153
       , C.,138
       , James,138
BITTLES, James,204
BIVENS, Arisbel,122
       , Avory,079
       , B.S.,122
       , Barney,100 ,104
       , Delilah Jane,122
       , Evan P.,122
       , F.C.,122
       , Franklin C.,122
       , George M.D.,122
       , Harriet A.,122
       , Jacob,150
       , James P.,122
       , James,153
       , Joseph,048 ,132,180,183,
              187
       , Martha A.,122
       , Mary,104
       , Nancy J.,122
       , Nathaniel,128
       , Susan A.,122
       , W.S.,090
BIVINS, Amanda J.,080 ,088
       , Avory,080 ,088
       , Barnabas,204
       , E.K.,150
       , Izza R.S.,080
       , J.S.,148
       , John B.,080,088
       , John,059
       , Joseph W.,080 ,088
       , Julia A.,080,088
       , Lydia S.,080,088
       , Margaret E.,080,088
       , Martha A.,080
       , Martha,088
       , Mary L.,080,088
       , Rebecca,080,088
       , S.,146
       , W.J.,145
       , Wm.,148

BLACK, H.G.,151
       , James G.,051
       , Jessie,204
       , Jno.,145
       , John,121,143
       , Margaret,101
       , William,047

BLACKARD, C.,148
       , Nancy,067
       , Willoughby,152
BLACKSHEAR, E.M.,147
       , Elijah,204
BLACKSHERE, E.M.,144
BLACKSHUE, J.H.,143
BLACKWELL, Dizzert,144
       , Jacob,002
       , Thos.,204
BLACKWOOD, Gideon,089
BLAGG, C.D.,064
BLAIR, John,141
       , Josiah,141
BLAKE, D.J.G.,055
BLAKELY, J.C.,093
       , John C.,016
       , Thomas,024,025,041,158,
              160,165,171,176,185,
              190
       , Thos,159
BLAKLY, Thomas,032
BLANKENSHIP, Abel,100 ,120,146
       , Abell,087
       , D.W.,094 ,112
       , Mary,112
       , P.,149
       , Pythias,114
       , Sarah A.,114
       , Thomas,100,120
BLANTON, Alexander,005 ,007
       , Lacy,007
       , Lucinda,007,015
       , Lucy Hix,015
       , Lucy,007
       , Ruth,015
       , Ruthy H.,007
       , W.T.,059 ,076,093,188,
              197
       , William T.,044,047,048,
              049,178,185,196,204
       , Wm.,204
       , Wm.T.,058 ,192
BLARINGIN, J.H.,136
BLEVIN, Abner,128
BLEVINS, Elijah,131
BLOUNT, A.G.,200
       , America,111
       , Ashley G.,120
       , Ashley,175
       , E.,200
       , E.P.,105,153
       , Emsley P.,035
       , Ensley,169
       , Floria,111
       , Henry R.,035
       , Henry,169
       , Isaac,204
       , James E.,035,109,140
       , James J.,111
       , James,169
       , John K.,035
       , John,057,169
       , Rebecca H.,035
       , Rebecca,057,169
       , Redden,035
       , Redding,169,178,185
       , Reden,194
       , Redin,188
       , Ridding,174,181
       , Susan Ann,035
       , Susan,169
       , William,205
BLUND, Lawson,153
BOALS, Cyntha,047
       , John W.,047
BOATWRIGHT, Stephen,144
BODES, H.G.,172
BODNY, Jas.,147
BOGGS, Isaac,139
BOHANNON, D.,153
       , David,205
BOLAN, W.P.,150
BOLLIN, J.B.,106
       , John,106
BOLTS, Alfred F.,142
BOND, Robert,143
       , Robt.E.,144
BONDS, R.E.,087
BOOKER, (Mrs),118
       , Eliza,116
       , L.F.,097,116,117,118
       , William,116
BOOKOUT, (Wid),026
       , Charles,130
       , Henry M.,158
       , Henry,026
       , Jesse,026 ,158
       , M.D.,127 ,137
       , Marman,130
       , Morman,128
BOON, Hiram,010
       , Watson,128,130
BOONE, Hiram,015
BOOTH, Andrei,138
       , Andrew,136 ,137,151
       , Samuel,136
       , Thomas A.,141
BOOTHE, Samuel,133
BOOTHS, L.S.,149
BORLAND, W.P.,142
BOSLEY, Beal,125,127
BOSTWICK, G.G.,072 ,141,194
       , G.L.,072
       , R.,072
BOSWELL, B.,150
       , R.B.,176
       , Sm.,152
       , Thomas,135
BOUGSSTER, Samuel,131
BOUNT, Ashley,170
       , Redding,170
BOURLAND, J.B.,114

BOURLAND, John B.,107
, John,096 ,102,103,114,
120
, O.,149
, Robert,108
, S.A.,120
, Samuel R.,107
, Susan A.,107
, W.P.,141 ,153
BOURTON, John,155
BOWEN, E.P.,147
BOWLIN, Washington,128
BOWLIS, J.P.,147
BOWLS, Nathan,205
, Synthia M.,182
BOWMAN, Jno.,142
BOWYAR, Adam,205
BOYCE, John,013
BOYD, Alfred,149
, Andrew R.,130
, Andrew,127 ,132
, James Jr.,205
, James Sr.,002,012,205
, James,002,007,008,012,205
, Jno.,002
, John,205
, R.H.,130 ,131,133,134,135
, Robt.H.,136
, T.P.,155
, W.C.,153
BRADEN, John G.,135
BRADFORD, George W.,101
BRADLEY, B.,155
, Francis A.,127
, Francis,053
BRADLY, Charles,137
BRADSHAW, William,004
BRADY, Charles,104 ,153
, Frederick,104
, Jno.,145
, John,147
, Wm.,153
BRAHAN, Thos.G.,126
BRAINE, James,144
, Joseph,144
BRANCH, Abraham,143,145
, Abram,141
, E.C.,137
, Eli,129,131,138
, Isaac,129 ,133,134
, Joseph,137 ,138
, Michal,153
BRANDEN, Philip,132
BRANDON, Phillip,134
BRANDT, George,135
BRANES, Wm.,137
BRANNON, C.C.,148
BRANNUM, C.C.,156
BRANON, P.,147
BRASFIELD, G.,205
, Wiley,126
BRASSFIELD, Elez.,142
BRASTFIELD, Alsey,156
, Asa,112
BRATON, William,128
BRATTENBOUCHER, John J.,025,026,
158,159,163,166
BRATTON, Paul,108
, Pulay,108
, Sterling,130
, Thomas,130
, Thos.,142
BRAUNT, Paul,151
BRAWLEY, C.W.,137
, T.G.,150
, Thos.G.,137
BRAY, Thomas J.,089
BRAZELTON, Hannah,205
BRECHIN, R.S.,128
BREWER, Mark,130
, Sterling,205
, Thomas S.,131
, Thomas,128 ,132,135
, Thos.,138
, Thos.S.,134
, William J.,131
, Wm.,135
BREWTON, Samuel S.,205
, Samuel,205
BRIAN, Joseph H.,188
, Mary,188
BRIANT, Aaron,015
, Elizabeth,015
, Joseph,040
BRICHEN, John,128
BRIDGES, James R.,109
BRIGGS, Jessie,205
BRILE, ,138
BRIM, Joseph,109
, Martha,167
, N.J.,109
, Newton J.,109
, Raleigh,056 ,189,190,197
, W.R.,131
, Walter,130
, William,037 ,053,135,167,
168,173,177,181,186,
188,193
BRISCOE, C.H.T.,148
, L.H.,194
BRIT, Leroy,137
BRITAIN, Jas.,142
BRITT, W.C.,155
BRITTON, America,200
, Charlotte,200
, Green,200
, J.B.,118 ,148,153
, James B.,097
, James,141
, John,200
, Parker,152
, Patsy,200
, W.M.,097

BRITTON, William,200,205
BROADAWAY, Wm.,150
BROADEN, Philip,131
BROADWAY, Wm.,135
BROGEL, S.G.,152
BROMLEY, William A.,084
BROOK, Richard,129
BROOKS, B.,188
, Bailey,205
, Bennett,050,055,082,090,
091,184,188,189,197,
205,206
, Browder,056,136,151,189
, Celest,082
, Charity,082,091,184
, Charles,206
, Isaac,142 ,206
, James M.,055,188,189,197

, Jeremiah,129
, John,129,132
, Madison,133,134,135
, Maria,055 ,082,188
, Richard,129,132
, Terrel,206
, Terril,132
, Thomas,132
, W.,145
, William,050,130,144,184
BROTHERTON, D.D.,120
BROUN, Andrew,156
BROUNT, Allen,012
BROWDER, Brooks,197
BROWN, ,135
, A.S.,127,130,133
, Daniel,140
, Danl.,141
, Dickson,206
, Ed,155
, G.H.,137,138
, George,129
, H.A.,152
, Hamilton,126,206
, Harry H.,126
, Henry H.,126,206
, Henry,155
, Hiram,141
, James,131,153,156
, Jasper,153
, Jessie,206
, John N.,152
, John,140,149,153
, L.Y.,097
, Lucius,151
, Sally,084
, Sampson,128
, Stephen,150
, W.,145 ,148
, Wallace,151
, William(N-Free),089
, William,144 ,206
, Wm.,136
BROWNERIN, Benjamin,018
BROYLES, C.S.,146
, Conway S.,092
, Conway,092
, Elizabeth,059
, John S.,010,021,064,206

, John,206
, Joseph,152
, L.H.,018 ,022,059,071,
089,185,194,206
, Lewis H.,007 ,012,019,
053,071,194,206
, Lewis H.Jr.,056
, Lewis H.Sr.,111
, Lewis N.,015
, Mary,080 ,081
BRUMLEY, James,132 ,134,145
, Jas.,147
, Jefferson C.,043
, John,134
, William,133
, Willis,031
BRUMLY, Bashabe,057
, William A.,061
BRUNCH, Eli,129
, Isaac,129
BRUTON, Nancy H.,048
, Nancy,181
, Samuel,048 ,181
BRYAN, Josiah,064
, Phillips,206
, Willis H.,064
BRYANT & CO., ,148
BRYANT, Aaron,003
, Bersheba,084
, Betsey,003
, Betsy,003
, Brooks P.,206
, Elisha,040 ,041,053,171,
173,174,180
, Hezekiah,143
, Jno.,142,145,147
, John,140,144
, Josiah H.,055 ,075,079,
084
, Josiah,075 ,078,079,084,
198
, Mahala,084 ,095
, Mary,055,198
, Peggy,040 ,171
, Peter,133 ,134,136,137,
145,147,149
, Polly,003
, W.H.,075
, William,078
, Willis A.,079
BUCHLER, Wilson,153
BUCKINGHAM, Joseph,012
BUCKMAN, David,206
BUGG, D.,142

BUGG, Geo.,142
, Jesse S.,065
BUIE, Cornelius,032,128,162
, D.R.,151
, Elizabeth,032
, John Sr.,021
, John,032 ,127,129,162
BULER, John,130
BULLARD, Peter,144
BUNCH, M.W.,145
, Richard L.,130
BUNCK, Richard,129
BUNDAY, John,027
BUNDY, Jno.,024
, John,096,206
BUNES, Eli,149
BURAM, Peter,125,126,206
BURDEN, J.A.,147
, Joseph,156
, N.B.,141
BURDS, H.J.,149
BURGE, Jeremiah,018,021
, Richard,018 ,206
, William,127
BURGESS, Elias,043 ,175,176
, Rachel,175
BURGS, Henry,207
BURIS, Jonathan,129
BURKS, B.H.,087
, Mary T.,094
, R.H.,094
BURLEY, Absalom,134
, George W.,134
BURN, Shepherd,130
BURNES, Richard,149
BURNETT, John D.,022
BURNS, F.M.,147
, J.W.,142
, Thos.S.,142
BURNY, Daniel,153
BUROGHS, J.,149
BURRIS, Jonathan,129
, Stephen,132
BURROW, P.F.,156
BURRYS, Jonathan,151
BURTON, George,156
, John Jr.,119
, John,021,119,207
, R.W.,152
, Squire,021
, Sterling,131,133,134,136

BURTWELL, George H.,019
, James,019
, John T.,207
BUSBY, Amos,044
, Levi,135,136
BUSELY, Amor,130
BUSHER, Thos.,207
BUTCHER, Thomas,207
BUTLER, B.D.,059,071
, Lemul,130
, Thos.,207
BYNAM, Mary,089
BYRD, D.E.,137 ,141,207
, David E.,132 ,133,136
, Elias,143,149
, John R.,024 ,031,167,184,
207
, John,135 ,136
, Lewis,128,130,136
, Liberty,127 ,134
, Lore(Wid),127 ,207
, M.H.,087
, N.C.,153
, Rebecca J.,065
, Robert,068
, Saml.,153
, Thomas,141
, Thos.,145
, W.B.,065 ,145
, W.C.,153
, William B.,052
, William,024 ,167
, Wm.,137 ,152
BYRUM, Peter,207

CABERT, ,149
CACKS, Isaac,137
CAGEL, Charles,041
CAGLE, George,207
, Jno.,146
, John S.,040
, John,044,129
CAIGLE, Henry,207
CAIRNS, W.M.,151
CALDER, Robert,207
CALDWELL, Q.P.,142
, T.,153
, Thomas,141
, W.P.,146 ,199
, William,131
, Wm.P.,137
CALENDS, William,143
CALLEN, Thomas,163
CALLINS, Green,119
, James,119
, John G.,119
, Josephine,119
, Lewis,119
, Mary,119
, William,119
CALWELL, Thos.R.,145
CAMBELL, Archibald A.,207
, Michel,125
CAMBLE, Collin,207
, Colling,208
CAMERSON, N.,198
CAMP(?), Thomas J.,045
CAMPBELL, A.,138,139
, A.B.,035 ,063,071,089,
118
, A.G.,112

CAMPBELL, A.J.,134
, A.W.,135
, Arthur B.,045,046,080,
112,174,175,179,182,
185,188,190,193,197
, C.J.,093
, Elizabeth,114
, G.W.,102 ,138
, Hutton,153
, Jacob,037
, John A.,114
, Ruth,037
, S.P.,135
, Samuel,208
, T.J.,106 ,200
, W.,126,139
, W.G.,032 ,054,058,065,
093,112,193,200
, W.S.,058
, Washington G.,107,200
, Washington,116
, William,125
CAMRON, Nahom,197
, Simon,145
CANNON, Naham,062
, Nahum,066
CANTRELL, Aaron V.B.,110,111
, Calisto L.,110
, Eleanor,110
, Eunice,110,111
, Harry,110
, J.W.,071
, James K.P.,110,111
, James W.,079 ,082,083,
084,089,110,111
, James,080
, John N.,110
, Lenoir W.,084
, Lenoir W.,084
, Lenoir,084
, Lenore,110
, Levi L.,110
, Manerva R.,111
, Minerva R.,110
, Olenor H.P.,110
, Olivia H.P.,111
, Theresa E.,110
, Therza,110
, William H.,111
CAREY, Joel,004
CARLISLE, James G.,164
, James,208
CAROTHERS, F.W.,128
CARPENTER, Ann Elizabeth,069
, Z.,151
, Zenith,069
CARR, J.M.,152
CARROLL, Francis(Negro),008
, Isaiah,041,059
, James,098
, John,041
, Joseph,084
, Martha P.,090
, Samuel,041
, Thomas,041,090
CARRON, John H.,126
CARRY, John,141
CARSON, Henry,136
, J.W.,153
CARTER, G.W.,137
, Jackson,133
, James M.,053
, Jesse,143
, Rachel,053
, Saml.,186
, Samuel,053
, William,053,119,139,208
, Wm.,186
CARTWRIGHT, Wm.H.,021 ,022
CASE, Chacy,129
, Chancy,129,131,133
, Chauncy,134
, J.R.,141
CASEY, J.W.,150
, Joel,005,011,092,146
, Riley,035,128,130,167,178
CASH, James,131,135,136,138,153,
156
, T.K.,131
CASHSTUE, Kenitre,151
CASSEY, Elizabeth,092 ,096
, Hubbard,092
, John,092,096
CASSOOL, James,102
CASTEEL, Jno.,147
, Kinith,150
, W.K.,147
, W.M.K.,150
CASTELL, K.,147
CASTIEL, Kindrick,144
CASTLEBERRY, Odom,070 ,078
, Syntha,070
CASTLEMAN, Andrew G.,208
CATHEY, Daniel,134
, Geo.,208
, George,125 ,126
, Wm. C.,208
CATHY, George,126
CEVENAUGH, P.,126
CHAMBERS, John,126 ,208
CHAMMES, A.P.,150
CHAMPION, ,141
CHANEY, C.C.,022
CHAPELL, Richard,208
CHAPMAN, ,147 ,149
CHARLES, Richard,129
CHERRY, Annie M.,111
, Columbus F.,041
, Daniel,010 ,015,208,209,
210
, Darling,210
, David,020 ,133,210

CHERRY, Eli,018,019,022,048,069,
090,153,158,159,160,
175,178,182,183,
185,190,193,198,210
, Frank,104
, Franklin,014
, H.L.,179
, Harrell L.,198
, Harrell,185,190,193
, Harry Bell,167
, Isham B.,069,167,190,193
,190
, Isham S.,041
, Isham,003 ,006,008,009,
011,012,013,014,015,
018,020,041,158,159,
160,210
, J.B.,179
, Jesse,020 ,041,158
, Joseph,014 ,134
, M.H.,077
, Margaret E.,041
, Margaret,019,022,083
, Mary Ann,179,185,193
, Mary,167
, Maryann,190
, Mazzell,013
, Nancy,159
, Noal,158
, Noel,017,022,159,162,163
,167,172,175,176,178
,183,185,190,193
, Nowel,182
, Nowell,179
, S.,142
, Sarah S.,071
, W.H.,061,062,077,087,090,
111,145,147,150,152
,194,195,197
, William H.,071 ,075,079,
197
, Wm.H.,197
CHESNEY, Thomas,050
CHILDERS, Burgess,136
, Joel,128 ,136
, Peter,210
, Robert,128,130
, William,095
CHILDRES, James,150
CHILDRESS, Harriet,116
, Hezekiah,127
, Joel,130
, John Sr.,211
, John,211
, Marion,144
, Sarah,116
, William,116
CHILDS, A.T.,148
CHISHOLM, James,211
, John,211
CHOAT, (Mrs),006
, Charles J.,004
, Christopher,006
, Eliza W.H.,004
, Jane J.C.,004
, Jno.,002
, Nicholas,138
CHRISHOLM, John,125
CHRISNEY, Thomas,135
CHRISTIAN, Harrison,067,080,129
CHURCH, J.M.,128
, Jonathan M.,008,019
, Joseph P.,132 ,133
, Pendleton,135
, R.N.,149
, R.S.,128
, Robert S.,071 ,104
CHURCHWELL, W.,149
, Wm.,139,143
CHURCHWILL, Candace,076
, W.,145
, William,129
, Wm.,140,147,151
CLACK, James A.,132
CLANCEY, J.H.,147
CLARK, A.I.,132
, A.J.,142
, Andrew,059 ,146
, Deacan,137
, Dickson,130
, Elbert,135
, H.,147
, Hiram,060,132,133,140,141
,142,145
, Kelso,195
, Kelsy,060
, Martha,059 ,192
, Riley,137
, W.A.,070,146
, William A.,188 ,192
, William H.,055
, William,049 ,131,195
, Wm.,147 ,211
CLARKE, Dickson,128
CLARY, Thos.,142
CLAUSEWELL, James,153
CLAYTON, S.,156
, S.N.,153
, W.D.,129
CLEM, Samuel,132
CLEMMONS, William,153
CLIFTON, Eldridge,057 ,062,211
, George B.,193
, James,101
, John M.,127
, Masion,143
, Thomas,147
, Turner C.,211
CLINE, James,138
, Samuel,138
CLINGAN, David,045
CLINGHAM, D.,153
CLINGMAN, Jno.F.,022

CLINKENBIRD, Wm.,211
CLOUD, Isaac,211
, J.P.,140
CLOUNCE, J.F.,148
COATNY, Sirzy,160
COATS, John,140
COB, Prsley,151
COBB, Edmond,152
, John B.,140
, John,152
COBLE, William,211
COBURN, Francis,034,054,170,174,
179,182,184,187
COCHRAN, F.A.,081 ,082,101,103,
104
COCKBUN, Headley,211
COCKBURN, H.,153
COCKRAN, F.A.,105
COCKURN, Canny(?),106
CODY, Curtis,134
COEY, Russell R.,011
COFFEE, Isaac N.,121
, Nathan,121
, William M.,121
COFFEY, H.,088
, Nathan,121
COFFMAN, Daniel,150
, J.D.,148
COL, Egar,148
COLBERT, A.J.,142
, Mrs.,107
, Owen,148 ,152
, Stephen,107
COLDER, Robert,211
COLDWELL, Thos.,138,139
, Wm.,133 ,136
COLE, Anderson,145
, Edwin,132
, Elizabeth,058
, John,058 ,116,141,195
, Mary,120
, Filmone,151
, Robert,151,153
, Stephen,120
, W.,155
, William,116 ,120
COLESON, William,135
COLLINS, John H.,130
, Thos.,211
COMBS, J.W.,002
, James W.,013
, Thomas,046 ,047,129,130
, W.G.,142
CONAWAY, D.B.,151
CONE, John,211
CONELLY, Ezekiel,135
CONLEY, Ezekiel,131,133,134,136,
138
CONNELLY, E.,145
, Ezekiel,153
, Peter,211
CONNER, Miles M.,133
, Samuel,133
, Thomas,130
CONROY, Michael,133
CONWAY, A.,140
COOK, Austin,135
, Benj.,152
, David,060,088,162,194
, Geo.,147
, J.C.,128
, John,132
, Martin,211
, Peter,211
, S.W.,140
, W.Main,138
, William,152
COOKE, David,061
, Isaac S.W.,002
COOPER, (Mrs),159 ,183
, (Wid),027
, Christopher C.,062
, D.L.,141
, Drussina,062,103
, E.H.,147
, Elizabeth,032 ,044,172,
193
, H.,147
, J.B.,102
, J.D.,159
, J.L.,147
, J.M.,146,153
, James,156
, Jasper B.,062
, Jno.,146
, John L.,062
, John,019,020,032,043,044
,051,062,103,172,175
,176,183,185,187,191
,193,194,198,211,212

, Jonathan,026,032,033,043
,159,162,163,166,171
,172,174,179,182,186
,189,193,198,212
, Patience,087
, R.H.,194
, Rachel R.,189
, Smith D.,063,198
, Susan,198
, Vach,193
, Vachel,032 ,044,172
COPELAND, James,155
, John W.,070
, John,102 ,116,131
, Malinda F.,089
, Martin,142
, Sal,150
, Solomon,038 ,039,067,
102,212
, W.C.,138
, William J.,089
, Wm.,139

COPELEN, Solomon,128
COPLAND, Thomas,149
CORBLEY, Paul,156
CORETIN, Robert M.,024
CORK, James,138
CORNHILL, Robt.,152
CORTNEY, Jonathan,212
CORTILLE, Denneth,153
CORY, Russell R.,212
COSSEY, H.,153
    , Herbert Jr.,118
    , James W.,151
    , John,129,130,133
    , Lenard,133
    , Lucretia,118
    , Luke Jr.,133
    , Luke,132,141
    , Mary,118
    , Sarah,118
    , W.H.D.,118
    , William,119
COUCH, James,062
    , Jas.,197
    , Moses P.,065
    , Moses W.,100
    , W.P.,153,156
COULTER, James,031
COULTON, George W.,003
    , Hartgrove,003
    , James,003
    , Milly,003
    , Nancy,003
    , Sally,003
    , Thomas,003
COUNCE, Cassell,152
    , Reddon,136
    , Ridding,133
    , W.J.,091
COUNTS, A.M.,146
    , William,101
COUPLAND, Alexd.,143
    , J.W.,143
    , Richd.,143
    , Thos.,147
    , W.C,145
COURTIS, George,150
    , Helory,150
    , W.F.,150
COURTNEY, Amos,136
    , Andrew,155
    , James,129,149
    , John,212
    , Jonathan,008 ,054,212
    , Tinsy,054
COURTNY, Conall,149
COVEY, A.B.M.,056
    , A.K.,118
    , Alfred K.,106
    , E.S.,062
    , Edward S.,198
    , Green S.,135
    , H.N.,108
    , Huldah,062 ,198
    , Jane,062
    , John M.,053
    , John Marshall,185
    , John T.,136
    , John,061,196
    , Joshua J.,052,186
    , Leon,062
    , Leven Ed.,177
    , Leven L.,045,177
    , Levin V.,187
    , Lewis G.W.,177
    , Margaret E.,052
    , Martha A.,062
    , Mary,177
    , May,062
    , Minerva,056
    , Minneford,062
    , N.W.,200
    , Nancy H.,053,185
    , Nancy,061,195
    , Noble H.,177
    , Noble W.,045,052,095,177,
        186,187
    , Rebecca E.,052 ,186
    , Robert,062
    , Roena,106
    , Russell R.,016 ,053,064,
        185,193,195
    , Russell,186
    , Sarah,095,177
    , Sophina,062
    , W.W.,191
    , Wesley,016 ,053,061,185,
        186,193,195,196
    , William W.,052 ,186
COVINGTON, Malinda,052
COVY, S.G.W.,140
COWAN, A.B.,081
COX, David,144
    , James,142
    , Joseph W.,026
    , Joseph,158
    , Merideth,158 ,212
    , Merideth,026
    , William,026,158,212
CRABB, Steven Wright,212
    , Steven,212
CRAFT, Geo.R.,216
CRAIG, Saml.,151
    , Samul.,153
CRAMPTON, John,212
CRANESHAM, Jackson,017
CRAWFORD, ,155
CREASEY, S.P.,148
CREASY, A.R.,137
    , Jno.,148
    , John,144,146,152
    , L.,142
    , S.P.,138,140,152

CREASY, Stephen P.,137 ,144
    , W.R.,146
    , William B.,144
CREEL, James M.,079,080,085,088,
        106
CREESY, Jeremiah,151
CRENSHAW, Elizabeth,018
    , Jackson,018 ,096,167,
        172
CRISSMAN, Jane,043
CROCKET, George,155
    , Mary L.E.,064
CROCKETT, Mary E.,098
    , Mary,086
CROMBY, H.,150
CRONK, Isaac,155
CROOK, D.D.,138,143
CROOKER, Willis,144
CROSS, Henry,212,213
    , W.C.,153
CROTTS, David,008
    , Eliza,008
    , Elizabeth,008
    , Joseph,008
    , Lewis,008 ,142
    , Polly,009
    , V.,147
    , Valentine,009
CROUCH, James,156
    , Willis,137
CROWDER, John,140 ,143
    , Joseph,156
    , Saml.,143
CROWNOVER, Joseph,213
CRUCY, Stephen P.,136
CRUMP, ,150
    , R.W.,093,095,103
CRUMSEY, Stephen P.,132
CRUMWELL, James,150
CRUNK, George,130
    , Wm.,213
CRUSEY, Ambrose,132
    , Stephen,134
CRUTCHFIELD, Jerry M.,143
CULLINS, John G.,115
    , Mary(Mrs),115
CUMBERLAND COLL.,126
CUMMINS, Christopher N.,213
CUNNINGHAM, Aarom,188
    , Aaron,020 ,197
    , Aron,055
    , J.M.,108,120
    , J.W.,114
    , L.H.,145
    , L.J.,142
    , Levi,050,055,066,163
        188,197,213
    , Thomas,013
    , Thos.,213
    , William,127
CURTIS, Moses,150
    , Samuel,153
    , Woodson,153
DALLUN, W.,149
DALTON, Elishia,213
    , Samuel,213
DAMERELL, Zachariah,078
DAMERIL, Joseph,130,139,140
DAMES, Delphia,129
DANIEL, J.W.,064,104
    , Jancy,064
    , Lewis,129
    , Nancy,104
    , Pompey,213
    , Robert,213
    , Watson,103
    , Wm.,142
DANIELS, (Mrs),148
    , Henry,151
    , J.,148
DARLTON, Davis,213
DARNES, Merideth,129
DARVEN, A.J.,147
    , P.P.,147
DAVEY, J.L.,122
    , John L.,016
    , R.,069
    , R.D.,095
    , Richard D.,164
    , Richard,034 ,164,175
    , S.E.,122
    , Sarah A.,122
    , Thomas,034
    , William T.,164
DAVI(?), Meridd,131
DAVID, Berry M.,184
    , Isaac,184
    , James(Heirs),125
DAVIDSON, George F.,091
    , George,186
    , J.J.,068
    , Jackson,141
    , Jacob,141
    , John,113
    , Robt.,155
    , S.S.,113
DAVIS, Archibald,166,213
    , Austin,087
    , B.A.,147
    , G.W.,153,156
    , H.M.,068,147,213
    , Henry W.,051,054
    , Isaiah(Heirs),126
    , J.D.,153
    , James D.,109
    , James,008,131,133
    , John,151
    , Joseph,199
    , M.W.,151
    , Margaret E.,195
    , Meredith,134

DAVIS, Merideth,137
    , Mourning,013
    , Samuel,060 ,195
    , William,109 ,138
    , Wm.,142
DAVISS, H.W.,183
DAVY, Bowen,021,041,047,063,064,
        074,151,172,175,180,
        187,213
    , J.L.,117
    , Jahu,034
    , Jehu,022 ,023,028,063,159
    , John,143 ,158,160,172,213
    , Katherine,091
    , R.D.,088 ,095
    , Richard S.,093
    , Richard,165
    , Thomas,063 ,086,088,103,108
        115,160,164
    , W.T.,016 ,088
DAY, Garland,174
    , John,127
    , L.F.,137
    , Moss,091
    , R.H.,151
    , R.T.,128
    , Reuben,041,174
    , Richard S.,099
    , Samel.,149
    , Saml.,143 ,151
DEAL, Nelson,134
DEAN, Bedford,008
    , Cornelious,008
    , Delpha,008
    , Jeremiah,008
    , Sherod,008
DEARIN, James,113
    , Larkin,137
    , N.P.,113
DEARING, Larkin,137,145
DEBERRY, Benjamin,053 ,054,186,
        195
    , Disha,054 ,186
    , Henry D.,053 ,186,195
    , L.W.,146 ,151,213
DELANEY, John W.,132
    , Joseph,151
    , Wesley,013
DELANY, John,213
DELLIAN, Jessee,128
DELOACH, James,135
DENHAM, ,143
    , William,137
DENISON, R.M.,135
DENNUM, Wilson,026
DESHAGO, Miles,130
DEVANEY, John,133
DEVEREAS, Thomas,126
DIAL, Jiremiah,135
DICKENS, Samuel,126
DICKERSON, Mat,153
    , Matthew,132
    , T.E.L.M.,143
    , T.E.S.M.,144
DICKEY, Alex.K.,147
    , Alexander,213
    , Alexd.,148
    , S.G.,136
    , Samuel,126
DICKS, Sampson,214
DICKSON, Alexander R.,176
    , Alexander,009
    , Ann,009
    , Elizabeth,009 ,028,044,
        176
    , Jane,176
    , John H.,009,044,176
    , John,032,162,168
    , M.M.,113 ,121
    , Matthew,133,136
    , Nancy,009
    , Sarah,009
    , T.E.S.M.,146
    , Thomas,126
    , Thos.,129
    , William N.,009,044,176
    , William,032,162,168
DICKY, A.K.,149
DICUS, William,129
DIFFEY, John,155
DILL, Asa,214
    , D.M.,090
    , J.A.,090
    , James,090,106,214
    , Patsy A.,106
    , Patsy,090
    , Susan,090
DILLIAN, John,127 ,128
    , Joseph,131
DILLON, Joseph,099 ,133,134
DINKINS, Edward G.,040 ,044
DINSON, A.W.,143
DISHAGA, Miles,140
DIXON, Abraham,127
DOBBIN, Jesse,082
DOBBINS, Jesse B.,130 ,131
DODD, Josiah,082
DODDS, Josiah,065 ,066,067,079,
        114,214
DOLLERSON, S.R.D.,146
DOLTON, J.H.,153
DONAHOO, John D.,069
    , John J.,077
    , William,077
    , William,078
DONAVAN, Jas.,145
DONAVEN, Sndras,126
DONHAU, W.,149
DONOHAU, William,066
DONOHOO, Angelina,054
    , Elinor,054
    , John D.,071
    , Polly,078

DONOHOO, Robt.,147
DONOVEN, Andrew,010,214,217
DORAN, A.,190
  , Alex.,189
  , Alexander,065,074,076,079
    ,187
  , Joseph,083
  , William,135
  , Wm.,146
DORCAS, James,130
DOREN, Alex.,175
  , Alexander,037,040,046,169
    ,176,179,180,182,195
  , James G.,037,169,176
DORMAN, John,152
DORNEL, Larthan,139
DOTY, Nathaniel,126
DOUGLAS, Jonathan,128
DOVE, W.H.,156
DOWDY, William,047
DOWING, Joseph,131
DOWNEY, D.H.,137
DOWNING, A.P.,082
  , Francis,151
  , J.M.,135
  , John,134
  , Josiah,128,130,133,134
  , W.,142
  , Wm,214
DUBERRY, Jesse,138
DUCAN, Jesse,130
DUCKWORTH, Anna,109
  , Elizabeth,109
  , Harriet,109
  , John W.,109
  , Mary A.,109
  , S.A.,134,142
  , Sarah J.,109
  , Thomas M.,007,011
  , W.H.,065,079,084,106,
    107,109
  , W.J.,214
  , Waldrip,151
  , Wilie J.,011
  , Willie J.,010
  , Wilson H.,194
  , Wm.S.,109
DUDLEY, A.L.,150
  , Guilford,129
  , J.J.,149
  , J.W.,156
  , Jackson,147
  , Jas.,147
  , S.S.,150
DUDLY, S.S.,149
DUFF, Alfred,142
  , James,021,032,033,163
  , Robert,021,214
DUGAN, Thomas,156
DUKE, Josiah,131
  , William B.,130
DULANEY, J.,148
  , Jacob,005
DULEEN, John,130
DULION, Jesse,130
DULLER, Polly,084
DUNAWAY, John,134
DUNCAN, D.S.,147
  , J.J.,148
  , Jesse D.,059
  , Jesse J.,056
  , Jesse,128
  , Jessee,146
  , Jos.,148
  , Jos.Jr.,108
  , Joseph,025 ,032,034,035,
    067,068,191
  , Lewis,145
  , Rebeca,068
  , Rebecca,067
  , Robt.,136
  , W.F.,144
  , W.S.D,149
  , William C.,054 ,056,059
  , William O.,054
DUNGAN, Nathan,092
DUNHAM, William,152
  , Wm.,152
DUNN, Willis,134
DURHAM, Thos.,145
DURMAN, W.,139
DYER, Joel,127

EADES, Leah,084
EADS, C.H.,163 ,167
  , Charles H.,033,036,169,176

  , Gabriel,003 ,005,006,012,
    013
  , William,136
EAKES, Harvey,066
  , Hovey,139
EAKS, Zachaiah,042
  , Zachariah,130,174
EARBY, William M.,082
EAGELEY, Saml.,144
EATON, Wm.,137
EAVES, Davis,133
  , William,133 ,135,137
EBERTON, John S.,127
EDDINGS, J.B.,141
  , James,139
EDMISTON, E.T.,142
EDWARD, Levi,129
EDWARDS, Elijah,006,007,008
  , Levi,132
  , Susan,100
  , Tatum,153
  , Thomas F.,013
  , W.M.,144
  , William,130,132
  , Willie B.,032

EDWARDS, Wm.,153
EELLIOT, William,128
ELDRIDGE, Elijah,003
  , James,147
ELIOT, Josep,150
ELKINS, Martha,152
ELLIOT, William,094
ELLIOTT, Jos.,147 ,148
  , Margaret,162
  , William,094
  , Wm.,145
ELLIS, (Capt) 110
  , G.G.,146
  , Green G.,144
  , J.J.,189
  , Jacob,145
  , Joseph W.,018,019,020,164
    ,167,172
EMBERSON, Isaac,214
  , J.D.,144
EMERSON, Isaac,133 ,214
  , Jas.,139
  , Thomas,130,214
EMMERSON, Eli,031 ,162,168,171,
    180
  , Isaac,128
  , James,008
  , John,155
  , M.T.,120
  , T.,140
  , Terence,031 ,162,168,
    171
  , Terrine,180
EMMET, Christopher,144
EMMITT, C.,147
ENGLAND, A.R.,083
  , Thos.,137
ENGLISH, James,010 ,214,215
EOFF, Dicy,017
  , Elijah,113
  , Eliza J.,113
  , James D.,113
  , Joseph,017,018
  , Nancy L.,113
  , Sena H.,113
  , Sena,113
  , Senah,108
  , Squire,108,113,128,133
  , Winny R.,113
  , Wm.,155
ERWIN, James B.,067
  , Nathaniel,021,158
  , Rebecca,067
ESSORY, John,156
ESTUS, Jas.D.,152
  , John B.,137
EVANS, Eger,033
  , Joseph,011
  , Stirling C.,092
  , William,134
EVES, Thos.,145
EVIS, Thoms,153
FALKNER, John,129 ,131
  , Lewis W.,011 ,013,018,
    215
FALLS, G.,151
  , Lettie,005
  , Lettis,015
  , William,126 ,215
FARRAR, Jefferson,003 ,215
  , John,017,215
FARRIS, L.E.,115
FAULKNER, W.W.,145
FAULTENBERRY, M.,150
FAWLS, William,125
FEDRICK, G.W.,153
FELLOWS, Thomas J.G.,040,180
FELOWS, Thomas J.G.,172
FENIO, Matthew,151
FERGISON, Jerimiah,151
FERIL, Mathew,149
FERILL, Wm.,150
FERREL, William,132
FERRELL, Vincent,140
FERRILL, William,215
FERRIS, J.D.,153
FIELD, Thos.,152
FIELDER, Andrew,127
FIGJERROL, R.L.,132
FILLOWS, Sarah,172
  , T.J.C.,172
  , Thomas J.G.,040
FINCH, Isaac,077
  , Wm.,147
FINGER, Robert,134
FINLAY, Joel,152
FINLEY, Joel,151
FISHER, Abraham,098
  , Caroline,073
  , Elizabeth,073
  , F.M.,098,115
  , Frances M.,090
  , Geo.,047
  , J.F.,148
  , J.M.,147
  , John F.,143,144
  , Jonathan H.,073
  , Lucy Ann,073
  , Lydia M.,073
  , Martin J.,073
  , Martin J.L.,073
  , Mary Jane,073 ,115
  , Paul H.,073
  , Thomas,155
  , William,023,136
  , Wm.,134
FISSHER, T.A.,150
FLAKE, J.L.,150
  , R.K.,148
  , Robert,150 ,153,155
FLANNARY, Daniel A.,215
FLAT, L.W.,137
  , Madison,137

FLATT, G.W.,149
  , J.S.,146
  , James,095,096
  , Solomon,062 ,197
  , Stephen W.,144
  , William,062 ,197
FLEMING, Elizabeth W.,095
  , John,129
  , Margaret,079
  , Phebe,079
  , Rebecca,079
  , W.D.,070 ,095
FLEMMING, Elizabeth,074
  , Phebe,074
  , W.D.,086
  , Wm.O.,177
FLOYD, Benjamin,155
  , M.,155
FORBES, Collin,020
  , James,215
  , Robert,091 ,215
FORBISH, Robert,106
FORCHAND, Elihu,147
FORD, John,215
  , Richard,007
FOREHAND, Martin,170
FOREST, James M.,122
FORESTER, Robert,128
FOSTER, Anthony,215
  , Robert,215
FOUDLES, Storling L.,062
FOWLER, Josiah,132
  , Lewis,132
  , M.R.,131
  , S.L.,090,100
  , S.T.,199
  , Sterling S.,079
  , Stirling L.,077
  , Terenze,134
  , Z.G.,142
FRAILEY, Marton,199
FRALEY, A.J.,163,170
  , Andrew J.,032 ,163
  , Caleb,052 ,176,182
  , D.,150
  , David,052 ,176,182
  , Elizabeth A.,052
  , Elizabeth,052 ,182
  , G.W.,142
  , Henderson G.,033,162,170

  , Henderson,163
  , J.C.,142
  , J.J.,065
  , James T.,119
  , James,052 ,176,182
  , John C.,182
  , John E.,052
  , Lucinda,162
  , Martin,032 ,039,052,065,
    163,170,171,176,179,
    182,184,187,189,193,
    215
  , Nancy,176
  , Sarah A.,052,182
  , Sarah,033 ,162,163,170,
    171
  , Sary,163
  , Thomas,176
  , Wm.Jackson,162
FRANCAM, Bryant,153
FRANCIS, Geo.M.,142
  , W.H.,065
FRAND, Joseph,131
FRANK, Eli,153
  , Frederic,116,117
  , John,117
  , Nancy,117
  , William G.,117
  , William,117
FRANKLIN, Betty(N-Free),050
  , Eliz.(N-Free),040
  , Nancy(N-Free),040
FRANKS, Bazzell,055
  , Edmund,135
  , J.W.,156
  , Jacob,128
  , James,144 ,156
  , Jas.,147
  , John,129,130,144
  , Joseph,129 ,156
  , Robt.,147
  , W.H.,094,119
  , William H.,057 ,079,084,
    115
  , William,063,127,130,132
  , Wm.,133,142,150
FRAZIER, Dock,155
  , W.S.,147
FREEMAN, Benjamin R.,032
  , Adaline C.,032,058
  , Adaline,037
  , B.R.,146,148,194,197
  , Benjamin A.,058
  , Benjamin R.,057
  , Elizabeth Ann,037
  , Elizabeth,037 ,058,168
  , H.A.,127
  , J.J.,146 ,148
  , James J.,032 ,054,140
  , James,037,052,058,151
  , John L.,036,037
  , John Lewis,032
  , John,047 ,127,142
  , Sarah,036 ,037
  , Sarah Jane,032,058
  , Tally,215
  , W.A.,143
  , William A.,032,037
  , William P.,032,037,041,
    162,168,173,177,181,
    185,188,193
  , William,194,197

FREEMAN, Wm.P.,029 ,030
FREEZE, Thomas,153
FRENCH, Daniel,077
    , Elizabeth,077
    , John Joseph,077
    , Wm.Jefferson,077
FRIE, A.B.,140
    , Alfred,140
    , J.,096
    , James G.,140
    , Jonathan,115
    , L.D.,133
    , W.G.,115
FRIELDS, Thomas,128
FRILEY, Martin,032 ,215
FRIS(?), Hugh,014
FRISE, John,152
FRLY, Andrew J.,032
    , Martin,032
    , Solomon,032
FROLER, H.,147
FRULDS, Thomas,131
    , Thos.,133
FRULES, Micky,135
FRULIY, Thomas,134
FRY, G.M.,145
FULLER, Emily,186 ,191
    , Jefferson,003 ,015
    , John,216
    , Joshua J.,191
    , Margaret,191
    , Noble W.,191
    , Rebecca E.,191
    , Sally,162
FURGERSON, Regal,216
GADSON, William,139
GAINES, Gabriel D.,140
GALLION, John,143
GALLORY, John,007
GAMAL, Rob.,150
GAMBILL, Benjamin,043
GAMMILL, Alfred,105
    , Archibald,134
    , Ebenezer,009 ,216
    , Elisha,042,173,175
    , F.G.,105
    , James P.,050
    , James T.,183
    , James,042 ,045,101,175,
        178
    , Jas.,101
    , Lewis,067 ,072,140
    , Margarett,050
    , Milas,139
    , Moses Jr.,142
    , Moses,050 ,216
    , Rebecca,173
    , Samuel,089,127
GAMMILL, Samuel,128
    , W.S.,101 ,183
    , William S.,050
    , William T.,142
    , William,130
    , Wm.,134,216
GANNT, Absolom B.,050
    , Andrew J.,050
    , Daniel P.,050
    , Elijah N.,050
    , James L.,050
    , Jesse B.,050
    , Jesse V.,050
    , Lucinda A.,050
    , Mary Ann,050
    , Nancy C.,050
    , Robert W.,050
    , William C.,050
GANT, A.J.,103
    , D.A.,149
    , Daniel P.,095
    , James L.,095
    , Jesse B.,216
    , Jesse,159
    , John,107
    , Robert W.,103
    , T.R.,149
GANTT, A.B.,064,073
    , A.T.,073
    , America,195
    , Andrews J.,063
    , Caroline M.,060
    , Daniel,085
    , David P.,073
    , E.N.,064
    , E.P.,064
    , Elijah,073 ,085
    , Elizabeth P.,057
    , Elizabeth W.,058
    , Elizabeth,070
    , G.V.,139
    , J.B.,057,058,065,085,191,
        192
    , James L.,063,064,073
    , Jesse B.,018,021,035,050,
        058,064,073,076,158,
        160,161,165,169,174,
        178,181,184,185,187,
        188,190,191
    , Jesse V.,060
    , Jesse,085,181
    , John,061,088,194
    , Jonathan W.,060 ,194
    , Jonathan(Heirs),140
    , Jonathan,075,195
    , L.H.,076
    , Levina A.,065
    , Main L.,058
    , Nancy E.,061,194
    , Nancy,064,088
    , Rachel,191
    , Robert W.,073
    , Robert,065 ,085
    , W.E.C.,065

GANTT, William C.,050 ,070,181,
        184,190
    , William,057
    , Wm.C.,058,193
GARDNER, C.H.,132
    , Thomas,125,126
GARLAND, John,125 ,126,216
GARNER, (Mrs),121
    , B.M.,147
    , D.E.G.,146
    , David,033 ,084,162
    , Elizabeth,024 ,026,057,
        161,191,192
    , Gabriel D.,084
    , H.,139
    , Harriet,084
    , Henry G.,008,072,161,177

    , Henry Sr.,161 ,186,190
    , Henry,024 ,026,065,072,
        084,093,131,138,159,
        160,161,165,169,173,
        181,216
    , James,026 ,065,084,161,
        165,169,177,181,186
    , John C.,145
    , John F.,084
    , John,002
    , Joshua,026 ,054,055,065,
        084,161,165,169,177,
        181,186
    , Mary Ann,093,095
    , Nancy,084
    , Peggy,084
    , Polly,084
    , Richard,132,139
    , William,092,093,095,121,
        143
GARRARD, D.M.,129
    , E.C.,119
    , Elizabeth,082
    , Henry,033 ,104,163,216
    , J.B.,144
    , James,139
    , Richard,137
    , Thos.B.,138
    , W.B.,130
    , William,082
GARRETT, Newman,117
    , W.T.,087
GARRISON, Arthur,057,151,191
    , Chisley,046 ,181,186
    , Ezekiel,216
    , Isaiah,067
GARSON, James,127
GARVILL, Elisha,216
GATIS, John,141
GATT, Joseph S.,131
GAY, John,128
GEORGE, John,101,150
GERARD, Daniel,129
GERMAN, Charles,008
GIBBS, (Wid),051
    , C.C.,051,135,183
    , Coonrod,014
    , Delila,185
    , Delilah,053
    , Isham P.,132,133
    , John,053,138,185
    , T.,085
    , W.T.,080
GIBON, J.J.,152
GIBSON, Hardin,194
    , J.,108
    , Jacob,216
BIDDINGS, J.P.,156
GIFFORD, Henderson,140
    , Jno.,146
    , Sitranus,216
GILBERT, E.A.,121
    , Eliza,112
    , J.W.,112
    , James H.,141
    , James,135
    , Jeremiah,216 ,217
    , Joseph W.,112
    , Pleasant,149
    , Pleast.,151
    , W.C.,147 ,149
    , Wm.,133
GILCHRIST, Cornelius,088,096
    , Daniel,137
    , John,088,096
    , Malcom,125
    , Nicholas,096
GILDCHRIST, John,094
GILL, George W.,131
    , James C.,131
    , W.B.,148
GILLES, John,217
GILLESPIE, Daniel,125
GILLIS, Alx.,023
    , D.W.N.,128
    , Dougal,017
    , Dougold,068
    , E.J.,115,117
GINNITTON, Sellers,065
GIVIN, William,128
GLENN, Moses,098
GLOVER, James D.,097
GOAD, Betty,149
GODWIN, Alfred,136 ,138,143,147,
        151
    , Jacob,129 ,133 134
    , Samuel,217
    , W.A.,153
    , W.C.,146
GOFF, Lewis,153,155
GOFORTH, Jerry,144 ,147
GOLD-, Denis,149
GOLDSMITH, John,134
    , Wesley,217
    , William,033 ,169

GOLDSMITH, Wm.,163
GOLLAIN, John,149
GOLLEHER, David,015
GOODIN, James,010 ,014
GOODLOE, John M.,126,127,217
GOODMAN, Samuel,126
GOODNER, Godfrey,018
GOODWIN, James,217
GORDAN, Nicholas,137
GORDEN, George,217
GORDON, Beverly,137
GORE, Jas.,148
GORFUTH, Alfred,050
GORVERE, John,152
GOSSETT, Henry,217
GOTILLY, J.T.,156
GOWEN, Cull,155
GOWERS, John,151
GRAHAM, A.H.,134
    , Charles,023
    , H.N.,131
    , Isaac,217
    , J.P.,141
    , James B.,159,160,162,166
        172,174
    , James,012 ,017,057,125,
        159,165,169,173,177,
        181,187,190,217
    , Richard,005
GRAVES, J.C.,145
    , Jacob,130
    , John,130,131
    , Lewis,156
GRAY, Franis,136
    , George,133
    , Henry L.,004
    , Jackson,103 ,143,144
    , John,140 ,141,143
    , Michel,156
    , Milton,034
    , Robert,019,127
    , Sarah A.,036
    , Sarah Ann,034,165
    , Sarah,167
    , T.P.,146
    , Thomas P.,144
    , Thomas,018,028,041,159
    , Thos.,217
    , Thos.P.,140 ,143
    , Wellis,155
    , William F.,132
    , Wm.F.,134,135,140
GRAYHAM, 129
GREARNER, James,094
GREEN, A.S.,143
    , Andrew,087 ,126,217
    , Andrw.T.,144
    , Daniel,131 ,133
    , E.W.,149
    , J.C.,151
    , J.M.,140,141
    , James C.,088,089,097,136,
        149
    , John,129,134
    , Miles,153
    , Nancy,087
    , William,135
GREENFIELD, Adam,131
GREENWOOD, A.L.,127
GREER, Burtwell,133
    , Daniel,131
    , John,125
GRESHAM, M.H.,150
    , Robert,073
GRIFFIN, Edbine,134
    , James,139
    , Kizziah,105
    , Thos.,152
    , William,136,150
GRIGGS, Alfred,127
GRIMES, James B.,026,032,037,045
        178,186
    , James,217
    , Rebecca,178
GRISAGE, James M.,035
BROGAN, L.B.,063,072,073,087,097
        153,194
    , Lewis B.,043,189
    , Lewis,193
    , Sarah H.,043
    , Sarah,174
GROSS, Isaac,156
    , John,105
GROVE, Henson,125
GROVES, Henson,126 ,217
    , Josiah,131
    , Matthewes,131
GUIN, Wiley,149
GUINN, B.F.,099
    , Champen,136
    , Champion,137
    , Martha,099
    , Mary,080
    , W.C.,137,144
GULLIN, Josiah S.,143
GULLUR, Samul,149
GUN, Jackson,132
GUTHRIE, George W.,014
GUTTERY, Lee,137
GUUNIN, John,153
GUY, W.C.,153
GWIN, B.F.,148
    , Mary,142
GWINN, Champin,142

H--, Jesse,131
HACKWORTH, Isabella,015
    , John,015
HACTNICK, Asa,135
HAGARTY, Wm.Jr.,140
HAGDEN, Elbert,080
    , Ephraim,080
    , Holley A.,080

HAGDEN, Martha,080
, Nancy Jane,080
, Thomas,080
HAGDON, Thomas,069
HAGERTY, Wm.,217
HAGEY, Jno.,148
HAGGARD, Henry,151
, James,068 ,072,130
, Jonathan,025
HAGGY, Henry,104
, John,190
, Lewis,104
HAGON, Jacob,218
HAGY, Celina,183
, Henry,172,183,195,218
, John,049 ,066,153,183,187, 195,198
, Lewis,109
, Rebecca,183
, Robert,109
, William,109 ,183,195
HAIL, Stephen S.,218
, Thomas,061,189,196
HAIN, T.P.,142
HAINES, Charles,218
, G.W.,218
HAIR, Abel,034
, Martha,034
HAIRE, Caion(?),017
, Martha,017
, Richard,026
, William,017
HALBERT, William,016,218
HALDIN, Joshua,127
HALE, Benjamin,012
, G.S.,218
, James,127,137
, Jasper,155
, R.C.,127
, Richard C.,023,218
HALEMAN, W.W.,110
HALES, John,140
HALETT, William,218
HALEY, Tilman,128
HALL, David,127
, Jackson,131
, James,129
, Thos.,054
, William,127
HALLEY, Eli,133
HAM, Jacob,053 ,076,132,186,196
, John P.,053
, Thomas B.,053
HAMBLETON, Joseph,166
HAMES, Alexander,155
, Charles,049 ,182
, Dillila,049
, J.T.,149
, John T.,049
, John,182
, Robert,097
, Weatherly,129
HAMIL, Alexander,194
HAMILTON, Andrew,110
, David,152
, Elizabeth,110
, G.M.,074 ,077,078,109, 110,200
, G.Miles,071
, Geo.M.,076,107,150
, George M.,057,070,097, 108,110,111
, George,131,130
, J.(Heirs),142
, J.A.R.,108,110
, J.J.,066
, James G.,090 ,105,108, 110
, John,218
, Jonathan,153
, Joseph,033,172
, Susannah,109
HAMMILL, Alexander,059
HAMMOCK, Robert,155
HAMMONDS, Thomas,011
HAMMONS, Joseph,127
, Thos.,218
HAMPTON, Isaiah,130,131
HANCOCK, J.C.,169 ,176
, Joel C.,037,167,176,177
, William,130
, Willis,070,084
HAND, Elkin,218
, J.W.,083
HANES, Samuel,128
, Witherbe,127
HANKS, John,137
HANLEY, E.Y.,218
HANNA, James,117
HANNAH, (Wid),027
, Abraham,140
, Alex.,162
, Alexander,026 ,029,030, 158
, Elizabeth,054
, John,019,038,046,159,218
, Robert,022
, Robt.,139
HANNERS, Timothy,058
HARBET, John A.,150
HARBOR, Elijah,011 ,013
, Elisha,013
HARBOUR, E.,197
, Elijah,024,053,056,057, 058,065,069,070,102, 120,189,191,193,194, 200,218,219
, Elisha,023,057,085,095, 191,219
, Elizabeth,192
, J.G.,149

HARBOUR, Metil C.,191
, Nancy,191
, S.B.,102
, Saml.,189
, Samuel Belle,191
, Samuel,003,015,016,021, 035,057,170,175,179, 185,191,219
HARDEN, Robt.,149
HARDIN, A.M.,061,069,073,074,075 ,077,194,196
, A.S.,100
, Alexander M.,047,070,071 ,072,181,187
, Alexander S.,054
, Amos,014,060,083,220
, B.M.,140
, Benj.,079
, Benjamin,007,021,060,070 ,098,101,194,219
, Bird,142
, Byrd,143
, Calloway,147
, Caloway,143
, Elizabeth J.,075
, Elizabeth,075 ,078
, G.G.,094
, George M.,075
, George,072
, Gibson G.,060 ,098
, Gibson,010 ,060,061,195, 219,220
, Gideon,100
, Grace,100
, James,002 ,003,007,010, 011,012,013,014,093, 220,221
, John,060,061,070,086,096 ,098,101
, Joseph,002 ,012,149,221
, Margaret E.,077
, Margaret,073
, Mark,022,098,100
, Martin,011 ,012,014
, Mary Ann,060
, Mary,012,100
, Robert,060 ,073,077,100
, S.G.,152
, S.P.,150
, Swan,012
, Thomas M.,021
, William K.,022 ,054,083, 115
, William,108,221
HARGERSON, Parris,136
HARGROVE, E.C.,119
, John H.,119
, John,143
, O.H.,119
, S.B.,081 ,082
, Samuel D.,119
, Stanley M.,066,190
, Valentine,021,082,221
HARIS, Hugh,149
, William H.,150
HARLAN, F.G.,108
, Felix G.,097
, J.B.,108
HARLUN, G.,142
HARMAN, James,108
HARNER, Philip,130
HARPER, Yancey,134
, Yancy,140
HARPOUR, Charles,151
HARRIS, 145
, Ada,216
, Euphrodinia A.,062
, Freedonia A.,198
, H.,147
, H.W.,146
, Jn.Sr.,140
, John,131,133,140,153
, Josephine,062 ,066,197
, Joseph,146
, Julianna M.,062
, Julianna,198
, Marinda,198
, Martha J.,062
, Martha Jane,066
, Martha,197
, Nathaniel,221
, Rebecca,055,066,197
, Rice,055,066,197,198
, Rich.C.,221
, Richard C.,126 ,221
, Thomas,125 ,126
, William Z.,062 ,198
, William,198
, Wm.O.,133
HARRISON, A.D.,109
, Alex.,151
, Colley,155
, D.E.,153
, J.H.,143 ,146
, Lawrence,142
, Mary Jane,109
, Mary,083
, Orville,128
, Smith H ,064 ,144
, William P.,064
, William,127
HARRISS, Rebecca,188
, Rice,188
HARROD, John,221
HART, James W.,221
HARTGROVES, Minerva,160
HARVEY, Jesse,135
HARVIL, Alexander,153
HARWON, Elisha,127
HASEY, James,129
HASLIN, Columbus,141
HASSEL, 150

HASSEL, James W.,164
HASSELL, Elizabeth,106
, J.D.,095
, J.W.,094 ,095
, James W.,221
, Joseph,106
, Mak(?),106
, Woods,088
HATLEY, Alston,055 ,188
, Elizabeth,165
, Green,221
, J.S.,180
, James S.,034,048,072,183 ,187
, James,165 ,174
, Jesse,089
, Mark Jr.,135,149
, Mark,134
, Sherrod,034,136,165,174
HATLY, Sherrod,169 ,170
, Stephen,169
HATTLEY, Sherrod,149
HATTON, Charles,084
, Martha A.,084
HATTY, Austin,221
HAUGH, Stephen,221
HAWK, John,031 ,162,168,171,180
HAWKINS, Elizabeth T.,172
, Elizabeth,096
, J.C.,222
, James O.,025 ,034,039, 041,164,172,174
, James,172
, Jno.T.,164
, John T.,025
, Lucy,172
, M.T.,130 ,132
, Martin,172
, Mary,172
, P.B.,023 ,064,072,074, 158,159,164,174
, Parry B.,024 ,025,161, 172
, Percerville S.,039
, Perces,041
, Perry D.,041 ,158
, R.T.,109
, Roland T.,172
, Scott,064
, Susan E.,020
, William J.,109
HAWKS, James W.,127
HAYNES, Darling,016,087
, Geo.,153
, George,156
, Henry,088
, Hiram,088
, Jack,145
, W.,088
, Weatherby,150
HAYS, C.L.,111
, Calista,111
, Dudly,111
, Henry Jr.,144
, Henry Sr.,144
, James,111
, Jesse,091
, Lawson,111
, Wallace,106
HEAD, Josiah,135
, William,035
HEATHCOCK, H.,147
HEATON, William,131
HEDGEPATH, Richd.,144
HEFTON, William,132
HEIK, Henry,004
HELMACK, H.,150
HELMS, Jonathan,127,129
HELTON, A.B.,149
, James,102 ,103,109
, Jno.R.,145
HEMPHILL, R.C.,066 ,067,081
HENDERSON, John,144,146,151,152
, Saml.,146,152
, Samuel,151
, Thos.,222
HENDRICK, Isaac,222
HENDRICKS, C.,146
HENDRIX, Isaac,127
, William,127
HENKIN, William,127
HENLEY, James,136
, Thomas,131
HENLY, Janes,137
, Thomas,128
HENRY, Jesse,070,130,133,134,135 ,136,137
, Jno.,145
, W.,146
, W.A.,149
, William,143
, Wm.,222
HERRELL, W.W.,146
HERRING, J.H.,071
HERROD, Catherine,023
, George W.,134
, Jno.,023
, John P.,134
, John,021
, Washington,132
HERRON, Collins,136
HESTER, J.K.,173
, Stephen,132
, Wm.,222
HEWLETT, Wm.,222
HEWITT, Eli C.,103
, W.T.A.,103
HIBBARD, Joseph,222
HIBBITS, Robert,125
HICHCOCK, Edwin,137
HICKEY, Wm.R.,222
HICKS, Alex.,131

HICKS, George W.,151
  , John,131,133,138
HIGGINS, Geo.,148
  , George,144
  , Powell,126
HIGHMAN, Martin,152
HILBERTS, Robt.H.,126
HILL, Benj.,152
  , W.B.,144 ,146
  , Wm.B.,143
HINDS, Jerry,138
HINIMAN, W.D.,142
HINKLE, Battis,082
  , Bollis,095
  , Jessie,065
  , Jonathan,082,108
  , Mary,085,086
  , William,086
HISE, J.B.,148
HITCHCOCK, Elizabeth,115
  , Irwin,136
  , Isaac,008,020
  , Jefferson,115
  , Lorenz,093
HITHCOCK, H.,150
HIX, Isaac,127
HOBBS, Barnabas,096,222
  , E.,142
HODGE, ,096
  , Robert,156
  , Robt.,153
  , Thomas,080 ,105,128
  , William F.,111
  , Wm.F.,089
HODGEN, Mary,043
HODGES, Jesse,142
  , Josiah,133
  , Thos.,101
  , William F.,199
  , William,128
HOGAN, John,009,017
  , Thomas,010
HOGDEN, James,129 ,132,133,135
HOGY, Henry C.,052
  , William C.,052
HOLDEN, Dewson,141
HOLDIN, Archibald,137
HOLLAN, Chisley,222
HOLLAND, ,149
  , Asa,013,025
  , Bannister,023
  , Chisley,199
  , Chisly,062
  , James M.,052
  , Jesse,025
  , Jno.,023
  , T.A.,148
  , T.J.,151
  , Thomas J.,052
  , Thomas,199
  , Thos.,062
  , William M.,052
  , William,131
HOLLANDSWORTH, John,035,167
HOLLINGSWORTH, J.B.,155
  , John,178
  , Jos.,146
HOLLINGWORTH, Joseph,152
HOLLIS, John,191
  , William L.,128
HOLT, A.J.,148
  , Amos,144
  , Anderson,151
  , David,222
  , Fielder S.,153
  , Giles,016,040,070,078,089,
      172,180
  , H.J.,153
  , James,139
  , Jennetta,200
  , John W.,040 ,172,180
  , Tilman,016
HOOD, Andrew,128
  , James,138
  , Robert,138
HOOK, James M.,120
HOOKS, Harry(N-Free),114
  , Harry,067
  , James M.,112,143
  , William C.,143
HOPKINS, E.L.,136
HOPPER, Avis,117
  , Charles Jr.,152
  , Charles,103
  , E.S.,106,117
  , Emily,117
  , Minda,117
  , T.E.,117
HORAM, S.P.,148
HORRELL, Joanna,109
  , Levi J.,109
HORTON, Henry,128
  , Lemuel,120
HOSEA, James,222
  , Jesse,222
HOSEY, Stephen,033 ,166,172
  , Stephen,127
HOUGE, Stephen,127
HOUGHTON, J.R.,155
HOUSE, Alice(Mrs),144
  , Mark,130,135,144
  , Martin,132
HOUSEY, Benjamin,139
HOUSTON, ,150 ,159
  , James H.,092
  , John,017 ,019,022,026,
      158,159
  , Matthew C.,022
  , Samuel,025
  , Wm.A.,092
HOWARD, G.,139
  , George,129 ,131,132,134,
      135,136,138
  , Susannah,105

HOWELL, ,101
  , Benj.F.,102
  , Benjamin,099,102
  , David P.,102
  , Doctor Riley,102
  , E.,137
  , Jonathan,102
  , Jourdan,222
  , Levi J.,102
  , Levi,099
  , Mary A.,102
  , Mary,102
  , Saml.,152
  , Samuel,151
  , William,125,126,129,133
HUALESS, R.,149
HUCKABEE, John,152
  , Shamet,152
HUCKABY, Isaac,137
HUDDLESTON, Benjamin,003
  , James,004 ,010,019,
      222
  , John,133
HUDEBURG, Solomon,038
HUDIBURG, Solomon,028 ,038,160
HUDIBURGH, Jane,060
  , Joseph A.,060
  , S.,171
  , Solomon S.,048 ,054,
      055
  , Solomon,039 ,166,170,
      179,222
  , Thos.,139
HUDSON, C.Y.,108
  , G.G.,153
  , H.M.,108,153
  , Joseph G.,047 ,181,187
  , Peter,108
HUGGINS, Geo.,152
  , John,115
  , L.E.,115
  , Thomas,129
  , Thos.,016
HUGHES, A.M.,021,222
  , Archilaws M.,005
  , B.B.,142
  , Colbert,155
  , J.H.,139
  , James N.,146
  , Stephen,222
  , Vistal,148
  , W.C.,077,139
  , William C.,029 ,030,074
HUGHLETT, William,125 ,126
HUGHLIN, Mary,118
HUGHLING, David,127
  , Reuben,223
HUGHLITS, W.T.A.,103
HUGHS, Alexander M.,049
  , J.M.,140
  , James,049
  , Wm.C.,223
HULERY, G.M.,143
HULETT, William,126
HULING, James,130
  , Ruben,134
  , S.M.,150
  , William,096,135
HUMBLE, Jacob,009
HUMPHEYS, C.,139
HUMPHRES, Thomas,138
HUMPHREYS, Michael,129
  , Michaiel,129
  , Thomas,129 ,131,132,
      143
HUMPHRIES, Thomas,135
  , Thos.,134,137
HUMPHRYS, T.,139
HUNDLEY, Edmund,129
  , J.Y.,036 ,129,176
  , Jas.,148
HUNDLY, Freeman,129
  , J.G.,024
HUNLEY, J.Y.,167
  , Jordan Y.,036
HUNT, Calvin,153
  , Jonathan,140
HUNTER, Daniel H.,028
  , Daniel,137
  , Danil,138
  , John,141
  , Malcolm,223
  , Robert,007
  , Samuel C.,150
HUNTON, Geo.,153
HUNTS, H.,148
HURLEY, Asa C.,049
  , Henry H.,049
  , Henry,155 ,183
  , James C.,049
  , James Jr.,145
  , James,083
  , John R.,049,172
  , John,223
  , Josiah,223
  , Polly,049 ,183
  , Rebecca,041,172,173,183
  , Thomas J.,049
  , Thomas,041 ,049,066,172,
      173,183,187,190,195
  , Thos.,075
HURST, Thompson,036,051,083,184,
      191,192
HURT, Jackson,135 ,136
HURTT, Thomas,134
HUSSELL, J.D.,152
HUSTON, Elizabeth,200
HUTCHENS, Mark,132 ,134
HUTCHINGS, A.,141
HUTCHINSON, Thomas,127
HUTCHISON, Amos,133
HUTON, Taswell,129
HUTSON, Charles,156

HUTSON, Eli,223
HUTTON, Charles,068
  , Charly,090
  , Daniel J.,144
  , Franklin,156
  , Martha Ann,068
  , Pricilla,070
  , Priscilla,084

INSEVY, Wm.,147
IRWIN, ,194
  , Alexander,129,132
  , Cornelia L.B.,111,112
  , Hail,132
  , Hattie L.,111
  , Hettie L.,112
  , J.S.,112,143
  , James W.,111,112,200
  , James,022,025,057,061,071
      ,111,112,158,164
  , Jas.,023
  , John S.,111
  , John,108
  , Juliet S.,111
  , Juliette S.,111
  , Linis B.,111
  , Mary D.,111 ,112
  , Nancy,111,112
  , Rebecca,068
  , Sim E.,111
  , Susannah,112
JACKSON, Aaron,223
  , Calvin,047
  , Isaiah,063
  , J.B.,129
  , James,143 ,145
  , John,150 ,223
  , Josiah,079
  , Martha,079,080
  , Robert,133,135
  , Robt.,136
JAMES, Andrew I.,142
  , Dalitha,170
  , Daniel,128
  , Dellilah,027
  , Elizabeth,027,170
  , Enoch,018,019
  , George W.,142
  , John,137,142,144,147
  , Jones H.,130
  , Mary A.,045 ,179,181,184,
      188,192,196
  , Mary Ann,168
  , Pricilla,027
  , Priscilla,170
  , Samuel,027 ,170
  , Sarah,019
  , Thomas,017 ,027,158,163,
      170,172,199
  , William R.,179
  , William,130 ,149
JANES, William R.,019
JARNAGAN, Hamilton,133
  , Hery,130
JAY, Isaac,223
JEFFERS, John A.,158,159
  , John,223
JENKINS, J.W.,093 ,112
  , Mary A.,081,112
JENL, John C.,138
JERNIGAN, Henry,128
  , William,129
JEWELL, James,128
  , Wm.,133
JINKING, J.W.,149
JOEL, R.B.,109
  , Richard,153
JOHN, Larkin,135
JOHNS, Samuel,127
JOHNSON, ,194
  , Abner,141 ,143
  , Benjamin,105 ,111,223
  , C.,022
  , Curtis,023
  , Dudley C.,019
  , Erasmus,052
  , George,019,024,052,053,
      058,161,186,189,193
  , Hugh,026 ,164
  , J.C.,022
  , Jno.C.,023
  , John,048 ,131,180,183,
      187
  , Larkin,130,131,133,140
  , Lewis,223
  , Lucinda,026,164
  , Mary Jane,073
  , Mary,052
  , Nancy,061 ,198,200
  , Presly,152
  , Sally,072 ,180
  , Samuel,223
  , Sarah A.,072
  , T.J.,072
  , Temple C.,021 ,223
  , Temple,144
  , Theoden,132
  , W.D.,146
  , William P.,143
  , William,061,198
  , Willie Rufus,009
  , Wm.,129,135,140,152
  , Wm.D.,134
  , Wm.H.,073 ,131
JOINER, David(Heirs),125
  , David,223
JONES, Allen W.,042
  , Andrew,134 ,137
  , Barrack,156
  , Calvin,125 ,126,222
  , Charles,137
  , D.M.,121
  , Daniel M.,122

JONES, Daniel,134 ,135
   , Danl.,141
   , E.J.(Mrs),114
   , Easter,194 ,197
   , Esther,059
   , Frank,153
   , Griffin,152
   , Henderson,125,126
   , Henry,007,223
   , Hester,223
   , Isaac,128
   , J.,121
   , Jeremiah,059,194,223
   , Jerim.,122
   , Jerm.,195
   , Jermiah,197
   , Jesse,002,012,013,100,223
       ,224
   , Jessie,006
   , John,127,135,224
   , Jonathan,045
   , Jones,194
   , Jonh,152
   , Joshua,177
   , Josiah,089
   , L.A.,121
   , Lodowick,013
   , Malecian,194
   , Melissa Ann,122
   , N.T.,114
   , R.B.,140
   , Rany,135
   , Riley,151
   , Sarah,102
   , T.A.,066,071,078,114
   , Thomas,224
   , Thos.,224
   , W.,146
   , William,050 ,058,089,153
       ,183,189,193
   , Wm.,137,147
JORRELL(?), Mary Jane,109
   , R.A.,109
JUDKINS, James W.,004 ,005
JULIUS, Seasor,129
KAGLE, George,025
KARR, Samuel,224
KEELAND, John,153
KEENAN, John,224
KEEP, Jessee,153
   , Wyle,153
KEESLING, Jacob,143
KEETON, Reason,068
KEITH, ,143
KELBY, Pleasant,141
KELLEY, ,153
   , Andrw.,144
   , Elisha,224
   , G.,148
   , Joseph,224
KELLISON, W.H.R.,144
KELLOGG, Eliza,023
   , S.,142
KELLY, Elizabeth,070
   , Kinchen,137
   , Lawson,061 ,196
   , Nancy H.,196
   , P.A.,070
KELOG, Samuel,027
KELSEY, Robert G.,002
   , Samuel,002
KELSY, Clark,059
KELTON, William,013,126,224
KEMP, H.,139
   , Henry,138,151
   , N.M.D.,116
   , P.C.,148
   , Solomon,077
   , T.J.,136
   , Wylie M.,147
KENDEL, John W.,098
KENDRICK, Allan,119
   , Allen,146,148
   , Nancy H.,119
KENEDY, W.M.,151
KENNIRY, Alfred,065
KERBY, R.P.,150
   , Richard P.,066
   , William,224
KERR, ,142
   , A.D.,091 ,092
   , Alfred D.,054
   , Anderson,140
   , Andrew,005,015,040,054,186

   , Caswell,138
   , Elizabeth,013
   , George,129
   , H-,151
   , Isabella,005 ,015
   , J.R.,143 ,151,153
   , J.W.A.,092
   , James,005,015,186
   , Jane,015 ,018,159,194
   , John,002
   , Margaret,005
   , Samuel,013
   , T.A.,069
   , Thomas A.,026,044,054,071,
       084,176,185,192,194,
       196
   , William,005 ,027
KETRON, Nancy,162
KEY, George,133
KEYTON, Wm.,140
KIDDY, ,153
   , Henry,152
KIDEL, Henry,155
KILCREASE, Davis,012
   , Mahala,012
KILLER, Andrew,126
KILLOUGH, Hezekiah,224

KILOUGH, Hezekiah,150
KILPATRICK, Presly,137
KIMMSEY, Alfred,076
KINCAID, A.J.,153
   , Patton,149
KINCANNON, Andrew,142
   , David,008,021,158,162
       ,167,224
   , Frances Sr.,011
   , Frances,099 ,162
   , Francis,009 ,015,033,
       098,162,163,164,169,
       183,190
   , James F.,113
   , James,005,010,162,224

   , Jesse C.,166
   , Jessie,224
   , Nancy E.,113
   , R.C.,155
   , Rebecca J.,113
   , Sarah,098
   , Thomas W.P.,113
   , W.C.,146,182
   , William C.,048
KINDEL, A.H.,081,096,101,103,184
       ,193,194
   , Alfred H.,048 ,056,081,
       117,189
   , J.N.,194
   , James A.,018
   , John N.,103
   , John,066
   , W.C.,019
KINDELL, A.H.,104 ,111,192
KINDLE, A.H.,081
   , Alfred H.,182 ,196
   , John,225
   , Lewis,073
   , Lucy Ann,073
   , Vianah,182
KINDRICK, Allen,148
KING, A.S.,142
   , Bolen,136
   , Calvin,155
   , Carroll,116
   , Edmund,088
   , Hezekiah,129
   , J.C.,150
   , James Jr.,225
   , John,127
   , Rebecca C.,116
   , Robertson,132
   , Siminon,135
   , Thomas R.,076
   , Thomas,088
   , William,046
   , Wm.,150
KINNERY, Alfred,142,191
KIRBY, J.,186
   , John,024,040,043,044,053,
       055,066,076,079,161,
       171,175,180,188,193,
       225
   , Nancy,175
   , Richard P.,079 ,175
   , William,022
KIRK, L.F.,127
KIRKPATRICK, John,125 ,126,225
KISER, Hannah Roann,191
   , Nancy E.,191
KIZER, Julan,225
   , Julian,137
   , Wm.,131
KNIGHT, Jonathan,225
KNOX, Daniel W.,135
KOGER, Jesse,113
   , William,113
KOONCE, Morrison,147
   , Ridding,225
   , Riding,137
KOUNCE, Redding,129
KYLE, Gilbert,106
   , William,106
LACEFIELD, J.H.,085
   , Jesse,011,126
   , Robert,004 ,007,225
   , Susan,085
   , Thomas,085
   , William,004
LACKEY, Eli,225
   , James,147
LACY, Climor,051
   , Eleanor,056
   , Ellen,055
   , Jacob,055,056
   , Mary,051 ,055,056
   , Rachel,051,056
LADEN, Cady,162,163
   , Eady,033
   , G-,149
   , George,033 ,162
   , Henry,163
   , J.L.W.,163
   , J.R.,119,120
   , John R.,060 ,198
   , Joseph,133
   , Mary J.,198
   , Mary Jane,060
   , Richard,163
   , Tabitha Cane,163
LAIN, Wm.T.,192
LAKES, William,156
LAKEY, James M.,096
   , Rachel,029 ,030
LAHY, John,139
LAMB, Benjamin,117
   , Henry,153
   , James H.,117
   , James,106,117
   , Jeremiah,117
   , Levicy E.,117

LAMB, M.A.,117
   , Nancy,105
   , Redding,225
   , Sarah E.,117
   , Stephen,153
LANAN, Mary E.,086
LANCASTER, Jesse,155
LANDRUM, Joseph,136
LANE, John,138
   , Richard,131
   , William T.,051,184,191
LANGH, Thos.,138
LANSON, Lucy C.,086
LANTON, Jesse,138
LANXTEN, Obediah,133,136
LANXTON, A.,136
LARKIN, Edmond,089
   , Edmund,097
LASSITER, Jesse,143
LATON, John,156
   , Priscilla,192,196
LAUDERDALE, Elijah,225
LAUN, Jason,138
LAVERY, Eliza,068
   , John D.,068
   , John,068
LAW, T.,139
LAWSON, Amos Sr.,145
   , Amos,147
LAXTEN, James,129
LAXTON, James,132 ,133,138
LAYTON, George Z.,168
   , M.,150
   , Martha A.,168
   , Pricilla,065
   , Priscilla,168 ,188
   , Priscilla,184
   , Priscilla,179
   , Priscilla,045 ,181
   , Thomas,038 ,065,168,171,
       178
   , Thos.,225
   , William L.,168
   , William,150,168
LEA, Matthew,132
LEAK, William H.,143
LEAKY, Mary,028
   , Phebe,028,031
   , Rachel,028
   , Rhody,028
LEDBETTER, Elizabeth F.,049
   , J.P.,128
   , James,022
LEDWILL, John,143
LEE, (Wid),029
   , Alford,190
   , Alfred C.,160
   , Alfred,029,030,082,162,164,
       173,174,175,179,185,
       193,197
   , D.R.,121
   , Dudley,147
   , Elizabeth,027 ,047,082,112,
       160,162,165,168,173
   , Emelia,193
   , Emily C.,072 ,160,190
   , Emily,029 ,030,082,162,164,
       173,174,175,179,185
   , Fanny,029 ,030,065,067,160,
       162,165,168,173
   , Felix G.,062
   , Felix,029 ,030,160,162,164,
       173,174,175,179,188
   , Francis,134
   , George W.,067
   , H.J.,067
   , James,153
   , Leay C.,067
   , M.B.,130 ,131,133,135,136
   , Martha,067
   , Nathan,067
   , Simpson,019,023,029,030,082,
       160,162,164,165,168,
       173,174,175,179,182,
       185,188,190,193,197

   , T.H.,063
   , Tarlino H.,135
   , William C.,047,180,187
LEETH, George D.,225
   , James S.,225
   , Josiah,225
LEFTWICK, A.,155
LEMBERSON, J.P.,142
LEMMON, George,127
LEMMONS, John,139
LEMONS, John,129,135
LEMORES, John,134
LESTER, Benjamin F.,047
   , Fountain,125,126
   , Fountaine,225
   , German,092 ,225
   , Mary E.,047
LETT, Dufield,142
   , John,138
LEWIS, C.,138
   , Henry,039
   , Joel D.,039
   , John,129
   , Polly,113
   , Quimby,152
   , William,009
LEZER, James,127
LIGHT, Samuel L.,225
LILEY, Wm.,153
LILLEY, Noah,226
   , R.,145
LILLY, John,191
   , Noah,009,010,060
LIMERICK, Andrew,135
LINDSAY, Isaac,226
LINDSEY, A.J.,152
   , Elizabeth,015

LINDSEY, Ezekiel,015,226
       , Isaac L.,015 ,081
       , Isaac S.,143
       , Isaac,015
       , J.L.,099
       , J.W.,146 ,153,198
       , John W.,015,063,198
       , Jonah G.,198
       , Josiah G.,015 ,198
       , Josiah W.,063
       , Phebe,015
       , Polly,015
       , William T.,015
LINDSY, J.L.,149
LINGO, G.W.,134
     , John,226
     , Michael,129 ,133
     , Moses,087
     , Pernell,129
     , Wm.,226
LINN, B.W.,120
LINSEY, Elizabeth,014
      , Ezekiel,014
      , Isaac,014
      , James,131
LITTLE, Joseph,152
      , Thomas,155
LODERDALE, Elijah,128
LOGAN, James,151
     , Jas.,146
     , John H.(Dr),090
     , John W.,066
LOGGINS, James,143
       , Jas.,148
LOID, Eli,150
LOMBS, A.M.,141
LONG, Daniel,052,184
    , David,129
    , Isaac,052,184
    , Lydia,103
    , Rebecca,052 ,184
    , Saml.,140
    , Sarner,149
    , Seamore,103
    , Seamoure,056
LOPP, Jacob,130
LOUD, D.L.,155
LOVE, Francis,226
    , John,116
    , Joseph,136,138
    , Thomas,143,155
    , Thos.,145
    , Wm.,226
LOVELADY, Thos.,226
LOVING, Jef,145
      , T.C.,145
LOW, Thomas,155
LOWE, Aquilla,007
    , Caleb,007
LOWERY, J.,151
      , John,226
      , Minerva,056
LOWRY, Delila,048
     , Delilah,182,189
     , I.T.,081
     , Isaac T.,101,103,182
     , J.,148
     , J.T.,082
     , Jno.,146
     , John H.,128
     , John,174
     , Kiziah,174
     , Lucinda,048 ,182,184
     , Minerva,182
     , Samuel,048 ,056,182,184
       189,192,193,196
     , Sarah A.,192 ,193,196
     , Sarah An,182
     , Sarah Ann,056
     , Sarah H.,145
     , Squin,182
LOYD, Eli,132 ,135,147
    , James H.,135
    , John,147
    , Owen,029 ,030,133,135
    , William,092 ,133
LUCAS, Eli,132
     , Isaac,115
     , J.H.,139
     , John,226,227
     , M.G.,153
     , Obidiah,151
     , T.W.,152
     , Willie,032 ,037,164,168
LUCUS, Harry,142
LUMPKINS, J.J.,149
LUSTER, Fontaine,227
LUTEN, Wylie,146
LUTHER, Jacob,017 ,085,113,119,
        145
      , Thomas W.,085

MACHIANS, Andrew,147
MACKEY, James,227
MACLIN, James C.,227
MADDIN, David,135
MADDOX, Ephraim,082,109
      , J.N.,082
      , John N.,082
      , John,025
      , Mary,025
      , N.,081
      , S.W.,133
      , Susannah,082
      , William,025
MADOX, Leonard,227
MAHAIR, Joseph,135
MAHAN, Henry,002
     , John,150
MAIM, William,135
MAJORS, Martha,071
      , Nelson,130
      , William H.,071

MALCOKS, R.J.,139
MALLEY, Joseph,131
MANAS, Richard,138
MANES, Henry,138
MANGRANO, Samuel,142
MANGUM, Harwell,115
      , Isaac,116
      , James,116
      , John E.,115
      , Lucy,116
      , Thomas C.,115
      , William W.,116
MANLEY, John,125,127,227
      , W.E.,145
MANUEL, John A.,138
MANUELS, John A.,138
MARK, Jesse,135
MARRIS, Wade M.,128
MARSH, S.,153
MARTIN, Eli J.,138
      , Fred,153
      , George,128 ,130
      , J.C.,031
      , J.G.,150,156
      , J.H.,071
      , J.M.,146
      , James D.,081,112,114
      , James,141 ,150,152,153
      , Jane,045,177,180,182
      , Joel,127,128
      , John B.,141
      , John,029,030,045,082,097
        ,112,161,166,177,180
        ,182,227
      , Jonathan W.,018,046,174,
        181,186
      , Joseph,136
      , L.D.,130
      , M.L.,156
      , Merdo,152
      , Murdock,153
      , Polly,129 ,131
      , R.,141
      , R.K.,156
      , Robert K.,045 ,177,180,
        182
      , S.T.,131
      , W.E.,153
      , Wm.,152
MASON, Thomas D.,022
     , William,136
MASSEY, Ausburn,227
      , J.B.,063
      , John B.,133
      , John,130,131,149
      , Lewis,130 ,132,133,138,
        139
      , Mark,147
      , P.,149
      , W.H.,130
MATHEWS, A.,149
       , Andrew,137,145
       , Andru,138
       , Andrw.,143
       , Benjamin,136 ,138
       , J.S.,153
       , James D.,141
       , James,155
       , Thomas,155
       , William,156
       , Wm.,138
MATHIS, Alsa,063
      , Alsey,086
      , Alsy,086
      , Elinor,068
      , James D.,086
      , James M.,197
      , James,062 ,068
      , John W.,086
      , Thomas W.,086
      , Wm.,145
MATLEY, J.F.,058
      , Joseph F.,111
      , Susan,058
MATTHEWS, Alsa,056 ,057,190
        , Benjamin,142
        , David,128,130
        , Dougald D.,068
        , Eleanor,056
        , Jackson,133
        , James,128,135
        , John,128 ,151
        , Joseph,136
        , W.,139
MATUS, John,150
MAXWELL, John,150
       , Thomas,056,071,104,107,
         108,109,111,116,118
MAY, Frances,092
   , Michael,105
   , Mitchel,104
MAYFIELD, J.,148
MAYFUL, N.J.,139
MAYSE, A.,155
MBOYSE, (Negro),073
MCAFEE, Harriet,116
MCALEXANDER,,141
MCALLEN,,148
MCBRIDE, Giles,055 ,163,188,192,
         198
       , J.D.,151 ,152
       , M.,141
       , Mary Jane,024
       , R.P.,142
       , Robert,024,040
       , Samuel,025,026
MCCAIG, Canst.,128
MCCALL, Alex.,125
      , Alexander,126 ,127,227
      , Daniel,104 ,127
      , David,103 ,127
      , Hu.,151
      , Hugh,127,144,147
      , James F.,132,135,137

MCCALL, Jno.,141
      , John B.,117
      , John,090
      , W.P.,139
MCCAMES, Pamelia,079
MCCAN, Joseph R.,019,227
MCCANDLESS, G.B.,094
         , Gideon,100
         , Isaac,134 ,135,136
         , William,083,100
MCCANLES, Isaac,131
MCCANLESS, A.J.,115
         , Isaac,129
MCCANLIS, G.B.,132
        , J.S.,133
MCCANN, Joseph R.,025
MCCARN, Cornelius,071
      , Daniel G.,068 ,115
      , Elizabeth,068 ,071
      , Hu.,021
      , Hugh,068,071,074,077,227
      , John D.,115
      , John,071
      , Nancy Manerva,071
      , Pamelia C.,071
      , Pormelia,077
      , Sarah Isabella,071
      , William C.,071
      , William,105
MCCARNS, Cornelius,071
       , Daniel,071
       , Hugh,071
MCCASLIN, Carroll,138
        , Grant A.,142
        , James,138
MCCASTIN, Elizabeth,038
MCCHAN, Joseph R.,017
MCCLAIN, A.S.,144
       , Emanuel,029,030
       , James,017 ,029,030,033,
         161,166
       , Kiziah,180
       , Kizziah,046
       , Manuel,046,072,161,166,
         180
       , Morris,227
       , William,045,132,178
MCCLAREN, James,088
MCCLEAN, Jno.,145
MCCLENTOCK, Alexander,227
MCCLINTOCK, A.,007
          , Alex,125
          , Alex.,007
MCCLINTON, James S.,153
MCCOLLUM, David,126
        , James Stephens,105
        , Martha A.,105
        , Nancy A.,105
        , Sarah A.,105
        , Susannah,105
        , Thomas,105
MCCOLUM, David,152
MCCONNELL, J.H.,066,080,091,151
         , John H.,057 ,092,192
         , Joshua,006 ,022,091
         , Mary,092
         , Polly,022
MCCORKLE, John,052
        , T.J.,143
MCCORMICK, J.H.,191
MCCOROSON, Robert,227
MCCOWEN, J.B.,133
MCCRARY, C.D.,142
       , James,098
       , M.J.,153
       , Sophia,098
       , T.B.,153
MCCRAW, Samuel,135
MCCREASY, C.B.,145
MCCROW, Mitchel,132
      , Samuel,132 ,133
MCCULLEN, D.G.,114
MCCULLOM, David,136
MCCURDY, James,136 ,143
MCDANIEL, ,145
        , Alexander,003
        , George,143
        , Hiram,227
        , Hugh,227
        , James,113
        , Joel,031 ,163
        , John,031 ,036,128,163,
          170,176,178
        , Jos.,031
        , L------,032
        , Lucy,031
        , Murdock,036 ,170,176,
          178
        , Nich.,233
        , Thomas,156
        , W.,150
        , W.P.,153
MCDONALD, Alex.,125,227,228
        , Alexander,229
        , John G.,228
        , John,228
MCDONOLD, Danl.,152
MCDOUGAL, A.G.,114 ,119
        , Archibald,112
        , John,115
        , W.R.,064
MCDOUGALL, Alex.,125
MCEADS, David,140
MCELRY, Thomas,131
MCFALLS, A.,146
MCFERREN, W.C.,146
MCFERRIN, Samuel,228
        , W.C.,144
        , William,033 ,171
        , Wm.C.,163
MCGASSOCK, Francis F.,127
MCGAVOCK, ,145

MCGAVOCK, David,125,228
, Francis,228 ,229
MCGAVOCK/MCDONALD, ,125
MCGAWS(?), Francis,143
MCGEE, Allen,153,156
, James G.,144
, John,122
, Sarah,122
MCGINNIS, C.H.,164
, Christopher H.,033,173
MCGOWEN, E.W.,150 ,152
MCGUIN, Frederick,136
, J.C.,133
, John,136
MCGUIRE, John,135
MCHAHAN, R.B.,146
MCINTOCH, T.S.,148
MCINTOSH, J.L.,141
, Lotty,200
, Thomas H.,116
MCIVER, John,126,127
MCIVES, John,126
MCKAY, ,139
MCKEE, Thomas,153
MCKEY, Robertson,136
, Wm.,229
MCKINDLEY, L.E.,137
MCKIRLEY, Charles,131
MCKISICK, Archibald,130
MCLAIN, Emanuel,187
, Kiziah,187
, Manuel,067 ,101
MCLEMORE, John C.,126 ,229
MCLIN, A.L.,155
, James C.,131
, James,127
, L.,142
MCMAHAN, Andrew,143
, Eleanor,167
, James F.,003 ,008,028,
160,167
, John D.,160
, Nelly,028 ,160
, R.R.,145
, Robert B.,160
, Wm.,097,129
MCMAHON, James F.,229
, Joseph,080,229
, Robert,084
MCMANAS, Wm.,140
MCMANUS, Wm.,148
MCMILLAN, Alfred,191
, John,098
, Neal,129 ,132
, William L.,229
MCMILLEN, Neal,129
MCMILLIAN, Alfred,199
MCMILLIN, Joseph,128
MCMILLON, John,131
, Joseph,130
MCMULLIN, Hugh,138
, J.F.,145
, J.H.,140
, John,138
, Neal,131
, William,130
, Wm.,133 ,140,141
MCMULLINS, J.J.,120
, William,132
MCNAIRY, John,125 ,229
MCNARNARD, George,140
MCNATT, F.M.,148,151
, Richard,151
MCNEALEY, J.W.,149
MCNEILL, Jas.,151
MCQUEEN, (Wid),059
, Daniel,136
, Hiram,064
, John,059 ,084
, Thomas,059 ,084
MCQUIN, Agnes,229
MCREYNOLDS, ,142
MCROSE, John,229
MCROSS, John,044,068,084,088,092
MCSWAIN, Ed,132
, Edmond,128
MCWALLACE, Alex.,136
MCWHERTER, George,194
, Matilda,194
MCWHORTER, Chardin A.,137
, George,059 ,072
, Matilda,059
, Narcissa,096
, Tabitha,096
MEADOW, M.G.,102,132
, Thomas W.,063
MEADOWS, J.S.,155
, Thos.,229
, W.S.,146
MEDCALF, Thomas,153
MEEK, A.,155
, Amaziah,136
, J.H.,155
, Jane,121
, John H.,110
, Josiah D.,082
, Mary A.,082
, Mary,070 ,078,080
, Moses,129
, Nancy E.,082
, Thomas P.,085
, Thomas S.,069
, Thomas,103
, W.M.B.,082
, William C.,080
, William,069 ,070,078,085,
103
MERCHIRSON, G.A.,156
MERIDETH, Andrew J.,229
, Jacob,229

MERIDETH, John,230
, Samuel,230
, Sarah,229,230
MERKINGON, Kenneth,021
METTERS, G.W.,136
MEYERIS, Richd.,152
MGAVOC, F.,145
MICKEL, David C.,126
, George,126
MIDDLETON, Perry,129
, T.J.,133
, Thomas,130
MIKY, Robert,138
MILAM, G.B.,153
, James M.,136
, James,144
, Thomas F.,086
, Thomas,134
, W.A.,140
, Wm.A.,141
MILAN, A.G.,088
, Thomas F.,088
MILES, Charles,230
, Harriet N.,085
, James,230
, Margaret,230
, Thomas,135
MILLAR, George,069
, L.D.,069,070
MILLER, Abraham D.,130
, Abraham,129,143,145
, Abram,230
, Allen,085
, Austin,005 ,007,010,230
, Dan,230
, J.D.,085
, J.O.,085
, Jacob,230
, James,085 ,113,145
, John,145
, Louis H.,085
MILLIGAN, Elinor,077
, G.M.,194
, Geo.M.,163
, George M.,027,060,113
, J.S.G.,159
, James S.,027 ,077
, Jas.,147
, William,015 ,027,159
, Wm.,163
MILLIKEIN, R.H.,142
MILLIS, L.D.,140
MILLOM, L.C.,153
MILLS, Adam,147,148
, Jacob,132,138
, Wilkinson,071
, William,153
MILTON, John,141
MIRES, James,136
MITCHEL, Jackson,046
, Manuel,051
, Nancy,045
, Zachariah,130
MITCHELL, Abagail (N-Free),075
, Abby,054
, Cyntha(N-Free),119
, David C.,125 ,230
, David R.,230
, David,125
, Elijah (N),062
, Elijah(N),055
, Elijah,057
, Geo.Wash(Mulatto),119
, George,126,230
, Henry T.,106
, Henry,230
, Jack (N-Free),118
, James(N-Free),119
, Jas.J.(Mulatto),119
, Jim,054
, Linda(Mulatto),119
, Manuel,054
, Maranda(Negro),097
, Martha E.,106
, Robert,128
, Sarah J.,106
, William H.,054
, William,132
MOHAIR, Joseph,134
MOLLETRLEL, ,147
MONDAY, J.O.,088
, Silas,087
MONK, Briant,137
, Bryant,142
, Felix G.,142
, Jesse,132,135,137,141
, Jessee,140
MONKS, Jessee,128
MONTGOMERY, A.,141
, Alf,155
, Alfred,091 ,107
, Caroline,107
, Cyntha,122
, E.E.,122
, Elizabeth,122
, Emily,107
, J.,149
, James,091 ,122,231
, John,122
, Joseph,107 ,122,231
, Katharine,107
, Mary,107
, Thomas F.,107 ,122
, Thos.J.,231
, William B.,122
, William,131
, Wm.,133
MOON, Templeton,136,137
MOORE, Elizabeth C.,038
, Elizabeth,049,070,198
, George,133 ,134
, Irvin,142
, James W.,074,087,119

MOORE, Jesse G.,006
, Jesse(N-Free),087
, Joseph,036 ,038,048,049,
060,168,171,175,180,
186,190,195
, Mary Ann,049
, Mary J.,038 ,198
, Mary Jane,060
, Michael,231
, Rebecca,038 ,039,171,179,
180
, Stephen,092
, Wm.,133
, Wm.P.,134,137
MOREHEAD, Peter,133
, Piter,131
MORGAN, John M.,127
, W.G.,144
, William,143
, Wm.,141
MORIER, Wm.F.,140
MORRIS, Benjmin,150
, C.M.,153
, C.W.,099,114,199
, Calvin,133 ,139
, Charles R.,093 ,112
, Charles W.,063 ,112
, Charles,231
, D.M.,140
, Henry,153
, J.T.,087
, James C.,130
, Jesse,002
, John Sr.,027
, John,128,130
, Nimrod,022 ,134
, R.G.J.,155
, Robert,029 ,030
, Roda,027
, Stephen,231
, Sterting,127
, Thomas,099
, W.H.,130,135
, William B.,112
, William,127,128,130,142,
231
MORRISON, Charles,153
MORRISS, C.M.,072
, Sarah,072
, T.J.,072
MORROW, G.D.,185
, Geo.D.,089
, George D.,029 ,030,034,
053,067,072,162,164,
165,175
, Nancy,164
, William,002,012
MORTIN, H.,168
, Mary W.,069
MORTON, H.,167
, Hezekiah,036
, Jas.M.,148
MOSELY, Elizabeth,025
, Henry(Heirs),125
, William,231
MOSES, James,141,153
, John,142,153
, W.,151
MOSLEY, Wm.,136
MOSS, David,003,007
MOSSES, John,137
MOTEN, William,131 ,133
MOZIER, W.F.,155
MUD, Joseph,126
MULLINS, Eli,140
, Elisa,087
, Eliza,088
, Silas,110
MULLUN, James,231
MUNDAY, James,231
, John O.,092
MURDOCK, William,132
, Wm.,134,135
MURKINSON, Kenneth,014
MURKISON, Kenneth,231
MURPHY, A.,088 ,092
, Archibald,089 ,100
, Barilla J.,089
, Berilla J.,089
, Burwell,092
, J.D.,138
, J.M.,146
, Jas.W.M.,089
, John W.,089
, M.,144
, Mary L.,089
, Mary,092,100
, N.G.,170
, Saml.,147
, W.H.,092
, Will,092
, William H.H.,092
, Wm.H.,089
MURREY, Philip,129
MURRY, Silas,129
MUSE, Thos.,147
MUSGROVE, Obadiah,127
, Samuel,133
MUTTON, Robert,231
NAIL, Thomas A.,076
NANCE, Allen,129,231
NAPIER, Richard C.,125 ,126
NCNAIRY, John,126
NEAL, James M.,149
NEELY, Hugh,129
, Paul H.,125 ,126
NEGRO, Daniel,190
, Jim(Free),094
, Ned,190
, Philis,190
NEIL, Alfred,117,118
, Andrew,005,186
, Gilbreath,186

NEIL, James,146
    , Thomas A.,118
NEILL, J.L.,151
NEILSON, C.B.,002
    , Charles B.,006,023
    , Robert,138
    , William,027
NELSON, Charles B.,231
    , R.S.,128
    , Robt.,137
    , Robt.S.,130
    , William,155
NESBITT, John,014
NETHERRY, Robert,012
NEVIL, T.E.,153
NEVILL, Alexander,026
NEWAL, Robert,150
NEWELL, H.F.,130
    , Hu.F.,020
NEWMAN, Clark,117
    , Garrett,117
    , Henry,105
    , Mary Ann,117
    , Nuby(?),105
    , R.P.,151
    , Samuel,024,158,161
    , Thomas,024,158
    , Thos.,161
NEWSOM, William,144
NEWSOME, Wm.,141
NEWSON, William,127
NEWTON, Henry,136
    , John D.,143
    , M.F.,143,145
    , M.G.,140
    , S.G.,062,140,199
NICHOLS, David,231
    , James A.,171
NICHOLLS, James,175
    , Nancy,166
NICHOLS, David,019
    , G.H.,072,078,079
    , J.A.,093
    , J.C.,128
    , J.G.,072
    , J.L.,093,120
    , J.Y.,075,078
    , James A.,036,093,168,180,231
    , James B.,035
    , James,147
    , Jefferson J.,138
    , John,140
    , Mary,035,175,176
    , Pinckney J.,138
    , William,035,166,175
NICKS, J.M.,153
NIEL, Thomas A.,083
    , Thos.A.,077
    , Washington,155
NIELSON, C.B.,022
NISBET, John,065,231
NIVILL, Alexander,028
    , Elizabeth,028
NIX, Elizabeth,172
    , Franklin,068
    , Joseph,040,130,172
NIXON, Henry,014
NOLEN, David,128
    , J.H.,148
    , J.W.,152
    , Joseph,021
    , Mack,140
    , Mark,139,142
    , Robert,140
    , Thomas,128
    , W.T.,147
    , William,133,153
    , Wm.,145
NORTHCUT, B.M.,153
    , J.W.,146
    , John H.,128
NORTHCUTT, Adrian,136
    , Alford,200
    , Anderson,130
    , Archibald,232
    , Isaac,004,061,198,200
    , J.W.Sr.,138
    , James K.P.,200
    , Jane,200
    , Jefferson,200
    , John W.,191
    , Lewis B.,200
    , Sarah Ann,200
NORTON, John,128
NORVIL, David J.,137
    , Wm.C.,137
NORVILL, David,145
    , J.P.,145
NORVILLE, James,021,158
NORWOOD, Fletcher,155
    , G.W.,138
    , John P.,188
    , John,055,192,198,232
    , W.F.,140
    , Washington,135
    , Wm.G.,232
NOVEL, D.,148
NOWELL, J.P.,148
    , L.P.,153
    , Wm.,141
NOWLER, Rufus,232
O'NEAL, Dennis,127
    , Mary,047,048
    , Thomas,155
OAKS, Henry,131
OBLESBY, Joseph,142
ODOM, Allen,232
OGLESBY, Joseph,079
    , William,128,130
    , Wm.,232

OLD, George,111
    , Isaac,111
    , William,111
OLDHAM, John,142
    , William,139
OLDS, William,105
OMENS, John,126
ONEIL, Elisha,232
ORNE, (Wid) Jno.,153
ORR, (Wid),159
    , Geo.W.,152
    , George W.,131
    , George,232
    , James,027,161,166
    , John,126
    , Richard,155
    , Thomas,076,082,085,132
ORTON, Richard,047
OSLEY, Thomas A.,153
OSTONE, Asa,232
OUTEN, J.N.,150
OUTLAW, (Widow),116
    ,101
    , A.,155
    , Alex.,152
    , Alexander,046,090
    , Emaline,046
    , Emeline,090
    , F.M.,090,155
    , Francis,046
    , James,102
    , Joseph,090,094,130
    , Lewis,040,046,047,048,049,055,090,094,116,155,171,180,183,188,192,232
    , Martha A,094
    , Martha E.,094
    , Mary J.,093,094
    , Matilda,171
    , Richard,046,090
    , Sarah,094
OVERTON, Miles,129
OWEIN, Daniel,130
OWEN, (Mrs),121
    , Alexander,094
    , Ann,038,169
    , Daniel,033,034,036,129,131,133,138,165,166,168,169,178
    , David,037,038,045,094,162
    , Jacob H.,076
    , John W.,121
    , John,232
    , Mary,034,036,037,038,094,165,169,176,177
    , T.J.,146
    , Thomas I.,170
    , Thomas J.,039
    , Thomas,037,064,143,169
    , Thos.,162
    , William H.,169
    , William,037
OWENS, Daniel,135
    , David,031,167,171,232
    , John,125,127
    , Mary,167
    , R.B.,143
    , Thomas I.,167
    , Thomas,031
    , William H.,167
    , Zach,147
PACE, Dempsey,085,086
    , James A.,086
    , John,135,137
    , Jonathan,086
    , Margaret L.,086
    , Thomas G.,086
    , William A.,086
PACK, Carroll,137
    , E.,160
    , Elisha,018,035,051,052,093,120,158,159,161,165,166,167,175,183,184,185,187,191,192,193,198,200,232
    , Francis A,200
    , Harret,200
    , Nancy,200
    , Peter,120,200
    , William,143
PAGET, Jesse,143
PAGGIT, Francis,147
    , Jessee,147
PAIN, George,130
    , Thomas I.,170
    , Thos.P.,130
PALE, John,135
PALMER, J.T.,153
    , John,153
    , M.H.,153
    , S.M.,153
    , W.P.,143
PARISANS, M.,139
PARISH, Green,066
    , Larkin,139
    , Sherwood,196
    , Wm.,232
PARK, Birton,150
PARKER, Aldridge,084
    , J.G.,149
    , O.M.,065
    , Pleasat,150
    , Polly,065
    , T.R.,152
    , William,144
PARKS, Richard,043,169,175,178
    , Sally,006
    , Samuel,006
    , Susan,75
PARMLEY, John,232
PARMLY, John,137
    , Samuel,140

PARRET, John,127
PARRIS, Mary,146
    , William,081,082
PARRISH, A.M.,128
    , Abel,108
    , Abel,107
    , C.R.,152
    , Cordy,023
    , Irvin,107,108
    , K.V.,022
    , L.,151
    , L.B.,106
    , Leonidas,132,133
    , Lewis B.,077,078
    , Linn,153
    , Lucious B.,092
    , Mimi,232
    , N.G.,071
    , W.,143
    , Wm.,128,152
    , Saml.,147
PARRONS, W.R.,156
PARSONS, Henry,232
    , Nancy L.,109
    , Samuel H.,109,117
PARTLE, Samuel S.,119
PATRICK, H.,141
    , R.,149
PATTERSON, Anguist,133
    , J.D.,142
    , Peter,233
PATTON, John R.,149
    , John,149
    , Richard T.,233
    , Sarah A.,122
PAUL, Lewis,138
PAULEY, Elijah,008
PAULK, Jason,103,104
PAULLY, Elijah,233
PAYNE, Israeil,134
    , M.H.,081
    , Mason,233
    , T.P.,072,139
    , Thomas P.,135
    , Thos.D.,233
    , Thos.P.,067,135
PAYTON, R.T.,233
PEA, Margaret E.,100
    , Thomas J.,100
PEACOCK, E.,149
    , Benajah,096
    , Benjiah,233
    , E.A.,121
    , J.N.,121
PEARCE, Henry,101
    , Mary,
PEARKS, Samuel,006
PEEPLES, H.W.,071,144
PELLY, Henry,154
PENN, G.H.G.,121
    , Margaret,121
PENNINGTON, H.,141,147
PENNY, Joel,156
PENSON, Joel,126
PERKINS, B.F.,150,152
    , Benj.,141
    , Daniel,200
    , David,083,233
    , E.L.M.,200
    , E.M.,077,088
    , Ebenezer M.,093
    , Ebenezer,084
    , Eliza,093
    , Elizabeth B.,083
    , H.,091
    , Hardeman,093
    , J.G.,078
    , J.S.,149
    , James,109
    , John G.,077
    , M.,146
    , Moses,140
    , Saml.,194
    , Samuel,034,057,060,093,164,172
    , Simion,093,145
    , W.S.,146
    , W.M.,091
    , William,153
    , Wm.M.,233
PERRY, Emily,121
    , Isaac,144
    , J.S.,121
    , James,153
    , Joel,083
    , Joseph,176,179,182,187
    , Josiah,150
    , Margaret,083
    , Marion,083
    , Sarah,083,170,187
    , Suvis,083
    , Wiley C.,137
PERSON, Wm.,153
PERU, V.W.,133
PETTIGREW, Lem.,233
PETTIGRU, Levi,143
PETTY, A.W.,141
    , Henry Sr.,233
    , Hubbard,126
    , Hubbert,125
    , James,139,140
    , John T.,031
    , Josiah,139
    , T.,146
    , W.B.,064,091
PHAROAH, Eliza,009
    , Jefferson,009
    , John,009
    , Madison,009
    , Rebecca,009
    , Samuel,009
PHELPS, Wm.N.,134
PHENIX, Henry,024

PHILIP, Nathan,128
PHILIPS, Beersheba,095
  , James,095
  , Joseph,126,233
  , Philip,125,126
  , William,091
  , Wm.,233
PHILLIPS, Dock,155
  , Geo.,152
  , Green,155
  , J.J.,155
  , J.T.,149 ,151
  , Polly,031
  , Samuel,135
  , William,139
PIBAS, John,233
PICKENS, (Mrs),119
  , A.G.,100 ,104
  , A.J.,146
  , Andrew J.,114 ,115
  , Archibald G.,029 ,030
  , David,155
  , Elizabeth B.,029 ,030
  , J.G.,108
  , J.H.,019 ,021
  , J.M.,146
  , J.R.,150
  , James G.,029 ,030,118
  , Jas.G.,142
  , Jeremiah H.,019
  , Jno.,146
  , John G.,103
  , John,103 ,153
  , Jonathan R.,008,029,030
    ,110,234
  , Jonathan,233 ,234
  , Martha,114
  , Mary Jane,029 ,030
  , Sion R.,029,030
  , W.,149
  , William,103
PICKING, A.G.,151
  , A.W.,152
  , Archibald G.,169
  , David,152
  , Elizabeth B.,169
  , Gabriel,234
  , Hezekiah,018
  , J.R.,234
  , James G.,169
  , Jeremiah H.,020
  , Jonathan R.,169
  , Mary J.,169
  , Saml.,141
  , Sion R.,169
  , Sion,141
  , William,018
PIERCE, H.,150
PIG, Jesse,057
  , Paul M.,057
  , Preston,057
PIGG, Nimrod,128
  , Prister,081
PIGGS, Davis,148
PIKE, Elisha,129
PILLOW, Abner,126
PINCKSTON, William,155
PINKEREY, D.,126
PIPER, N.A.,127
  , William,234
PITTS, Alfred,096 ,107,114,119
  , C.,096
  , J.B.,114
  , John F.,086 ,102
  , Mary,114
  , Sarah E.,114
  , W.F.,114
PITTY, Joel,129
PLUMMER, E.B.,136
  , Emsley,200
  , Jesse,177 ,200
  , Mary A.S.,200
POINDEXTER, Henry,156
  , Julius,153
  , P.P.,067
  , T.W.,022,094,234
  , Thomas W.,018 ,057,
    190
  , Thomas,106
  , Thos.W.,044
  , William,155
POLK, ,142
  , C.M.,189
  , Cassander,160,165,176,179,
    185,190
  , Catherine,165
  , Charles M.,047,049,180,182
    ,192
  , Charles T.,014,033,034,164
    ,165,173,177
  , Charles,188
  , Eliza J.,037
  , Elizabeth J.,028 ,171,176
  , Elizabeth Jane,161,165
  , Elizabeth,183,187
  , Ezekiel,135 ,161,165,171,
    176,179,183,187
  , Feraby,180
  , G.A.(Guardian),145
  , G.H.,066
  , G.W.,070
  , George H.,060,062,078,100,
    182,186,195,198
  , George M.,049,198
  , George,071
  , Green H.,080 ,085,086,091,
    092,173,177,181,184,
    187,192,197
  , Green M.,164
  , Green W.,033 ,175
  , John,037,158,159,160,161,
    165,171,176,179,185,
    187,190

POLK, Joseph,126
  , Joshua,142
  , Margaret,090
  , Marian A.,177
  , Marian,071,184,187,192,197

  , Martha,052,059,182,192
  , Martin A.,181
  , Mary A.,099
  , Mary,182
  , Michael L.,047,050
  , Michael Lee,182
  , Pharily,182
  , Pheraby,049
  , Polly Ann,024,160,165,176,
    185,190
  , Robert M.,099
  , S.,126
  , Samuel,125,126
  , T.A.,192 ,199
  , Thomas A.,047,052,066,087,
    090,099,182
  , Thomas,028,039,070,125,126
    ,130,155,161,165,171
    ,176,179,183,187
  , Thos.,067
  , Thos.A.,065
  , W.H.,143
  , William H.,049,062,078,099
    ,182,198
  , William,047 ,048,049,052,
    059,180,182,188,189,
    192,198
  , Wm.,180
  , Wm.J.,132
POLL, Geo.,147
POLLARD, George,130
  , J.B.,136 ,234
  , James,018 ,021,165,166
  , John B.,130,132,133,135

  , John,135
  , Louisa,166
  , Nancy,166
POLLEY, Martin,133
POLLG, Martin,129
POLLICK, Caroline,089
  , Samuel J.,089
POLLOCK, J.K.,153
POLLSY, Martin,134
POND, James R.,146
PONELLO, George,077
POOL, A.,149
  , A.P.,071
  , Aaron,113
  , Archibald,033,104,109,163
  , Caroline M.,109
  , Catherine,104
  , Geo.,151 ,153
  , J.C.,072
  , John C.,068 ,084
  , Joseph,155
  , L.C.,141
  , M.L.P.,071
  , Robinson W.,155
  , William,136
  , Wrollam,153
POOLE, Riddley,137
POPE, Riley,136
POPLES, Jackson,234
POR, James,149
PORTER, E.M.,061
  , E.W.,071,196
  , Eleanor,028,160,166
  , Elias W.,072,078,080
  , Jackson,132
  , R.J.,150
  , W.H.,088
  , William,028,166
  , Wm.,160
PORTERFIELD, ,142
  , C.L.,097
  , Chas.L.,112
  , John D.,019,127,159

  , Nancy,112
  , W.C.,082
POTTER, Thos.,234
POTTS, Geo.,151
  , Joshua,234
POWELL, Benjamin,127
  , George,067
  , Hardin,129
  , Jno.,144
  , Lewis,129
  , William,132
  , Wm.,134,144
POWER, Isham,151
  , Jesse,113
POWERS, E.M.,145
  , Jesse,057 ,191,200
PRATT, G.W.,087
  , Joseph,153
  , Patrick,141
PRESSLEY, C.,148
PRESTON, J.A.,102
  , J.L.,102
  , John,102
  , M.E.,102
  , P.B.,102
  , R.W.,153
  , W.J.,102
PREWIT, James,134
PRICE, ,139
  , J.,149
  , T.J.,156
PRIM, A.M.,146 ,148
PRINCE, C.A.,144
  , Calvin M.,143
  , Jno.,147
PRISTON, P.V.,152
PRISTOW, P.V.,149
PRUIT, James,135

PUCKETT, Robt.,155
PULUM, Isham,153
PURDY, John,125
PURLEY, Green,127
PURVIS, Cullen,017
PYBAS, John,013
PYBURN, Christopher,234
  , Elizabeth,166 ,184
  , Jane,043
  , Mary Jane,047
  , Samuel W.,047
  , Samuel,043
  , Susan,184
  , William,007,043,047,166,
    184,234
QUALLS, William,133,138
QUICK, Lodwick,141
  , M.K.,104
QUILLEY, Allen,141

RAMBO, Elizabeth,162
RAMLY, James,139
RAMSEY, Zadach,140
RANDOLPH, R.A.,038 ,170
  , Rix A.,020,033,039,171
    ,180,234
RANEY, Doctor,234
RANSEY, Richard,138
RASBERRY, Joseph,138
RASPBERRY, J.L.,141
RATCLIFF, William R.,078
RATLIFF, Watkins(Negro),097
RATTAFF, Sarah Ann,234
RATTLE, Libby Jane(N-Free),075
RAWLINGS, Jane L.,020
RAY, Elizabeth,068 ,112,114
  , J.,138
  , Jno.,147
  , John C.,112
  , Joseph,153
  , Richard,127
  , Robert,130
RAYBURNE, John,234
RAYNES, Thomas,150
REA, E.M.,107
  , Elizabeth M.,074 ,109
  , Elizabeth,086
  , Ginsey,199
  , Hanna,086
  , Jincy,063 ,074,076,086,099
  , Joanna,074,086,109
  , John A.,188
  , John C.,029,030,063,064,074
    ,075,087,107,109,199

  , John,086 ,137
  , Lidia Jane,109
  , Lydia Jane,074,086
  , T.F.,107
  , Thomas T.,109
  , Thomas,074
  , William,148
READ, David,127
  , William,126
READEN, M.C.,148
REAMS, Joshua,164
REAVES, Drewry,175
  , F.T.,141
  , George,234
  , Jas.,148
  , Stephen,148
RECORD, Sion,169
REDDEN, H.,141
REDDING, Isaac,102
  , James M.,035
  , James,181
  , Jane,050 ,183
  , John,081 ,132
  , M.C.,144
  , Nelly,081
  , Samuel,050,181,183,189
  , William,132
REDDON, George,137
REDIC, Richard,139
REDIN, Ezekiel,130
REED, Amzi,023 ,235
  , Angie,235
  , D.K.,097 ,098
  , David K.,052 ,098,099
  , E.R.,098
  , James,235
  , John,126
  , Mary,098
  , Ozzi,023
  , W.D.,097 ,098
REEDS, David R.,184
REEVES, W.H.,155
RENFROE, George,155
  , James W.,155
  , Stephen C.,235
  , Thomas J.,155
RENI, James A.,131
RENTFROW, Geo.,153
  , J.N.,153
  , T.G.,153
REY, Robert,132
REYNOLDS, A.,192
  , Alexander,011
  , B.F.,031
  , Benjamin F.,049
  , Colan,235
  , Elizabeth,014,077
  , Gharky,031,077
  , Henry Vernon,017
  , Henry,017,018,034,035,
    046,062,158,159,160,
    161,165,169,170,172,
    174,177,178,179,181,
    182,184,185,187,188,
    192,235
  , Irise,134
  , John C.,018
  , John D.,049 ,077,165

REYNOLDS, John,009 ,014,031,032,
              076,077,159,161,165,
              235
        , Joseph,031,032,039,165
              ,171,235
        , Mary,031
        , Matilda,017 ,160,161
        , Polly Perry,017
        , R.W.,076
        , Redden Wash.,017
        , Redding W.,034,169,172
              ,177
        , Rita Caroline,017
        , Samuel,189
        , Sarah A.,062 ,197
        , Sarah Ann,017,035,046,
              169,170
        , Sarah,034,056,175,179,
              185,189
        , Tabitha J.,034,046,169
              ,170,179,182,184
        , Tabitha Jane,017
        , Tabitha,174 ,187
        , Telitha J.,054
        , W.N.,138
RHOADS, Thomas,021 ,022
RHODES, James,235
RICE, C.O.,155
    , Carroll M.,185
    , Carroll,049
    , Charles O.,185
    , Henry,116
    , John A.,038 ,049,169,178,
              185,192,196,235
    , John,049 ,125,138
    , Jonathan T.,185
    , Mary,185
    , Oliver,152,155
    , Olliver,049
    , Richard,153 ,155
RICHARD, William,137
RICHARDS, Clark,031,235
        , J.G.W.,153
        , James C.,135
        , James,135
RICHERSON, John,235
RICHIE, Samuel,002
RICKETS, A.,155
       , John,141 ,143,155
RIDDEN, Jacob,144
      , Joseph,155
RIDDLE, Britton,041,173
      , Charles,033
      , Delila,041 ,173
      , John,130
      , Nathaniel,039 ,171,175,
              179
RIDLEY, Britton,235
      , Wilson,155
RIGGINS, Powell,235
RILEY, Jas.,148
     , Elisha,147
     , Geo.,147
RINCK, George,144
RINK, H.A.,017
RINKLE, Morgan,127
RIRDIN, N.G.,138
RITTON, Jas.,148
RIVES, F.F.,143
ROACH, Caledonia,089
     , Daniel,037 ,038,043,167,
              169,179
     , David,067,077
     , Emily,077
     , John,037,038,043,169,176,
              177,178,179
     , Mary,043
     , Matilda Ann,077
     , Stephen,003 ,007,235
     , Virginia,037,167
     , W.B.,089
     , Wm.Henry,077
ROAN, Hastin,139
    , Solomon,068
ROANE, A.,140
     , Isaac,153
     , John,136
ROARD, Henikiah,136
ROBBINS, C.,147
       , John,021
ROBERSON, David,236
        , John,236
        , Michael,236
        , Richard,236
        , Samuel Jr.,236
        , W.E.,140
        , William,156
ROBERTS, D.A.,087 ,112
       , David,081
       , J.C.,068 ,072
       , Margaret,029 ,030
       , R.H.,087
       , Stephen,087
       , William C.,058,059
ROBERTSON, Ann,086
         , C.S.,107,109
         , Christopher,236
         , Daniel,144
         , David,236
         , Felix,126
         , J.W.,098
         , Jack(N-Free),050
         , Jas.,141
         , Jessee,143
         , John W.,117
         , Samuel,026 ,162
         , Thomas,128
         , Thos.,153
         , W.G.,098
         , Wm.,236
ROBINS, H.K.,145
      , M.,141
      , Sarah Alex.,044

ROBINS, W.G.,150
      , W.J.,145
      , Wm.,150
ROBINSON, A.L.,178 ,195,196
        , Aaron,071
        , Absalom L.,043,174,177
              ,179
        , Absalom,175
        , Absolom L.,182
        , Alexander F.,034 ,063,
              066,078,164,166,171
        , Ann,140
        , Cathahill,122
        , Christian,007
        , Christopher,143
        , D.(Heirs),145
        , D.,166
        , D.H.,016
        , D.V.,197
        , David D.,003
        , David V.,061 ,079,174,
              195,196
        , David,005,009,010,011,
              021,023,036,043,044,
              061,072,078,158,167,
              174,175,177,178,179,
              182,196,236
        , Dawson H.,032
        , Dorson H.,036,164,171
        , Felix,125
        , J.C.,152
        , J.H.,153
        , J.W.,091
        , Jack,050
        , James W.,236
        , James,019,021,025,158,
              160,162,164,168,173,
              216,236
        , Jas.,176
        , Jesse,237
        , Jessee,145
        , John M.,237
        , Lawson,034
        , Linis,132
        , Major,237
        , Mary A.,109
        , Matilda Cro,191
        , Rebecca,174
        , Richard,007 ,128,134
        , S.A.,148 ,149
        , Samuel,158
        , Sarah A.,063 ,066,078
        , Thomas,035,167,237
        , Thos.,175
        , Unity,050
        , W.A.,074 ,075
        , W.R.,146 ,151
        , William,121 ,155
        , Wily G.,091
        , Wm.,011
ROBISON, John W.,097
       , Wiley G.,097
RODEN, Ezekiel,132
     , Nathan,134
     , Stephen,133
RODES, Abner,127
     , James,127
     , William G.,039
RODGERS, A.J.,137
RODNEY, Dorton,129
ROGERS, Kiziah T.,056
      , L.C.,141
      , T.H.,237
      , Thos.H.,237
      , William E.,237
ROMINES, A.J.,152
       , S.G.R.,127
RORIE, F.A.,133
ROSE, Eli,137
    , Enos,071 ,085,146
    , Frederick,237
    , Henry,151
    , J.F.,140
    , James C.,146
    , James,152
    , Jas.,148
    , John,153
    , Sarah,010,200
    , W.J.,145
ROSS, A.B.,237
    , Alfred,095
    , Charles M.,057
    , Charles W.,011,021
    , Charles,237
    , D.L.,128
    , David L.,127
    , F.W.,127
    , Francis,237
    , Geo.,145
    , George G.,064,102,144
    , George,023,074,141,237
    , Isaac W.,112
    , Isabell,149
    , Isabella,077
    , J.C.,144 ,148
    , J.M.,237
    , James,137
    , Jessie L.,237
    , Jno.Mc.,024
    , John B.,132
    , John M.,112
    , John Mc.,007 ,011,023,096
    , Lucinda,121
    , M.H.,114
    , Morgan H.,077,079,106,121
    , T.A.,083
    , Theodore,076 ,077
    , W.M.,153
    , W.N.,116
    , William B.,014,237,238
    , William T.,238
ROUSEY, J.H.,155
      , Joseph,155

ROUSEY, Morgan,137
      , Richardson,137
ROWSEY, Franklin,141
      , G.W.,141
      , H.,097
      , Henry C.,064
      , J.H.,106
      , James H.,087,117
      , John,238
      , Morgan,131 ,132,134,139,
              238
      , Richard,132
      , Thomas,087
      , Z.,142 ,145
ROY, Emanuel F.,068
RUDLE, James,135
RUNNELLS, Hamilton,238
RUSHING, C.C.,141
       , G.W.,152
       , Mark,078
RUSSELL, (Mrs),025
       , Albert,020,029,030
       , Alexander,020 ,028,029,
              030,038,055,072,160,
              161,166,167,170,179,
              238
       , Alexd.,148
       , Alx.,023
       , Benjamin P.,076
       , Delilah J.,086
       , Delilah,023,160,166
       , Elinor A.,061
       , Eliz.Jane,086
       , Elizabeth,020
       , Hugh,029 ,030,105
       , J.R.,190
       , J.T.,158
       , James R.,056
       , James W.,061
       , James,016 ,020,028,029,
              030,044,081,086,102,
              108,160,161,167,184,
              188,192,195,238
       , Joab A.,075,080,121
       , Joab,073 ,074,075
       , John T.,020,025,158
       , John,029 ,030
       , Larcent,061
       , Martha Ann,044
       , Martha,184
       , Mary A.,081,178,184,188
              ,192,195
       , Mary Ann,044 ,140
       , Mary Jane,141
       , Matilda,086
       , Nancy,105
       , Polly,029 ,030
       , R.P.,145
       , Robert P.,075 ,076,080
       , Robert R.,029 ,030,073,
              086
       , Robert,012,072,073,074,
              075,238,244
       , Robt.,143 ,145,151
       , Samuel,153
       , Sarah A.E.,081
       , Susan A.,184
       , Susan C.T.,081
       , Susannah C.,044
       , T.M.,098
       , Thomas M.,056 ,190
       , W.,071
       , William,029,030,038,061
              ,105,112,139
       , Wyatt,038 ,170
       , Wyatte,038 ,179
RUSTIY, Ezekiel,134
RUTLEDGE, (Heirs),147
        , George,238
        , Robt.,238
RYLIE, A.A.,142

SAMUEL, Achilles W.,024
SANDERS, Adeline,093
       , Austin,147
       , John,138
       , Thos.,136
       , W.R.,148
SANDERSON, Wm.,136
SANER, John,153
SANSON, Peter,126
SATON, Geo.Z.,145
SATTERFIELD, Jeremiah,019 ,161
           , R.S.,130 ,131
SAUNDERS, N.W.,135
        , Thomas,135
SAWYERS, Riley,174
SCHARF, John,101
SCHEABER, Mo.,148
SCHUBERT, Jno.,145
SCHWARTS, Joseph,136
SCIRRATT, Jacob,056
SCOTT, A.B.,145
     , Andrew,138
     , G.B.,054,055
     , James A.,140
     , James,010,025,113,158,178

     , Jas.,148
     , Jeremiah,128,238
     , John,017,020,027,038,053,
              056,066,125,126,158,
              163,170,172,185,186,
              199,239
     , Margaret,054,055
     , Martha A.,104
     , Martin,130
     , Rosamond,126
     , Rosanond P.,125
     , Rosomond P.,239
     , Rosseman P.,170
     , Saml.,151
     , W.C.,136

SCOTT, William,056 ,066
     , Winfield B.,081
     , Winfield,083,113
     , Wm.C.,134
SEAGO, Simeon,151
     , Simon,133
SEAL, John,094
SEAMAN, Thomas,052 ,061,070,075,
        079,080
     , W.H.H.,148
     , William H.H.,080
     , Wm. H.H.,061
     , Wm.H.H.,142
SEATON, George,119
SEAY, Leven,137
     , Lewis,140,199
SEGO, S.,147
     , Samuel,150
     , Seaman,130
     , Siamon,132
SELLERS, John(N),069
     , Riley(N-Free),061
SEMORE, Cannon,137
SERATT, Wm.,152
SETTLE, John E.,143
SEWEL, John,186
     , Newton,186
SEWELL, Geo.,153
     , Jno.,148
     , Thos.F.,145,147
     , William,130
SHADER, J.R.,144
SHANNON, Aaron,134
     , Benj.F.,239
     , E.E.,093
     , George W.,020
     , George,120,122
     , Hedley,136
     , James,153
     , Jane K.,122
     , John,153
     , Mary,077
     , N.E.,076
     , Nathan E.,020 ,039,077,
        171
     , Robert,077
     , Robt.,126 ,147,153
     , Sarah A.,020 ,034,164
     , T.S.,148 ,152
     , Thomas Sr.,018
     , Thomas J.,020
     , Thomas,020
     , W.R.,149
     , William G.,076,077
     , William H.,025
     , Wm.,239
     , Wm.H.,020
SHARP, ,153
     , J.F.,156
     , John,150
SHAW, J.D.,141
     , Richard,134
     , Robert,131
SHEAN, David,153
SHEARLEY, E.G.,132
     , E.W.,132
SHEARMAN, James,132
SHEARS, Robert,239
SHEILD, W.B.,109
SHELBY, A.C.,150
     , Archibald C.,100
     , R.F.,117,146
     , Eli,100
     , Elizabeth J.,042,173,181
     , Elizabeth,196
     , Ely,239
     , George,134
     , John,134
     , Levi,039,082,117,179
     , M.W.,173,181
     , Mary A.,181,185
     , Mary Amanda,042
     , Mary M.,173
     , Mary,196
     , Moses A.,017,018,042,173
        177,181
     , Moses W.,042
     , Moses,185 ,188,196
     , Sarah Ann,042 ,173
     , Thomas D.,036 ,042,087,
        109,167,171,177,178,
        181,185,188,194,196
     , Thomas,173
     , Thos.D.,060,090,099,188
     , Virginia A.,109
SHELL, John R.,197
     , Joseph,068
SHELLEY, Washington,153
     , William,043,132
SHELLY, William,042
SHELTON, E.H.,060 ,071,084,195
     , W.T.,147
SHEPHERD, William,126
SHERFIELD, Ephraim,137
SHERLEY, E.S.,129
SHERLING, James,146
SHERMAN, William,144
SHIELDS, G.W.,139
     , George W.,149
     , H.R.,188
     , Jessee,147
     , W.B.,071 ,153
SHINON, Joseph M.,135
SHIPMAN, E.H.,199
     , Edward,133
SHIRLEY, E.W.,140
     , Thos.,149
SHIRLING, M.,148
SHITTAN, Jesse,149
SHIVE, John,149
SHORT, Johnathan,150
     , R.C.,153

SHORTS, Elmira B.,089
SHOULTS, Martin,133
SHUIN, John D.,239
SHULL, A.E.,133,135
     , A.M.,155
     , David,017
     , Enoch,239
     , Jno.,136,153
     , John,056,139,239
     , Joseph,086 ,239
     , Robert,139
     , W.W.,147
SHURLEY, E.F.,152
     , E.S.,130
     , James,239
     , Lake,126
     , Luke,126
SHUTE, Jehu Davy,025
     , Philip,022 ,025
     , Thomas,023 ,125,126,127,
        239
SIBZINGER, J.,141
SIFIIS, W.R.,147
SIMINGTON, John,125,126
SIMMONS, Henry,138
     , James H.,083 ,106
     , James,153
     , Lemuel,137
     , M.L. (Widow),118
     , S.,147
     , William,118,136
     , Wm.,133,137,145
SIMPSON, Eliza,099
     , George W.,099
     , James M.,099
     , Jno.Jr.,146
     , John C.,240
     , John P.,099
     , M.P.,139
     , Maclean,099
     , Margarett,099
     , Martha,099
     , Mary E.,099
     , Mathew A.,099
     , Mathew K.,099
     , Rebecca Jane,099
     , Sarah M.,099
     , Susan,099
     , Thomas,099
     , W.R.,099
     , William,085,139
SLAKE, Robt.,152
SLAUGHTER, J.B.,141
SLAYMAKER, E.,141
SLIDER, James,139
SLOAN, Alexander,015
     , James,137
     , Jno.,144
     , John M.,149
     , John,142,143
     , Ruth,015
     , William,013
SLONE, Thomas,128 ,129
SMIDDY, Samuel,128
SMITH, Absolom,240
     , Berry,140
     , Caswell,152
     , Charles,143
     , Connall,149
     , D.M.,146
     , Daniel,010 ,018,020,023,
        033,034,038,041,047,
        054,058,073,074,075,
        076,111,162,163,169,
        172,173,177,179,180,
        182,183,188,189,190,
        191,192,240
     , Danl.,189
     , David,136
     , Drewery,128
     , F.D.,141
     , Edward M.,155
     , Elisha,170
     , Elizabeth,046,178
     , G.K.,141
     , Geo.W.,240
     , Hardin,131
     , Henry H.,112,113
     , Hiram R.,133
     , Hiram,114,115,134
     , Isaac,139,240
     , J.M.,085
     , J.P.,155
     , J.W.,108,147,153
     , James B.,134
     , James N.,145
     , James L.,049,061,083,116,
        117,182,194
     , James M.,112
     , James P.,240
     , James S.,083
     , James,012,240
     , Jarrard,046
     , Jarrod,178
     , Jesse,023,240
     , Joel,134,240
     , John A.,092 ,119,135
     , John E.,152
     , John Jr.,128,151
     , John L.,092
     , John,045,046,134,138,178,
        180,190
     , Jordan,240
     , Joseph,053 ,076,115,186,
        196
     , Lem,130
     , Levi,085
     , Lucy,115,116
     , M.,149
     , Madison H.,134
     , Moses,013
     , P.M.,114
     , Payton,240

SMITH, Peyton,085
     , Richard,125 ,126
     , Saml.,152
     , Sarah(Mrs),115
     , Stephen,145
     , Susan,068
     , Thomas W.,131
     , Thomas,028
     , Thos.,152
     , Thos.W.,133
     , W.B.,142
     , Wiley,090
     , William H.,240
     , William,128 ,240
SMITHWICK, John,142
     , Jordan,130 ,132,133,
        240
     , Jourdan,134
     , Mary,122
SMOOT, M.M.,153
SMYTH, Zachariah,018
SNAGUE, J.W.,149
SNEED, Henley,140
SNELGROVE, William,153
SNELLGROVE, Saml.,145 ,147
SNODGRASS, D.F.,147
     , Danl.,144
     , John,143
     , L.,149
     , Larkin,143
     , Will,144
     , Wm.,141
SNOW, Elizabeth,200
     , William,130 ,153
     , Wm.,146
SOLOMON, John,136 ,142
     , Saml.,136
     , Wiley,142
     , Wm.,142
     , Wylie,143
SONDEN, L.H.,142
SORRELLS, David,127
SORRELS, Jacob,142
SOUTH, Andrew M.,083
     , John,108
     , Levi,108
     , Philip,150
     , Samuel,150
SOUTHERLAND, Peter,153
SOUTHION, Pieter,151
SOUTHIORN, Jacob,151
SOWELL, John,046,118,120,178,187
     , Newton,046 ,178,187
     , Susannah,118,120
SPAAR, Edward Y.,132
SPAIN, Charlotte,200
     , Elizabeth,200
     , Hannah D.,111
     , J.D. (Heirs),150
     , J.D.,148,150
     , J.H.D.,134
     , James D.,200
     , James W.,093 ,095,200,240
     , John D.,093 ,095,200,240
     , John M.D.,111
     , John,200
     , Marshell D.,100 ,104,111,
        200,240
     , Peter D.,200,241
     , Solomon D.,241
SPANN, M.,148
SPARKES, W.H.,151
SPARKS, J.F.,118
     , J.L.,118
     , J.N.,118
     , Mary,118
     , S.E.,118
     , W.H.,194
     , W.J.,118
SPEAR, Edmund,135
SPEARE, Isaiah,140
SPEARMAN, James,128
     , William,142
SPEARS, William,141
SPENCER, Charles,025,126
     , Hiram,130
     , Thomas S.,116
     , Thomas,042
     , Thos.S.,110
     , Wm.,194
SPENCR, F.J.,144
SPENSER, James,130
SPRAGGINS, Samuel,125 ,126,127
SPRAKS, W.,149
SPRIGGINS, Samuel,241
STACK, Jno.,148
STAMFORD, G.W.,141
STAMIS, John,140
STAND, Thomas,083
STANDEN, John,134
STANDER, John S.,130
     , John,131
STANDERS, John,133
STANDFIELD, George W.,151
     , M.,150
STANFIELD, G.W.,143,148
     , H.D.,148
     , J.D.,146
     , Polly,003
STANTON, Robert,143
STARLING, Wiley,059
STARN, Jack A.,140
     , John,152
STARR, George,241
     , Wm.,140
STAY, C.S.,156
STEADMAN, S.S.,153
STEEL, William,149
STEELE, Nancy J.,122
     , W.J.,122
STEELY, J.C.,064,097

STEELY, J.J.,150
STELL, J.J.,140
STEMMILL, James,102
STEPHENS, Elizabeth,016,032,168
  , Geo.,153 ,155
  , Henry,032,037,168
  , J.H.T.,152
  , Joseph,089
STEPHENSON, E.H.,065,085,104,121
  ,162,163,184,189,193
  ,198
  , Elbert H.,052
  , Elihu,085 ,104
  , Elmarine,132
  , Emerine,137
  , Hardin,085 ,104
  , James,085 ,104,155
  , John,121 ,155
  , Mary A.,104
  , Mary Ann,085
  , W.H.,137
  , William,085,104
STEVENS, Arisbel,122
  , Elizabeth,161 ,164
  , Henry,032 ,161,164
  , Thomas,135
  , W.R.,122
STEVENSON, Elbert H.,241
STEWART, J.B.,142
STEWELL, H.C.,145
STILLGIL, Martin,147
STILLWILL, H.C.,147
STINNETT, Jesse,155
STOBUCK, C.,146
STOCKTON, Daniel L.,036,167
  , Daniel,170,173
  , Thomas J.,061
  , Thomas,036,167,168,170
  ,173
STOGDEN, Amilinth,052
STONE, E.F.,145
  , Hardeman,131
  , Meredith,144
  , Pryor,241
  , R.B.,029
STOOP, John A.,128
STOUT, Alexd.,144
  , Andrew,020 ,024,241
  , Isaiah,024
  , J.S.,153
  , John,241
  , Robert,021 ,024
  , W.,153
  , William,138
STOVEALL, J.T.,141
STRATON, James R.,144
STRATTEN, John,042
STRATTON, Henry,140
  , John R.,051 ,184
STRAUN, Mary,032,033
  , William,022
STRAWN, Anthony,151
  , Richard,128,133,136,241
  , W.,192
  , William,023,051,184
  , Wm.,192,241
STRAYHON, William,107
STREET, D.A.,071,083
  , D.T.,069
  , Daniel A.,083
  , David A.,069
  , David T.,071
  , John T.,071
  , Lucy M.,069,071
  , R.W.,152
  , Sarah C.,071
  , Sarah,069
  , Thomas,069
STRICKLAND, Wm.C.,082
STRICKLIN, John,071
  , William C.,071
  , William,020
STRIVIN, William,241
STROUD, Aaron,136
  , Hampton,135,136
STUART, Elizabeth,005
  , John,131
  , William,005
STUMPH, J.W.,155
SUGGINS, James,144
SULLIVAN, Elijah,241
SUMNER, Benjamin,114
  , Martha,114
  , Mary,114
SURRAT, Jacob,066
SURRATT, Jacob,241
GUTHERLAND, Cantin,129
SUTTILL, Henry,152
SUTTON, Hugh,143,145
  , J.D.,071
  , Jesse D.,142
  , John,136,142
  , Joseph,131
  , Lemuel,021
SWANFORD(?), Biven,144
SWANNEN, Lacy G.,148
SWEENEY, A.W.,011 ,015
  , James,028
SWEENY, A.W.,008,010
SWENEY, A.W.,006
  , Joseph,132
SWINEY, M.J.,071
SWINNEY, Gyle,155
SWINSON, Wm.,148

TAB, John,241
TACKER, Delice,103
  , Homer(?),103
  , W.R.,147,150
TACKET, Thos.,145
TACKETT, Geo.,150
  , George,137
TALIAFERRO, C.W.,093,113,145,200

TALIAFERRO, George,141
TALLEY, R.J.,135
  , William M.,155
  , William,130
TALLY, Anderson,031
TANKERELY, Thornton,130
TANKERLEY, James,027
TANKERSLEY, Caledonia,116
  , F.,147
  , Fountain,067
  , James,134
  , Jane,166,184
TANKERSLY, George,140
TANKESLEY, Fountain,108
  , J.D.,150
  , J.H.,241
TANKESLY, Caledonia,108
TARBEET, H.,190
TARBET, Hu.,025,180,182
TARBETT, Hu.,046
  , Hugh,081
TARBIT, H.,159
TARKENTON, Isaac,241
TARKINGTON, A.J.,135,140
TARKINTON, A.T.,138
  , Isaac,024,070
  , Wm.,138
TARNTON, N.M.,149
TATUM, Edward,117
TAYLOR, C.,150
  , H.,126
  , Caswell,101
  , Denis,136
  , George W.,241
  , George,127
  , Isaac,006
  , John P.,126,242
  , John,126,137,241
  , Richard,040
  , Sarah L.,096
  , Thomas,153
  , Wm.,242
TEAGE, James,134 ,242
TEAGUE, Thomas,134
  , Wm.,242
TEAL, Timothy,242
TEMPLES, A.W.,083
  , Allan,075 ,172
  , Allen A.,095
  , Allen W.,084
  , Allen,066
TENESON, Ezekiel,042
TENINNOR, Eli,142
TENNESON, W.H.,140
TENNISON, Ezekiel,051 ,184
TEPPER, Jacob,139
  , William,139
TERLEY, R.J.,150
TERRELL, John,141
  , Wm.,133
TERRY, David,153
  , E.,242
  , George W.,128,134
  , J.C.,148
  , James H.,144,145
  , M.C.,148
  , T.S.,086
TEVERY, J.H.,150
THACKER, J.R.,153
THAXTON, Martha S.,048 ,166
  , Martha,182
  , W.B.,166
  , William W.,166
THOM, Harbet,131
THOMAS, Andrew,024
  , Bennett,151
  , David,143
  , George,147
  , Jacob,144 ,151
  , James,127
  , John,127,151
  , M.A.,145,148
  , Miles A.,132,137
  , Miles,135
  , Polly,024
  , Richard,127
  , W.W.,149
  , William,037,127
THOMPSON, A.J.,141
  , David,137,190,242
  , Frances,013
  , Francis,006 ,011,013
  , George,150
  , I.T.,138
  , J.C.,148
  , J.T.,104 ,130
  , Jackson(N-Free),035
  , James,242
  , Jesse T.,131 ,133,135
  , Jesse,129,136
  , Jessee,144
  , Jessi,242
  , John,009 ,011,012,242
  , Judah,013
  , Lucinda K.,004
  , Mary,013
  , Nancy C.,013
  , Richard,164 ,242
  , Robert,126,136
  , Tempy,200
  , William,005 ,006,013,
    114,131,200
THORN, Harbert,133
THORNTON, Daniel,221
  , Isaac B.,075
  , Isaac,032,037,044,073,
    074,075,078,168,173,
    177,179,181,182,185,
    186,188,189,193,198
  , J.B.,143
  , Josiah,016

THORNTON, Mary Ann,057
  , N.M.,065,073,147
  , Nancy,073,075,078
  , Newton M.,064,196
  , Newton,057,073
  , S.R.,016 ,085
  , Silas,073
  , Thursday M.,075
  , W.W.,071
  , William,094 ,143
  , Wm.,139
THRASHER, Joseph,020,242
  , Robert,005,018,128
TICER, John,133
  , Richd.G.,143
TIDWELL, C.W.,142
  , E.S.,116
  , Jno.,145
  , Simeon,152
  , W.M.,156
TILLEY, Samuel,131
TIMS, Thomas,140
TINES, Sidney,135
TINSLEY, Emily F.,092
  , James T.,091 ,092
TIPPA, Silas,141
TISDALE, Polly,017
TISLLEY, Abbert,138
TOBOTT, Ross,242
TODD, Caroline,121
TOLIVER, Malsiah,135
TOMKINS, Harrison,242
TOMLINSON, Peter,242
TOMPKINS, Harrison,004 ,242
  , Mary Ann,004
TOODMAN, C.,138
TOPPER, Silas,138
TORE, Levi,141
TORIEE, Wm.,128
TOWERY, John,042,183
  , Kiziah,042 ,183
TOWNY, Isaac,242
TOWRY, E.,150
  , J.C.,153
  , John,044,056
TRACE, W.L.,243
TREASE, Charity,091
TREES, Jacob,137
TRENTHAM, Sarah,042,174
  , Zachariah,042,174
TREVILLIAN, H.,148
  , J.†.,144
TRICE, John,150
TRUCE, Jacob,132
TRURE, William,130
TRUSE, William,131
TRUSTY, James,128 ,130
TUBBS, (Mr)153
TUCKER, 153
  , Allen,134
  , J.R.,122
  , Margaret S.,074
  , P.M.,104,105
  , Petser M.,111
  , R.W.,090,091,092,097,10
    ,118
  , Susan A.,122
  , T.,163
  , Thomas,020 ,028,136,161
    167
  , Thos.,243
  , Wilson,135
TUER, John,132
TUMBLESTON, Henry,144
  , Hiram,128
  , Peter,128
TURNBAUGH, A.,141
TURNBO, Samuel,127
TURNER, James,099
  , Jesse,134
  , John,099,128,243
  , Thos.,148
  , Washington,029 ,030
  , Wasking B.,025
  , William,171
  , Wm.,147,153
TURPENS, R.P.,153
TURTOW, Joseph,136
TUTEN, W.,149
TUTON, Benjamin,138
TUTOR, Bynum,155
TYCER, John,153
TYSEN, William,083
TYSON, Elizabeth Ann,083
  , John M.,083
  , Martha Jane,083
UMBORGO, John,139
USSING, A.W.P.,243
UTLEY, John,128
VAIL, Daniel,135
VANCE, ,125
  , Adam,191
VANCLAVE, J.B.,144
VANCLEAVE, J.B.,143
VANDERGRIFT, W.M.,152
VANHOOSE, Jacob,043,058,174,175
    181
  , Mark,139 ,153
VARICK, W.E.,148
VARNER, Adam,051,183
VASLER, J.G.,138
VASSER, G.,139
  , John,131
VAUGHN, Reuben,014
VAWN, Alexander,184
VAWNEY, Isaac,043 ,175
  , Joel,175
  , Mary Susan,175
  , Mary,175
VERMILLION, J.H.,150,151
  , Saml.,144 ,145
VIARS, Rebecca,024 ,161
  , William F.,144

VICER, Isaac,153
VINCENT, Abraham,133,134
       , Catherine,099
       , Isaac,156
       , Jordan,099
VIRES, William F.,139
WADE, David K.,025
    , H.B.,077 ,078,093,099
    , John,130
    , Noah,040 ,145
    , O.P.,153
    , Richard,243
    , Samuel,243
    , W.B.S.,147
    , Wm.H.,130
WAGGONER, Daniel,028,029,160,163
                ,165,168,169,173,177
                ,181,184
        , Danl.,193
        , Elizabeth,184
        , F.G.R.,183
        , Francis,163 ,169,181
        , John,243
        , Martha,028,029,160,162
          ,183
        , Mathias,169
        , Matthias,163 ,183
        , Nancy,163,169
        , Susan,184
WAGNER, Daniel,023
      , Martha,023
WAGONER, Daniel,187
       , Francis,187
       , Martha,192
       , Matthias,192
WALDO, Wilie,153
WALDRIP, Abel,243
       , Thos.,243
WALDRUP, John,130
       , Abel,127
WALKER, Archilans,097
      , Charles R.,014
      , G.M.,129
      , George W.,243
      , James G.,159
      , James,138 ,143,243
      , Jas.G.,216
      , Jesse B.,114
      , Mark,243
      , Robert,125 ,126,243
      , William B.,243
      , Williamson,132
WALLACE, (Wid),174
       , B.F.,152
       , Hugh,050 ,135,136
       , Hughes,137
       , James,141 ,143
       , Janutt,050
       , Jas.W.,142
       , Jennette,199
       , John,151
       , Joseph,009
       , Lawron,140
       , Lewis,141
       , Peter,143
       , Rachel,043,175,181
       , Thomas,129
       , Thos.,244
       , Walter,141
       , Wesley,136,137
       , William,042,043,129,175
         ,181
WALLIS, America G.,244
      , Hugh,134
      , James E.,135
      , John,129,131
      , Newton,127
WALLS, Reuben,153
WARD, (Wid),038
    , E.W.,150
    , George,156
    , James T.,131
    , James,037,102,177,194
    , Jane,102 ,194
    , Swain,018,057,165,166,168,
      173,177
WARDEN, W.J.,152
WARE, Jame,053
    , James,019,029,030,161,168
    , Jas.,185
WARREN, Elias,140 ,142
      , Jacob,144 ,145
      , Jas.,160
      , Joshua,140 ,153
      , Leroy,044
      , W.J.,145
WARSON, William,128
WASHBURN, Gabriel,134
WASHINGTON, Thomas,126 ,244
WASSON, Abner,126
WATERS, Robert,033
WATKINS, A.,148
       , Benjamin,117
WATSON, James L.,038,104,170
      , James,179 ,192
      , John W.,045
      , John,038,039,153,170,179
        ,192,244
      , Margaret,200
      , Martah G.,045
      , Mitalda R.D.,045
      , Samuel,038 ,045,162,163,
        167,170,172,176,178,
        179,200
WATT, (Dr),194
    , Polly,194
    , William,127
WEAKS, C.,153
WEATHERFORD, Hill K.,117
          , J.M.,156
          , J.W.,150
          , John,133 ,244

WEATHERSPOON, M.C.,091
WEAVER, Green,004
      , Matthew,132
WEBB, Calvin,144,145,151
    , Joseph,244
    , William,244
WEBBS, C.,148
WEBSTER, John,129
WEEMS, W.J.,142
WELBANKS, Wm.,142
WELBORN, John J.,119
       , T.P.,149
WELBURN, Alexd.,144
WELCH, E.C.,103
     , James,153
     , John C.,117
     , John J.,099
     , John,128,132,244
     , Joseph,149
     , T.J.,147
     , William,139
WELLBANKS, Jno.,145
WELLBORN, Jon.,161
        , Jonathan,160 ,162
WELLBUNK, Jno.,141
WELLS, Abraham,012
     , Elizabeth,159,161
     , Isaac,127
     , James,017,163
     , John,142
     , L.H.,194
     , Lewis K.,081
     , Lucinda G.,081
     , Margaret,060,083
     , N.S.,081
     , Samuel,171
     , Samuel,011 ,014,036,163,
       167,178
     , Sarah Jane,032 ,033,163
     , Washington,094 ,108
     , William,010 ,018,032,050,
       077,159,161,165
     , Woodson,060 ,083,095,098
WELSH, Philip,141
WEST, Alexander,134
    , Anderson,127
    , Felix,133,136
    , James,038,131,168
    , William,135
    , Wm.,244
WESTLY, Wm.,146
WETHERFORD, John,132
         , W.,141
WETHERLY, Job,023
        , Margaret,023
WHEAT, Wyley,131
WHITE, (Wid),044
     , Abraham,112
     , Abrahm,151
     , Andrew,020 ,177,244
     , Archibald,090
     , C.R.,151
     , Dallas,076 ,085
     , Dempsey,092
     , Elijah,130 ,131,133,136
     , Elisabeth P.,200
     , Elizabeth,090
     , Emily C.,058,076
     , Emily,085,121
     , Geo.,151
     , George M.D.,058
     , George,018 ,128,244
     , Henry A.,059
     , Henry,057,076,153,196
     , Isaac N.,058,076
     , James D.,058
     , James,027,057,131,196,244

     , Jas.,149
     , Jno.,155
     , Jno.D.,145
     , John D.,112
     , John,018,038,039,041,045,
       053,055,058,085,086,
       091,121,161,166,170,
       173,174,178,179,180,
       183,186,189,193,244
     , Jonathan,138,139
     , King,044,168,176
     , Levi,170
     , M.,148
     , Margaret A.,058
     , Margaret S.,055 ,186,189
     , Margaret,058,076,121,186
     , Margarette,085
     , Marshall,058,076
     , Martha A.,058,076
     , Martha,085 ,099
     , Matilda,072
     , Milly Fenas,057
     , Milly Francis,196
     , N.,176
     , Nancy J.,075,076
     , Nancy,052,168,176,184
     , Nicy,057,076
     , Noel,130
     , Nowell,044 ,052,144,184
     , Pernecy,057
     , Perniecy,196
     , Perry,130
     , Recisk(?),091
     , Rednick,092
     , Reuben,057 ,196
     , Rider M.,091
     , Samuel,018 ,039,048,130,
       170,179,182
     , Sherod,034
     , Sherrod,035
     , T.B.,144
     , Thomas B.,128
     , Thomas,040 ,057,172,196
     , W.J.,149
     , William,010

WHITEHEAD, William,126
WHITEHED, William,126
WHITEHURST, E.,221
WHITESIDE, Jenkin,126
WHITLOW, Antiwithe,171
       , Calvin,153
       , Coleman,049
       , Eyre,049
       , Ezra Forrest,170
       , Grandville,118
       , Henderson,039 ,049,118,
         170,172,183,196,197
       , Joshua,101
       , Milton,039,049,118,170,
         171,172,196,197
       , Paschal,036,047,170
       , Permelia,171
       , Sally,171
       , Sarah,118 ,172
       , W.C.,072
WHITSETT, William G.,090
WHITSON, Harriet,080,117,142
       , James,117
       , M.C.,156
WHITWORTH, William,127
WHORLEY, Abraham,181
       , George,181
WHORTON, S.,148
WICKER, Calvin,153
      , Levi,156
      , R.G.,148
WIDEMAN, Mark,006
       , Martha,006
WIGGINS, H.,126
WIGGS, Probate,136 ,138,143
     , Robert,135
WILBANKS, Jno.,147
WILBORN, Jonathan,167
WILDS, Jas.S.,148
WILIS, T.F.,150
WILFERSON, R.J.,064
         , Thomas,132
WILKINS, William,022
WILKINSON, R.J.,154
WILLAMS, Elizabeth,059
       , John J.,059
WILLBANKS, Bennett,019
         , Wm.,151
WILLER, Logan,137
WILLETT, R.H.,137
WILLIAM, Isaac,127
       , J.G.,149
       , William L.,030
WILLIAMS, ,149
        , A.,144,147
        , Ambrose H.,237
        , Anderson,133 ,145
        , C.C.,112
        , Charlotte,004
        , Clayburn,126
        , Daniel,028,165,181,187
        , Eli,129 ,130,132,133
        , Elizabeth,028,165,181,
          187
        , George,127
        , Green D.,145
        , H.D.,122
        , Hardin,004
        , J.A.,010
        , J.J.,058 ,071,148,152,
          160,165,173,184,187,
          194
        , J.S.,148
        , James A.,004 ,011
        , James,127,141,153
        , Jane,122
        , Jesse G.,071
        , Jno.,145
        , Jno.J.,023
        , John G.,010
        , John J.,028 ,060,140,
          165,168,173,177,181,
          193,194
        , John,097 ,132,134,135,
          142,144,230
        , Joseph,010,011,012
        , Julia,028,165,184,187
        , July,181
        , Lewis,025,035,052,166,
          176,184,192
        , Lora Lucinda,004
        , Lucinda Eliza,004
        , M.,148
        , M.I.,152
        , Maria,126
        , Matilda,004
        , Nancy,166
        , R.J.,088 ,120,121
        , Robert J.,109
        , Robinson,142
        , Sally,004
        , Sampson,126
        , Samuel H.,006,008,010,
          126
        , Samuel,014,035,043,125
          ,126,166,176
        , Sarah,028
        , Sebastine C.,004
        , Susan,058,165,181,187
        , Thomas H.,126
        , Thomas J.,126
        , W.,151
        , William L.,029,160,161
          ,168
        , Wm.,133 ,134
        , Wright,059,195
WILLIAMSON, (Heirs),149
          , Elizabeth,083
          , J.M.,080
          , J.W.,083
          , James M.,083

WILLIAMSON, John M.,083
         , John W.,066,066,080
         , Josephus,083
WILLIS, A.,099
      , Archibald,057 ,064
      , David,062 ,099
      , Joel,057,064
      , Martha,062
      , Mary,057,064,099
      , Talbot,062
      , Tolbert,096
WILLITT, R.H.,137
WILLOUGH, James G.,076
WILLOUGHBY, James G.,015,027
          , James,077
          , Margaret,015
WILLS, James,132
     , Samuel,064
     , W.C.,147
     , Wm.J.,145
WILSON, Adam,009
      , Alex.,131
      , Benjamin,007
      , Columbia,007
      , Cornelius(N-Free),049
      , David,125 ,126
      , Green,007
      , James,008   ,009,126,244
      , John,007,008,020
      , Madison,007
      , Nelson,131
      , Samuel,083 ,126
      , T.P.,147
      , Unity(N-Free),050
      , William H.,093
      , William,126
      , Willie B.,007 ,008
WIMMS, Wm.,137
WINBORN, Elihu,181
       , James,128
       , Katherine,181
       , Rebecca,181
       , Samuel,181
WINBURN, Catharine,048
       , Eliha,048
       , J.S.,071
       , James S.,133
       , James,128
WINBUURN, Catharine,048
WINCHESTER, B.,139 ,149,153
          , Benjn.,147
          , Daniel,133 ,134,244
          , James,131 ,133
          , John,131,135,136,138
            ,139,155
          , Maden,130
          , R.R.,113
          , Robertson,073
          , Robinson,131
          , Robirson,130
          , Robt.,145
          , Russell,119,133
          , S.,153
          , Sarah,113
          , Thomas,136
          , Thos,244,245
          , Thos.,145
          , William,131
          , Wm.,134,135,138,153
          , Wm.Jr.,133
          , Wm.Sr.,133
WINDSOR, Jonathan,022 ,028,031,
          037,160,161,162,168,
          173,177
       , Martha,031,162
       , W.B.,061 ,189
       , William B.,037,168,173,
          177
       , William D.,054
WINGO, C.W.,148
     , Josiah,140
     , O.W.,146
     , Wm.,150
WINN, J.B.,082 ,086,098
    , L.,150
WINNINGHAM, Esperana,075
          , G.B.,075,100
WINSLOW, Joseph,017,018,164
WINSOR, Jonathan,181
      , William B.,181
WIRT, James,137,138,143
WISDOM, Alfred,134
      , G.M.,144
      , J.H.,155
      , J.M.,153
      , J.R.,140
      , Thomas,132 ,135
      , Thos.,145
WISEMAN, Thomas D.,132
       , William,132
WITHERSPOON, Francis,080
           , Moses,097 ,098
WOLF, A.H.,076
    , Charles H.,076
    , Charlse,076
    , G.W.,076 ,087
    , George W.,072
    , J.J.,067
    , J.P.,072 ,076,087
    , Jacob J.,076
    , Jacob,067,075,076,194
    , James A.,067
    , James Alvis,076
    , John,076 ,245
    , Jonathan,076
    , Nicholas,128
    , Peter,076,087
    , Richard,076
    , Washington,076
    , William,067
    , Wm.,076 ,134
    , Wm.C.,076
    , Z.,141

WOLFE, J.J.,064
     , J.P.,152
     , Jonathan,245
WOLVERTON, John,089,112
         , Laura Jane,089
         , Wiley Green,089
WONBURN, William,138
WOOD, Caledonia,116
    , Charles,027   ,035,166,176
    , Daniel G.,043,056,189
    , David G.,197
    , E.J.,152
    , Geo.,142 ,145,148
    , George,141
    , John C.,116
    , John H.,105 ,120
    , Joseph,139
    , Josiah,120
    , L.B.,142 ,152,153
    , Mary,166
    , Moses,139
    , Nancy,166
    , Peter,152
    , Saml.,152
    , Samuel,153
    , Walter,012,014
WOODARD, Fiedler,165
WOODBIN, Thomas,081
WOODBUN, Calvin G.,149
WOODBURN, Alonzo A.,099
        , Patience,099
        , Ranzo(?),099
        , Sarah C.,099
        , William K.,099
WOODEY, Robert,129
WOODS, Charles,184
     , Danl.G.,145
     , George,129 ,140,150
     , J.E.,150
     , James,104,105
     , L.B.,150
     , M.L.,023
     , Mary,184
     , Nancy,184
     , Sarah,106
     , Washington,139
     , William,126
WOODWARD, ,122
        , Fiedler,037   ,045,178,
          186
        , Jno.,147
        , John,129
        , Moses,199
        , William,143
WOODWY, Joseph,129
WOODY, Joseph,128 ,130
     , William,129
WOOLF, Nicholas,151
WOORDWARD, Fiedler,045
WORLEY, Abraham,058,174,175
      , Abram,043
      , Anna,079,174
      , Elizabeth,079 ,174
      , George,174 ,175
      , J.G.,153
      , Jacob,148
      , Jno.(Heirs),147
      , Joel M.W.,069
      , John V.A.,069
      , John,010,058,080,174,193
      , Juranner,174
      , Louisa M.,069
      , Lucinda M.,069
      , Lydia M.,069
      , M.,141
      , Margaret Ann,069
      , Mary W.,069
      , Michael,010,069,072
      , Rebecca Casey,069
      , Stephen S.,079
      , Stephen,105,112
      , Susannah Eliz.,069
WORLEYL, George,043
WORT, Jones,136
WRIGHT, (Heirs),141
      , (Mr),127
      , Ann,162
      , Elias,133
      , Euphemia,023
      , Isaac,025 ,046,139,179,
          185
      , James Sr.,159 ,185
      , James,019   ,025,046,159,
          178,179,185,212
      , John E.,143
      , Mary,162
      , Nancy,178
      , Rachel,025 ,185
      , William,019,025
      , Wm.,159
WYAN, Bannister,127
WYATT, C.,155
     , Ephraim,137
     , Washington,141
     , William,035 ,055,062,197
WYATTE, A.,153
      , William,066,188
WYATTS, Daniel,143
YANCY, A.J.,150
YARBERRY, Wm.,150
YARBORO, W.,155
YARBREY, Benjamin,135
YARBROUGH, ,138
         , Ambrose,245
         , Benjamin,138
         , William,152
YOAKHAM, David,137
YOCUM, Dan,155
YOUNG, (Widow),116
     , D.,153
     , David,104
     , Evlin,216

YOUNG, Franklin,151,153
     , Isaac H.,110,116
     , Isaac R.,104
     , Isaac,245
     , J.H.,146
     , James W.,104
     , James,245
     , Margaret J.,104
     , R.G.,110,117
     , William N.,104
YOUNT, Eliza,108
     , Larkin,016 ,038,069,094,
       101,108
ZA(?), Drew,128
ZACHARIAH, Olivia(N-Free),040

SLAVE, Abraham,161
, Adaline,194
, Adam,194
, Aelsey,167
, Agga,011
, Agnes,022
, Alfred,167
, Almeda,086
, Ambrose,191
, Amelia,108
, Amra,167
, Amy,005
, Ann,174 ,195
, Anny,185
, Anthony,174 ,178
, Antionette,086
, Ben,182 ,184
, Betsy,191
, Billy,086
, Calvin,194
, Carolin,162
, Caroline,185
, Charles,086
, Charlotte,006
, Cynthia,024
, Daniel,191
, David,165
, Delilah,167
, Dilcey,174
, Diley(f),195
, Dinah,076,079,194
, Dorcas,174
, Dulcina,161
, Edd,100
, Edeline,191
, Eli,167
, Elias,191
, Elihu,194
, Eliza,079
, Ellis,194
, Emiline,022
, Ester,191
, Eve,161
, Ezekiel,161
, Fanny,194
, Fetney,194
, Frank,194
, Gabriel,195
, George,086 ,167,182,194
, Green,166,191
, Handy,086
, Hannah,011 ,182
, Harriet,166
, Harry,020,161
, Henderson,162,185
, Henrita,161
, Henry,167,174
, Hugh,198
, Isaac,167,182,184,191
, Isaiah,167
, James,006,191
, Jemima,086
, Jeremiah,191
, Jerry,086,115
, Jim,108
, Jo,164
, John Jackson,178
, John,086,191
, Jonathan,191
, Jos.,162
, Joseph,006 ,185
, Julius,161
, Killis,020
, King,100
, Kizziah,194
, Kyer(f),191
, Letha Ann,178
, Lis,182
, Lissa,167
, Louisa,195
, Low,167
, Lucy,166
, Luiza,161
, Mabe(m),195
, Mabe,174
, Malinda,167 ,194
, Manda,185
, Manerva,161 ,174
, Manuel,167
, Margaret,166
, Marion,178
, Martha,161
, Mary Ann,034
, Mary,100,166,167,174
, Masse,164
, Matilda,162 ,185
, Mille,194
, Milly,174
, Minerva,100
, Minny,162
, Molly,174
, Morse,069
, Nancy,174
, Ned,190
, Nelly,006
, Orange(m),191
, Owen,191
, Patsey,198
, Peter,162,191,198
, Phebe,194
, Philip,191
, Philli,164
, Polly Ann,191
, Polly,006
, R.M.,194
, Rachel,162 ,185
, Riley,161
, Robert,161
, Rodah,006
, Rose,022
, Rutter,100
, Sally,159,162

SLAVE, Sam,100 ,164,198
, Sampson,191
, Samuel,176
, Sarah,006,162,185
, Sibby,182
, Sintha,167
, Smart,182
, Solomon,006
, Sophia,178
, Sphiah,191
, Tilby,038
, Tom,100
, W.H.,194
, Washington,110 ,167
, Wesley,161 ,165
, Willie,161
, Windd,167
, Winn,185
, Winny,006
, Wm.Gorden,191
, Zichariah,167

www.ingramcontent.com/pod-product-compliance
Lightning Source LLC
Chambersburg PA
CBHW020645300426
44112CB00007B/240